Mackenzie River and the Yukon, dow.. .. important part of the Company's history.

For the task thus undertaken the author is well fitted. He has had special opportunities for becoming acquainted with the history, position, and inner life of the Hudson's Bay Company. He has lived for nearly thirty years in Winnipeg, for the whole of that time in sight of Fort Garry, the fur traders' capital, or what remains of it; he has visited many of the Hudson's Bay Company's posts from Fort William to Victoria, in the Lake Superior and the Lake of the Woods region, in Manitoba, Assiniboia, Alberta, and British Columbia; in those districts he has run the rapids, crossed the portages, surveyed the ruins of old forts, and fixed the localities of long-forgotten posts; he is acquainted with a large number of the officers of the Company, has enjoyed their hospitality, read their journals, and listened with interest to their tales of adventure in many out-of-the-way posts; he is a lover of the romance, and story, and tradition of the fur traders' past.

The writer has had full means of examining documents, letters, journals, business records, heirlooms, and archives of the fur traders both in Great Britain and Canada. He returns thanks to the custodians of many valuable originals, which he has used, to the Governor of the Hudson's Bay Company in 1881, Right Hon. G. J. Goschen, who granted him the privilege of consulting all Hudson's Bay Company records up to the date of 1821, and he desires to still more warmly acknowledge the permission given him by the distinguished patron of literature and education, the present Governor of the Hudson's Bay Company, Lord Strathcona and Mount Royal, to read any documents of public importance in the Hudson's Bay House in London. This unusual opportunity granted the author was largely used by him in 1896 and again in 1899.

Taking the advice of his publishers, the author, instead of publishing several volumes of annals of the Company, has condensed the important features of the history into one fair-sized volume, but has given in an Appendix references and authorities which may afford the reader, who desires more detailed information on special periods, the sources of knowledge for fuller research.

The Remarkable History of the Hudson's Bay Company
George Bryce

PREFACE

THE Hudson's Bay Company! What a record this name represents of British pluck and daring, of patient industry and hardy endurance, of wild adventure among savage Indian tribes, and of exposure to danger by mountain, precipice, and seething torrent and wintry plain!

For two full centuries the Hudson's Bay Company, under its original Charter, undertook financial enterprises of the greatest magnitude, promoted exploration and discovery, governed a vast domain in the northern part of the American Continent, and preserved to the British Empire the wide territory handed over to Canada in 1870. For nearly a generation since that time the veteran Company has carried on successful trade in competition with many rivals, and has shown the vigour of youth.

The present History includes not only the record of the remarkable exploits of this well-known Company, but also the accounts of the daring French soldiers and explorers who disputed the claim of the Company in the seventeenth century, and in the eighteenth century actually surpassed the English adventurers in penetrating the vast interior of Rupert's Land.

Special attention is given in this work to the picturesque history of what was the greatest rival of the Hudson's Bay Company, viz, the North-West Fur Company of Montreal, as well as to the extraordinary spirit of the X Y Company and the Astor Fur Company of New York.

A leading feature of this book is the adequate treatment for the first time of the history of the well-nigh eighty years just closing, from the union of all the fur traders of British North America under the name of the Hudson's Bay Company. This period, beginning with the career of the Emperor-Governor, Sir George Simpson (1821), and covering the life, adventure, conflicts, trade, and development of the vast region stretching from Labrador to Vancouver Island, and north to the

THE HUDSON'S BAY COMPANY

CHAPTER I.

CHARLES LAMB—"delightful author"—opens his unique "Essays of Elia"
with a picturesque description of the quaint "South Sea House."
Threadneedle Street becomes a magnetic name as we wander along it
toward Bishopsgate Street "from the Bank, thinking of the old house
with the oaken wainscots hung with pictures of deceased governors and
sub-governors of Queen Anne, and the first monarchs of the Brunswick
dynasty—huge charts which subsequent discoveries have made
antiquated—dusty maps, dim as dreams, and soundings of the Bay of
Panama." But Lamb, after all, was only a short time in the South Sea
House, while for more than thirty years he was a clerk in the India
House, partaking of the genius of the place.

The India House was the abode of a Company far more famous than
the South Sea Company, dating back more than a century before the
"Bubble" Company, having been brought into existence on the last day
of the sixteenth century by good Queen Bess herself. To a visitor,
strolling down Leadenhall Street, it recalls the spirit of Lamb to turn
into East India Avenue, and the mind wanders back to Clive and Burke
of Macaulay's brilliant essay, in which he impales, with balanced
phrase and perfect impartiality, Philip Francis and Warren Hastings
alike.

The London merchants were mighty men, men who could select their
agents, and send their ships, and risk their money on every sea and on

every shore. Nor was this only for gain, but for philanthropy as well. Across yonder is the abode of the New England Company, founded in 1649, and re-established by Charles II. in 1661—begun and still existing with its fixed income "for the propagation of the Gospel in New England and the adjoining parts of America," having had as its first president the Hon. Robert Boyle; and hard by are the offices of the Canada Company, now reaching its three-quarters of a century.

Not always, however, as Macaulay points out, did the trading Companies remember that the pressure on their agents abroad for increased returns meant the temptation to take doubtful or illicit methods to gain their ends. They would have recoiled from the charge of Lady Macbeth,—

> "Wouldst not play false,
> And yet wouldst wrongly win."

Yet on the whole the Merchant Companies of London bear an honourable record, and have had a large share in laying the foundations of England's commercial greatness.

Wandering but a step further past East India Avenue, at the corner of Lime and Leadenhall Streets, we come to-day upon another building sitting somewhat sedately in the very heart of stirring and living commerce. This is the Hudson's Bay House, the successor of the old house on Fenchurch Street, the abode of another Company, whose history goes back for more than two centuries and a quarter, and which is to-day the most vigorous and vivacious of all the sisterhood of companies we have enumerated. While begun as a purely trading Company, it has shown in its remarkable history not only the shrewdness and business skill of the race, called by Napoleon a "nation of shopkeepers," but it has been the governing power over an empire compassing nearly one half of North America, it has been the patron of science and exploration, the defender of the British flag and name, and the fosterer, to a certain extent, of education and religion.

Not only on the shores of Hudson Bay, but on the Pacific coast, in the prairies of Red River, and among the snows of the Arctic slope, on the rocky shores of Labrador and in the mountain fastnesses of the Yukon, in the posts of Fort William and Nepigon, on Lake Superior, and in far distant Athabasca, among the wild Crees, or greasy Eskimos, or treacherous Chinooks, it has floated the red cross standard, with the well-known letters H. B. C.—an "open sesame" to the resources of a wide extent of territory.

The founding of the Company has features of romance. These may well be detailed, and to do so leads us back several years before the incorporation of the Company by Charles II. in 1670. The story of the first voyage and how it came about is full of interest.

Two French Protestant adventurers—Medard Chouart and Pierre Esprit Radisson—the former born near Meaux, in France, and the other a resident of St. Malo, in Brittany—had gone to Canada about the middle of the seventeenth century. Full of energy and daring, they, some years afterwards, embarked in the fur trade, and had many adventures.

Radisson was first captured by the Iroquois, and adopted into one of their tribes. After two years he escaped, and having been taken to Europe, returned to Montreal. Shortly afterwards he took part in the wars between the Hurons and Iroquois. Chouart was for a time assistant in a Jesuit mission, but, like most young men of the time, yielded to the attractions of the fur trade. He had married first the daughter of Abraham Martin, the French settler, after whom the plains of Abraham at Quebec are named. On her death Chouart married the widowed sister of Radisson, and henceforth the fortunes of the two adventurers were closely bound up together. The marriage of Chouart brought him a certain amount of property, he purchased land out of the proceeds of his ventures, and assumed the title of Seignior, being known as "Sieur des Groseilliers." In the year 1658 Groseilliers and Radisson went on the third expedition to the west, and returned after an absence of two years, having wintered at Lake Nepigon, which they called "Assiniboines." It is worthy of note that Radisson frankly states in the account of his third voyage that they had not been in the Bay of the North (Hudson Bay).

The fourth voyage of the two partners in 1661 was one of an eventful kind, and led to very important results. They had applied to the Governor for permission to trade in the interior, but this was refused, except on very severe conditions. Having had great success on their previous voyage, and with the spirit of adventure inflamed within them, the partners determined to throw off all authority, and at midnight departed without the Governor's leave, for the far west. During an absence of two years the adventurers turned their canoes northward, and explored the north shore of Lake Superior.

It is in connection with this fourth voyage (1661) that the question has been raised as to whether Radisson and his brother-in-law Groseilliers visited Hudson Bay by land. The conflicting claim to the territory about Hudson Bay by France and England gives interest to this question. Two French writers assert that the two explorers had visited Hudson Bay by land. These are, the one, M. Bacqueville de la Potherie, Paris; and the other, M. Jeremie, Governor of the French ports in Hudson Bay. Though both maintain that Hudson Bay was visited by the two Frenchmen, Radisson and Groseilliers, yet they differ entirely in details, Jeremie stating that they captured some Englishmen there, a plain impossibility.

Oldmixon, an English writer, in 1708, makes the following statement:—"Monsieur Radisson and Monsieur Gooselier, meeting with some savages in the Lake of the Assinipouals, in Canada, they learnt of them that they might go by land to the bottom of the bay, where the English had not yet been. Upon which they desired them to conduct them thither, and the savages accordingly did it." Oldmixon is, however, inaccurate in some other particulars, and probably had little authority for this statement.

THE CRITICAL PASSAGE.

The question arises in Radisson's Journals, which are published in the volume of the Prince Society.

For so great a discovery the passage strikes us as being very short and inadequate, and no other reference of the kind is made in the voyages. It is as follows, being taken from the fourth voyage, page :—

"We went away with all hast possible to arrive the sooner at ye great river. We came to the seaside, where we finde an old house all demolished and battered with boullets. We weare told yt those that came there were of two nations, one of the wolf, and the other of the long-horned beast. All those nations are distinguished by the representation of the beasts and animals. They tell us particularities of the Europians. We know ourselves, and what Europ is like, therefore in vaine they tell us as for that. We went from isle to isle all that summer. We pluckt abundance of ducks, as of other sort of fowles; we wanted not fish, nor fresh meat. We weare well beloved, and weare overjoyed that we promised them to come with such shipps as we invented. This place has a great store of cows. The wild men kill not except for necessary use. We went further in the bay to see the place that they weare to pass that summer. That river comes from the lake, and empties itself in ye river of Sagnes (Saguenay) called Tadou-sack, wch is a hundred leagues in the great river of Canada, as where we are in ye Bay of ye North. We left in this place our marks and rendezvous. The wild men yt brought us defended us above all things, if we would come quietly to them, that we should by no means land, & so goe to the river to the other side, that is to the North, towards the sea, telling us that those people weare very treacherous."

THE CLAIM INVALID.

We would remark as follows:—

1. The fourth voyage may be traced as a journey through Lake Superior, past the pictured rocks on its south side, beyond the copper deposits, westward to where there are prairie meadows, where the Indians grow Indian corn, and where elk and buffalo are found, in fact in the region toward the Mississippi River.

2. The country was toward that of the Nadoneseronons, i.e. the Nadouessi or Sioux; north-east of them were the Christinos or Crees; so

that the region must have been what we know at present as Northern Minnesota. They visited the country of the Sioux, the present States of Dakota, and promised to visit the Christinos on their side of the upper lake, evidently Lake of the Woods or Winnipeg.

3. In the passage before us they were fulfilling their promise. They came to the "seaside." This has given colour to the idea that Hudson Bay is meant. An examination of Radisson's writing shows us, however, that he uses the terms lake and sea interchangeably. For example, in, he speaks of the "Christinos from the bay of the North Sea," which could only refer to the Lake of the Woods or Lake Winnipeg. Again, on, Radisson speaks of the "Lake of the Hurrons which was upon the border of the sea," evidently meaning Lake Superior. On the same page, in the heading of the third voyage, he speaks of the "filthy Lake of the Hurrons, Upper Sea of the East, and Bay of the north," and yet no one has claimed that in this voyage he visited Hudson Bay. Again, elsewhere, Radisson uses the expression, "salted lake" for the Atlantic, which must be crossed to reach France.

4. Thus in the passage "the ruined house on the seaside" would seem to have been one of the lakes mentioned. The Christinos tell them of Europeans, whom they have met a few years before, perhaps an earlier French party on Lake Superior or at the Sault. The lake or sea abounded in islands. This would agree with the Lake of the Woods, where the Christinos lived, and not Hudson Bay. Whatever place it was it had a great store of cows or buffalo. Lake of the Woods is the eastern limit of the buffalo. They are not found on the shores of Hudson Bay.

5. It will be noticed also that he speaks of a river flowing from the lake, when he had gone further in the bay, evidently the extension of the lake, and this river empties itself into the Saguenay. This is plainly pure nonsense. It would be equally nonsensical to speak of it in connection with the Hudson Bay, as no river empties from it into the Saguenay.

Probably looking at the great River Winnipeg as it flows from Lake of the Woods, or Bay of Islands as it was early called, he sees it flowing north-easterly, and with the mistaken views so common among early voyageurs, conjectures it to run toward the great Saguenay and to empty into it, thence into the St. Lawrence.

6. This passage shows the point reached, which some interpret as Hudson Bay or James Bay, could not have been so, for it speaks of a further point toward the north, toward the sea.

7. Closely interpreted, it is plain that Radisson had not only not visited Hudson or James Bay, but that he had a wrong conception of it altogether. He is simply giving a vague story of the Christinos.

On the return of Groseilliers and Radisson to Quebec, the former was made a prisoner by order of the Governor for illicit trading. The two partners were fined 4000*l.* for the purpose of erecting a fort at Three Rivers, and 6000*l.* to go to the general funds of New France.

A GREAT ENTERPRISE.

Filled with a sense of injustice at the amount of the fine placed upon them, the unfortunate traders crossed over to France and sought restitution. It was during their heroic efforts to secure a remission of the fine that the two partners urged the importance, both in Quebec and Paris, of an expedition being sent out to explore Hudson Bay, of which they had heard from the Indians. Their efforts in Paris were fruitless, and they came back to Quebec, burning for revenge upon the rapacious Governor.

Driven to desperation by what they considered a persecution, and no doubt influenced by their being Protestant in faith, the adventurers now turned their faces toward the English. In 1664 they went to Port Royal, in Acadia, and thence to New England. Boston was then the centre of English enterprise in America, and the French explorers brought their case before the merchants of that town. They asserted that having been on Lake Assiniboine, north of Lake Superior, they had there been assured by the Indians that Hudson Bay could be reached.

After much effort they succeeded in engaging a New England ship, which went as far as Lat. 61, to the entrance of Hudson Straits, but on account of the timidity of the master of the ship, the voyage was given up and the expedition was fruitless.

The two enterprising men were then promised by the shipowners the use of two vessels to go on their search in 1665, but they were again discouraged by one of the vessels being sent on a trip to Sable Isle and the other to the fisheries in the Gulf of St. Lawrence. Groseilliers and Radisson, bitterly disappointed, sought to maintain their rights against the shipowners in the Courts, and actually won their case, but they were still unable to organize an expedition.

At this juncture the almost discouraged Frenchmen met the two Royal Commissioners who were in America in behalf of Charles II. to settle a number of disputed questions in New England and New York. By one of these, Sir George Carteret, they were induced to visit England. Sir George was no other than the Vice-Chamberlain to the King and Treasurer of the Navy. He and our adventurers sailed for Europe, were captured by a Dutch ship, and after being landed on the coast of Spain, reached England.

Through the influence of Carteret they obtained an audience with King Charles on October 25th, 1666, and he promised that a ship should be supplied to them as soon as possible with which to proceed on their long-planned journey.

Even at this stage another influence came into view in the attempt of De Witt, the Dutch Ambassador, to induce the Frenchmen to desert England and go out under the auspices of Holland. Fortunately they refused these offers.

The war with the Dutch delayed the expedition for one year, and in the second year their vessel received orders too late to be fitted up for the voyage. The assistance of the English ambassador to France, Mr. Montague, was then invoked by Groseilliers and Radisson, now backed up by a number of merchant friends to prepare for the voyage.

Through this influence, an audience was obtained from Prince Rupert, the King's cousin, and his interest was awakened in the enterprise.

It was a remarkable thing that at this time the Royal House of England showed great interest in trade. A writer of a century ago has said, "Charles II., though addicted to pleasure, was capable of useful exertions, and he loved commerce. His brother, the Duke of York, though possessed of less ability, was endowed with greater perseverance, and by a peculiar felicity placed his chief amusement in commercial schemes whilst he possessed the whole influence of the State." "The Duke of York spent half his time in the business of commerce in the city, presiding frequently at meetings of courts of directors."

It will be seen that the circumstances were very favourable for the French enthusiasts who were to lead the way to Hudson Bay, and the royal personages who were anxious to engage in new and profitable schemes.

The first Stock Book (1667) is still in existence in the Hudson's Bay House, in London, and gives an account of the stock taken in the enterprise even before the Company was organized by charter. First on the list is the name of His Royal Highness the Duke of York, and, on the credit side of the account, "By a share presented to him in the stock and adventure by the Governor and Company, 300l."

The second stockholder on the list is the notable Prince Rupert, who took 300l. stock, and paid it up in the next two years, with the exception of 100l. which he transferred to Sir George Carteret, who evidently was the guiding mind in the beginning of the enterprise. Christopher, Duke of Albemarle—the son of the great General Monk, who had been so influential in the restoration of Charles II. to the throne of England, was a stockholder for 500l.

Then came as stockholders, and this before the Company had been formally organized, William, Earl of Craven, well known as a personal friend of Prince Rupert; Henry, Earl of Arlington, a member of the ruling cabal; while Anthony, Earl of Shaftesbury, the versatile minister of Charles, is down for 700l. Sir George Carteret is charged with between six and seven hundred pounds' worth of stock; Sir John

Robinson, Sir Robert Vyner, Sir Peter Colleton and others with large sums.

As we have seen, in the year 1667 the project took shape, a number of those mentioned being responsible for the ship, its cargo, and the expenses of the voyage. Among those who seem to have been most ready with their money were the Duke of Albemarle, Earl of Craven, Sir George Carteret, Sir John Robinson, and Sir Peter Colleton. An entry of great interest is made in connection with the last-named knight. He is credited with 96*l.* cash paid to the French explorers, who were the originators of the enterprise. It is amusing, however, to see Groseilliers spoken of as "Mr. Gooseberry"—a somewhat inaccurate translation of his name.

Two ships were secured by the merchant adventurers, the *Eaglet*, Captain Stannard, and the *Nonsuch Ketch*, Captain Zachariah Gillam. The former vessel has almost been forgotten, because after venturing on the journey, passing the Orkneys, crossing the Atlantic, and approaching. Hudson Straits, the master thought the enterprise an impossible one, and returned to London.

Special interest attaches to the *Nonsuch Ketch*. It was the successful vessel, but another notable thing connected with it was that its New England captain, Zachariah Gillam, had led the expedition of 1664, though now the vessel under his command was one of the King's ships.

It was in June, 1668, that the vessels sailed from Gravesend, on the Thames, and proceeded on their journey, Groseilliers being aboard the *Nonsuch*, and Radisson in the *Eaglet*. The *Nonsuch* found the Bay, discovered little more than half a century before by Hudson, and explored by Button, Fox, and James, the last-named less than forty years before. Captain Gillam is said to have sailed as far north as 75° N. in Baffin Bay, though this is disputed, and then to have returned into Hudson Bay, where, turning southward, he reached the bottom of the Bay on September 29th. Entering a stream, the Nemisco, on the southeast corner of the Bay—a point probably not less than 150 miles from the nearest French possessions in Canada—the party took possession of it, calling it, after the name of their distinguished patron, Prince Rupert's River.

Here, at their camping-place, they met the natives of the district, probably a branch of the Swampy Crees. With the Indians they held a parley, and came to an agreement by which they were allowed to occupy a certain portion of territory. With busy hands they went to work and built a stone fort, in Lat. 51° 20' N., Long. 78° W., which, in honour of their gracious sovereign, they called "Charles Fort."

Not far away from their fort lay Charlton Island, with its shores of white sand, and covered over with a growth of juniper and spruce. To this they crossed on the ice upon the freezing of the river on December 9th. Having made due preparations for the winter, they passed the long and dreary time, finding the cold excessive. As they looked out they saw "Nature looking like a carcase frozen to death."

In April, 1669, however, the cold was almost over, and they were surprised to see the bursting forth of the spring. Satisfied with their journey, they left the Bay in this year and sailed southward to Boston, from which port they crossed the ocean to London, and gave an account of their successful voyage.

The fame of the pioneer explorer is ever an enviable one. There can be but one Columbus, and so for all time this voyage of Zachariah Gillam, because it was the expedition which resulted in the founding of the first fort, and in the beginning of the great movement which has lasted for more than two centuries, will be memorable. It was not an event which made much stir in London at the time, but it was none the less the first of a long series of most important and far-reaching activities.

CHAPTER II.

Royal charters—Good Queen Bess—"So miserable a wilderness"—Courtly stockholders—Correct spelling—"The nonsense of the Charters"—Mighty rivers—Lords of the territory—To execute justice—War on infidels—Power to seize—"Skin for skin"—Friends of the red man.

THE success of the first voyage made by the London merchants to Hudson Bay was so marked that the way was open for establishing the Company and carrying on a promising trade. The merchants who had given their names or credit for Gillam's expedition lost no time in applying, with their patron, Prince Rupert, at their head, to King Charles II. for a Charter to enable them more safely to carry out their plans. Their application was, after some delay, granted on May 2nd, 1670.

The modern method of obtaining privileges such as they sought would have been by an application to Parliament; but the seventeenth century was the era of Royal Charters. Much was said in England eighty years after the giving of this Charter, and again in Canada forty years ago, against the illegality and unwisdom of such Royal Charters as the one granted to the Hudson's Bay Company. These criticisms, while perhaps just, scarcely cover the ground in question.

As to the abstract point of the granting of Royal Charters, there would probably be no two opinions to-day, but it was conceded to be a royal prerogative two centuries ago, although the famous scene cannot be forgotten where Queen Elizabeth, in allowing many monopolies which she had granted to be repealed, said in answer to the Address from the House of Commons: "Never since I was a queen did I put my pen to any grant but upon pretext and semblance made to me that it was both good and beneficial to the subject in general, though private profit to some of my ancient servants who had deserved well. . . Never thought was cherished in my heart that tended not to my people's good."

The words, however, of the Imperial Attorney-General and Solicitor-General, Messrs. Bethel and Keating, of Lincoln's Inn, when appealed to by the British Parliament, are very wise: "The questions of the validity and construction of the Hudson's Bay Company Charter cannot be considered apart from the enjoyment that has been had under it during nearly two centuries, and the recognition made of the rights of the Company in various acts, both of the Government and Legislature."

The bestowal of such great privileges as those given to the Hudson's Bay Company are easily accounted for in the prevailing idea as to the royal prerogative, the strong influence at Court in favour of the applicants for the Charter, and, it may be said, in such opinions as that expressed forty years after by Oldmixon: "There being no towns or plantations in this country (Rupert's Land), but two or three forts to defend the factories, we thought we were at liberty to place it in our book where we pleased, and were loth to let our history open with the description of so wretched a Colony. For as rich as the trade to those parts has been or may be, the way of living is such that we cannot reckon any man happy whose lot is cast upon this Bay."

The Charter certainly opens with a breath of unrestrained heartiness on the part of the good-natured King Charles. First on the list of recipients is "our dear entirely beloved Prince Rupert, Count Palatine of the Rhine, Duke of Bavaria and Cumberland, etc," who seems to have taken the King captive, as if by one of his old charges when he gained the name of the fiery Rupert of Edgehill. Though the stock book of the Company has the entry made in favour of Christopher, Duke of Albemarle, yet the Charter contains that of the famous General Monk, who, as "Old George," stood his ground in London during the year of the plague and kept order in the terror-stricken city. The explanation of the occurrence of the two names is found in the fact that the father died in the year of the granting of the Charter. The reason for the appearance of the name of Sir Philip Carteret in the Charter is not so evident, for not only was Sir George Carteret one of the promoters of the Company, but his name occurs as one of the Court of Adventurers in the year after the granting of the Charter. John Portman, citizen and goldsmith of London, is the only member named who is neither nobleman, knight, nor esquire, but he would seem to have been very useful to the Company as a man of means.

The Charter states that the eighteen incorporators named deserve the privileges granted because they "have at their own great cost and charges undertaken an expedition for Hudson Bay, in the north-west parts of America, for a discovery of a new passage into the South Sea, and for the finding of some trade for furs, minerals, and other considerable commodities, and by such their undertakings, have already made such discoveries as to encourage them to proceed farther in pursuance of their said design, by means whereof there may probably arise great advantage to Us and our kingdoms."

The full name of the Company given in the Charter is, "The Governor and Company of Adventurers of England, trading into Hudson Bay." They have usually been called "The Hudson's Bay Company," the form of the possessive case being kept in the name, though it is usual to speak of the bay itself as Hudson Bay. The adventurers are given the powers of possession, succession, and the legal rights and responsibilities usually bestowed in incorporation, with the power of adopting a seal or changing the same at their "will and pleasure"; and this is granted in the elaborate phraseology found in documents of that period. Full provision is made in the Charter for the election of Governor, Deputy-Governor, and the Managing Committee of seven. It is interesting to notice during the long career of the Company how the simple machinery thus provided was adapted, without amendment, in carrying out the immense projects of the Company during the two and a quarter centuries of its existence.

The grant was certainly sufficiently comprehensive. The opponents of the Company in later days mentioned that King Charles gave away in his sweeping phrase a vast territory of which he had no conception, and that it was impossible to transfer property which could not be described. In the case of the English Colonies along the Atlantic coast it was held by the holders of the charters that the frontage of the seaboard carried with it the strip of land all the way across the continent. It will be remembered how, in the settlement with the Commissioners after the American Revolution, Lord Shelburne spoke of this theory as the "nonsense of the charters." The Hudson's Bay Company was always very successful in the maintenance of its claim to the full privileges of the Charter, and until the time of the surrender of its territory to Canada kept firm possession of the country from the shore of Hudson Bay even to the Rocky Mountains.

The generous monarch gave the Company "the whole trade of all those seas, streights, and bays, rivers, lakes, creeks, and sounds, in whatsoever latitude they shall be, that lie within the entrance of the streights commonly called Hudson's Streights, together with all the lands, countries, and territories upon the coasts and confines of the seas, streights, bays, lakes, rivers, creeks, and sounds aforesaid, which are not now actually possessed by any of our subjects, or by the subjects of any other Christian prince or State."

The wonderful water system by which this great claim was extended over so vast a portion of the American continent has been often described. The streams running from near the shore of Lake Superior find their way by Rainy Lake, Lake of the Woods, and Lake Winnipeg, then by the River Nelson, to Hudson Bay. Into Lake Winnipeg, which acts as a collecting basin for the interior, also run the Red River and mighty Saskatchewan, the latter in some ways rivalling the Mississippi, and springing from the very heart of the Rocky Mountains. The territory thus drained was all legitimately covered by the language of the Charter. The tenacious hold of its vast domain enabled the Company to secure in later years leases of territory lying beyond it on the Arctic and Pacific slopes. In the grant thus given perhaps the most troublesome feature was the exclusion, even from the territory granted, of the portion "possessed by the subjects of any other Christian prince or State." We shall see afterwards that within less than twenty years claims were made by the French of a portion of the country on the south side of the Bay; and also a most strenuous contention was put forth at a later date for the French explorers, as having first entered in the territory lying in the basin of the Red and Saskatchewan Rivers. This claim, indeed, was advanced less than fifty years ago by Canada as the possessor of the rights once maintained by French Canada.

The grant in general included the trade of the country, but is made more specific in one of the articles of the Charter, in that "the fisheries within Hudson's Streights, the minerals, including gold, silver, gems, and precious stones, shall be possessed by the Company." It is interesting to note that the country thus vaguely described is recognized as one of the English "Plantations or Colonies in America," and is called, in compliment to the popular Prince, "Rupert's Land."

Perhaps the most astounding gift bestowed by the Charter is not that of the trade, or what might be called, in the phrase of the old Roman law, the "usufruct," but the transfer of the vast territory, possibly more than one quarter or a third of the whole of North America, to hold it "in free and common socage," i.e., as absolute proprietors. The value of this concession was tested in the early years of this century, when the Hudson's Bay Company sold to the Earl of Selkirk a portion of the territory greater in area than the whole of England and Scotland; and in this the Company was supported by the highest legal authorities in England.

To the minds of some, even more remarkable than the transfer of the ownership of so large a territory was the conferring upon the Company by the Crown of the power to make laws, not only for their own forts and plantations, with all their officers and servants, but having force over all persons upon the lands ceded to them so absolutely.

The authority to administer justice is also given in no uncertain terms. The officers of the Company "may have power to judge all persons belonging to the said Governor and Company, or that shall live under them, in all causes, whether civil or criminal, according to the laws of this kingdom, and execute justice accordingly." To this was also added the power of sending those charged with offences to England to be tried and punished. The authorities, in the course of time, availed themselves of this right. We shall see in the history of the Red River Settlement, in the very heart of Rupert's Land, the spectacle of a community of several thousands of people within a circle having a radius of fifty miles ruled by Hudson's Bay Company authority, with the customs duties collected, certain municipal institutions established, and justice administered, and the people for two generations not possessed of representative institutions.

One of the powers most jealously guarded by all governments is the control of military expeditions. There is a settled unwillingness to allow private individuals to direct or influence them. No qualms of this sort seem to have been in the royal mind over this matter in connection with the Hudson's Bay Company. The Company is fully empowered in the Charter to send ships of war, men, or ammunition into their plantations, allowed to choose and appoint commanders and officers, and even to issue them their commissions.

There is a ludicrous ring about the words empowering the Company to make peace or war with any prince or people whatsoever that are not Christians, and to be permitted for this end to build all necessary castles and fortifications. It seems to have the spirit of the old formula leaving Jews, Turks, and Saracens to the uncovenanted mercies rather than to breathe the nobler principles of a Christian land. Surely, seldom before or since has a Company gone forth thus armed *cap-à-pie* to win glory and profit for their country.

An important proviso of the Charter, which was largely a logical sequence of the power given to possess the wide territory, was the grant of the "whole, entire, and only Liberty of Trade and Traffick." The claim of a complete monopoly of trade was held most strenuously by the Company from the very beginning. The early history of the Company abounds with accounts of the steps taken to prevent the incoming of interlopers. These were private traders, some from the English colonies in America, and others from England, who fitted out expeditions to trade upon the Bay. Full power was given by the Charter "to seize upon the persons of all such English or any other subjects, which sail into Hudson's Bay or inhabit in any of the countries, islands, or territories granted to the said Governor and Company, without their leave and license in that behalf first had and obtained."

The abstract question of whether such monopoly may rightly be granted by a free government is a difficult one, and is variously decided by different authorities. The "free trader" was certainly a person greatly disliked in the early days of the Company. Frequent allusions are made in the minutes of the Company, during the first fifty years of its existence, to the arrest and punishment of servants or employés of the Company who secreted valuable furs on their homeward voyage for the purpose of disposing of them. As late as half a century ago, in the more settled parts of Rupert's Land, on the advice of a judge who had a high sense of its prerogative, an attempt was made by the Company to prevent private trading in furs. Very serious local disturbances took place in the Red River Settlement at that time, but wiser counsels prevailed, and in the later years of the Company's regime the imperative character of the right was largely relaxed.

The Charter fittingly closes with a commendation of the Company by the King to the good offices of all admirals, justices, mayors, sheriffs, and other officers of the Crown, enjoining them to give aid, favour, help, and assistance.

With such extensive powers, the wonder is that the Company bears, on the whole, after its long career over such an extended area of operations, and among savage and border people unaccustomed to the restraints of law, so honourable a record. Being governed by men of high standing, many of them closely associated with the operations of government at home, it is very easy to trace how, as "freedom broadened slowly down" from Charles II. to the present time, the method of dealing with subjects and subordinates became more and more gentle and considerate. As one reads the minutes of the Company in the Hudson's Bay House for the first quarter of a century of its history, the tyrannical spirit, even so far at the removal of troublesome or unpopular members of the Committee and the treatment of rivals, is very evident.

This intolerance was of the spirit of the age. In the Restoration, the Revolution, and the trials of prisoners after rebellion, men were accustomed to the exercise of the severest penalties for the crimes committed. As the spirit of more gentle administration of law found its way into more peaceful times the Company modified its policy.

The Hudson's Bay Company was, it is true, a keen trader, as the motto, "Pro Pelle Cutem"—"skin for skin"—clearly implies. With this no fault can be found, the more that its methods were nearly all honourable British methods. It never forgot the flag that floated over it. One of the greatest testimonies in its favour was that, when two centuries after its organization it gave up, except as a purely trading company, its power to Canada, yet its authority over the wide-spread Indian population of Rupert's Land was so great, that it was asked by the Canadian Government to retain one-twentieth of the land of that wide domain as a guarantee of its assistance in transferring power from the old to the new regime.

The Indian had in every part of Rupert's Land absolute trust in the good faith of the Company. To have been the possessor of such absolute powers as those given by the Charter; to have on the whole "borne their faculties so meek"; to have been able to carry on government and trade so long and so successfully, is not so much a commendation of the royal donor of the Charter as it is of the clemency and general fairness of the administration, which entitled it not only officially but also really, to the title "The Honourable Hudson's Bay Company."

CHAPTER III.

THE generation that lived between the founding of the Company and the end of the century saw a great development in the trade of the infant enterprise. Meeting sometimes at the place of business of one of the Committee, and afterwards at hired premises, the energetic members of the sub-committee paid close attention to their work. Sir John Robinson, Sir John Kirke, and Mr. Portman acted as one such executive, and the monthly, and at times weekly meetings of the Court of Adventurers were held when they were needed. It brings the past very close to us as we read the minutes, still preserved in the Hudson's Bay House, Leadenhall Street, London, of a meeting at Whitehall in 1671, with His Highness Prince Rupert in the chair, and find the sub-committee appointed to carry on the business. Captain Gillam for a number of years remained in the service of the Company as a trusted captain, and commanded the ship Prince Rupert. Another vessel, the *Windingoo*, or *Wyvenhoe Pinck*, was soon added, also in time the *Moosongee Dogger*, then the *Shaftsbury*, the *Albemarle*, and the *Craven Bark*—the last three named from prominent members of the Company. Not more than three of these ships were in use at the same time.

The fitting out of these ships was a work needing much attention from the sub-committee. Year after year its members went down to Gravesend about the end of May, saw the goods which had been purchased placed aboard the ships, paid the captain and men their wages, delivered the agents to be sent out their commissions, and exercised plenary power in regard to emergencies which arose. The articles selected indicate very clearly the kind of trade in which the Company engaged. The inventory of goods in 1672 shows how small an affair the trade at first was. "Two hundred fowling-pieces, and powder and shot; 200 brass kettles, size from five to sixteen gallons; twelve gross of knives; 900 or 1000 hatchets," is recorded as being the estimate of cargo for that year.

A few years, however, made a great change. Tobacco, glass beads, 6,000 flints, boxes of red lead, looking-glasses, netting for fishing, pewter dishes, and pewter plates were added to the consignments. That some attention was had by the Company to the morals of their employés is seen in that one ship's cargo was provided with "a book of common prayer, and a book of homilies."

About June 1st, the ship, or ships, sailed from the Thames, rounded the North of Scotland, and were not heard of till October, when they returned with their valuable cargoes. Year after year, as we read the records of the Company's history, we find the vessels sailing out and returning with the greatest regularity, and few losses took place from wind or weather during that time.

The agents of the Company on the Bay seem to have been well selected and generally reliable men. Certain French writers and also the English opponents of the Company have represented them as timid men, afraid to leave the coast and penetrate to the interior, and their conduct has been contrasted with that of the daring, if not reckless, French explorers. It is true that for about one hundred years the Hudson's Bay Company men did not leave the shores of Hudson Bay, but what was the need so long as the Indians came to the coast with their furs and afforded them profitable trade! By the orders of the Company they opened up trade at different places on the shores of the Bay, and we learn from Oldmixon that fifteen years after the founding of the Company there were forts established at (1) Albany River; (2) Hayes Island; (3) Rupert's River; (4) Port Nelson; (5) New Severn. According to another authority, Moose River takes the place of Hayes Island in this list. These forts and factories, at first primitive and small, were gradually increased in size and comfort until they became, in some cases, quite extensive.

The plan of management was to have a governor appointed over each fort for a term of years, and a certain number of men placed under his direction. In the first year of the Hudson's Bay Company's operations as a corporate body, Governor Charles Bailey was sent out to take charge of Charles Fort at Rupert's River. With him was associated the French adventurer, Radisson, and his nephew, Jean Baptiste Groseilliers. Bailey seems to have been an efficient officer, though fault was found with him by the Company. Ten years after the founding of the Company he died in London, and was voted a funeral by the Company, which took place by twilight to St. Paul's, Covent Garden. The widow of the Governor maintained a contention against the Company for an allowance of 400*l*., which was given after three years' dispute. Another Governor was William Lydall, as also John Bridgar, Governor of the West Main; and again Henry Sargeant, Thomas Phipps, Governor of Fort Nelson, and John Knight, Governor of Albany, took an active part in the disputes of the Company with the French. Thus, with a considerable amount of friction, the affairs of the Company were conducted on the new and inhospitable coast of Hudson Bay.

To the forts from the vast interior of North America the various tribes of Indians, especially the Crees, Chipewyans, and Eskimos, brought their furs for barter. No doubt the prices were very much in favour of the traders at first, but during the first generation of traders the competition of French traders from the south for their share of the Indian trade tended to correct injustice and give the Indians better prices for their furs.

The following is the standard fixed at this time:—

Guns	twelve winter beaver skins for largest, ten for medium, eight for smallest.
Powder	a beaver for ½ lb.
Shot	a beaver for 4 lbs.
Hatchets	a beaver for a great and little hatchet.
Knives	a beaver for eight great knives and eight jack knives.

Beads	a beaver for ½ lb. of beads.
Laced coats	six beavers for one.
Plain coats	live beavers for one plain red coat.
Coats for women, laced, 2 yds	six beavers.
Coats for women, plain	five beavers.
Tobacco	a beaver for 1 lb.
Powder-horn	a beaver for a large powder-horn and two small ones.
Kettles	a beaver for 1 lb, of kettle.
Looking-glass and comb	two skins.

The trade conducted at the posts or factories along the shore was carried on by the local traders so soon as the rivers from the interior—the Nelson and the Churchill—were open, so that by the time the ship from London arrived, say in the end of July or beginning of August, the Indians were beginning to reach the coast. The month of August was a busy month, and by the close of it, or early in September, the ship was loaded and sent back on her journey.

By the end of October the ships arrived from Hudson Bay, and the anxiety of the Company to learn how the season's trade had succeeded was naturally very great. As soon as the vessels had arrived in the Downs or at Portsmouth, word was sent post haste to London, and the results were laid before a Committee of the Company. Much reference is made in the minutes to the difficulty of preventing the men employed in the ships from entering into illicit trade in furs. Strict orders were given to inspect the lockers for furs to prevent private trade. In due time the furs were unladen from the ships and put into the custody of the Company's secretary in the London warehouse.

The matter of selling the furs was one of very great importance. At times the Company found prices low, and deferred their sales until the outlook was more favourable. The method followed was to have an auction, and every precaution was taken to have the sales fair and aboveboard. Evidences are not wanting that at times it was difficult for the Court of Adventurers to secure this very desirable result.

The matter was not, however, one of dry routine, for the London merchants seem to have encouraged business with generous hospitality. On November 9th, 1681, the sale took place, and the following entry is found in the minutes: "A Committee was appointed to provide three dozen bottles of sack and three dozen bottles of claret, to be given to buyers at ye sale. Dinner was also bespoken at 'Ye Stillyard,' of a good dish of fish, a loyne of veal, two pullets, and four ducks."

As the years went on, the same variations in furs that we see in our day took place. New markets were then looked for and arrangements made for sending agents to Holland and finding the connections in Russia, that sales might be effected. In order to carry out the trade it was necessary to take large quantities of hemp from Holland in return for the furs sent. The employment of this article for cordage in the Navy led to the influence of important members of the Company being used with the Earl of Marlborough to secure a sale for this commodity. Pending the sales it was necessary for large sums of money to be advanced to carry on the business of the Company. This was generally accomplished by the liberality of members of the Company itself supplying the needed amounts.

The Company was, however, from time to time gratified by the declaration of handsome dividends. So far as recorded, the first dividend was declared in 1684, and judged by modern standards it was one for which a company might well wait for a number of years. It was for 50 per cent. upon stock. Accordingly, the Earl of Craven received 150*l.*, Sir James Hayes 150*l.*, and so on in proportion. In 1688 another dividend of a like amount of 50 per cent. on the stock resulted, and among others, Hon. Robert Boyle, Earl Churchill, and Sir Christopher Wren had their hearts gladdened. In 1689 profits to the extent of 25 per cent. on the stock were received, and one of the successful captains was, in the exuberance of feeling of the stock-holders, presented with a silver flagon in recognition of his services. In 1690, however, took place by far the most remarkable event of a financial kind in the early history of the

Company. The returns of that year from the Bay were so large that the Company decided to treble its stock. The reasons given for this were:—

(1) The Company has in its warehouse about the value of its original stock (10,500*l*.). (2) The factories at Fort Nelson and New Severn are increasing in trade, and this year the returns are expected to be 20,000*l*. in beaver. (3) The factories are of much value. (4) Damages are expected from the French for a claim of 100,000*l*.

The Company then proceeded to declare a dividend of 25 per cent., which was equivalent to 75 per cent. on their original stock.

It was a pleasing incident to the sovereign of the realm that in all these profits he was not forgotten. In the original Charter the only recompense coming to the Crown, for the royal gift, was to be the payment, when the territory was entered upon, of "two elks and two black beavers." This may have been a device for keeping up the royal claim, but at any rate 300*l*. in the original stock-book stood to the credit of the sovereign. It had been the custom to send a deputation to present in person the dividends to His Majesty, and the pounds sterling were always changed to guineas.

On this occasion of the great dividend, King William III. had but lately returned from his victories in Ireland. The deputation, headed by Sir Edward Dering, was introduced to the King by the Earl of Portland, and the following address, hitherto, so far as known to the writer, unpublished, was presented along with the noble gift:—

"Your Majestie's most Loyal and Dutiful subjects beg leave to congratulate your Majestie's Happy Return here with Honor and Safety. And we do daily pray to Heaven (that Hath God wonderfully preserved your Royall Person) that in all your undertakings Your Majestic may be as victorious as Caesar, as beloved as Titus, and (after all) have the long and glorious Reigne and Peacefull end of Augustus."

On this happy occasion we desire also most humbly to present to your Majestic a dividend of *Two Hundred and twenty-five guineas* upon three hundred pounds stock in the Hudson's Bay Company, now Rightfully delivered to your Majestie. And although we have been the greatest sufferers of any Company from those common enemies of all mankind the French, yet when your Majestie's just Arms shall have given Repose to all Christendom, we also shall enjoy our share of these great Benefits and do not doubt but to appeare often with this golden fruit in our hands, under the happy influence of Your Majestie's most gracious protection over us and all our Concerns."

It is true that towards the end of the seventeenth century, as we shall afterwards see, the trade of the Company was seriously injured by the attacks of the French on the Bay, but a quarter of a century in which the possibility of obtaining such profits had been shown was sufficient to establish the Company in the public favour and to attract to it much capital. Its careful management from the first led to its gaining a reputation for business ability which it has never lost during two and a quarter centuries of its history.

CHAPTER IV.

Men of high station—Prince Rupert primus—Prince James, "nemine contradicente"—The hero of the hour—Churchill River named—Plate of solid gold—Off to the Tower.

THE success of the Hudson's Bay Company, and the influence exerted by it during so long a period, has often been attributed to the union of persons of station and high political influence with the practical and far-seeing business men of London, who made up the Company. A perusal of the minutes of the first thirty years of the Company's history impresses on the mind of the reader that this is true, and that good feeling and patriotism were joined with business tact and enterprise in all the ventures. From the prosperous days of Queen Elizabeth and her sea-going captains and explorers, certainly from the time of Charles II., it was no uncommon thing to see the titled and commercial classes co-operating, in striking contrast to the governing classes of France, in making commerce and trade a prominent feature of the national life.

The first Governor of the Hudson's Bay Company, Rupert, Prince of Bavaria, grandson by the mother's side of James I. of England, is a sufficiently well-known character in general history to require no extended notice. His exploits on the Royalist side in the Civil War, his fierce charges and his swiftness in executing difficult military movements, led to his name being taken as the very embodiment of energy and prowess. In this sense the expression, "the fiery Rupert of debate" was applied to a prominent parliamentarian of the past generation.

After the restoration of Charles II., Prince Rupert took up his abode in England, finding it more like home to him than any Continental country. Enjoying the plaudits of the Cavaliers, for whom he had so strenuously fought, he was appointed Constable of Windsor, a no very onerous position. From the minutes of the Hudson's Bay Company we find that he had lodgings at Whitehall, and spent much of his time in business and among scientific circles—indeed, the famous toys called "glass tears," or "Rupert's drops," were brought over by him to England from the Continent to interest his scientific friends.

We have seen already the steps taken by the returned Commissioners from the American Colonies to introduce Radisson and Groseilliers to Prince Rupert, and through him to the royal notice.

The success of the expedition of Gillam and the building of Charles Fort on Hudson Bay led to the Prince consenting to head the new Company. He had just passed the half century of his age when he was appointed Governor of the vast terra *incognita* lying to the west of the Bay to which, in his honour, was given the name Rupert's Land.

The Company lost no time in undertaking a new expedition. Prince Rupert's intimate friend, the Earl of Craven, was one of the incorporators, and it was with this nobleman that Prince Rupert's widowed mother, the Princess Elizabeth, had found a home in the days of adversity.

The close connection of the Hudson's Bay Company with the Court gave it, we see very plainly, certain important advantages. Not only do the generous terms of the Charter indicate this, but the detailing of certain ships of the Royal Navy to protect the merchantmen going out to Hudson Bay shows the strong bond of sympathy. Certainly nothing less than the thorough interest of the Court could have led to the firm stand taken by the English Government in the controversies with Franco as to the possession of Hudson Bay.

Several excellent paintings of the Prince are in existence, one by Vandyke in Warwick Castle, showing his handsome form, and another in Knebworth, Hertford. The Prince was unfortunately not free from the immorality that was so flagrant a feature of the Court of Charles II. At that time this was but little taken into account, and the fame of his military exploits, together with the fixing of his name upon so wide an extent of the earth's surface, have served to give posterity an interest in him.

For twelve successive years Prince Rupert was chosen Governor at the General Court of Adventurers, and used his great influence for the Company. He died on November 29th, 1682, at the comparatively early age of sixty-three.

The death of the first Governor was a somewhat severe trial for the infant Company. The Prince's name had been one to conjure by, and though he had been ably supported by the Deputy-Governor, Sir James Hayes, yet there was some fear of loss of prestige to the Adventurers on his unexpected death.

The members of the Company were anxious to keep up, if possible, the royal connection, but they were by no means clear as to the choice of the only available personage who came before their view. James, Duke of York, was a man with a liking for business, but he was not a popular favourite. The famous *jeu d'esprit* of Charles II. will be remembered. When James informed Charles II. that there was a conspiracy on foot to drive him from the throne, "No, James," said Charles, "they will never kill me to make you king."

The minutes of the Company show that much deliberation took place as to the choice of a successor to Prince Rupert, but at length, in January, 1683, at a General Court, the choice was made, and the record reads:—"His Royal Highness the Duke of York was chosen Governor of the Company, Nemine contradicente.' " The new Governor soon had reasons to congratulate himself on his election, for on April 21st, 1684, Sir James Hayes and Sir Edward Dering reported to the Adventurers their having paid 150 guineas to His Royal Highness as a dividend on the stock held by him. Prince James was chosen Governor for three successive years, until the year when, on the death of Charles, he became King. While James was not much in favour as a man, yet he possessed decided administrative ability, and whether this was the cause or not, certainly the period of his governorship was a successful time in the history of the Company.

Failing a prince or duke, the lot could not have fallen upon a more capable man than was chosen as the Duke of York's successor for the governorship. On April 2nd, 1685, at a General Court of the Adventurers, the choice fell upon one of the most remarkable men of his time, the Right Hon. John Lord Churchill, afterwards Duke of Marlborough. Lord Churchill had not yet gained any of his great victories. He was, however, at this time a favourite of the Duke of York, and no doubt, on the recommendation of James, had been brought before the Court of Adventurers. He was one of the most adroit men of his time, he was on the highway to the most distinguished honours, and the Adventurers gladly elected him third governor.

On April 2nd, 1685, the new governor threw himself heartily into the work of the Company. No doubt one so closely connected with the public service could be of more practical value than even a royal duke. The great dividend of which we have already spoken followed the years of his appointment.

The success attained but stimulated the Company to increase their trade and widen the field of their operations. The river running into the west side of the Bay, far to the north, was named in honour of the new governor, Churchill River, and in 1686 expansion of trade was sought by the decision to settle at the mouth of this river and use it as a new trading centre for the north and west. Without any desire to annoy the French, who claimed the south end of the Bay, it was determined to send a ship to the southern part of Hudson Bay, and a few months later the *Yonge*, frigate was dispatched. The fear of attacks from the French, who were known to be in a very restless condition, led to the request being made to the Government to station a military force at each fort in Hudson Bay. It was also the desire of the Company that steps should be taken to protect them in their Charter rights and to prevent illegal expeditions from going to trade in the Bay. All this shows the energy and hopefulness of the Company under the leadership of Lord Churchill.

The part taken by Lord Churchill in the opposition to James, and his active agency in inducing William of Orange to come to England, are well known. He was a worshipper of the rising sun. On the arrival of

William III., Lord Churchill, who was soon raised to the peerage as Earl of Marlborough, was as popular, for the time, with the new king as he had been with his predecessor. His zeal is seen in his sending out in June, 1689, as governor, the instructions that William and Mary should be proclaimed in the posts upon the shores of Hudson Bay. He was able shortly after to report to his Company that 100 marines had been detailed to protect the Company's ships on their way to Hudson Bay. The enthusiasm of the Company at this mark of consideration obtained through the influence of Lord Churchill, was very great, and we learn from the minutes that profuse thanks were given to the governor, and a piece of plate of solid gold, of the value of 100 guineas, was presented to him for his distinguished services. Legislation was also introduced at this time into Parliament for the purpose of giving further privileges to the Adventurers.

But the rising tide of fortune was suddenly checked. Disaster overtook the Governor. William had found some reason for distrusting this versatile man of affairs, and he suspected him of being in correspondence with the dethroned James. No doubt the suspicion was well founded, but the King had thought it better, on account of Marlborough's great talents, to overlook his unfaithfulness. Suddenly, in May, 1692, England was startled by hearing that the Earl of Marlborough had been thrown into the Tower on an accusation of high treason. For seven years this determined soldier had led the Company to success, but his imprisonment rendered a change in the governorship a necessity. Marlborough was only imprisoned for a short time, but he was not re-elected to the position he had so well filled. At the General Court of Adventurers in November of the year of Marlborough's fall, Sir Stephen Evance was chosen Governor. This gentleman was re-elected a number of times, and was Governor of the Company at the close of the century.

Two decades, and more, of the formative life of the Company were thus lived under the aegis of the Court, the personal management of two courtly personages, and under the guidance of the leading general of his time. As we shall see afterwards, during a part of this period the affairs of the Company were carried on in the face of the constant opposition of the French. Undoubtedly heavy losses resulted from the French rivalry, but the pluck and wisdom of the Company were equally manifested in the confidence with which they risked their means, and the strong steps taken to retain their hold on Hudson Bay. This was the golden age of the Hudson's Bay Company. When money was needed it was often cheerfully advanced by some of the partners; it was an honour to have stock in a Company which was within the shadow of the throne; its distinguished Governors were reelected so long as they were eligible to serve; again and again the Committee, provided with a rich purse of golden guineas, waited on His Majesty the King to give return for the favour of the Royal Charter; and never afterward can the historian point in the annals of the Company to so distinguished a period.

CHAPTER V.

A MYSTERIOUS interest gathers around two of the most industrious and,
it must be added, most diplomatic and adroit of the agents of the
Company, the two Frenchmen, Pierre Esprit Radisson and Medard
Chouart, afterwards the Sieur de Gro-seilliers. Acquainted with the far
northern fur trade, their assistance was invaluable. We have seen in a
former chapter that finding little encouragement either in New France
or their mother country, they had transferred their services to England,
and were largely instrumental in founding the Hudson's Bay Company.

In the first voyage of the adventurers to Hudson's Bay, it came about
that while Groseilliers was lucky in being on the *Nonsuch* ketch, which
made its way into the Bay, on the other hand, Radisson, to his great
chagrin, was on board the companion ship, the *Eaglet*, which, after
attempting an entrance and failing, returned to England.

It has been stated that during the time of his enforced idleness in
London, while the party was building Charles Fort on Prince Rupert's
River, Radisson was busy interesting the leading men of the city in the
importance of the adventure. Immediately on the return of the company
of the *Nonsuch*, steps were taken for the organization of the Hudson's
Bay Company. This, as we have seen, took place in May, 1670, and in
the same year Radisson and Groseilliers went out with Governor Bailey,
and assisted in establishing trade on the shores of the Bay.

On their return, in the autumn of 1671, to London, the two
adventurers spent the winter there, and, as the minutes of the
Company show, received certain money payments for their
maintenance. In October, 1673, the sloop *Prince Rupert* had arrived at

Portsmouth from Hudson Bay, and there are evidences of friction between Radisson and Captain Gillam. Radisson is called on to be present at a meeting of the General Court of the Company held in October, and afterwards Gillam is authorized to advance the amounts necessary for his living expenses.

In the Company minutes of June 25th, 1674, is found the following entry:—"That there be allowed to Mr. Radisson 100 pounds per annum from the time of his last arrival in London, in consideration of services done by him, out of which to be deducted what hath been already paid him since that time, and if it shall please God to bless this Company with good success hereafter that they shall come to be in a prosperous condition they will then re-assume the consideration thereof."

During the next month a further sum was paid Radisson.

The restless Radisson could not, however, be satisfied. No doubt he felt his services to be of great value, and he now illustrated what was really the weakness of his whole life, a want of honest reliability. The Company had done as well for him as its infant resources would allow, but along with Groseilliers he deserted from London, and sought to return to the service of France under the distinguished Prime Minister Colbert.

The shrewd Colbert knew well Radisson's instability. This feature of his character had been further emphasized by another event in Radisson's life. He had married a daughter of Sir John Kirke, one of the Hudson's Bay Company promoters, and a member of the well-known family which had distinguished itself in the capture of Canada, nearly fifty years before. This English and domestic connection made Colbert suspicious of Radisson. However, he agreed to pay Radisson and Groseilliers the sum of their debts, amounting to 400*l*., and to give them lucrative employment. The condition of his further employment was that Radisson should bring his wife to France, but he was unable to get either his wife or her father to consent to this. The Kirke family, it must be remembered, were still owners of a claim amounting to 341,000*l*.

against France, which had been left unsettled during the time of Champlain, when England restored Canada to France.

For seven years Radisson vacillated between the two countries. Under the French he went for one season on a voyage to the West Indies, and was even promised promotion in the French marine. At one time he applied again to the Hudson's Bay Company for employment, but was refused. The fixed determination of his wife not to leave England on the one hand, and the settled suspicion of the French Government on the other, continually thwarted him. At length, in 1681, Radisson and Groseilliers were sent by the French to Canada, to undertake a trading expedition to Hudson Bay. The lack of money, and also of full confidence, led to their venture being poorly provided for. In July, 1682, rendezvous was made at Ile Percee, in the lower St. Lawrence, by Radisson in a wretched old vessel of ten tons, and by Groseilliers in a rather better craft of fifteen tons burthen.

No better could be done, however, and so, after many mishaps, including serious mutinies, dangers of ice and flood, and hairbreadth escapes, the two vessels reached the mouth of the Hayes River on Hudson Bay. They determined to trade at this point. Groseilliers undertook to build a small fort on this river, and Radisson went inland on a canoe expedition to meet the natives. In this Radisson was fairly successful and gathered a good quantity of furs.

The French adventurers were soon surprised to find that an English party had taken possession of the mouth of the Nelson River, and were establishing a fort. Radisson opened communication with the English, and found them in charge of Governor Bridgar, but really led by young Gillam, son of the old captain of the Nonsuch. The versatile Frenchman soon met a fine field for his diplomatic arts. He professed great friendship for the new comers, exchanged frequent visits with them, and became acquainted with all their affairs. Finding the English short of provisions, he supplied their lack most generously, and offered to render them any service.

Governor Bridgar was entirely unable to cope with the wiles of Radisson. Matters were so arranged that Jean Baptiste Groseilliers, his nephew, was left in charge of the forts, to carry on the trade during the next winter, and with his brother-in-law, Groseilliers, and Governor Bridgar, somewhat of a voluntary prisoner, Radisson sailed away to Canada in Gillam's ship. On reaching Canada Governor De la Barre restored the ship to the English, and in it Bridgar and Gillam sailed to New England, whence in due time they departed for England. The whole affair has a Quixotic appearance, and it is not surprising that Radisson and Groseilliers were summoned to report themselves to Colbert in France and to receive his marked displeasure. Their adventure had, however, been so successful, and the prospects were so good, that the French Government determined to send them out again, in two ships, to reap the fruits of the winter's work of the younger Groseilliers.

Now occurred another of Radisson's escapades. The French expedition was ready to start in April. The day (24th) was fixed. Radisson asked for delay, pleading important private business in England. On May 10th he arrived in England, and we find him, without any compunction, entering into negotiations with the Hudson's Bay Company, and as a result playing the traitor to his engagements in France, his native country.

The entry in the Company's minutes bearing on this affair is as follows:—

"May 12th, 1684."

Sir James Hayes and Mr. Young, that Peter Esprit Radisson has arrived from France; that he has offered to enter their service; that they took him to Windsor and presented him to His Royal Highness; that they had agreed to give him 50*l.* per annum, 200*l.* worth of stock, and 20*l.* to set him up to proceed to Port Nelson; and his brother (in-law) Groseilliers to have 20*s.* per week, if he come from France over to Britain and be true. Radisson took the oath of fidelity to the Company."

A few days later Radisson took the ship *Happy Return* to Hudson Bay. Sailing immediately to Hayes River, Radisson found that his nephew, J. Baptiste Groseilliers, had removed his post to an island in the river. On his being reached, Radisson explained to him the change that had taken place, and that he proposed to transfer everything, establishment and peltry, to the Hudson's Bay Company. Young Groseilliers, being loyal to France, objected to this, but Radisson stated that there was no option, and he would be compelled to submit* The whole quantity of furs transferred to Radisson by his nephew was 20,000—an enormous capture for the Hudson's Bay Company. In the autumn Radisson returned in the Hudson's Bay Company's ship, bringing the great store of booty.

At a meeting of the Committee of the Company (October 7th), "a packet was read from Pierre Radisson showing how he had brought his countrymen to submit to the English. He was thanked, and a gratuity of 100 guineas given him." It is also stated that "a promise having been made of 20s. per week to Groseilliers, and he not having come, the same is transferred to his son in the bay." The minute likewise tells us that "Sir William Young was given a present of seven musquash skins for being instrumental in inviting Radisson over from France." From this we infer that Sir William, who, as we shall afterwards see, was a great friend and promoter of Radisson, had been the active agent in inducing Radisson to leave the service of France and enter that of the English Company.

The Company further showed its appreciation of Radisson's service by voting him 100*l.* to be given to four Frenchmen left behind in Hudson Bay. Jean Baptiste Groseilliers, nephew of Radisson, was also engaged by the Company for four years in the service at 100*l.* a year. Radisson seems to have had some dispute with the Company as to the salary at this time. On May 6th, 1685, his salary when out of England was raised to 100l a year, and 300*l.* to his wife in case of his death. Radisson refused to accept these terms. The Company for a time would not increase its offer, but the time for the ship to sail was drawing nigh, and the Committee gave way and added to the above amount 100*l*. of stock to be given to his wife. John Bridgar was appointed Governor at Port Nelson for three years, and Radisson superintendent of the trade there. Radisson was satisfied with the new terms, and that the Company was greatly impressed with the value of his services is seen in the following entry: "A hogshead of claret being ordered for Mr. Radisson, 'such as Mr. R. shall like.'"

In the year 1685-6 all hitherto printed accounts of Radisson leave our redoubtable explorer. We are, for the history up to this date, much indebted to the Prince Society of Boston for printing an interesting volume containing the Journals of Radisson, which are preserved in the British Museum in London and in the Bodleian Library in Oxford.

Dr. N. E. Dionne, the accomplished librarian of the Legislative Library, Quebec, has contributed to the proceedings of the Royal Society of Canada very appreciative articles entitled, "Chouart and Radisson." In these he has relied for the detail of facts of discovery almost entirely on the publication of the Prince Society. He has, however, added much genealogical and local Canadian material, which tends to make the history of these early explorers more interesting than it could otherwise be.

A resident of Manitoba, who has shown an interest in the legends and early history of Canada, Mr. L. A. Prudhomme, St. Boniface, Judge of the County, has written a small volume of sixty pages on the life of Radisson. Like the articles of Dr. Dionne, this volume depends entirely for its information on the publication of the Prince Society.

Readers of fiction are no doubt familiar with the appearance of Radisson in Gilbert Parker's novel, "The Trail of the Sword." It is unnecessary to state that there seems no historic warrant for the statement, "Once he attempted Count Frontenac's life. He sold a band of our traders to the Iroquois." The character, thoroughly repulsive in this work of fiction, does not look to be the real Radisson; and certainly as we survey the bloody scene, which must have been intended for a period subsequent to Frontenac's return to Canada in 1689, where

Radisson fell done to death by the dagger and pistol of the mutineer Bucklaw and was buried in the hungry sea, we see what was purely imaginary. Of course, we do not for a moment criticize the art of the historic novelist, but simply state that the picture is not that of the real Radisson, and that we shall find Radisson alive a dozen or more years after the tragic end given him by the artist.

These three works, as well as the novel, agree in seeing in Radisson a man of remarkable character and great skill and adroitness.

FURTHER HISTORY.

The Prince Society volume states: "We again hear of Radisson in Hudson Bay in 1685, and this is his last appearance in public records as far as is known." The only other reference is made by Dionne and Prudhomme in stating that Charlevoix declares "that Radisson died in England."

Patient search in the archives of the Hudson's Bay Company in London has enabled the writer to trace the history of Radisson on for many years after the date given, and to unearth a number of very interesting particulars connected with him; indeed, to add some twenty-five years hitherto unknown to our century to his life, and to see him pass from view early in 1710.

In 1687, Radisson was still in the employ of the Company, and the Committee decided that he should be made a denizen or subject of England. He arrived from Hudson Bay in October of this year, appeared before the Hudson's Bay Company Committee, and was welcomed by its members. It was decided that 50*l*. be given as a gratuity to the adventurer till he should be again employed. On June 24th, 1688, Radisson again sailed in the ship for Hudson Bay, and during that year he was paid 100*l*. as 50 per cent. dividend on his 200*l*. worth of stock, and in the following year 50*l*. as 25 per cent. dividend on his stock. As the following year, 1690, was the time of the "great dividend," Radisson was again rejoiced by the amount of 150*l*. as his share of the profits.

The prosperity of the Company appears to have led to an era of extravagance, and to certain dissensions within the Company itself. The amounts paid Radisson were smaller in accordance with the straits in which the Company found itself arising from French rivalry on the Bay. In 1692 Sir William Young is seen strongly urging fuller consideration for Radisson, who was being paid at the reduced rate of 50*l*. a year.

In the Hudson's Bay Company letter-book of this period we find a most interesting memorial of Sir William Young's in behalf of Radisson, with answers by the Company, on the whole confirming our narrative, but stating a few divergent points.

We give the memorial in full.

Dated December 20th, 1692, being plea of William Young, in behalf of Pierre Esprit Radisson:—

"Radisson, born a Frenchman, educated from a child in Canada, spent youth hunting and commercing with the Indians adjacent to Hudson Bay, master of the language, customs, and trade.

"Radisson being at New England about twenty-seven or twenty-eight years past, met there with Colonel Nichols, Governor of New York, and was by him persuaded to go to England and proffer his services to King Charles the Second, in order to make a settlement of an English factory in that bay.

"At his arrival, the said King, giving credit to Radisson for that undertaking, granted to Prince Rupert, the Duke of Albemarle, and others, the same Charter we do still claim by, thereby constituting them the proprietors of the said bay, under which authority he, the said Radisson, went immediately and made an English settlement there according to his promises.

"On his return to England the King presented him with a medal and gold chain. When rejected by the Company, he was compelled to return to Canada, his only place of abode. Joined the French and led an expedition to Hudson Bay. With the aid of Indians destroyed Company's factory and planted a New England factory in Port Nelson River.

"During the winter Radisson did no violence to the English, but supplied them with victuals, powder, and shot when their ship was cast away. Refused a present from the Indians to destroy the English, and gave them a ship to convey them away. Afterwards settled the French factory higher up the same river, where his alliance with the Indians was too strong for New England or Old England, and immediately after he went to France. Mr. Young, member of the Hudson's Bay Company, with leave from Sir James Hayes, deputy-governor, tried to hire him back to Hudson's Bay Company's service with large promises. During negotiations, Radisson unexpectedly arrived in London. Company's ships were ready to sail. Had just time to kiss the King's hand at Windsor and that of the Duke of York, then governor. They commended him to the care and kindness of Sir James Hayes and the Hudson's Bay Company, and commanded that he should be made an English citizen, which was done in his absence.

"Before sending him, the Company gave him two original actions in Hudson's Bay Company stock, and 50l. for subsistence money, with large promises of future rewards for expected service.

"Arriving at Port Nelson he put Company in entire possession of that river, brought away the French to England, and took all the beavers and furs they had traded and gave them to the Company without asking share of the profits, although they sold for 7,000l.

"He was kindly welcomed in England and again commended by the King. Committee presented him with 100 guineas, and entered in the books that he should have 50l. added to the former 50l., until the King should find him a place, when the last 50l. should cease. Had no place given him. Sir Edward Dering, deputy governor, influenced Committee to withdraw 50l., so he had only 50l. to maintain self, wife, and four or five children, and servants, 24l. of this going for house-rent. When chief factor at Nelson, was tempted by servants to continue to cheat the Company, was beaten because he refused.

"Prays for payment of 100l. and arrears, because:

"1. All but Sir Edward Dering think it just and reasonable.

"2. No place was given in lieu of 50l.

"3. Of fidelity to the Company in many temptations.

"4. He never asked more than the Company chose to give.

"5. Imprisoned in bay in time of trade for not continuing to cheat the Company.

"6. The Company received from Port Nelson, after he gave it them, 100,000*l.* worth of furs, which is now believed would have been lost, with their whole interest in the bay, if he had not joined them when invited.

"7. The original actions and the 100*l.* revert to the Company at his death.

"8. Income inadequate to maintain wife and children in London.

"9. Debts great from necessity. Would be compelled to leave wife and children and shift for himself.

"10. He cannot sell original actions, since they cease with his life.

"11. Of King Charles' many recommendations to kindness of Company.

"12. French have a price on his head as a traitor, so that he cannot safely go home.

"13. Mr. Young further pleads that as Mr. Radisson was the author of the Company's prosperity, so he (Mr. Young) was the first to persuade him to join their service. That he (Mr. Young) had been offered a reward for his services in persuading him, which he had utterly refused. But now that this reward be given in the form of maintenance for Radisson in his great necessity, &c."

The Committee passes over the sketch of Radisson's life, which they do not gainsay.

In the second paragraph, they observe that Mr. Young stated their neglect to maintain Mr. Radisson without mentioning their reasons for so doing, which might have shown whether it was their unkindness or Radisson's desert.

They go on to take notice of the fact that about 1681 or 1682, Radisson and Groseilliers entered into another contract with the Company and received 20*l.* Soon afterwards they absconded, went to France, and thence to Canada. Next year they joined their countrymen in an expedition to Port Nelson, animated by the report of Mr. Abram to the Company that it was the best place for a factory. They took their two barks up as far as they durst for fear of the English. Then the French in the fall built a small hut, which Mr. Young says was too strong for either New England or Old England without guns or works— a place merely to sleep in, manned only with seven French.

This expedition, Mr. Young saith, was at first prejudicial to the Company, but afterward of great advantage, which he cannot apprehend.

In another place Mr. Young is pleased to state that the New England settlement was so strong that the Old could not destroy it. Old England settlement was only a house unfortified, which Bridgar built to keep the goods dry, because Gillam's boat arrived late.

"1. Mr. Young says all are in favour of Radisson but Sir Edward Dering, we have not met with any who are in favour but Mr. Young. Those who give gratuity should know why.

"2. That he had no place or honour given him is no reason for giving gratuity, there being no contract in the case.

"3. Never found him accused of cheating and purloining, but breach of contract with Company, after receiving their money, we do find him guilty of.

"4. Says he never did capitulate with the Company. Find he did (see minutes), May 6th, 1685.

"5. Cannot believe Radisson was beaten by the Company's servants. Greater increase of furs after he left, &c., &c., &c."

This memorial and its answer show the rather unreasonable position taken by the Company. In the time of its admiration for Radisson and of fat dividends, it had provided liberal things; but when money became scarce, then it was disposed to make matters pleasing to itself, despite the claims of Radisson. In the year following the presenting of the memorial, it is stated in the minutes that "Radisson was represented to the Company as in a low and mean condition." At this time it was ordered that 50*l.* be paid Radisson and to be repaid out of the next dividend.

The unreasonable position assumed by the Company, in withholding a part of the salary which they had promised in good faith, filled Radisson with a sense of injustice. No doubt guided by his friend, Sir William Young, who, on account of his persistence on behalf of the adventurer, was now dropped from the Committee of the Company, Radisson filed a bill in Chancery against the Company, and in July, 1694, notice of this was served upon the Committee.

Much consternation appears to have filled their minds, and the Deputy-Governor, Sir Samuel Clark, reported shortly after having used 200*l.* for secret service, the matter being seemingly connected with this case.

Notwithstanding the great influence of the Company, the justice of Radisson's claims prevailed, and the Court of Chancery ordered the payment of arrears in full. The Committee afterwards met Sir William Young and Richard Craddock, who upheld Radisson's claim. It is reported that they agreed to settle the matter by paying Radisson 150*l.*, he giving a release, and that he should be paid, under seal, 100*l.* per annum for life, except in those years when the Company should make a dividend, and then but 50*l.* according to the original agreement. Radisson then received, as the minutes show, his salary regularly from this time.

In 1698, the Company asked for the renewal by Parliament of its Charter. Radisson petitioned Parliament for consideration, asking that before the request made by the Company for the confirmation of the privileges sought were granted, a clause should be inserted protecting him in the regular payment of the amounts due to him from time to time by the Company.

At the time of his petition to Parliament he states that he has four young children, and has only the 100*l.* a year given by the Company to live on. In the year 1700 he was still struggling with his straitened circumstances, for in that year he applied to the Company to be appointed warehouse-keeper for the London promises, but his application was refused. His children, of whom he is said to have had nine, appear to have passed over to Canada and to have become a part of the Canadian people. His brother-in-law, Groseilliers, had also returned to his adopted Canada, but is stated to have died before 1698.

Regularly during the succeeding years the quarterly amount is voted to Radisson by the Company, until January 6th, 1710, when the last quota of 12*l.* 10s. was ordered to be given. About this time, at the ripe ago of seventy-four, passed away Pierre Esprit Radisson, one of the most daring and ingenious men of his time. We know nothing of his death, except from the fact that his pension ceased to be paid.

Judge Prudhomme, to whose appreciative sketch of Radisson in French we have already referred, well summarizes his life. We translate:—

"What a strange existence was that of this man! By turns discoverer, officer of marine, organizer and founder of the most commercial company which has existed in North America, his life presents an astonishing variety of human experiences.

"He may be seen passing alternately from the wigwams of the miserable savages to the court of the great Colbert; from managing chiefs of the tribes to addressing the most illustrious nobles of Great Britain.

"His courage was of a high order. He looked death in the face more than a hundred times without trepidation. He braved the tortures and the stake among the Iroquois, the treacherous stratagems of the savages of the West, the rigorous winters of the Hudson Bay, and the tropical heat of the Antilles.

"Of an adventurous nature, drawn irresistibly to regions unknown, carried on by the enthusiasm of his voyages, always ready to push out into new dangers, he could have been made by Fennimore Cooper one of the heroes of his most exciting romances.

"The picture of his life consequently presents many contrasts. The life of a brigand, which he led with a party of Iroquois, cannot be explained away.

"He was blamable in a like manner for having deserted the flag of France, his native country. The first time we might, perhaps, pardon him, for he was the victim of grave injustice on the part of the government of the colony.

"No excuse could justify his second desertion. He had none to offer, not one. He avowed very candidly that he sought the service of England because he preferred it to that of France.

"In marrying the daughter of Mr. John Kirke, he seems to have espoused also the nationality of her family. As for him, he would have needed to change the proverb, and, in the place of one who marries a husband takes his country.' to say, 'One who marries a wife takes her country.'

"The celebrated discover of the North-West, the illustrious Le Verandrye, has as much as Radisson, and even more than he, of just reason to complain of the ingratitude of France; yet how different was his conduct!

"Just as his persecutions have placed upon the head of the first a new halo of glory, so they have cast upon the brow of the second an ineffaceable stain.

"Souls truly noble do not seek in treason the recompense for the rights denied them."

CHAPTER VI.

The golden lilies in danger—"To arrest Radisson"—The land called "Unknown"—A chain of claim—Imaginary pretensions—Chevalier de Troyes—The brave Lemoynes—Hudson Bay forts captured—A litigious governor—Laugh at treaties—The glory of France—Enormous claims—Consequential damages.

THE two great nations which were seeking supremacy in North America came into collision all too soon on the shores of Hudson Bay. Along the shore of the Atlantic, England claimed New England and much of the coast to the southward. France was equally bent on holding New France and Acadia. Now that England had begun to occupy Hudson Bay, France was alarmed, for the enemy would be on her northern as well as on her southern border. No doubt, too, France feared that her great rival would soon seek to drive her golden lilies back to the Old World, for New France would be a wedge between the northern and southern possessions of England in the New World.

The movement leading to the first voyage to Hudson Bay by Gillam and his company was carefully watched by the French Government. In February, 1668, at which time Gillam's expedition had not yet sailed, the Marquis de Denonville, Governor of Canada, appointed an officer to go in search of the most advantageous posts and occupy the shores of the Baie du Nord and the embouchures of the rivers that enter therein. Among other things the governor gave orders "to arrest especially the said Radisson and his adherents wherever they may be found."

Intendant Talon, in 1670, sent home word to M. Colbert that ships had been seen near Hudson Bay, and that it was likely that they were English, and were "under the guidance of a man des Grozeliers, formerly an inhabitant of Canada."

The alarm caused the French by the movements of the English adventurers was no doubt increased by the belief that Hudson Bay was included in French territory. The question of what constituted ownership or priority of claim was at this time a very difficult one among the nations. Whether mere discovery or temporary occupation could give the right of ownership was much questioned. Colonization would certainly be admitted to do so, provided there had been founded "certain establishments." But the claim of France upon Hudson Bay would appear to have been on the mere ground of the Hudson Bay region being contiguous or neighbouring territory to that held by the French.

The first claim made by France was under the commission, as Viceroy to Canada, given in 1540 by the French King to Sieur de Roberval, which no doubt covered the region about Hudson Bay, though not specifying it. In 1598 Lescarbot states that the commission given to De La Roche contained the following: "New France has for its boundaries on the west the Pacific Ocean within the Tropic of Cancer; on the south the islands of the Atlantic towards Cuba and Hispaniola; on the east, the Northern Sea which washes its shores, embracing in the north the land called Unknown toward the Frozen Sea, up to the Arctic Pole."

The sturdy common sense of Anglo-Saxon England refused to be bound by the contention that a region admittedly "Unknown" could be held on a mere formal claim.

The English pointed out that one of their expeditions under Henry Hudson in 1610 had actually discovered the Bay and given it its name; that Sir Thomas Button immediately thereafter had visited the west side of the Bay and given it the name of New Wales; that Captain James had, about a score of years after Hudson, gone to the part of the Bay which continued to bear his name, and that Captain Fox had in the same year reached the west side of the Bay. This claim of discovery was opposed to the fanciful claims made by France. The strength of the English contention, now enforced by actual occupation and the erection of Charles Fort, made it necessary to obtain some new basis of objection to the claim of England.

It is hard to resist the conclusion that a deliberate effort was made to invent some ground of prior discovery in order to meet the visible argument of a fort now occupied by the English. M. de la Potherie, historian of New France, made the assertion that Radisson and Groseilliers had crossed from Lake Superior to the Baie du Nord (Hudson Bay). It is true, as we have seen, that Oldmixon, the British writer of a generation or two later, states the same thing. This claim is, however, completely met by the statement made by Radisson of his third voyage that they heard only from the Indians on Lake Superior of the Northern Bay, but had not crossed to it by land. We have disposed of the matter of his fourth voyage. The same historian also puts forward what seems to be pure myth, that one Jean Bourdon, a Frenchman, entered the Bay in 1656 and engaged in trade. It was stated also that a priest, William Couture, sent by Governor D'Avaugour of New France, had in 1663 made a missionary establishment on the Bay. These are unconfirmed statements, having no details, and are suspicious in their time of origination. The Hudson's Bay Company's answer states that Bourdon's voyage was to another part of Canada, going only to 53° N., and not to the Bay at all. Though entirely unsupported, these claims were reiterated as late as 1857 by Hon. Joseph Cauchon in his case on behalf of Canada v. Hudson's Bay Company. M. Jeremie, who was Governor of the French forts in Hudson Bay in 1713, makes the statement that Radisson and Groseilliers had visited the Bay overland, for which there is no warrant, but the Governor does not speak of Bourdon or Couture. This contradiction of De la Potherie's claim is surely sufficient proof that there is no ground for credence of the stories, which are purely apocryphal. It is but just to state, however, that the original claim of Roberval and De la Roche had some weight in the negotiations which took place between the French and English Governments over this matter.

M. Colbert, the energetic Prime Minister of France, at any rate made up his mind that the English must be excluded from Hudson Bay. Furthermore, the fur trade of Canada was beginning to feel very decidedly the influence of the English traders in turning the trade to their factories on Hudson Bay. The French Prime Minister, in 1678, sent word to Duchesnau, the Intendant of Canada, to dispute the right of the English to erect factories on Hudson Bay. Radisson and Groseilliers, as we have seen, had before this time deserted the service of England and returned to that of France. With the approval of the French Government, these facile agents sailed to Canada and began the organization, in 1681, of a new association, to be known as "The Northern Company." Fitted out with two small barks, *Le St. Pierre* and *La Ste. Anne*, in 1682, the adventurers, with their companions, appeared before Charles Fort, which Groseilliers had helped to build, but do not seem to have made any hostile demonstration against it. Passing away to the west side of the Bay, these shrewd explorers entered the River Ste. Therese (the Hayes River of to-day) and there erected an establishment, which they called Fort Bourbon.

This was really one of the best trading points on the Bay. Some dispute as to even the occupancy of this point took place, but it would seem as if Radisson and Groseilliers had the priority of a few months over the English party that came to establish a fort at the mouth of the adjoining River Nelson. The two adventurers, Radisson and Groseilliers, in the following year came, as we have seen, with their ship-load of peltries to Canada, and it is charged that they attempted to unload a part of their cargo of furs before reaching Quebec. This led to a quarrel between them and the Northern Company, and the adroit fur traders again left the service of France to find their way back to England. We have already seen how completely these two Frenchmen, in the year 1684, took advantage of their own country at Fort Bourbon and turned over the furs to the Hudson's Bay Company.

The sense of injury produced on the minds of the French by the treachery of these adventurers stirred the authorities up to attack the posts in Hudson Bay. Governor Denonville now came heartily to the aid of the Northern Company, and commissioned Chevalier de Troyes to organize an overland expedition from Quebec to Hudson Bay. The love of adventure was strong in the breasts of the young French noblesse in Canada. Four brothers of the family Le Moyne had become known for their deeds of valour along the English frontier. Leader among the valorous French-Canadians was Le Moyne D'Iber-ville, who, though but twenty-four years of age, had already performed prodigies of daring. Maricourt, his brother, was another fiery spirit, who was known to the Iroquois by a name signifying "the little bird which is always in motion." Another leader was Ste. Helene. With a party of chosen men these intrepid spirits left the St. Lawrence in March, 1685, and threaded the streams of the Laurentian range to the shore of Hudson Bay.

After nearly three months of the most dangerous and exciting adventures, the party reached their destination. The officers and men of the Hudson's Bay Company's service were chiefly civilians unaccustomed to war, and were greatly surprised by the sudden appearance upon the Bay of their doughty antagonists. At the mouth of the Moose River one of the Hudson's Bay Company forts was situated, and here the first attack was made. It was a fort of considerable importance, having four bastions, and was manned by fourteen guns. It. however, fell before the fierce assault of the forest rangers. The chief offence in the eyes of the French was Charles Fort on the Rupert River, that being the first constructed by the English Company. This was also captured and its fortifications thrown down. At the same time that the main body were attacking Charles Fort, the brothers Le Moyne, with a handful of picked men, stealthily approached in two canoes one of the Company's vessels in the Bay and succeeded in taking it.

The largest fort on the Bay was that in the marshy region on Albany River. It was substantially built with four bastions and was provided with forty-three guns. The rapidity of movement and military skill of the French expedition completely paralyzed the Hudson's Bay Company officials and men. Governor Sargeant, though having in Albany Fort furs to the value of 50,000 crowns, after a slight resistance surrendered without the honours of war. The Hudson's Bay Company employés were given permission to return to England and in the meantime the Governor and his attendants were taken to Charlton Island and the rest of the prisoners to Moose Fort. D'Iberville afterwards took the prisoners to France, whence they came back to England.

A short time after this the Company showed its disapproval of Governor Sargeant's course in surrendering Fort Albany so readily. Thinking they could mark their disapprobation more strongly, they brought an action against Governor Sargeant in the courts to recover 20,000*l*. After the suit had gone some distance, they agreed to refer the matter to arbitration, and the case was ended by the Company having to pay to the Governor 350*l*. The affair, being a family quarrel, caused some amusement to the public.

The only place of importance now remaining to the English on Hudson Bay was Port Nelson, which was near the French Fort Bourbon. D'Iberville, utilizing the vessel he had captured on the Bay, went back to Quebec in the autumn of 1687 with the rich booty of furs taken at the different points.

These events having taken place at a time when the two countries, France and England, were nominally at peace, negotiations took place between the two Powers.

Late in the year 1686 a treaty of neutrality was signed, and it was hoped that peace would ensue on Hudson Bay. This does not seem to have been the case, however, and both parties blame each other for not observing the terms of the Act of Pacification. D'Iberville defended Albany Fort from a British attack in 1689, departed in that year for Quebec with a shipload of furs, and returned to Hudson Bay in the following year. During the war which grew out of the Revolution, Albany Fort changed hands again to the English, and was afterwards retaken by the French, after which a strong English force (1692) repossessed themselves of it. For some time English supremacy was maintained on the Bay, but the French merely waited their time to attack Fort Bourbon, which they regarded as in a special sense their own. In 1694 D'Iberville visited the Bay, besieged and took Fort Bourbon, and reduced the place with his two frigates. His brother De Chateauguay was killed during the siege.

In 1697 the Bay again fell into English hands, and D'Iberville was put in command of a squadron sent out for him from Prance, and with this he sailed for Hudson Bay. The expedition brought unending glory to France and the young commander. Though one of his warships was crushed in the ice in the Hudson Straits and his remaining vessels could nowhere be seen when he reached the open waters of the Bay, yet he bravely sailed to Port Nelson, purposing to invest it in his one ship, the *Pelican*. Arrived at his station, he observed that he was shut in on the rear by three English men-of-war. His condition was desperate; he had not his full complement of men, and some of those on board were sick. His vessel had but fifty guns; the English vessels carried among them 124. The English vessels, the *Hampshire*, the *Dering*, and the *Hudson's Bay*, all opened fire upon him. During a hot engagement, a well-aimed broadside from the *Pelican* sank the *Hampshire* with all her sails flying, and everything on board was lost; the *Hudson's Bay* surrendered unconditionally, and the *Dering* succeeded in making her escape. After this naval duel D'Iberville's missing vessels appeared, and the commander, landing a sufficient number of men, invested and took Port Nelson. The whole of the Hudson Bay territory thus came into the possession of the French. The matter has always, however, been looked at in the light of the brilliant achievement of this scion of the Le Moynes.

Few careers have had the uninterrupted success of that of Pierre Le Moyne D'Iberville, although this fortune reached its climax in the exploit in Hudson Bay. Nine years afterwards the brilliant soldier died of yellow fever at Havana, after he had done his best in a colonization enterprise to the mouth of the Mississippi which was none too successful. Though the treaty of Ryswick, negotiated in this year of D'Iberville's triumphs, brought for the time the cessation of hostilities, yet nearly fifteen years of rivalry, and for much of the time active warfare, left their serious traces on Hudson's Bay Company affairs. A perusal of the minutes of the Hudson's Bay Company during this period gives occasional glimpses of the state of war prevailing, although it must be admitted not so vivid a picture as might have been expected. As was quite natural, the details of attacks, defences, surrenders, and parleys come to us from French sources rather than from the Company's books. That the French accounts are correct is fully substantiated by the memorials presented by the Company to the British Government, asking for recompense for losses sustained.

In 1687 a petition was prepared by the Hudson's Bay Company, and a copy of it is found in one of the letter-books of the Company. This deals to some extent with the contention of the French king, which had been lodged with the British Government, claiming priority of ownership of the regions about Hudson Bay. The arguments advanced are chiefly those to which we have already referred. The claim for compensation made upon the British Government by the Company is a revelation of how seriously the French rivalry had interfered with the progress of the fur trade. After still more serious conflict had taken place in the Bay, and the Company had come to be apprehensive for its very existence, another petition was laid before His Majesty William III., in 1694. This petition, which also contained the main facts of the claim of 1687, is so important that we give some of the details of it. It is proper to state, however, that a part of the demand is made up of what has since been known as "consequential damages," and that in consequence the matter lingered on for at least two decades.

The damages claimed were:—

	£	s.	d.
1682. Captain Gillara and cargo on *Prince Rupert*. (Captain and a number of men, cargo, and ship all lost in hostilities.) Governor Bridgar and men seized and carried to Quebec............................ Moderate damages	25,000	0	0
September, 1684. French with two ships built a small house and interrupted Indian trade .... Damages	10,000	0	0
1685. French took *Perpetuana* and cargo to Quebec............................... Damages	5,000	0	0
For ship, master, and men..Damages	1,255	16	3
1686. French destroyed three of Company's ships at bottom of Bay, and also three ships' stores, &c., and took 50,000 beaver skins, and	50,000	0	0

turned out to sea a number of His Majesty's subjects..................			
1682-6. Five years' losses about Forts (10,000 beaver skins yearly)	20,000	0	0
1688. Company's ships *Churchill* and *Young* seized by French	10,000	0	0
1692. Company sent out expedition to retake Forts, which cost them	20,000	0	0
1686-93. French possessed bottom of the Bay for seven years. Loss, 10,000*l.* a year	70,000	0	0
Damages	20,000	0	0
Total damages claimed	£211,255	16	3

CHAPTER VII.

The "Grand Monarque" humbled—Caught napping—The Company in peril—Glorious Utrecht—Forts restored—Damages to be considered—Commission useless.

LOUIS XIV. of France, by his ambition and greed in 1690, united against himself the four nations immediately surrounding him—Germany, Spain, Holland, and England, in what they called "The Grand Alliance." Battles, by land and sea for six years, brought Louis into straits, unrelieved by such brilliant episodes as the naval prodigies wrought by D'Iberville on Hudson Bay. In 1696, "Le Grand Monarque" was sufficiently humbled to make overtures for peace. The opposing nations accepted these, and on May 9th, 1697, the representatives of the nations met at William III.'s Chateau of Neuberg Hansen, near the village of Ryswick, which is in Belgium, a short distance from the Hague.

Louis had encouraged the Jacobite cause, James III. being indeed a resident of the Castle of St. Germain, near Paris. This had greatly irritated William, and one of the first things settled at the Treaty was the recognition of William as rightful King of England.

Article VII. of the Treaty compelled the restoration to the King of France and the King of Great Britain respectively of "all countries, islands, forts, and colonies," which cither had possessed before the declaration of war in 1690. However satisfactory this may have been in Acadia and Newfoundland, we find that it did not meet the case of the Hudson Bay, inasmuch as the ownership of this region was, as we have seen, claimed by both parties before the war. In the documents of the Company there is evidence of the great anxiety caused to the adventurers when the news reached London, as to what was likely to be the basis of settlement of the Treaty. The adventurers at once set themselves to work to bring influence to bear against the threatened result. The impression seemed to prevail that they had been "caught napping," and possibly they could not accomplish anything. Their most influential deputation came to the Hague, and, though late in the day, did avail somewhat.

No doubt Article VII. of the Treaty embodies the results of their influence. It is so important for our purpose that we give it in full:— "Commissioners should be appointed on both sides to examine and determine the rights and pretensions which either of the said Kings have to the places situated in Hudson Bay; but the possession of those places which were taken by the French during the peace that preceded this war, and were retaken by the English during this war, shall be left to the French, by virtue of the foregoing articles. The capitulation made by the English on September 5th, 1695, shall be observed according to the form and tenor; the merchandises therein mentioned shall be restored; the Governor at the fort taken there shall be set at liberty, if it be not already done; the differences which have arisen concerning the execution of the said capitulation and the value of the goods there lost, shall be adjudicated and determined by the said commissioners; who immediately after the ratification of the present Treaty, shall be invested with sufficient authority for the setting of the limits and confines of the lands to be restored on either side by virtue of the foregoing article, and likewise for exchanging of lands, as may conduce to the mutual interest and advantage of both Kings."

This agreement presents a few salient points:—

1. The concession to France of rights (undefined, it is true), but of rights not hitherto acknowledged by the English.

2. The case of the Company, which would have been seriously prejudiced by Article VII., is kept open, and commissioners are appointed to examine and decide boundaries.

3. The claim for damages so urgently pressed by the Hudson's Bay Company receives some recognition in the restoration of merchandize and the investigation into the "value of the goods lost."

4. On the whole, the interests of the Hudson's Bay Company would seem to have been decidedly prejudiced by the Treaty.

The affairs of the Company were in a very unfortunate condition for fifteen years after the Treaty of Ryswick. The Treaty took place in the very year of D'Iberville's remarkable victories in the Bay. That each nation should hold that of which it was in actual possession meant that of the seven Hudson's Bay Company forts, only Fort Albany was left to the Company. The Company began to petition at once for the appointment of the Commissioners provided by the Treaty, to settle the matter in dispute. The desperate condition of their affairs accounts for the memorials presented to the British Government by the Company in 1700 and in the succeeding year, by which they expressed themselves as satisfied to give the French the southern portion of the Bay from Rupert's River on the east and Albany Fort on the west. About the time of the second of these proposals the Hudson's Bay Company sent to the British Government another petition of a very different tone, stating their perilous condition, arising from their not receiving one-fifth of the usual quantity of furs, even from Fort Albany, which made their year's trade an absolute loss; they propose that an expedition of "three men-of-war, one bomb-vessel, and 250 soldiers" should be sent to dislodge the French and to regain the whole Bay for them, as being the original owners. No steps on the part of the Ryswick Commissioners seem to have been taken toward settling the question of boundaries in Hudson Bay.

The great Marlborough victories, however, crushed the power of France, and when Louis XIV. next negotiated with the allies at Utrecht—"The Ferry of the Rhine"—in 1713, the English case was in a very different form from what it had been at the Treaty of Ryswick. Two years before the Treaty, when it was evident that the war would be brought to an end, the Hudson's Bay Company plucked up courage and petitioned strongly to be allowed the use of the whole of Hudson Bay, and to have their losses on the Bay repaid by France. Several times during the war had France sued for peace at the hands of the allies, but the request had been refused. To humble France seemed to be the fixed policy of all her neighbours. At the end of the war, in which France was simply able to hold what she could defend by her fortresses, the great kingdom of Louis XIV. found itself "miserably exhausted, her revenue greatly fallen off, her currency depreciated thirty per cent., the choicest of her nobles drafted into the army, and her merchants and industrious artisans weighed down to the ground by heavy imposts." This was England's opportunity, and she profited by it. Besides "the balance of power" in Europe being preserved, Great Britain received Nova Scotia, Newfoundland, certain West India Islands, and the undisturbed control of the Iroquois.

Sections X. and XI. of the Treaty are of special value to us in our recital. By the former of these the entire west coast of Hudson Bay became British; the French were to evacuate all posts on the Bay and surrender all war material within six months; Commissioners were to be appointed to determine within a year the boundary between Canada and the British possessions on Hudson Bay. Section XI. provided "that the French King should take care that satisfaction be given, according to the rule of justice and equity, to the English Company trading to the Bay of Hudson, for all damages and spoil done to their colonies, ships, persons, and goods, by the hostile incursions and depredations of the French in time of peace." This was to be arrived at by Commissioners to be appointed.

If the Hudson's Bay Company, to quote their own language in regard to the Treaty of Ryswick, had been left "the only mourners by the peace," they were to be congratulated on the results of the Treaty of Utrecht. As in so many other cases, however, disputed points left to be settled by Commissioners lingered long before results were reached. Six years after the Treaty of Utrecht, the Memorial of the Hudson's Bay Company shows that while they had received back their forts, yet the line of delimitation between Canada had not been drawn and their losses had not been paid.

In the preceding chapter we have a list of the claims against the French as computed in 1694, amounting to upwards of 200,000*l*.; now, however, the amount demanded is not much above 100,000*l*., though the Memorial explains that in making up the above modest sum, they had not counted up the loss of their forts, nor the damage done to their trade, as had been done in the former case. Immediately after the time of this Memorial of the Company, the Commissioners were named by Great Britain and France, and several meetings took place. Statements were then given in, chiefly as to the boundaries between the British and French possessions in the neighbourhood of Hudson Bay and Canada. The Commissioners for several years practised all the arts of diplomacy, and were farther and farther apart as the discussions went on. No result seems to have been reached, and the claims of the Hudson's Bay Company, so far as recorded, were never met. Peace, however, prevailed in Hudson Bay for many years; the Indians from the interior, even to the Rocky Mountains, made their visits to the Bay for the first forty years of the eighteenth century, and the fur trade, undisturbed, became again remunerative.

CHAPTER VIII.

WHEN peace had been restored by the Treaty of Utrecht, the shores of the Bay, which had been in the hands of the French since the Treaty of Ryswick, were given over to Great Britain, according to the terms of the Treaty; they have remained British ever since. The Company, freed from the fears of overland incursions by the French from Canada, and from the fleets that had worked so much mischief by sea, seems to have changed character in the *personnel* of the stockholders and to have lost a good deal of the pristine spirit. The charge is made that the stockholders had become very few, that the stock was controlled by a majority, who, year after year, elected themselves, and that considering the great privileges conferred by the Charter, the Company was failing to develop the country and was sleeping in inglorious ease on the shores of Hudson Bay. Certain it is that Sir Bibye Lake was re-elected Governor year after year, from 1720 to 1740.

It would appear, however, to have been a spirit of jealousy which animated those who made these discoveries as to the Company's inaction. The return of peace had brought prosperity to the traders; and dividends to the stockholders began to be a feature of company life which they had not known for more than a quarter of a century. As we shall see, the stock of the Company was greatly increased in 1720, and preparations were being made by the Committee for a wide extension of their operations.

About this time a man of great personal energy appears on the scene of English commercial life, who became a bitter opponent of the Company, and possessed such influence with the English Government that the Company was compelled to make a strenuous defence. This was Arthur Dobbs, Esq., an Irishman of undoubted ability and courage. He conducted his plan of campaign against the Company along a most ingenious and dangerous line of attack.

He revived the memory among the British people of the early voyages to discover a way to the riches of the East, and appealed to the English imagination by picturing the interior of the North American Continent, with its vast meadows, splendid cascades, rich fur-bearing animals, and numberless races of Indians, picturesquely dressed, as opening up a field, if they could be reached, of lucrative trade to the London merchants. To further his purpose he pointed out the sluggish character of the Hudson's Bay Company, and clinched his arguments by quoting the paragraph in the Charter which stated that the great privileges conferred by generous Charles II. were bestowed in consideration of their object having been "The Discovery of a New Passage into the South Sea." Dobbs appealed to the sacrifices made and the glories achieved in earlier days in the attempt to discover the North-West Passage. In scores of pages, the indefatigable writer gives the accounts of the early voyages.

We have but to give a passage or two from another author to show what a powerful weapon Dobbs wielded, and to see how he succeeded in reviving a question which had slumbered well nigh a hundred years, and which again became a living question in the nineteenth century.

This writer says:—"It would lead us far beyond our limits were we to chronicle all the reasons urged, and the attempts made to 'finde out that short and easie passage by the Northwest, which we have hitherto so long desired.' Under the auspices of the 'Old Worthies' really—though ostensibly countenanced by kings, queens, and nobles—up rose a race of men, daring and enthusiastic, whose names would add honour to any country, and embalm its history."

Commencing with the reign of Henry VII., we have first, John Cabot (1497), ever renowned; for he it was who first saw and claimed for the 'Banner of England,' the American continent. Sebastian, his son, follows in the next year—a name honourable and wise. Nor may we omit Master Robert Thorne of Bristol (1527); Master Hore (1536); and Master Michael Lok (1545), of London—men who knew - cosmography' and the 'weighty and substantial reasons' for 'a discovery even to the North Pole.' For a short time Arctic energy changed its direction from the North-west to the Northeast (discoveries of the Muscovy Company), but wanting success in that quarter, again reverted to the North-west. Then we find Martin Frobisher, George Best, Sir Humphrey Gilbert, James Davis, George Waymouth, John Knight, the cruelly treated Henry Hudson, James Hall, Sir Thomas Button, Fotherbye, Baffin and Bylot, 'North-west' Luke Fox, Thomas James, &c."

Thus, in the course of sixty years—now breaking the icy fetters of the North, now chained by them; now big with high hope 'of the Passage,' then beaten back by the terrific obstacles, as it were, guarding it— notwithstanding, these men never faltered, never despaired of finally accomplishing it. Their names are worthy to be held in remembrance; for, with all their faults, all their strange fancies and prejudices, still they were a daring and glorious race, calm amid the most appalling dangers; what they did was done correctly, as far as their limited means went; each added something that gave us more extended views and a better acquaintance with the globe we inhabit—giving especially large contributions to geography, with a more fixed resolution to discover the 'Passage.' By them the whole of the eastern face of North America was made known, and its disjointed lands in the North, even to 77 deg. or 78 deg. N. Their names will last while England is true to herself."

Mr. Dobbs awakened much interest among persons of rank in England as to the desirability of finding a North-West Passage. Especially to the Lords of the Admiralty, on whom he had a strong hold, did he represent the glory and value of fitting out an expedition to Hudson Bay on this quest.

Dobbs mentions in his book the unwilling efforts of the Hudson's Bay Company to meet the demand for a wider examination of the Bay which took place a few years after the Peace of Utrecht. In 1719, Captain

James Knight received orders from the Company to fit out an expedition and sail up the west coast of the Bay. This he did in two ships, the *Albany* frigate, Captain George Barlow, and the *Discovery*, Captain David Vaughan. Captain John Scroggs, in the ship *Whalebone*, two years afterward, sailed up the coast in search of the expedition. It is maintained by the opponents of the Company that these attempts were a mere blind to meet the search for a North-West Passage, and that the Company was averse to any real investigation being made.

It is of course impossible to say whether this charge was deserved or not. The fact that no practicable North-West Passage has ever been discovered renders the arguments drawn from the running of the tides, &c., of no value, and certainly justifies the Company to some extent in its inaction. The fact that in 1736 the Hudson's Bay Company yielded to the claim raised by Dobbs and his associates, is to be noted in favour of the Company's contention that while not believing in the existence of the North-West Passage, they were willing to satisfy the excited mind of the English public. Their expedition of the *Churchill* sloop, Captain Napper, and the *Musquash* sloop, Captain Crow, accomplished nothing in solving the question in dispute.

Disappointed with the efforts made by the Company at his request, Dobbs, in 1737, took in hand to organize an expedition under Government direction to go upon the search of the "Passage." At this time he opened communication with Captain Christopher Middleton, one of the best known captains in the service of the Hudson's Bay Company. Middleton, being satisfied with the Company's service, refused to leave it. Dobbs then asked him to recommend a suitable man, and also arranged with Middleton to be allowed to examine the records kept of his voyages, upon the Hudson's Bay Company ships. This, however, came to nothing. About 1740 Captain Middleton had cause to differ with the Company on business matters, and entertained Dobbs' proposition, which was that he should be placed in command of a British man-of-war and go in search of the long-sought North-West

Passage. Middleton gave the Hudson's Bay Company a year's notice, but found them unwilling to let him retire.

He had taken the step of resigning deliberately and adhered to it, though he was disappointed in his command not being so remunerative as he expected. In May, 1741, Captain Middle-ton received his orders from the Lords of the Admiralty to proceed upon his journey and to follow the directions given him as to finding a North-West Passage. These had been prepared under Dobbs' supervision. Directions are given as to his course of procedure, should he reach California, and also as to what should be done in case of meeting Japanese ships. Middleton was placed in charge of Her Majesty's sloop the *Furnace*, and had as a companion and under his orders the *Discovery Pink*, William Moore, Master. In due time, Hudson Bay was reached, but in August the season seemed rather late to proceed northward from "Cary's Swan's Nest," and it was decided to winter in the mouth of Churchill River.

On July 1st, 1742, the expedition proceeded northward. Most complete observations were made of weather, land, presence of ice, natives of the coast, depth of bay, rivers entering bay, tides, and any possible outlets as far as 88 deg. or 89 deg. W. longitude. Observations were continued until August 18th, when the expedition sailed home to report what it had found.

Captain Middleton read an important paper on "The Extraordinary Degrees and Surprising Effects of Cold in Hudson Bay," before the Royal Society in London.

No sooner had Middleton reached the Orkneys on his return voyage than he forwarded to Dobbs, who was in Ireland, a letter and an abstract of his journal. Lest this should have gone astray, he sent another copy on his arrival in the Thames. The report was, on the whole, discouraging as to the existence of a north-west passage.

Dobbs, however, was unwilling to give up his dream, and soon began to discredit Middleton. He dealt privately with the other officers of the ships, Middleton's subordinates, and with surprising skill turned the case against Captain Middleton.

The case of Dobbs against Captain Middleton has been well stated by John Barrow. Middleton was charged with neglect in having failed to explore the line of coast which afforded a probability of a passage to the north-west. The principal points at issue appear to have been in respect to the following discoveries of Middleton, viz. the Wager River, Repulse Bay, and the Frozen Strait. As regards the first, Mr. Dobbs asserted that the tide came through the so-called river from the westward; and this question was settled in the following year by Captain Moore, who entirely confirmed Captain Middleton's report.

Repulse Bay, which well deserves the name it bears, was no less accurately laid down by Captain Middleton, and of the Frozen Strait, Sir Edward Parry remarks, "Above all, the accuracy of Captain Middleton is manifest upon the point most strenuously urged against him, for our subsequent experience has not left the smallest doubt of Repulse Bay and the northern part of Welcome Bay being filled by a rapid tide, flowing into it from the eastward through the Frozen Strait."

Dobbs, by a high order of logic chopping, succeeded in turning the case, for the time being, against Captain Middleton. Seldom has greater skill been used to win a cause. He quotes with considerable effect a letter by Sir Bibye Lake, addressed to the Governor of the Prince of Wales Fort, Churchill River, reading: "Notwithstanding an order to you, if Captain Middleton (who is sent ahead in the Government's service to discover a passage north-west) should by inevitable necessity be brought into real distress and danger of his life and loss of his ship, in such case you are then to give him the best assistance and relief you can." Dobbs' whole effort seems to be to show that Middleton was hiding the truth, and this, under the influence of his old masters, the Hudson's Bay Company. A copy of Dobbs' Criticisms, laid before the Lords of the Admiralty, was furnished Captain Middleton, and his answer is found in "Vindication of the Conduct," published in 1743."

An Account of the Countries adjoining to Hudson Bay" by Arthur Dobbs, Esq., is a book published in the year after, and is really a book of note. A quarto, consisting of upwards of 200 pages, it showed a marvellous knowledge of colonization in America, of the interior of the continent at that time, and incidentally deals with Captain Middleton's journal. Its account of the journey of "Joseph La France, a French Canadese Indian," from Lake Superior by way of Lake Winnipeg to Hudson Bay, is the first detailed account on record of that voyage being made. Evidently Arthur Dobbs had caught the ear of the English people, and the Company was compelled to put itself in a thorough attitude of defence.

Dobbs with amazing energy worked up his cause, and what a writer of the time calls, "The long and warm dispute between Arthur Dobbs, Esq. and Captain Middleton," gained much public notice. The glamour of the subject of a north-west passage, going back to the exploits of Frobisher, Baffin, and Button, touched the national fancy, and no doubt the charge of wilful concealment of the truth made against the Hudson's Bay Company, repeated so strenuously by Dobbs, gained him adherents. Parliament took action in the matter and voted 20,000*l*. as a reward for the discovery of a north-west passage. This caused another wave of enthusiasm, and immediately a subscription was opened for the purpose of raising 10,000*l*. to equip an expedition for this popular enterprise. It was proposed to divide the whole into 100 shares of 100*l*. each. A vigorous canvass was made to secure the amount, and the subscription list bears the names of several nobles, an archbishop, a bishop, and many esquires. A perusal of the names suggests that a number of them are Irish, and no doubt were obtained by Mr. Dobbs, who was often at Lisburn in Ireland. The amount raised was 7,200*l*. The expedition, we hear afterwards, cost upwards of 10,000*l*., but the money needed was, we are told, willingly contributed by those who undertook the enterprise. Mr. Dobbs, as was suitable, was a leading spirit on the Committee of Management.

Two ships were purchased by the Committee, the Dobbs galley, 180 tons burden, Captain William Moore, and the *California*, 140 tons, Captain Francis Smith. On May 24th, 1746, the two vessels, provisioned and well fitted out for the voyage, left the mouth of the

Thames, being in company with the two ships of the Hudson's Bay Company going to the Bay, the four ships being under the convoy of the ship *Loo*, of forty guns, as France was at this time at war with England. The voyage was rather prosperous, with the exception of a very exciting incident on board the *Dobbs* galley. A dangerous fire broke out in the cabin of the vessel, and threatened to reach the powder-room, which was directly underneath, and contained "thirty or forty barrels of powder, candles, spirits, matches, and all manner of combustibles." Though, as the writer says, "during the excitement, you might hear all the varieties of sea eloquence, cries, prayers, curses, and scolding, mingled together, yet this did not prevent the proper measures being taken to save the ship and our lives."

The story of the voyage is given to us in a very interesting manner by Henry Ellis, gentleman, agent for the proprietors of the expedition. Though nearly one hundred pages are taken up with the inevitable summaries of "The Several Expeditions to discover a North-West Passage," yet the remaining portion of the book is well written. After the usual struggle with the ice in Hudson Strait, as it was impossible to explore southward during the first season, the *Dobbs* galley and the *California* sailed for Port Nelson, intending to winter there. They arrived on August 26th. Ellis states that they were badly received by the Hudson's Bay officers at the first. They, however, laid up their ships in Hayes River, and built an erection of logs on the shore for the staff. The officers' winter quarters were called "Montague House," named after the Duke of Montague, patron of the expedition. After a severe winter, during which the sailors suffered with scurvy, and, according to Ellis, received little sympathy from the occupants of York Fort, the expedition left the mouth of the Hayes River on June 24th, to prosecute their discovery. After spending the summer coasting Hudson Bay and taking careful notes, the officers of the vessels gladly left the inhospitable shore to sail homeward, and the two ships arrived in Yarmouth Roads on October 14th, 1747."

Thus ended," says Ellis, "this voyage, without success indeed, but not without effect; for though we did not discover a north-west passage . . . we returned with clearer and fuller proofs . . . that evidently such a passage there may be." It will be observed that Ellis very much confirms Captain Middleton's conclusions, but Mr. Dobbs no doubt made the best of his disappointment, and, as we shall see, soon developed what had been from the first his real object, the plan for founding a rival company.

CHAPTER IX.

THE INTERESTING BLUE-BOOK OF 1749

"Le roi est mort"—Royalty unfavourable—Earl of Halifax—"Company asleep"—
Petition to Parliament—Neglected discovery—Timidity or caution—Strong "Prince
of Wales"—Increase of stock—A timid witness—Claims of discovery—To make
Indians Christians—Charge of disloyalty—New Company promises largely—Result
nil.

ARTHUR DOBBS, ESQ,, was evidently worsted in his tilt with the
Hudson's Bay Company. His fierce onslaught upon Captain Middleton
was no doubt the plan of attack to enable him to originate the
expedition of the *Dobbs* galley and *California*. Even this voyage had
brought little better prospect of the discovery of a north-west passage,
except the optimistic words of Ellis, the use of which, indeed, seemed
very like the delectable exercise of "extracting sunbeams from
cucumbers."

But the energy of the man was in no way dampened. Indeed, the
indications are, as we survey the features of the time, that he had
strong backing in the governing circles of the country. Time was when
the Hudson's Bay Company basked in the sunshine of the Court. It is,
perhaps, the penalty of old institutions that as rulers pass away and
political parties change, the centre of gravity of influence shifts.
Perhaps the Hudson's Bay Company had not been able to use the
convenient motto, "Le Roi est mort: Vive le Roi!" At any rate the strong
Court influence of the Company had passed away, and there is hardly a
nobleman to be found on the list of stockholders submitted by the
Company to the Committee of the Lords.

On the other hand, when Henry Ellis, the historian of the expedition,
writes his book in the year after his return, he is permitted to dedicate
it to His Royal Highness Frederick, Prince of Wales, is privileged to
refer in his dedication to a "gracious audience" allowed him by the
Prince after his return, and to speak of "the generous care" expressed by
the Prince "for the happy progress of his design." Again, in a similar

dedication of a book written four years afterwards by Joseph Robson, a former employé of the Hudson's Bay Company, but a book full of hostility to the Company, allusion is made to the fact that the Earl of Halifax, Lord Commissioner of Trade and Plantations, gave his most hearty approval to such plans as the expedition sought to carry out. It is said of Lord Halifax, who was called the Father of Colonies: "He knows the true state of the nation—that it depends on trade and manufactures; that we have more rivals than ever; that navigation is our bulwark and Colonies our chief support; and that new channels should be industriously opened. Therefore, we survey the whole globe in search of fresh inlets which our ships may enter and traffic." Those familiar with the work of Lord Halifax will remember that the great colonization scheme by which Nova Scotia was firmly grappled to the British Empire and the City of Halifax founded, was his; and the charge made by Dobbs that for a generation the "Company had slept on the shores of the Bay," would appeal with force to a man of such energetic and progressive nature as the Lord Commissioner.

Accordingly, Dobbs now came out boldly; not putting the discovery of the North-West Passage in the front of his plan, but openly charging the Hudson's Bay Company with indolence and failure, and asking for the granting of a charter to a rival company.

As summed up by the sub-committee to which the petition of Dobbs and his associates was submitted, the charges were:—

I. The Company had not discovered, nor sufficiently attempted to discover, the North-West Passage into the southern seas.

II. They had not extended their settlements to the limits given them by their Charter.

III. They had designedly confined their trade within very narrow limits:

(*a*) Had abused the Indians.

(*b*) Had neglected their forte.

(*c*) Ill-treated their own servants.

(*d*) Encouraged the French.

The Hudson's Bay Company, now put on their mettle, exhibited a considerable amount of activity, and filed documents before the Committee that in some respects met the charges against them. They claimed that they had in the thirty years preceding the investigation done a fair amount of exploratory work and discovery. In 1719, they had sent out the *Albany* frigate and *Discovery* to the northern regions, and neither of them returned to tell the tale. In the same year its vessels on the Bay, the *Prosperous* and the *Success*, one from York Factory, the other from Prince of Wales Fort, had sailed up the coast on exploratory expeditions. Two years afterward, the *Prosperous*, under Kelsey, made a voyage, and the *Success*, under Captain Napper, had sailed from York Fort and was lost. In the same year the *Whalebone*, under Captain John Scroggs, went from England to Prince of Wales Fort, and after wintering there, in the following year made a decided effort on behalf of the Passage, but returned unsuccessful. In the year when Dobbs became so persistent (1737) James Napper, who had been saved from the wreck of the Success sixteen years before, took command of the *Churchill* from 'Prince of Wales Fort, but on the exploration died, and the vessel returned. The *Musquash*, under Captain Crow, accompanied the *Churchill*, but returned with no hope of success. This was the case presented by the Hudson's Bay Company. It was still open to the opponents of the Company to say, as they did, that the Hudson's Bay Company was not in earnest, wanted nothing done to attract rivals, and were adepts in concealing their operations and in hoodwinking the public.

A more serious charge was that they had not sought to reach the interior, but had confined their trade to the shores of the Bay. Here it seems that the opponents of the Company made a better case. It is indeed unaccountable to us to-day, as we think that the Company had now been eighty years trading on the Bay and had practically no knowledge of the inheritance possessed by them. At this very time the French, by way of Lake Superior, had journeyed inland, met Indian tribes, traded with them, and even with imposing ceremonies buried metal plates claiming the country which the Hudson's Bay Company Charter covered as lying on rivers, lakes, &c., tributary to Hudson Bay. It is true they had submitted instructions to the number of twenty or thirty, in which governors and captains had been urged to explore the interior and extend the trade among the Indian tribes. But little evidence could be offered that these communications had been acted on.

The chief dependence of the Company seems to have been on one Henry Kelsey, who went as a boy to Hudson Bay, but rose to be chief officer there. The critics of the Company were not slow to state that Kelsey had been a refugee from their forts and had lived for several seasons among the Indians of the interior. Even if this were so, it is still true that Kelsey came to be one of the most enterprising of the wood-runners of the Company. Dobbs confronted them with the fact that the voyage from Lake Superior to Hudson Bay had been only made once in their history, and that by Joseph La France, the Canadian Indian. Certainly, whether from timidity, caution, inertia, or from some deep-seated system of policy, it was true that the Company had done little to penetrate the interior.

The charge that the Company abused the Indians was hardly substantiated. The Company was dependent on the goodwill of the Indians, and had they treated them badly, their active rivals, the French, would simply have reaped the benefit of their folly. That the price charged the Indians for goods was as large as the price paid for furs was small, is quite likely to have been true. Civilized traders all the world over, dealing with ignorant and dependent tribes, follow this policy. No doubt the risks of life and limb and goods in remote regions are great, and great profits must be made to meet them. It is to be remembered, however, that when English and French traders came into competition, as among the Iroquois in New York State, and afterwards in the Lake Superior district, the quality of the English goods was declared by the Indians better and their treatment by the English on the whole more honest and aboveboard than that by the French.

That traders should neglect their own forts seems very unlikely. Those going to the Hudson Bay Main expected few luxuries, and certainly did not have an easy life, but there was on the part of the Company a vast difference in treatment as compared with that given to the fur traders in New France as they went to the far west. No doubt pressure for dividends prevented expenditure that was unnecessary, but a perusal of the experience of Champlain with his French fur company leads us to believe that the English were far the more liberal and considerate in the treatment of employés.

The fortress of the River Churchill, known as the Prince of Wales Fort, with its great ruins to be seen to-day, belonging to this period, speaks of a largo expense and a high ideal of what a fort ought to be. During the examination of witnesses by the Committee, full opportunity was given to show cases of ill-treatment of men and poor administration of their forts. Twenty witnesses were examined, and they included captains, merchants, and employés, many of whom had been in the service of the Company on the Bay, but whether, as Robson says, "It must be attributed either to their confusion upon appearing before so awful an assembly, or to their having a dependence on the Company and an expectation of being employed again in their service," little was elicited at all damaging to the Company.

The charge of the fewness of the forts and the smallness of the trade was more serious. That they should have a monopoly of the trade, and should neither develop it themselves, nor allow others to develop it, would have been to pursue a "dog in the manger" policy. They stated that they had on an average three ships employed solely on their business, that their exports for ten years immediately preceding amounted to 40,240l. and their imports 122,835l., which they claimed was a balance of trade satisfactory to England.

The objection that the whole capital of the Company at the commencement, 10,500l., was trifling, was perhaps true, but they had made great profits, and they used them in the purchase of ships and the building of forts, and now had a much more valuable property than at the beginning. That they had been able to increase their stock so largely was a tribute to the profits of their business and to its ability to earn dividends on a greatly increased capital stock.

The increase of stock as shown by the Company was as follows:—

Original stock.	. . . .	£10,500 . . . . . .
Trebled in 1690.	. . . . . .	.31,500. . . . . .
Trebled in 1720.	. . . . . .	.94,500. . . . . .

At this time there was a movement to greatly increase the stock, but the stringency of the money market checked this movement, and subscriptions of ten per cent. were taken, amounting to 3,150l. only. This was also trebled and added to the original 94,500l., making a total stock of 103,950l.

Some three years after the investigation by the Committee, one of the witnesses, Joseph Robson, who gave evidence of the very mildest, most non-committal character, appears to have received new light, for he published a book called, "An Account of Six Years' Residence in Hudson's Bay." He says in the preface, speaking of the evidence given by him in the investigation, "For want of confidence and ability to express myself clearly, the account I then gave was far from being so exact and full as that which I intended to have given." What the influence was that so effectually opened Robson's eyes, we do not know. The second part of this work is a critique of the evidence furnished by the Company, and from the vigour employed by this writer as compared with the apathy shown at the investigation, it is generally believed that in the meantime he had become a dependent of Dobbs.

The plea put forward by the petitioners for the granting of a charter to them contained several particulars. They had, at their own cost and charges, fitted out two ships, the *Dobbs* galley and *California*, in search of the North-West Passage to the West and Southern Ocean. Their object was, they claimed, a patriotic one, and they aimed at extending the trade of Great Britain. They maintained that though the reward offered had been 20,000l., it was not sufficient to accomplish the end, as they had already spent more than half of that sum. Notwithstanding this, they had discovered a number of bays, inlets, and coasts before unknown, and inasmuch as this was the ground of the Charter issued by Charles II. to the Hudson's Bay Company, they claimed like consideration for performing a similar service.

The petitioners made the most ample promise as to their future should the charter be granted. They would persevere in their search for the passage to the Southern Ocean of America, of which, notwithstanding the frequent failures in finding it, they had a strong hope. The forward policy of Lord Halifax of extensive colonization they were heartily in favour of, and they undertook to settle the lands they might discover. The question had been raised during the investigation, whether the Company had done anything to civilize the natives. They had certainly done nothing. Probably their answer was that they were a trading company, and never saw the Indians except in the months of the trading season, when in July and August they presented-themselves from the interior at the several factories. The petitioners promised, in regard to the natives, that they would "lay the foundation for their becoming Christians and industrious subjects of His Majesty." Beyond the sending out of a prayer-book from time to time, which seemed to indicate a desire to maintain service among their servants, the Company had taken no steps in this direction.

The closing argument for the bestowal of a charter was that they would prevent French encroachments upon British rights and trade on the continent of America. The petition makes the very strong statement that the Hudson's Bay Company had connived at, or allowed French and English to encroach, settle, and trade within their limits on the south side of the Bay. Whatever may have been in the mind of the petitioners on this subject of conniving with the French, a perusal of the minutes of the Company fails to show any such disposition. The Company in Charles II.'s times was evidently more anti-French than the Government. They disputed the claim of the French to any part of the Bay, and strongly urged their case before the English Commissioners at the Treaty of Ryswick. One of their documents, seemingly showing them to be impressed with the claim of priority of ownership of the French King, did propose a division of the Bay, giving the south part of the Bay to the French and the remainder to themselves. It is easy to understand a trading company wishing peace, so that trade might go on, and knowing that Hudson Bay, with its enormous coast line, afforded wide room for trade, proposing such a settlement.

No doubt, however, the reference is to the great competition which was, in a few years, to extend through the interior to the Rocky Mountains. This was to be indeed a battle royal. Arthur Dobbs, judging by his book, which shows how far ahead he was of his opponents in foresight, saw that this must come, and so the new Company promises to penetrate the interior, cut off the supply of furs from the French, and save the trade to Britain. A quarter of a century afterwards, the Hudson's Bay Company, slow to open their eyes, perceived it too, and as we shall see, rose from their slumbers, and entered the conflict.

The Report was made to the Privy Council, expressing appreciation of the petition, and of the advanced views enunciated, but stating that the case against the Hudson's Bay Company had not yet been made out. So no new charter was granted!

CHAPTER X.

EVEN the French in Canada were animated in their explorations by the
dream of a North-West Passage. The name Lachine at the rapids above
Montreal is the memorial of La Salle's hope that the Western Sea was
to be reached along this channel. The Lake Superior region seems to
have been neglected for twenty years after Radisson and Groseilliers
had visited Lake Nepigon, or Lake Assiniboines, as they called it.

But the intention of going inland from Lake Superior was not lost
sight of by the French explorers, for on a map (Parl. Lib. Ottawa) of
date 1680, is the inscription in French marking the Kaministiquia or
Pigeon River, "By this river they go to the Assinepoulacs, for 150
leagues toward the north-west, where there are plenty of beavers."

The stirring events which we have described between 1682 and 1684,
when Radisson deserted from the Hudson's Bay Company and founded
for the French King Fort Bourbon on the Bay, were accompanied by a
new movement toward Lake Superior, having the purpose of turning
the stream of trade from Hudson Bay southward to Lake Superior.

At this time Governor De La Barre writes from Canada that the
English at Hudson Bay had that year attracted to them many of the
northern Indians, who were in the habit of coming to Montreal, and
that he had despatched thither Sieur Duluth, who had great influence
over the western Indians. Greysolon Duluth was one of the most daring
spirits in the service of France in Canada. Duluth writes (1684) to the
Governor from Lake Nepigon, where he had erected a fort, seemingly
near the spot where Radisson and Groseilliers had wintered.

Duluth says in his ardent manner: "It remains for me, sir, to assure
you that all the savages of the north have great confidence in me, and

that enables me to promise you that before the lapse of two years not a single savage will visit the English at Hudson Bay. This they have all promised me, and have bound themselves thereto, by the presents I have given, or caused to be given them. The Klistinos, Assinepoulacs, &c., have promised to come to my fort. . . . Finally, sir, I wish to lose my life if I do not absolutely prevent the savages from visiting the English."

Duluth seems for several years to have carried on trade with the Indians north and west of Lake Nepigon, and no doubt prevented many of them from going to Hudson Bay. But he was not well supported by the Governor, being poorly supplied with goods, and for a time the prosecution of trade by the French in the Lake Superior region declined. The intense interest created by D'Iberville in his victorious raids on Hudson Bay no doubt tended to divert the attention of the French explorers from the trade with the interior. The Treaties of Ryswick and Utrecht changed the whole state of affairs for the French King, and deprived by the latter of these treaties of any hold on the Bay, the French in Canada began to turn their attention to their deserted station on Lake Superior.

Now, too, the reviving interest in England of the scheme for the discovery of the North-West Passage infected the French. Six years after the Treaty of Utrecht, we find (MSS. Ottawa) it stated: "Messrs. de Vaudreuil and Begin having written last year that the discovery of the Western Sea would be advantageous to the Colony, it was approved that to reach it M. de Vaudreuil should establish these posts, which he had proposed, and he was instructed at the same time to have the same established without any expense accruing to the King—as the person establishing them would be remunerated by trade."

In the year 1717 the Governor sent out a French lieutenant, Sieur De la Noue, who founded a fort at Kaministiquia. In a letter, De la Noue states that the Indians are well satisfied with the fort he has erected, and promise to bring there all those who had been accustomed to trade at Hudson Bay. Circumstances seem to have prevented this explorer from going and establishing a fort at Tekamiouen (Rainy Lake), and a third at the lake still farther to the north-west-It is somewhat notable that during the fifty years succeeding the early voyages of Radisson and Groseilliers on Lake Superior, the French were quite familiar with the names of lakes and rivers in the interior which they had never visited. It will be remembered, however, that the same thing is true of the English on Hudson Bay. They knew the names Assiniboines, Christinos, and the like as familiar terms, although they had not left the Bay.

The reason of this is easily seen. The North-West Indian is a great narrator. He tells of large territories, vast seas, and is, in fact, in the speech of Hiawatha, "Iagoo, the great boaster." He could map out his route upon a piece of birch-bark, and the maps still made by the wild North-Western Indians are quite worthy of note.

It will be observed that the objection brought by the French against the Hudson's Bay Company of clinging to the shores of the Bay, may be equally charged against the French on the shore of Lake Superior, or at least of Lake Nepigon, for the period from its first occupation of at least seventy years. No doubt the same explanation applies in both cases, viz. the bringing of their furs to the forts by the Indians made inland exploration at that time unnecessary.

But the time and the man had now come, and the vast prairies of the North-West, hitherto unseen by the white man, were to become the battle-ground for a far greater contest for the possession of the fur trade than had yet taken place either in Hudson Bay or with the Dutch and English in New York State.

The promoting cause for this forward movement was again the dream of opening up a North-West Passage. The hold this had upon the French we see was less than that upon Frobisher, James, Middleton, or Dobbs among the English. Speaking of the French interest in the scheme, Pierre Margry, keeper of the French Archives in Paris, says: "The prospect of discovering by the interior a passage to the *Grand Océan*, and by that to China, which was proposed by our officers under Henry IV., Louis XIII., and Louis XIV., had been taken up with renewed ardour during the Regency. Memorial upon memorial had been presented to the Conseil de Marine respecting the advisability and the advantage of making this discovery. Indeed, the Père de Charlevoix was sent to America, and made his great journey from the north to the south of New France for the purpose of reliably informing the Council as to the most suitable route to pursue in order to reach the Western Sea. But the ardour which during the life of Philip of Orleans animated the Government regarding the exploration of the West became feeble, and at length threatened to be totally extinguished, without any benefit being derived from the posts which they had already established in the country of the Sioux and at Kaministiquia."

"The Regent, in choosing between the two plans that Father Charlevoix presented to him at the close of his journey for the attainment of a knowledge of the Western Sea, through an unfortunate prudence, rejected the suggestion, which, it is true, was the most expensive and uncertain, viz. an expedition up the Missouri to its source and beyond, and decided to establish a post among the Sioux. The post of the Sioux was consequently established in 1727. Father Gonor, a Jesuit missionary who had gone upon the expedition, we are told, was, however, obliged to return without having been able to discover anything that would satisfy the expectations of the Court about the Western Sea."

At this time Michilimackinac was the depot of the West. It stood in the entrance of Lake Michigan—the Gitche Gumee of the Indian tribes, near the mouth of the St. Mary River, the outlet of Lake Superior; it was at the head of Lake Huron and Georgian Bay alike. Many years afterwards it was called the "Key of the North-West" and the "Key of the Upper Lakes." A round island lying a little above the lake, it appealed to the Indian imagination, and, as its name implies, was likened by them to the turtle. To it from every side expeditions gathered, and it became the great rendezvous.

At Michilimackinac, just after the arrival of Father Gonor, there came from the region of Lake Superior a man whose name was to become illustrious as an explorer, Pierre Gaultier de Varennes, Sieur de la Verandrye. We have come to know him simply by the single name of Verandrye.

This great explorer was born in Three Rivers, the son of an old officer of the French army. The young cadet found very little to do in the New World, and made his way home to France. He served as a French officer in the War of the Spanish Succession, and was severely wounded in the battle of Malplaquet. On his recovery, he did not receive the recognition that he desired, and so went to the western wilds of Canada and took up the life of a "coureur de bois."

Verandrye, in pursuing the fur trade, had followed the somewhat deserted course which Radisson and Groseilliers had long before taken, and which a decade before this La Noue had, as we have seen, selected. The fort on Lake Nepigon was still the rendezvous of the savages from the interior, who were willing to be turned aside from visiting the English on Hudson Bay. From the Indians who assembled around his fort on Lake Nepigon, in 1728, Verandrye heard of the vast interior, and had some hopes of reaching the goal of those who dreamt of a Western Sea.

An experienced Indian leader named Ochagach undertook to map out on birch bark the route by which the lakes of the interior could be reached, and the savage descanted with rapture upon the furs to be obtained if the journey could be made. Verandrye, filled with the thought of western discovery, went to Quebec, and discussed his purpose with the Governor there. He pointed out the route by way of the river of the Assiniboels, and then the rivers by which Lake Ouinipegon might be reached. His estimate was that the Western Sea might be gained by an inland journey from Lake Superior of 500 leagues.

Governor Beauharnois considered the map submitted and the opinions of Verandrye with his military engineer, Chaussegros Do Lory; and their conclusions were favourable to Verandrye's deductions. Verandrye had the manner and character which inspired belief in his honesty and competence. He was also helped in his dealings with the

Governor at Quebec by the representations of Father Gonor, whom we have seen had returned from the fort established among the Sioux, convinced that the other route was impracticable.

Father Gonor entirely sympathized with Verandrye in the belief that the only hope lay in passing through the country of the Christinos and Assiniboels of the North. The Governor granted the explorer the privilege of the entire profit of the fur trade, but was unable to give any assistance in money. Verandrye now obtained the aid of a number of merchants in Montreal in providing goods and equipment for the journey, and in high glee journeyed westward, calling at Michilimackinac to take with him the Jesuit Father Messager, to be the companion of his voyage. Near the end of August, 1731, the expedition was at Pigeon River, long known as Grand Portage, a point more than forty miles south-westward of the mouth of the Kaministiquia.

This was a notable event in history when Verandrye and his crew stood ready to face the hardships of a journey to the interior. No doubt the way was hard and long, and the men were sulky and discouraged, but the heroism of their commander shone forth as he saw into the future and led the way to a vast and important region.

Often since that time have important expeditions going to the North-West been seen as they swept by the towering heights of Thunder Cape, and, passing onward, entered the uninviting mouth of Kaministiquia.

Eighty-five years afterward, Lord Selkirk and his band of one hundred De Meuron soldiers appeared here in canoes and penetrated to Red River to regain the lost Fort Douglas.

One hundred and twenty-six years after Verandrye, according to an account given by an eye-witness—an old Hudson's Bay Company officer—a Canadian steamer laden high above the decks appeared at the mouth of the Kaministiquia, bearing the Dawson and Hind expedition, to explore the plains of Assiniboia and pave the way for their admission to Canada.

One hundred and thirty-nine years after Verandrye, Sir Garnet Wolseley, with his British regulars and Canadian volunteers, swept through Thunder Bay on their way to put down the Red River rebellion.

And now one hundred and sixty-nine years after Verandrye, the splendid steamers of the Canadian Pacific Railway Company thrice a week in summer carry their living cargo into the mouth of the Kaministiquia to be transported by rail to the fast filling prairies of the West.

Yes! it was a great event when Verandrye and his little band of unwilling voyageurs started inland from the shore of Lake Superior.

Verandrye, his valiant nephew, De La Jemeraye, and his two sons, were the leaders of the expedition. Grand Portage avoids by a nine mile portage the falls and rapids at the mouth of the Pigeon River, and northward from this point the party went, and after many hardships reached Rainy Lake in the first season, 1731. Here, at the head of Rainy River, just where it leaves the Lake, they built their first fort, St. Pierre. The writer has examined the site of this fort, just three miles above the falls of Rainy River, and seen the mounds and excavations still remaining. This seems to have been their furthest point reached in the first season, and they returned to winter at Kaministiquia. In the next year the expedition started inland, and in the month of June reached their Fort St. Pierre, descended the Rainy River, and with exultation saw the expanse of the Lake of the Woods.

The earliest name we find this lake known by is that given by Verandrye. He says it was called Lake Minitie (Cree, Ministik) or Des Boîs. (1) The former of these names, Minitie, seems to be Ojibway, and to mean Lake of the Islands, probably referring to the largo number of islands to be found in the northern half of the Lake. The other name (2), Lac des Boîs, or Lake of the Woods, would appear to have been a mistranslation of the Indian (Ojibway) name by which the Lake was known. The name (3) was "Pikwedina Sagaigan," meaning "the inland lake of the sand hills." referring to the skirting range of sand hills running for some thirteen miles along the southern shore of the Lake to the east of the mouth of Rainy River, its chief tributary.

Another name found on a map prepared by the Hudson's Bay Company in 1748 is (4) Lake Nimigon, probably meaning the "expanse," referring to the open sheet of water now often called "La Traverse." Two other names, (5) Clearwater Lake and (6) Whitefish Lake, are clearly the extension of Clearwater Bay, a north-western part of the Lake, and Whitefish Bay, still given by the Indians to the channel to the east of Grande Presqu'île.

On the south-west side of the Lake of the Woods Verandrye's party built Fort St. Charles, probably hoping then to come in touch with the Sioux who visited that side of the lake, and with whom they would seek trade. At this point the prospect was very remote of reaching the Western Sea. The expenses were great, and the fur trade did not so far give sufficient return to justify a further march to the interior. Unassisted they had reached in 1733 Lake Ouinipegon (Winnipeg), by descending the rapid river from Lake of the Woods, to which they gave the name of Maurepas.

The government in Quebec informed the French Minister, M. de Maurepas, that they had been told by the adventurous Jemeraye that if the French King would bear the expense, they were now certain that the Western Sea could be reached. They had lost in going to Lake Ouinipegon not less than 43,000 livres, and could not proceed further without aid. The reply from the Court of France was unfavourable; nothing more than the free privilege of the fur trade was granted the explorers.

In the following year Verandrye built a fort near Lake Ouinipegon, at the mouth of the Maurepas River (which we now know as Winnipeg River), and not far from the present Fort Alexander. The fort was called Fort Maurepas, although the explorers felt that they had little for which to thank the French Minister. Still anxious to push on further west, but prevented by want of means, they made a second appeal to the French Government in 1735. But again came the same reply of refusal. The explorers spent their time trading with the Indians between Lake Winnipeg and Grand Portage, and coming and going, as they had occasion, to Lake Superior, and also to Michilimackinac with their cargoes.

While at Fort St. Charles, on the shores of the Lake of the Woods, in 1736, a great disaster overtook the party. Verandrye's eldest son was very anxious to return to Kaministiquia, as was also the Jesuit priest, Anneau, who was in company with the traders. Verandrye was unwilling, but at last consented. The party, consisting of the younger Verandrye and twenty men, were ruthlessly massacred by an ambush of the Sioux on a small island some five leagues from Fort St. Charles, still known as Massacre Island.

A few days afterwards the crime was discovered, and Verandrye had difficulty in preventing his party from accepting the offer of the Assiniboines and Christinos to follow the Sioux and wreak their vengeance upon them. During the next year Fort Maurepas was still their farthest outpost.

Though no assistance could be obtained from the French Court for western discovery, and although the difficulties seemed almost insurmountable, Verandrye was unwilling to give up the path open to him. He had the true spirit of the explorer, and chafed in his little stockade on the shores of Lake Winnipeg, seeking new worlds to conquer.

If it was a great event when Verandrye, in 1731, left the shores of Lake Superior to go inland, it was one of equal moment when, penniless and in debt, he determined at all hazards to leave the rocks and woods of Lake Winnipeg, and seek the broad prairies of the West. His decision being thus reached, the region which is now the fertile Canadian prairies was entered upon.

We are fortunate in having the original journal of this notable expedition of 1738, obtained by Mr. Douglas Brymner, former Archivist at Ottawa. This, with two letters of Bienville, were obtained by Mr.

Brymner from a French family in Montreal, and the identity of the documents has been fully established.

This journal covers the time from the departure of Verandrye from Michilimackinac on July 20th, till say 1739, when he writes from the heart of the prairies. On September 22nd the brave Verandrye left Fort Maurepas for the land unknown. It took him but two days with his five men to cross in swift canoes the south-east expanse of Lake Winnipeg, enter the mouth of Red River, and reach the forks of the Red and Assiniboine Rivers, where the city of Winnipeg now stands.

It was thus on September 24th of that memorable year that the eyes of the white man first fell on the site of what is destined to be the great central city of Canada. A few Crees who expected him met the French explorer there, and he had a conference with two chiefs, who were in the habit of taking their furs to the English on Hudson Bay.

The water of the Assiniboine River ran at this time very low, but Verandrye was anxious to push westward. Delayed by the shallowness of the Assiniboine, the explorer's progress was very slow, but in six days he reached the portage, then used to cross to Lake Manitoba on the route to Hudson Bay. On this portage now stands the town of Portage la Prairie.

The Assiniboine Indians who met Verandrye here told him it would be useless for him to ascend the Assiniboine River further, as the water was so low. Verandrye was expecting a reinforcement to join his party, under his colleague, M. de la Marque. He determined to remain at Portage la Prairie and to build a fort. Verandrye then assembled the Indians, gave them presents of powder, ball, tobacco, axes, knives, &c., and in the name of the French King received them as the children of the great monarch across the sea, and repeated several times to them the orders of the King they were to obey.

It is very interesting to notice the skill with which the early French explorers dealt with the Indians, and to see the formal way in which they took possession of the lands visited. Verandrye states that the Indians were greatly impressed, "many with tears in their eyes." He adds with some *naïveté*, "They thanked me greatly, promising to do wonders."

On October 3rd, Verandrye decided to build a fort. He was joined shortly after by Messrs. de la Marque and Nolant with eight men in two canoes. The fort was soon pushed on, and, with the help of the Indians, was finished by October 15th. This was the beginning of Fort de la Reine. At this stage in his journal Verandrye makes an important announcement, bearing on a subject which has been somewhat discussed.

Verandrye says, "M. de la Marque told me he had brought M. de Louviere to the forks with two canoes to build a fort there for the accommodation of the people of the Red River. I approved of it if the Indians were notified." This settles the fact that there was a fort at the forks of the Red and Assiniboine Rivers, and that it was built in 1738.

In the absence of this information, we have been in the habit of fixing the building of Fort Rouge at this point from 1735 to 1737. There can now be no doubt that October, 1738, is the correct date. From French maps, as has been pointed out, Fort Rouge stood at the mouth of the Assiniboine, on the south side of the river, and the portion of the city of Winnipeg called Fort Rouge is properly named.

It is, of course, evident that the forts erected by these early explorers were simply winter stations, thrown up in great haste.

Verandrye and his band of fifty-two persons, Frenchmen and Indians, set out overland by the Mandan road on October 18th, to roach the Mandan settlements of the Missouri. It is not a part of our work to describe that journey. Suffice it to say that on December 3rd he was at the central fort of the Mandans, 250 miles from his fort at Portage la Prairie.

Being unable to induce his Assiniboine guides and interpreters to remain for the winter among the Mandans, Verandrye returned somewhat unwillingly to the Assiniboine River. He arrived on February 10th at his Fort de la Reine, as he says himself, "greatly fatigued and very ill."

Verandrye in his journal gives us an excellent opportunity of seeing the thorough devotion of the man to his duty. From Fort Michilimackinac to the Missouri, by the route followed by him, is not less than 1,200 miles, and this he accomplished, as we have seen with the necessary delay of building a fort, between July 20th and December 3rd—136 days—of this wonderful year of 1738.

Struggling with difficulties, satisfying creditors, hoping for assistance from France, but ever patriotic and single-minded, Verandrye became the leading spirit in Western exploration. In the year after his great expedition to the prairies, he was summoned to Montreal to resist a lawsuit brought against him. The prevailing sin of French Canada was jealousy. Though Verandrye had struggled so bravely to explore the country, there were those who whispered in the ear of the Minister of the French Court that he was selfish and unworthy. In his heart-broken reply to the charges, he says, "If more than 40,000 livres of debt which I have on my shoulders are an advantage, then I can flatter myself that I am very rich."

In 1741 a fruitless attempt was made to reach the Mandans, but in the following year Verandrye's eldest surviving son and his brother, known as the Chevalier, having with them only two Canadians, loft Forte de la Reine, and made in this and the succeeding year one of the most famous of the Verandrye discoveries. This lies beyond the field of our inquiry, being the journey to the Missouri, and up to an eastern spur of the Rocky Mountains. Parkman, in his "A Half Century of Conflict," has given a detailed account of this remarkable journey.

Going northward over the Portage la Prairie, Verandrye's sons had discovered what is now known as Lake Manitoba, and had reached the Saskatchewan River. On the west side of Lake Manitoba they founded Fort Dauphin, while at the west end of the enlargement of the Saskatchewan known as Cedar Lake, they built Fort Bourbon and ascended the Saskatchewan to the forks, which were known as the Poskoiac. Tardy recognition of Verandrye's achievements came from the French Court in the explorer being promoted to the position of captain in the Colonial troops, and a short time after he was given the Cross of the Order of St. Louis. Beauharnois and his successor Galissionière had both stood by Verandrye and done their best for him. Indeed, the explorer was just about to proceed on the great expedition which was to fulfil their hopes of finding the Western Sea, when, on December 6th, he passed away, his dream unrealized. He was an unselfish soul, a man of great executive ability, and one who dearly loved his King and country. He stands out in striking contrast to the Bigots and Jonquières, who disgraced the name of France in the New World.

From the hands of these vampires, who had come to suck out the blood of New France, Verandrye's sons received no consideration. Their claims were coolly passed by, their goods shamelessly seized, and their written and forcible re-monstrance made no impression. Legardeur de St. Pierre, more to the mind of the selfish Bigot, was given their place and property, and in 1751 a small fort was built on the upper waters of the Saskatchewan, near the Rocky Mountains, near where the town of Calgary now stands. This was called in honour of the Governor, Fort La Jonquiere. A year afterward, St. Pierre, with his little garrison of five men, disgusted with the country, deserted Fort La Reine, which, a few weeks after, was burned to the ground by the Assiniboines.

The fur trade was continued by the French in much the same bounds, so long as the country remained in the hands of France.

We are fortunate in having an account of these affairs given in De Bougainville's Memoir, two years before the capture of Canada by Wolfe. The forts built by Verandrye's successors were included under the "Post of the Western Sea" (La Mer de l'Ouest). Bougainville says, "The Post of the Western Sea is the most advanced toward the north; it is situated amidst many Indian tribes, with whom we trade and who have intercourse with the English, toward Hudson Bay. We have there several forts built of stockades, trusted generally to the care of one or two officers, seven or eight soldiers, and eighty *engagés Canadians*. We can push further the discoveries we have made in that country, and communicate even with California."

This would have realized the dream of Verandrye of reaching the Western Sea."

The Post of La Mer de l'Ouest includes the forts of St. Pierre, St. Charles, Bourbon, De la Reine, Dauphin, Poskoiac, and Des Prairies (De la Jonquiere), all of which are built with palisades that can give protection only against the Indians.""The post of La Mer de l'Ouest merits special attention for two reasons: the first, that it is the nearest to the establishments of the English on Hudson Bay, and from which their movements can be watched; the second, that from this post, the discovery of the Western Sea may be accomplished; but to make this discovery it will be necessary that the travellers give up all view of personal interest."

Two years later, French power in North America came to an end, and a generation afterward, the Western Sea was discovered by British fur traders.

CHAPTER XI.

THE SCOTTISH MERCHANTS OF MONTREAL

Unyielding old Cadot—Competition—The enterprising Henry—Leads the way—
Thomas Curry—The older Finlay—Plundering Indians—"Grand Portage"—A famous
mart—The plucky Frobishers—The Sleeping Giant aroused—Fort Cumberland—
Churchill River—Indian rising—The deadly smallpox—The whites saved.

THE capture of Canada by General Wolfe in 1759 completely changed
the course of affairs in the Western fur country. Michilimackinac and
Sault Ste. Marie had become considerable trading centres under the
French *régime*, but the officers and men had almost entirely been
withdrawn from the outposts in the death struggle for the defence of
Quebec and Montreal.

The conquest of Canada was announced with sorrow by the chief
captain of the West, Charles de Langlade, on his return after the
capitulation of Montreal. The French Canadians who had taken Indian
wives still clung to the fur country. These French half-breed settlements
at Michilimackinac and neighbouring posts were of some size, but
beyond Lake Superior, except a straggler here and there, nothing
French was left behind. The forts of the western post fell into decay, and
were in most cases burnt by the Indians. Not an army officer, not a
priest, not a fur trader, remained beyond Kaministiquia.

The French of Michilimackinac region were for a time unwilling to
accept British rule. Old trader, Jean Baptiste Cadot, who had settled
with his Indian wife, Anastasie, at Sault Ste. Marie, and become a man
of wide influence, for years refused to yield, and a French Canadian
author says: "So the French flag continued to float over the fort of Sault
Ste. Marie long after the *fleur-de-lis* had quitted for over the ramparts
of Quebec. Under the shadow of the old colours, so fruitful of tender
memories, he was able to believe himself still under the protection of
the mother-country." However, Cadot ended by accepting the situation,
and an author tells us that like Cadot, "were the La Cornes, the
Langlades, the Beaujeus, the Babys, and many others who, after

fighting like lions against England, were counted a little later among the number of her most gallant defenders." For several years, however, the fur trade was not carried on.

The change of flag in Canada brought a number of enterprising spirits as settlers to Quebec and Montreal. The Highland regiments under Generals Amherst and Wolfe had seen Montreal and Quebec. A number of the military became settlers. The suppression of the Jacobite rebellion in Scotland in 1745 had led to the dispersion of many young men of family beyond the seas. Some of these drifted to Montreal. Many of the Scottish settlements of the United States had remained loyal, so that after the American Revolution parties of these loyalists came to Montreal. Thus in a way hard to explain satisfactorily, the English-speaking merchants who came to Canada were largely Scottish. In a Government report found in the Haldimand papers in 1784, it is stated that "The greater part of the inhabitants of Montreal (no doubt meaning English-speaking inhabitants) are Presbyterians of the Church of Scotland." It was these Scottish merchants of Montreal who revived the fur trade to the interior.

Washington Irving, speaking of these merchants, says, "Most of the clerks were young men of good families from the Highlands of Scotland, characterized by the perseverance, thrift, and fidelity of their country." He refers to their feasts "making the rafters resound with bursts of loyalty and old Scottish songs."

The late Archbishop Taché, a French Canadian long known in the North-West, speaking of this period says, "Companies called English, but generally composed of Scotchmen, were found in Canada to continue to make the most of the rich furs of the forests of the North. Necessity obliged them at first to accept the co-operation of the French Canadians, who maintained their influence by the share they took in the working of these companies. . . . This circumstance explains how, after the Scotch, the French Canadian element is the most important, "The first among these Scottish merchants to hie away from Montreal to the far West was Alexander Henry, whose "Travels and Adventures in

Canada and the Indian Territories between the years 1760 and 1766" have the charm of narrative of an Irving or a Parkman. He knew nothing of the fur trade, but he took with him an experienced French Canadian, named Campion. He appeared at Michilimackinac two years after the conquest by Wolfe, and in the following year visited Sault Ste. Marie with its stockaded fort, and formed a friendship with trader Cadot. In the following year, Henry was a witness of the massacre at Michilimackinac, so graphically described by Parkman in his "Conspiracy of Pontiac." Henry's account of his own escape is a thrilling tale.

In 1765 Henry obtained from the Commandant at Michilimackinac licence of the exclusive trade of Lake Superior. He purchased the freight of four canoes, which he took at the price of 10,000 good, merchantable beavers. With his crew of twelve men, and supplies of fifty bushels of prepared Indian corn, he reached a band of Indians on the Lake who were in poverty, but who took his supplies on trust, and went off to hunt beaver. In due time the Indians returned, and paid up promptly and fully the loans made to them. By 1768 he had succeeded in opening up the desired route of French traders, going from Michilimackinac to Kaministiquia on Lake Superior and returning. His later journeys we may notice afterwards.

Of the other merchants who followed Henry in reviving the old route, the first to make a notable adventure was the Scotchman Thomas Curry. Procuring the requisite band of voyageurs and interpreters, in 1766 he pushed through with four canoes, along Verandrye's route, even to the site of the old French Fort Bourbon, on the west of Cedar Lake, on the lower Saskatchewan River. Curry had in his movement something of the spirit of Verandrye, and his season's trip was so successful that, according to Sir Alexander Mackenzie, his fine furs gave so handsome a return that "he was satisfied never again to return to the Indian country."

Another valorous Scotchman, James Finlay, of Montreal, took up the paddle that Curry had laid down, and in 1768, with a force equal to that of Curry, passed into the interior and ascended the Saskatchewan to Nipawi, the farthest point which Verandrye had reached. He was rewarded with a generous return for his venture.

But while these journeys had been successful, it would seem that the turbulent state of the Indian tribes had made other expeditions disastrous. In a memorial sent by the fur traders a few years later to the Canadian Government, it is stated that in a venture made from Michilimackinac in 1765 the Indians of Rainy Lake had plundered the traders of their goods, that in the next year a similar revolt followed, that in the following year the traders were compelled to leave a certain portion of their goods at Rainy Lake to be allowed to go on to Lake Ouinipique. It is stated that the brothers, Benjamin and James Frobisher, of Montreal, who became so celebrated as fur traders, began a post ten years after the conquest. These two merchants were Englishmen. They speedily took the lead in pushing forward far into the interior, and were the most practical of the fur traders in making alliances and in dealing successfully with the Indians. In their first expedition they had the same experience in their goods being seized by the thievish Indians of Rainy Lake; but before they could send back word the goods for the next venture had reached Grand Portage on Lake Superior, and they were compelled to try the route to the West again. On this occasion they managed to defy the pillaging bands, and reached Fort Bourbon on the Saskatchewan. They now discovered that co-operation and a considerable show of force was the only method of carrying on a safe trade among the various tribes. It was fortunate for the Montreal traders that such courageous leaders as the Frobishers had undertaken the trade.

The trade to the North-West thus received a marvellous development at the hands of the Montreal merchants. Nepigon and the Kaministiquia, which had been such important points in the French *régime*, had been quite forgotten, and Grand Portage was now the place of greatest interest, and so continued to the end of the century.

It is with peculiar interest a visitor to-day makes his way to Grand Portage. The writer, after a difficult night voyage over the stormy waters of Lake Superior, rowed by the keeper of a neighbouring lighthouse, made a visit a few years ago to this spot. Grand Portage ends on a bay of Lake Superior. It is partially sheltered by a rocky island which has the appearance of a robber's keep, but has one inhabitant, the only white man of the region, a French Canadian of very fair means. On the bay is to-day an Indian village, chiefly celebrated for its multitude of dogs. A few traces of the former greatness of the place may be seen in the timbers down in the water of the former wharves, which were extensive. Few traces of forts are now, a century after their desertion by the fur traders, to be seen.

The portage, consisting of a road fairly made for the nine or ten miles necessary to avoid the falls on Pigeon River, can still be followed. No horse or ox is now to be found in the whole district, where at one time the traders used this means of lightening the burden of packing over the portage. The solitary road, as the traveller walks along it, with weeds and grasses grown up, brings to one a melancholy feeling. The bustle of voyageur and trader and Indian is no more; and the reflection made by Irving comes back, "The lords of the lakes and forests have passed away."

And yet Grand Portage was at the time of which we are writing a place of vast importance. Here there were employed as early as 1783, by the several merchants from Montreal, 500 men. One half of these came from Montreal to Grand Portage in canoes of four tons burden, each managed by from eight to ten men. As these were regarded as having the least romantic portion of the route, meeting with no Indians, and living on cured rations, they were called the "mangeurs de lard," or pork eaters. The other half of the force journeyed inland from Grand Portage in canoes, each carrying about a ton and a half. Living on game and the dried meat of the buffalo, known as pemmican, these were a more independent and daring body. They were called the "coureurs de bois."

For fifteen days after August 15th these wood-runners portaged over the nine or ten miles their burdens. Men carrying 150 lbs. each way have been known to make the portage and return in six hours. When the canoes were loaded at the west end of the portage with two-thirds goods and one-third provisions, then the hurry of the season came, and supplies for Lake Winnipeg, the Saskatchewan, and far distant Athabasca were hastened on apace. The difficulties of the route were at many a décharge, where only the goods needed to be removed and the canoes taken over the rapids, or at the portage, where both canoes and load were carried past dangerous falls and fierce rapids. The dash, energy, and skill that characterized these mixed companies of Scottish traders, French voyageurs, half-breed and Indian *engagés*, have been well spoken of by all observers, and appeal strongly to the lovers of the picturesque and heroic.

A quarter of a century after the conquest we have a note of alarm at the new competition that the Company from Hudson Bay had at last under taken. In the Memorial before us it is stated that disturbance of trade is made by "New Adventurers." It is with a smile we read of the daring and strong-handed traders of Montreal saying, "Those adventurers (evidently H. B. Co.), consulting their own interests only, without the least regard to the management of the natives or the general welfare of the trade, soon occasioned such disorders, &c. . . . Since that time business is carried on with great disadvantages." This reference, so prosaically introduced, is really one of enormous moment in our story. The Frobishers, with their keen business instincts and daring plans, saw that the real stroke which would lead them on to fortune was to divert the stream of trade then going to Hudson Bay southward to Lake Superior. Accordingly, with a further aggressive movement in view, Joseph Frobisher established a post on Sturgeon Lake, an enlargement of the Saskatchewan, near the point known by the early French as Poskoiac.

A glance at the map will show how well chosen Sturgeon Lake Fort was. Northward from it a watercourse could be readily followed, by which the main line of water communication from the great northern districts to Hudson Bay could be reached and the Northern Indians be interrupted in their annual pilgrimage to the Bay. But, as we shall afterward see, the sleeping giant of the Bay had been awakened and was about to stretch forth his arms to grasp the trade of the interior with a new vigour. Two years after Frobisher had thrown down the pledge of battle, it was taken up by the arrival of Samuel Hearne, an officer of the Hudson's Bay Company, and by his founding Fort Cumberland on Sturgeon Lake, about two miles below Frobisher's Fort. Hearne returned to the Bay, leaving his new fort garrisoned by a number of Orkney men under an English officer.

During the same year an explorer, on behalf of the Hudson's Bay Company, visited Red River, but no fort was built there for some time afterward. The building of Fort Cumberland led to a consolidation on the part of the Montreal merchants. In the next year after its building, Alexander Henry, the brothers Frobisher, trader Cadot, and a daring trader named Pond, gathered at Sturgeon Lake, and laid their plans for striking a blow in retaliation, as they regarded it, for the disturbance of trade made by the Hudson's Bay Company in penetrating to the interior from the Bay.

Cadot, with four canoes, went west to the Saskatchewan; Pond, with two, to the country on Lake Dauphin; and Henry and the Frobisher brothers, with their ten canoes and upwards of forty men, hastened northward to carry out the project of turning anew the Northern Indians from their usual visit to the Bay. On the way to the Churchill River they built a fort on Beaver Lake. In the following year, a strong party went north to Churchill or English River, as Joseph Frobisher now called it. When it was reached they turned westward and ascended the Churchill, returning at Serpent's Rapid, but sending Thomas Frobisher with goods on to Lake Athabasca.

From the energy displayed, and the skill shown in seizing the main points in the country, it will be seen that the Montreal merchants were not lacking in ability to plan and decision to execute. The two great forces have now met, and for fifty years a battle royal will be fought for the rivers, rocks, and plains of the North Country. At present it is our duty to follow somewhat further the merchants of Montreal in their agencies in the North-West.

There can be no doubt that the competition between the two companies produced disorder and confusion among the Indian tribes. The Indian nature is excitable and suspicious. Rival traders for their own ends played upon the fears and cupidity alike of the simple children of the woods and prairies. They represented their opponents in both cases as unreliable and grasping, and party spirit unknown before showed itself in most violent forms. The feeling against the whites of both parties was aroused by injustices, in some cases fancied, in others real. The Assiniboines, really the northern branch of the fierce Sioux of the prairies, were first to seize the tomahawk. They attacked Poplar Fort on the Assiniboine. After some loss of life, Bruce and Boyer, who were in charge of the fort, decided to desert it. Numerous other attacks were made on the traders' forts, and it looked as if the prairies would be the scene of a general Indian war.

The only thing that seems to have prevented so dire a disaster was the appearance of what is ever a dreadful enemy to the poor Indian, the scourge of smallpox. The Assiniboines had gone on a war expedition against the Mandans of the Missouri River, and had carried back the smallpox infection which prevailed among the Mandan lodges. This disease spread over the whole country, and several bands of Indians were completely blotted out. Of one tribe of four hundred lodges, only ten persons remained; the poor survivors, in seeking succour from other bands, carried the disease with them. At the end of 1782 there were only twelve traders who had persevered in their trade on account of the discouragements, but the whole trade was for two or three seasons brought to an end by this disease.

The decimation of the tribes, the fear of infection by the traders, and the general awe cast over the country turned the thoughts of the natives away from war, and as Masson says, "the whites had thus escaped the danger which threatened them."

Two or three years after the scourge, the merchants of Montreal revived the trade, and, as we shall see, made a combination which, in the thoroughness of its discipline, the energy of its operations, the courage of its promoters, and the scope of its trade, has perhaps never been equalled in the history of trading companies.

CHAPTER XII.

SUCH an agitation as that so skilfully planned and shrewdly carried on by Arthur Dobbs, Esq., could not but affect the action of the Hudson's Bay Company. The most serious charge brought against the Company was that, while having a monopoly of the trade on Hudson Bay, it had taken no steps to penetrate the country and develop its resources. It is of course evident that the Company itself could have no reason for refusing to open up trade with the interior, for by this means it would be expanding its operations and increasing its profits. The real reason for its not doing so seems to have been the inertia, not to say fear, of Hudson's Bay Company agents on the Bay who failed to mingle with the bands of Indians in the interior.

Now the man was found who was to be equal to the occasion. This was Samuel Hearne. Except occasional reference to him in the minutes of the Company and works of the period, we know little of Samuel Hearne. He was one of the class of men to which belonged Norton, Kelsey, and others—men who had grown up in the service of the Company on the Bay, and had become, in the course of years, accustomed to the climate, condition of life, and haunts of the Indians, thus being fitted for active work for the Company.

Samuel Hearne became so celebrated in his inland expeditions, that the credit of the Hudson's Bay Company leaving the coast and venturing into the interior has always been attached to his name. So greatly, especially in the English mind, have his explorations bulked, that the author of a book of travels in Canada about the beginning of this century called him the "Mungo Park of Canada." In his "Journey," we have an account of his earlier voyages to the interior in search of the Coppermine River. This book has a somewhat notable history.

In the four-volume work of La Perouse, the French navigator, it is stated that when he took Prince of Wales Fort on the Churchill River in 1782, Hearne, as governor of the fort, surrendered it to him, and that the manuscript of his "Journey" was seized by the French commander. It was returned to Hearne on condition that it should be published, but the publication did not take place until thirteen years afterwards. It is somewhat amusing to read in Perouse's preface (1791) the complaint that Hearne had not kept faith with him in regard to publishing the journal, and the hope is expressed that this public statement in reminding him of his promise would have the desired effect of the journal being published.

Four years afterwards Hearne's "Journey" appeared. A reference to this fine quarto work, which is well illustrated, brings us back in the introduction to all the controversies embodied in the work of Dobbs, Ellis, Robson, and the "American Traveller."

Hearne's orders were received from the Hudson's Bay Company, in 1769, to go on a land expedition to the interior of the continent, from the mouth of the Churchill as far as 70 deg. N. lat., to smoke the calumet of peace with the Indians, to take accurate astronomical observations, to go with guides to the Athabasca country, and thence northward to a river abounding with copper ore and "animals of the fur kind," &c.

It is very noticeable, also, that his instructions distinctly tell him" to clear up the point, if possible, in order to prevent further doubt from arising hereafter respecting a passage out of Hudson Bay into the Western Ocean, as hath lately been represented by the 'American Traveller.'" The instructions made it plain that it was the agitation still continuing from the days of Dobbs which led to the sending of Hearne to the north country.

Hearne's first expedition was made during the last months of the year 1769. It is peculiarly instructive in the fact that it failed to accomplish anything, as it gives us a glimpse of the difficulties which no doubt so long prevented the movement to the interior. In the first place, the bitterly severe months of November and December were badly chosen for the time of the expedition. On the sixth day of the former of these months Hearne left Prince of Wales Fort, taking leave of the Governor, and being sent off with a salute of seven guns. His guide was an Indian chief, Chawchinahaw. Hearne ascertained very soon, what others have found among the Indians, that his guide was not to be trusted; he "often painted the difficulties in the worst colours" and took every method to dishearten the explorer. Three weeks after starting, a number of the Indians deserted Hearne.

Shortly after this mishap, Chawchinahaw and his company ruthlessly deserted the expedition, and two hundred miles from the fort set out on another route, "making the woods ring with their laughter." Meeting other Indians, Hearne purchased venison, but was cheated, while his Indian guide was feasted. The explorer remarks:—"A sufficient proof of the singular advantage which a native of this country has over an Englishman, when at such a distance from the Company's factories as to depend entirely on them for subsistence."

Hearne arrived at the fort after an absence of thirty-seven days, as he says, "to my own mortification and the no small surprise of the Governor." Hearne was simply illustrating what has been shown a hundred times since, in all foreign regions, viz., native peoples are quick to see the inexperience of men raw to the country, and will heartlessly maltreat and deceive them. However, British officers and men in all parts of the world become at length accustomed to dealing with savage peoples, and after some experience, none have ever equalled British agents and explorers in the management and direction of such peoples.

Early in the following year Hearne plucked up courage for another expedition. On this occasion he determined to take no Europeans, but to trust to Indians alone. On February 23rd, accompanied by five Indians, Hearne started on his second journey. Following the advice of the Governor, the party took no Indian women with them, though Hearne states that this was a mistake, as they were "needed for hauling the baggage as well as for dressing skins for clothing, pitching our tent, getting firing, &c." During the first part of the journey deer were plentiful, and the fish obtained by cutting holes in the ice of the lakes were excellent.

Hearne spent the time of the necessary delays caused by the obtaining of fish and game in taking observations, keeping his journal and chart, and doing his share of trapping. Meeting, as soon as the spring opened, bands of Indians going on various errands, the explorer started overland. He carried sixty pounds of burden, consisting of quadrant, books and papers, compass, wearing apparel, weapons and presents for the natives. The traveller often made twenty miles a day over the rugged country.

Meeting a chief of the Northern Indians going in July to Prince of Wales Fort, Hearne sent by him for ammunition and supplies. A canoe being now necessary, Hearne purchased this of the Indians. It was obtained by the exchange of a single knife, the full value of which did not exceed a penny. In the middle of this month the party saw bands of musk oxen. A number of these were killed and their flesh made into pemmican for future use. Finding it impossible to reach the Coppermine during the season, Hearne determined to live with the Indians for the winter.

The explorer was a good deal disturbed by having to give presents to Indians who met him. Some of them wanted guns, all wanted ammunition, iron-work, and tobacco; many were solicitous for medicine; and others pressed for different articles of clothing. He thought the Indians very inconsiderate in their demands.

On August 11th the explorer had the misfortune to lose his quadrant by its being blown open and broken by the wind. Shortly after this disaster, Hearne was plundered by a number of Indians who joined him.

He determined to return to the fort. Suffering from the want of food and clothing, Hearne was overtaken by a famous chief, Matonabbee, who was going eastward to Prince of Wales Fort. The chief had lived several years at the fort, and was one who knew the Coppermine.

Matonabbee discussed the reasons of Hearne's failure in his two expeditions. The forest philosopher gave as the reason of these failures the misconduct of the guides and the failure to take any women on the journey. After maintaining that women were made for labour, and speaking of their assistance, said Matonabbee, "women, though they do everything, are maintained at a trifling expense, for as they always stand cook, the very licking of their fingers in scarce times is sufficient for their subsistence." Plainly, the northern chief had need of the ameliorating influence of modern reformers. In company with the chief, Hearne returned to the fort, reaching it after an absence of eight months and twenty-two days, having, as he says, had "a fruitless or at least an unsuccessful journey."

Hearne, though beaten twice, was determined to try a third time and win. He recommended the employment of Matonabbee as a guide of intelligence and experience. Governor Norton wished to send some of the coast Indians with Hearne, but the latter refused them, and incurred the ill-will of the Governor. Hearne's instructions on this third journey were "in quest of a North-West Passage, copper-mines, or any other thing that may be serviceable to the British nation in general, or the Hudson's Bay Company in particular." The explorer was now furnished with an Elton's quadrant.

This third journey was begun on December 7th, 1770. Travelling sometimes for three or four days without food, they were annoyed, when supplies were secured, by the chief Matonabbee taking so ill from over-eating that he had to be drawn upon a sledge. Without more than the usual incidents of Indian travelling, the party pushed on till a point some 19 deg. west of Churchill was reached, according to the calculations of the explorer. It is to be noted, however, that Hearne's observations, measurements, and maps, do not seem to be at all accurate.

Turning northward, as far as can be now made out, about the spot whore the North-West traders first appeared on their way to the Churchill River, Hearne went north to his destination. His Indian guides now formed a large war party from the resident Indians, to meet the Eskimos of the river to which they were going and to conquer them.

The explorer announces that having left behind "all the women, children, dogs, heavy baggage, and other encumbrances," on June 1st, 1771, they pursued their journey northward with great speed. On June 21st the sun did not set at all, which Hearne took to be proof that they had reached the Arctic Circle. Next day they met the Copper Indians, who welcomed them on hearing the object of their visit.

Hearne, according to orders, smoked the calumet of peace with the Copper Indians. These Indians had never before seen a white man. Hearne was considered a great curiosity. Pushing on upon their long journey, the explorers reached the Coppermine River on July 13th. Hearne was the witness of a cruel massacre of the Eskimos by his Indian allies, and the seizure of their copper utensils and other provisions, and expresses disgust at the enormity of the affair. The mouth of the river, which flows into the Arctic Ocean, was soon reached on July 18th, and the tide found to rise about fourteen feet.

Hearne seems in the narrative rather uncertain about the latitude of the mouth of the Coppermine River, but states that after some consultation with the Indians, he erected a mark, and took possession of the coast on behalf of the Hudson's Bay Company.

In Hearne's map, dated July, 1771, and purporting to be a plan of the Coppermine, the mouth of the river is about 71 deg. 54′ N. This was a great mistake, as the mouth of the river is somewhere near 68 deg. N. So great a mistake was certainly unpardonable. Hearne's apology was that after the breaking of his quadrant on the second expedition, the instrument which he used was an old Elton's quadrant, which had been knocking about the Prince of Wales Fort for nearly thirty years.

Having examined the resources of the river and heard of the mines from which the Copper Indians obtained all the metal for the manufacture of hatchets, chisels, knives, &c., Hearne started southward on his return journey on July 18th. Instead of coming by the direct route, he went with the Indians of his party to the north side of Lake

Athabasca on December 24th. Having crossed the lake, as illustrating the loneliness of the region, the party found a woman who had escaped from an Indian band which had taken her prisoner, and who had not seen a human face for seven months, and had lived by snaring partridges, rabbits, and squirrels. Her skill in maintaining herself in lonely wilds was truly wonderful. She became the wife of one of the Indians of Hearne's party. In the middle of March, 1772, Hearne was delivered a letter, brought to him from Prince of Wales Fort and dated in the preceding June. Pushing eastward, after a number of adventures, Hearne reached Prince of Wales Fort on June 30th, 1772, having been absent on his third voyage eighteen months and twenty-three days. Hearne rejoices that he had at length put an end to the disputes concerning a North-West Passage through Hudson Bay. The fact, however, that during the nineteenth century this became again a living question shows that in this he was mistaken.

The perseverance and pluck of Hearne have impressed all those who have read his narrative. He was plainly one of the men possessing the subtle power of impressing the Indian mind. His disasters would have deterred many men from following up so difficult and extensive a route. To him the Hudson's Bay Company owes a debt of gratitude. That debt consists not in the discovery of the Coppermine, but in the attitude presented to the Northern Indians from the Bay all the way to Lake Athabasca, Hearne does not mention the Montreal fur traders, who, in the very year of his return, reached the Saskatchewan and were stationed at the Churchill River down which he passed.

First of white men to reach Athapuscow, now thought to have been Great Slave Lake, Samuel Hearne claimed for his Company priority of trade, and answered the calumnies that his Company was lacking in energy and enterprise. Ho took what may be called "seizen" of the soil for the English traders. We shall speak again of his part in leading the movement inland to oppose the Nor'-Westers in the interior. His services to the Hudson's Bay Company received recognition in his promotion, three years after his return home from his third voyage, to the governorship of the Prince of Wales Fort. To Hearne has been largely given the credit of the new and adventurous policy of the Hudson's Bay Company.

Hearne does not, however, disappear from public notice on his promotion to the command of Prince of Wales Fort. When war broke out a few years later between England and France, the latter country, remembering her old successes under D'Iber-ville on Hudson Bay, sent a naval expedition to attack the forts on the Bay. Umfreville gives an account of the attack on Prince of Wales Fort on August 8th and 9th, 1772. Admiral de la Perouse was in command of these war vessels, his flagship being *Le Sceptre*, of seventy-four guns. The garrison was thought to be well provided for a siege, and La Perouse evidently expected to have a severe contest. However, as he approached the fort, there seemed to be no preparations made for defence, and, on the summons to surrender, the gates were immediately thrown open.

Umfreville, who was in the garrison and was taken prisoner on this occasion, speaks of the conduct of the Governor as being very reprehensible, but severely criticizes the Company for its neglect. He says:—"The strength of the fort itself was such as would have resisted the attack of a more considerable force; it was built of the strongest materials, the walls were of great thickness and very durable (it was planned by the ingenious Mr. Robson, who went out in 1742 for that purpose), it having been forty years in building and attended with great expense to the Company. In short, it was the opinion of every intelligent person that it might have made an obstinate resistance when attacked, had it been as well provided in other respects; but through the impolitic conduct of the Company, every courageous exertion of their servants must have been considered as imprudent temerity; for this place, which would have required four hundred men for its defence, the Company, in its consummate wisdom, had garrisoned with only thirty-nine."

In this matter, Umfreville very plainly shows his animus to the Company, but incidentally he exonerates Hearne from the charge of cowardice, inasmuch as it would have been madness to make defence against so large a body of men. As has been before pointed out, we can hardly charge with cowardice the man who had shown his courage and determination in the three toilsome and dangerous journeys spoken of; rather would we see in this a proof of his wisdom under unfortunate circumstances. The surrender of York Factory to La Perouse twelve days afterwards, without resistance, was an event of an equally discouraging kind. The Company suffered great loss by the surrender of these forts, which had been unmolested since the Treaty of Utrecht.

CHAPTER XIII.

THE new policy of the Company that for a hundred years had carried on its operations in Hudson Bay was now to be adopted. As soon as the plan could be developed, a long line of posts in the interior would serve to carry on the chief trade, and the forts and factories on Hudson Bay would become depots for storage and ports of departure for the Old World.

It is interesting at this point to have a view of the last days of the old system which had grown up during the operations of a century. We are fortunate in having an account of these forts in 1771 given by Andrew Graham, for many years a factor of the Hudson's Bay Company. This document is to be found in the Hudson's Bay Company house in London, and has been hitherto unpublished. The simplicity of description and curtness of detail gives the account its chief charm.

PRINCE OF WALES FORT.—On a peninsula at the entrance of the Churchill River. Most northern settlement of the Company. A stone fort, mounting forty-two cannon, from six to twenty-four pounders. Opposite, on the south side of the river, Cape Merry Battery, mounting six twenty-four pounders with lodge-house and powder magazine. The river 1,006 yards wide. A ship can anchor six miles above the fort. Tides carry salt water twelve miles up the river. No springs near; drink snow water nine months of the year. In summer keep three draught horses to haul water and draw stones to finish building of forts.

Staff:—A chief factor and officers, with sixty servants and tradesmen. The council, with discretionary power, consists of chief factor, second factor, surgeon, sloop and brig masters, and captain of Company's ship when in port. These answer and sign the general letter, sent yearly to directors. The others are accountant, trader, steward, armourer, ship-wright, carpenter, cooper, blacksmith, mason, tailor, and labourers. These must not trade with natives, under penalties for so doing. Council mess together, also servants. Called by bell to duty, work from six to six in summer; eight to four in winter. Two watch in winter, three in summer. In emergencies, tradesmen must work at anything. Killing of partridges the most pleasant duty.

Company signs contract with servants for three or five years, with the remarkable clause: "Company may recall them home at any time without satisfaction for the remaining time. Contract may be renewed, if servants or labourers wish, at expiry of term. Salary advanced forty shillings, if men have behaved well in first term. The land and sea officers' and tradesmen's salaries do not vary, but seamen's are raised in time of war."

A ship of 200 tons burden, bearing provisions, arrives yearly in August or early September. Sails again in ten days, wind permitting, with cargo and those returning. Sailors alone get pay when at home.

The annual trade sent home from this fort is from ten to four thousand made beaver, in furs, felts, castorum, goose feathers, and quills, and a small quantity of train oil and whalebone, part of which they receive from the Eskimos, and the rest from the white whale fishery. A black whale fishery is in hand, but it shows no progress.

YORK FACTORY.—On the north bank of Hayes River, three miles from the entrance. Famous River Nelson, three miles north, makes the land between an island. Well-built fort of wood, log on log. Four bastions with sheds between, and a breastwork with twelve small carriage guns. Good class of quarters, with double row of strong palisades. On the bank's edge, before the fort, is a half-moon battery, of turf and earth, with fifteen cannon, nine-pounders. Two miles below the fort, same side, is a battery of ten twelve-pounders, with lodge-house and powder magazine. These two batteries command the river, but the shoals and sand-banks across the mouth defend us more. No ship comes higher than five miles below the fort.

Governed like Prince of Wales Fort. Complement of men: forty-two. The natives come down Nelson River to trade. If weather calm, they paddle round the point. If not, they carry their furs across. This fort sends home from 7,000 to 33,000 made beaver in furs, &c., and a small quantity of white whale oil.

SEVERN FORT.—On the north bank of Severn River. Well-built square house, with four bastions. Men: eighteen. Commanded by a factor and sloop master. Eight small cannon and other warlike stores. Sloop carries furs in the fall to York Factory and delivers them to the ship, with the books and papers, receiving supply of trading goods, provisions, and stores. Severn full of shoals and sand banks. Sloop has difficulty in getting in and out. Has to wait spring tides inside the point. Trade sent home, 5,000 to 6,600 made beaver in furs, &c.

ALBANY FORT.—On south bank of Albany River, four miles from the entrance. Large well-built wood fort. Four bastions with shed between. Cannon and warlike stores. Men: thirty; factor and officers. River difficult. Ship rides five leagues out and is loaded and unloaded by large sloop. Trade, including two sub-houses of East Main and Henley, from 10,000 to 12,000 made beaver, &c. (This fort was the first Europeans had in Hudson Bay, and is where Hudson traded with natives.)

HENLEY HOUSE.—One hundred miles up the river from Albany. Eleven men, governed by master. First founded to prevent encroachments of the French, when masters of Canada, and present to check the English.

EAST MAIN HOUSE.—Entrance of Slude River. Small square house. Sloop master and eleven men. Trade: 1000 to 2000 made beaver in furs, &c. Depth of water just admits sloop.

MOOSE FACTORY.—South bank of Moose River, near entrance. Well-built wood fort—cannon and warlike stores. Twenty-five men. Factor and officers. River admits ship to good harbour, below fort. Trade, 3,000 to 4,000 made beavers in furs, &c. One ship supplies this fort, along with Albany and sub-forts.

These are the present Hudson's Bay Company's settlements in the Bay. "All under one discipline, and excepting the sub-houses, each factor receives a commission to act for benefit of Company, without being answerable to any person or persons in the Bay, more than to consult for good of Company in emergencies and to supply one another with trading goods, &c., if capable, the receiver giving credit for the same."

The movement to the interior was begun from the Prince of Wales Fort up the Churchill River. Next year, after his return from the discovery of the Coppermine, Samuel Hearne undertook the aggressive work of going to meet the Indians, now threatened from the Saskatchewan by the seductive influences of the Messrs. Frobisher, of the Montreal fur traders. The Governor at Prince of Wales Fort, for a good many years, had been Moses Norton. He was really an Indian born at the fort, who had received some education during a nine years' residence in England. Of uncultivated manners, and leading far from a pure life, he was yet a man of considerable force, with a power to command and the ability to ingratiate himself with the Indians. He was possessed of undoubted energy, and no doubt to his advice is very much due the movement to leave the forts in the Bay and penetrate to the interior of the country. In December of the very year (1773) in which Hearne went on his trading expedition inland, Norton died.

In the following year, as we have seen, Hearne erected Cumberland House, only five hundred yards from Frobisher's new post on Sturgeon Lake. It was the intention of the Hudson's Bay Company also to make an effort to control the trade to the south of Lake Winnipeg. Hastily called away after building Cumberland House, Hearne was compelled to leave a colleague, Mr. Cockings, in charge of the newly-erected fort, and returned to the bay to take charge of Prince of Wales Fort, the post left vacant by the death of Governor Norton.

The Hudson's Bay Company, now regularly embarked in the inland trade, undertook to push their posts to different parts of the country, especially to the portion of the fur country in the direction from which the Montreal traders approached it. The English traders, as we learn from Umfreville, who was certainly not prejudiced in their favour, had the advantage of a higher reputation in character and trade among the Indians than had their Canadian opponents. From their greater nearness to northern waters, the old Company could reach a point in the Saskatchewan with their goods nearly a month earlier in the spring than their Montreal rivals were able to do. We find that in 1790 the Hudson's Bay Company crossed south from the northern waters and erected a trading post at the mouth of the Swan River, near Lake Winnipegoosis. This they soon deserted and built a fort on the upper waters of the Assiniboine River, a few miles above the present Hudson's Bay Company post of Fort Pelly.

A period of surprising energy was now seen in the English Company's affairs. "Carrying the war into Africa," they in the same year met their antagonists in the heart of their own territory, by building a trading post on Rainy Lake and another in the neighbouring Red Lake district, now included in North-Eastern Minnesota. Having seized the chief points southward, the aroused Company, in the next year (1791), pushed north-westward from Cumberland House and built an establishment at Ile à la Crosse, well up toward Lake Athabasca.

Crossing from Lake Winnipeg in early spring to the head waters of the Assiniboine River, the spring brigade of the Hudson's Bay Company quite outdid their rivals, and in 1794 built the historic Brandon House, at a very important point on the Assiniboine River. This post was for upwards of twenty years a chief Hudson's Bay Company centre until it was burnt. On the grassy bank of the Assiniboine, the writer some years ago found the remains of the old fort, and from the well-preserved character of the sod, was able to make out the line of the palisades, the exact size of all the buildings, and thus to obtain the ground plan.

Brandon House was on the south side of the Assiniboine, about seventeen miles below the present city of Brandon, Its remains are situated on the homestead of Mr. George Mair, a Canadian settler from Beauharnois, Quebec, who settled here on July 20th, 1879. The site was well chosen at a bend of the river, having the Assiniboine in front of it on the east and partially so also on the north. The front of the palisade faced to the east, and midway in the wall was a gate ten feet wide, with inside of it a look-out tower (guérite) seven feet square. On the south side was the long store-house. In the centre had stood a building said by some to have been the blacksmith's shop. Along the north wall were the buildings for residences and other purposes. The remains of other forts, belonging to rival companies, are not far away, but of these we shall speak again.

The same activity continued to exist in the following year, for in points so far apart as the Upper Saskatchewan and Lake Winnipeg new forts were built. The former of these was Edmonton House, built on the north branch of the Saskatchewan. The fort erected on Lake Winnipeg was probably that at the mouth of the Winnipeg River, near where Fort Alexander now stands.

In 1796, another post was begun on the Assiniboine River, not unlikely near the old site of Fort de la Reine, while in the following year, as a half-way house to Edmonton on the Saskatchewan, Carlton House was erected. The Red River proper was taken possession of by the Company in 1799. Alexander Henry, junr., tells us that very near the boundary line (49 degrees N.) on the east side of the Red River, there were in 1800 the remains of a fort.

Such was the condition of things, so far as the Hudson's Bay Company was concerned, at the end of the century.

In twenty-five years they had extended their trade from Edmonton House, near the Rockies, as far as Rainy Lake; they had made Cumberland House the centre of their operations in the interior, and had taken a strong hold of the fertile region on the Red and Assiniboine Rivers, of which to-day the city of Winnipeg is the centre.

Undoubtedly the severe competition between the Montreal merchants and the Hudson's Bay Company greatly diminished the profits of both. According to Umfreville, the Hudson's Bay Company business was conducted much more economically than that of the merchants of Montreal. The Company upon the Bay chiefly employed men obtained in the Orkney Islands, who were a steady, plodding, and reliable class. The employés of the Montreal merchants were a wild, free, reckless people, much addicted to drink, and consequently less to be depended upon.

The same writer states that the competition between the two rival bodies of traders resulted badly for the Indians. He says: "So that the Canadians from Canada and the Europeans from Hudson Bay met together, not at all to the ulterior advantage of the natives, who by this means became degenerated and debauched, through the excessive use of spirituous liquors imported by these rivals in commerce."

One thing at any rate had been clearly demonstrated, that the inglorious sleeping by the side of the Bay, charged by Dobbs and others against the old Company, had been overcome, and that the first quarter of the second century of the history of the Hudson's Bay Company showed that the Company's motto, "Pro Pelle Cutem," "Skin for Skin," had not been inappropriately chosen.

CHAPTER XIV.

Hudson's Bay Company aggressive—The great McTavish—The Fro-bishers—Pond and Pangman dissatisfied—Gregory and McLeod—Strength of the North-West Company—Vessels to be built—New route from Lake Superior sought—Good-will at times—Bloody Pond—Wider union, 1787—Fort Alexandria—Mouth of the Souris—Enormous fur trade—Wealthy Nor'-Westers—"The Haunted House."

THE terrible scourge of smallpox cut off one-half, some say one-third of the Indian population of the fur country. This was a severe blow to the prosperity of the fur trade, as the traders largely depended on the Indians as trappers. The determination shown by the Hudson's Bay Company, and the zeal with which they took advantage of an early access to the Northern Indians, were a surprise to the Montreal traders, and we find in the writings of the time, frequent expressions as to the loss of profits produced by the competition in the fur trade.

The leading fur merchants of Montreal determined on a combination of their forces. Chief among the stronger houses were the Frobishers. Joseph Frobisher had returned from his two years' expedition in 1776, "having secured what was in those days counted a competent fortune," and was one of the "characters" of the commercial capital of Canada.

The strongest factor in the combination was probably Simon McTavish, of whom a writer has said "that he may be regarded as the founder of the famous North-West Company." McTavish, born in 1750, was a Highlander of enormous energy and decision of character. While by his force of will rousing opposition, yet he had excellent business capacity, and it was he who suggested the cessation of rivalries and strife among themselves and the union of their forces by the Canadian traders.

Accordingly the North-West Company was formed 1783-4, its stock being apportioned into sixteen parts, each stockholder supplying in lieu of money a certain proportion of the commodities necessary for trade, and the Committee dividing their profits when the returns were made from the sale of furs. The united firms of Benjamin and Joseph Frobisher and Simon McTavish administered the whole affair for the traders and received a commission as agents.

The brightest prospect lay before the new formed Company, and they had their first gathering at Grand Portage in the spring of 1784. But union did not satisfy all. A viciously-disposed and self-confident trader, Peter Pond, had not been consulted. Pond was an American, who, as we have seen in 1775, accompanied Henry, Cadot, and Frobisher to the far North-West. Two years later he had gone to Lake Athabasca, and forty miles from the lake on Deer River, had built in 1778 the first fort in the far-distant region, which became known as the Fur Emporium of the North-West. Pond had with much skill prepared a great map of the country for presentation to the Empress Catherine of Russia, and at a later stage gave much information to the American commissioners who settled the boundary line under the Treaty of Paris.

Pond was dissatisfied and refused to enter the new Company. Another trader, Peter Pangman, an American also, had been overlooked in the new Company, and he and Pond now came to Montreal, determined to form a strong opposition to the McTavish and Frobisher combination. In this they were successful.

One of the rising merchants of Montreal at this time was John Gregory, a young Englishman. He was united in partnership with Alexander Norman McLeod, an ardent Highlander, who afterwards rose to great distinction as a magnate of the fur trade. Pangman and Pond appealed to the self-interest of Gregory, McLeod & Company, and so, very shortly after his projected union of all the Canadian interests, McTavish saw arise a rival, not so large as his own Company, but in no way to be despised.

To this rival Company also belonged an energetic, strong-willed Scotchman, who afterwards became the celebrated Sir Alexander Mackenzie, his cousin Roderick McKenzie—a notable character, a trader named Ross, and also young Finlay, a son of the pioneer so well known twenty years before in the fur trading and civil history of

Canada. Pond signalized himself by soon after deserting to the older Company.

The younger Company acted with great vigour. Leaving McLeod behind to manage the business in Montreal, the other members found themselves in the summer at Grand Portage, where they established a post. They then divided up the country and gave it to the partners and traders. Athabasca was given to Ross; Churchill River to Alexander Mackenzie; the Saskatchewan to Pangman; and the Red River country to the veteran trader Pollock.

The North-West Company entered with great energy upon its occupation of the North-West country. We are able to refer to an unpublished memorial presented by them, in 1784, to Governor Haldimand, which shows very well their hopes and expectations. They claim to have explored and improved the route from Grand Portage to Lake Ouinipique, and they ask the governor to grant them the exclusive privilege of using this route for ten years.

They recite the expeditions made by the Montreal traders from their posts in 1765 up to the time of their memorial. They urge the granting of favours to them on the double ground of their having to oppose the "new adventurers," as they call the Hudson's Bay Company, in the north, and they claim to desire to oppose the encroachments of the United States in the south. They state the value of the property of the Company in the North-West, exclusive of houses and stores, to be 25,303*l.* 3*s.* 6*d.*; the other outfits also sent to the country will not fall far short of this sum. The Company will have at Grand Portage in the following July 50,000*l.* (original cost) in fur. They further ask the privilege of constructing a small vessel to be built at Detroit and to be taken up Sault Ste. Mario to ply on Lake Superior, and also that in transporting their supplies on the King's ships from Niagara and Detroit to Michilimackinac, they may have the precedence on account of the shortness of their season and great distance interior to be reached.

They state that they have arranged to have a spot selected at Sault Ste. Marie, whither they may have the fort transferred from

Michilimackinac, which place had been awarded by the Treaty of Paris to the Americans. They desire another vessel placed on the lakes to carry their furs to Detroit. This indicates a great revival of the fur trade and vigorous plans for its prosecution.

A most interesting statement is also made in the memorial: that on account of Grand Portage itself having been by the Treaty of Paris left on the American side of the boundary on Lake Superior, they had taken steps to find a Canadian route by which the trade could be carried on from Lake Superior to the interior. They state that they had sent off on an expedition a canoe, with provisions only, navigated by six Canadians, under the direction of Mr. Edward Umfreville, who had been eleven years in the service of the Hudson's Bay Company, and who along with his colleague, Mr. Verrance, knew the language of the Indians.

We learn from Umfreville's book that "he succeeded in his expedition much to the satisfaction of the merchants," along the route from Lake Nepigon to Winnipeg River. The route discovered proved almost impracticable for trade, but as it was many years before the terms of the treaty were carried into effect, Grand Portage remained for the time the favourite pathway to the interior.

The conflict of the two Montreal companies almost obscured that with the English traders from Hudson Bay. True, in some districts the competition was peaceful and honourable. The nephew of Simon McTavish, William McGillivray, who afterwards rose to great prominence as a trader, was stationed with one of the rival company, Roderick McKenzie, of whom we have spoken, on the English River. In 1786 they had both succeeded so well in trade that, forming their men into two brigades, they returned together, making the woods resound with the lively French songs of the voyageurs.

The attitude of the traders largely depended, however, on the character of the men. To the Athabasca district the impetuous and intractable Pond was sent by the older Company, on his desertion to it. Here there was the powerful influence of the Hudson's Bay Company to contend against, and the old Company from the Bay long maintained its hold on the Northern Indians. To make a flank movement upon the Hudson's Bay Company he sent Cuthbert Grant and a French trader to Slave Lake, on which they established Fort Resolution, while, pushing on still farther, they reached a point afterwards known as Fort Providence.

The third body to be represented in Athabasca Lake was the small North-West Company by their *bourgeois*, John Ross. Ross was a peaceable and fair man, but Pond so stirred up strife that the employés of the two Companies were in a perpetual quarrel. In one of these conflicts Ross was unfortunately killed. This added to the evil reputation of Pond, who in 1781 had been charged with the murder of a peaceful trader named Wadin, in the same Athabasca region.

When Roderick Mckenzie heard at Ile à la Crosse of the murder, he hastened to the meeting of the traders at Grand Portage. This alarming event so affected the traders that the two Companies agreed to unite. The union was effected in 1787, and the business at headquarters in Montreal was now managed by the three houses of McTavish, Frobisher, and Gregory. Alexander Mackenzie was despatched to Athabasca to take the place of the unfortunate trader Ross, and so became acquainted with the region which was to be the scene of his triumphs in discovery.

The union of the North-West fur companies led to extension in some directions. The Assiniboine Valley, in one of the most fertile parts of the country, was more fully occupied. As in the case of the Hudson's Bay Company, the occupation of this valley took place by first coming to Lake Winnipeg and ascending the Swan River (always a fur trader's paradise), until, by a short portage, the Upper Assiniboine was reached.

The oldest fort in this valley belonging to the Nor'-Westers seems to have been built by a trader, Robert Grant, a year or two after 1780. It is declared by trader John McDonnell to have been two short days' march from the junction of the Qu'Appelle and Assiniboine.

Well up the Assiniboine, and not far from the source of the Swan River, stood Fort Alexandria, "surrounded by groves of birch, poplar, and aspen," and said to have been named after Sir Alexander Mackenzie. It was 256 feet in length by 196 feet in breadth; the "houses, stores, &c., being well built, plastered on the inside and outside, and washed over with a white earth, which answers nearly as well as lime for whitewashing."

Connected with this region was the name of a famous trader, Cuthbert Grant, the father of the leader of the half-breeds and Nor'-Westers, of whom we shall speak afterwards. At the mouth of Shell River on the Assiniboine stood a small fort built by Peter Grant in 1794.

When the Nor'-Westers became acquainted with the route down the Assiniboine, they followed it to its mouth, and from that point, where it joined the Red River, descended to Lake Winnipeg and crossed to the Winnipeg River.

In order to do this they established in 1785, as a halting place, Pine Fort, about eighteen miles below the junction of the Souris and Assiniboine Rivers. At the mouth of the Souris River, and near the site of the Brandon House, already described as built by the Hudson's Bay Company, the North-West Company built in 1795 Assiniboine House. This fort became of great importance as the depot for expeditions to the Mandans of the Missouri River.

The union of the Montreal Companies resulted, as had been expected, in a great expansion of the trade. In 1788 the gross amount of the trade did not exceed 40,000*l*., but by the energy of the partners it reached before the end of the century more than three times that amount—a remarkable showing.

The route now being fully established, the trade settled down into regular channels. The agents of the Company in Montreal, Messrs. McTavish & Co., found it necessary to order the goods needed from England eighteen months before they could leave Montreal for the West. Arriving in Canada in the summer, they were then made up in packages for the Indian trade. These weighed about ninety pounds each, and were ready to be borne inland in the following spring.

Then being sent to the West, they were taken to the far points in the ensuing winter, where they were exchanged for furs. The furs reached Montreal in the next autumn, when they were stored to harden, and were not to be sold or paid for before the following season. This was forty-two months after the goods were ordered in Canada. This trade was a very heavy one to conduct, inasmuch as allowing a merchant one year's credit, he had still two years to carry the burden after the value of the goods had been considered as cash.

Toward the end of the century a single year's produce was enormous. One such year was represented by 106,000 beavers, 32,000 marten, 11,800 mink, 17,000 musquash, and, counting all together, not less than 184,000 skins.

The agents necessary to carry on this enormous volume of trade were numerous. Sir Alexander Mackenzie informs us that there were employed in the concern, not including officers or partners, 50 clerks, 71 interpreters and clerks, 1,120 canoe-men, and 35 guides.

The magnitude of the operations of this Company may be seen from the foregoing statements. The capital required by the agents of the concern in Montreal, the number of men employed, the vast quantities of goods sent out in bales made up for the western trade, and the enormous store of furs received in exchange, all combined to make the business of the North-West Company an important factor in Canadian life.

Canada was then in her infancy. Upper Canada was not constituted a province until the date of the formation of the North-West Company. Montreal and Quebec, the only places of any importance, were small towns. The absence of manufactures, agriculture, and means of inter-communication or transport, led to the North-West Company being the chief source of money-making in Canada. As the fur merchants became rich from their profits, they bought seigniories, built mansions, and even in some cases purchased estates in the old land.

Simon McTavish may be looked upon as a type. After a most active life, and when he had accumulated a handsome competence, Simon McTavish owned the Seigniory of Terrobonne, receiving in 1802 a grant of 11,500 acres in the township of Chester. He was engaged at the time of his death, which took place in 1804, in erecting a princely mansion at the foot of the Mountain in Montreal. For half a century the ruins of this building were the dread of children, and were known as McTavish's "Haunted House." The fur-trader's tomb may still be recognized by an obelisk enclosed within stone walls, near "Ravenscrag," the residence of the late Sir Hugh Allan, which occupies the site of the old ruin. *Surely the glory of the lords of the lakes and the forest has passed away.*

CHAPTER XV.

ONE of the chiefs of the fur traders seems to have had a higher ambition than simply to carry back to Grand Portage canoes overflowing with furs. Alexander Mackenzie had the restless spirit that made him a very uncertain partner in the great schemes of McTavish, Frobisher & Co., and led him to seek for glory in the task of exploration. Coming as a young Highlander to Montreal, he had early been so appreciated for his ability as to be sent by Gregory, McLeod & Co. to conduct their enterprise in Detroit. Then we have seen that, refusing to enter the McTavish Company, he had gone to Churchill River for the Gregory Company. The sudden union of all the Montreal Companies (1787) caused, as already noted, by Pond's murder of Ross, led to Alexander Mackenzie being placed in charge in that year of the department of Athabasca.

The longed-for opportunity had now come to Mackenzie. He hoard from the Indians and others of how Samuel Hearne, less than twenty years before, on behalf of their great rivals, the Hudson's Bay Company, had returned by way of Lake Athabasca from his discovery of the Coppermine River. Ho longed to reach the Arctic Sea by another river of which he had heard, and eclipse the discovery of his rival. He even had it in view to seek the Pacific Ocean, of which he was constantly hearing from the Indians, where white men wearing armour were to be met—no doubt meaning the Spaniards.

Mackenzie proceeded in a very deliberate way to prepare for his long journey. Having this expedition in view, he secured the appointment of his cousin, Roderick McKenzie, to his own department. Reaching Lake Athabasca, Roderick McKenzie selected a promontory running out some three miles into the lake, and here built (1788) Fort Chipewyan, it being called from the Indians who chiefly frequented the district. It became the most important fort of the north country, being at the converging point of trade on the great watercourses of the north-west.

On June 3rd, 1789, Alexander Mackenzie started on his first exploration. In his own birch-bark canoe was a crew of seven. His crew is worthy of being particularized. It consisted of four French Canadians, with the wives of two of them. These voyageurs were François Barrieau, Charles Ducette, or Cadien, Joseph Landry, or Cadien, Pierre de Lorme. To complete the number was John Steinbruck, a German. The second canoe contained the guide of the expedition, an Indian, called the "English chief," who was a great trader, and had frequented year by year the route to the English, on Hudson Bay. In his canoe were his two wives, and two young Indians. In a third canoe was trader Leroux, who was to accompany the explorer as far north as Slave Lake, and dispose of the goods he took for furs. Leroux was under orders from his chief to build a fort on Slave Lake.

Starting on June 3rd, the party left the lake, finding their way down Slave River, which they already knew. Day after day they journeyed, suffered from myriads of mosquitoes, passed the steep mountain portage, and, undergoing many hardships, reached Slave Lake in nine days.

Skirting the lake, they departed north by an unknown river. This was the object of Mackenzie's search. Floating down the stream, the Horn Mountains were seen, portage after portage was crossed, the mouth of the foaming Great Slave Lake River was passed, the snowy mountains came in view in the distance, and the party, undeterred, pressed forward on their voyage of discovery.

The usual incidents of early travel were experienced. The accidents, though not serious, were numerous; the scenes met with were all new; the natives were surprised at the bearded stranger; the usual deception and fickleness were displayed by the Indians, only to be overcome by the firmness and tact of Mackenzie; and forty days after starting, the expedition looked out upon the floating ice of the Arctic Ocean. Mackenzie, on the morning of July 14th, erected a post on the shore, on which he engraved the latitude of the place (69 deg. 14′ N.), his own name, the number of persons in the party, and the time they remained there.

His object having been thus accomplished, the important matter was to reach Lake Athabasca in the remaining days of the open season. The return journey had the usual experiences, and on August 24th they came upon Leroux on Slave Lake, where that trader had erected Fort Providence. On September 12th the expedition arrived safely at Fort Chipewyan, the time of absence having been 102 days. The story of this journey is given in a graphic and unaffected manner by Mackenzie in his work of 1801, but no mention is made of his own name being attached to the river which he had discovered.

We have stated that Peter Pond had prepared a map of the north country, with the purpose of presenting it to the Empress of Russia. Being a man of great energy, he was not deterred from this undertaking by the fact that he had no knowledge of astronomical instruments and little of the art of map-making. His statements were made on the basis of reports from the Indians, whose custom was always to make the leagues short, that they might boast of the length of their journeys. Computing in this way, he made Lake Athabasca so far from Hudson Bay and the Grand Portage that, taking Captain Cook's observations on the Pacific Coast four years before this, the lake was only, according to his calculations, a hundred or a hundred and fifty miles from the Pacific Ocean.

The effect of Pond's calculations, which became known in the Treaty of Paris, was to stimulate the Hudson's Bay Company to follow up Hearne's discoveries and to explore the country west of Lake Athabasca. They attempted this in 1785, but they sent out a boy of fifteen, named George Charles, who had been one year at a mathematical school, and had never made there more than simple observations. As was to have been expected, the boy proved incompetent. Urged on by the Colonial Office, they again in 1791 organized an expedition to send Astronomer Philip to Turner to make the western journey. Unaccustomed to the Far West, and poorly provided for this journey, Turner found himself at Fort Chipewyan entirely dependent for help and shelter on the Nor'-Westers. He was, however, qualified for his work, and made correct observations, which settled the question of the distance of the Pacific Ocean. Mr. Roderick McKenzie showed him every hospitality. This expedition served at least to show that the Pacific was certainly five times the distance from Lake Athabasca that Pond had estimated.

After coming back from the Arctic Sea, Alexander Mackenzie spent his time in urging forward the business of the fur trade, especially north of Lake Athabasca; but there was burning in his breast the desire to be the discoverer of the Western Sea. The voyage of Turner made him still more desirous of going to the West.

Like Hearne, Alexander Mackenzie had found the want of astronomical knowledge and the lack of suitable instruments a great drawback in determining his whereabouts from day to day. With remarkable energy, he, in the year 1791, journeyed eastward to Canada, crossed the Atlantic Ocean to London, and spent the winter in acquiring the requisite mathematical knowledge and a sufficient acquaintance with instruments to enable him to take observations.

He was now prepared to make his journey to the Pacific Ocean. He states that the courage of his party had been kept up on their reaching the Arctic Sea, by the thought that they were approaching the Mer de l'Ouest, which, it will be remembered, Verandrye had sought with such passionate desire.

In the very year in which Mackenzie returned from Great Britain, his great purpose to reach the Pacific Coast led him to make his preparations in the autumn, and on October 10th, 1792, to leave Fort Chipewyan and proceed as far up Peace River as the farthest settlement, and there winter, to be ready for an early start in the following spring. On his way he overtook Mr. Finlay, the younger, and called upon him in his camp near the fort, where he was to trade for the winter. Leaving Mr. Finlay "under several volleys of musketry." Mackenzie pushed on and reached the spot where the men had been despatched in the preceding spring to square timber for a house and cut palisades to fortify it. Here, where the Boncave joins the main branch of the Peace River, the fort was erected. His own house was not ready for occupation before December 23rd, and the body of the men went on after that date to erect five houses for which the material had been prepared. Troubles were plentiful; such as the quarrelsomeness of the natives, the killing of an Indian, and in the latter part of the winter severe cold. In May, Mackenzie despatched six canoes laden with furs for Fort Chipewyan.

The somewhat cool reception that Mackenzie had received from the other partners at Grand Portage, when on a former occasion he had given an account of his voyage to the Arctic Sea, led him to be doubtful whether his confreres would fully approve the great expedition on which he was determined to go. He was comparatively a young man, and he knew that there were many of the traders jealous of him. Still, his determined character led him to hold to his plan, and his great energy urged him to make a name for himself.

Mackenzie had found much difficulty in securing guides and voyageurs. The trip proposed was so difficult that the bravest shrank from it. The explorer had, however, great confidence in his colleague, Alexander Mackay, who had arrived at the Forks a few weeks before the departure. Mackay was a most experienced and shrewd man. After faithfully serving his Company, he entered, as we shall see, the Astor Fur Company in 1811, and was killed among the first in the fierce attack on the ship *Tonquin*, which was captured by the natives. Mackenzie's crew was the best he could obtain, and their names have become historic. There were besides Mackay, Joseph Landry and Charles Ducette, two voyageurs of the former expedition, Baptiste Bisson, François Courtois, Jacques Beauchamp, and François Beaulieu, the last of whom died so late as 1872, aged nearly one hundred years, probably the oldest man in the North-West at the time. Archbishop Taché gives an interesting account of Beaulieu's baptism at the age of seventy. Two Indians completed the party, one of whom had been so idle a lad, that he bore till his dying day the unenviable name of "Cancre"— the crab.

Having taken, on the day of his departure, the latitude and longitude of his winter post, Mackenzie started on May 9th, 1793, for his notable voyage. Seeing on the banks of the river elk, buffalo, and bear, the expedition pushed ahead, meeting the difficulties of navigation with patience and skill. The murmurs of his men and the desire to turn back made no impression on Mackenzie, who, now that his Highland blood was up, determined to see the journey through. The difficulties of navigation became extreme, and at times the canoes had to be drawn up stream by the branches of trees.

At length in longitude 121° W. Mackenzie reached a lake, which he considered the head of the Ayugal or Peace River. Here the party landed, unloaded the canoes, and by a portage of half-a-mile on a well-beaten path, came upon another small lake. From this lake the explorers followed a small river, and here the guide deserted the party. On June 17th the members of the expedition enjoyed, after all their toil and anxiety, the "inexpressible satisfaction of finding themselves on the bank of a navigable river on the west side of the first great range of mountains."

Running rapids, breaking canoes, re-ascending streams, quieting discontent, building new canoes, disturbing tribes of surprised Indians, and urging on his discouraged band, Mackenzie persistently kept on his way. He was descending on Tacoutche Tesse, afterwards known as the Fraser River. Finding that the distance by this river was too great, he turned back. At the point where he took this step (June 23rd) was afterwards built Alexandria Fort, named after the explorer. Leaving the great river, the party crossed the country to what Mackenzie called the West Road River. For this land journey, begun on July 4th, the explorers were provided with food. After sixteen days of a most toilsome journey, they at length came upon an arm of the sea. The Indians near the coast seemed very troublesome, but the courage of Mackenzie never failed him. It was represented to him that the natives "were as numerous as mosquitoes and of a very malignant character."

His destination having been reached, the commander mixed up some vermilion in melted grease and inscribed in large characters on the south-east face of the rock, on which they passed the night, "Alexander Mackenzie, from Canada, by land the twenty-second of July, one thousand seven hundred and ninety-three."

After a short rest the well-repaid explorers began their homeward journey. To ascend the Pacific slope was a toilsome and discouraging undertaking, but the energy which had enabled them to come through an unknown road easily led them back by a way that had now lost its uncertainty. Mackenzie says that when "we reached the downward current of the Peace River and came in view of Fort McLeod, we threw out our flag and accompanied it with a general discharge of firearms, while the men were in such spirits and made such an active use of their paddles, that we arrived before the two men whom we left in the spring could recover their senses to answer us. Thus we landed at four in the afternoon at the place which we left in the month of May. In another month (August 24th) Fort Chipewyan was reached, where the following winter was spent in trade.

It is hard to estimate all the obstacles overcome and the great service rendered in the two voyages of Alexander Mackenzie. Readers of the "North-West Passage by Land" will remember the pitiable plight in which Lord Milton and Dr. Cheadle, nearly seventy years afterwards, reached the coast. Mackenzie's journey was more difficult, but the advantage lay with the fur-traders in that they were experts in the matters of North-West travel. Time and again, Mackenzie's party became discouraged. When the Pacific slope was reached, and the voyageurs saw the waters begin to run away from the country with which they were acquainted, their fears were aroused, and it was natural that they should be unwilling to proceed further.

Mackenzie had, however, all the instincts of a brave and tactful leader. On one occasion he was compelled to take a stand and declare that if his party deserted him, he would go on alone. This at once aroused their admiration and sympathy, and they offered to follow him. At the point on the great river where he turned back, the Indians were exceedingly hostile. His firmness and perfect self-control showed the same spirit that is found in all great leaders in dealing with savage or semi-civilized races. Men like Frontenac, Mackenzie, and General Gordon seemed to have a charmed life which enabled them to exercise a species of mesmeric influence over half-trained or entirely uncultivated minds.

From the wider standpoint, knowledge was supplied as to the country lying between the two great oceans, and while it did not, as we know from the voyages seeking a North-West Passage in this century, lay the grim spectre of an Arctic channel, yet it was a fulfilment of Verandrye's dream, and to Alexander Mackenzie, a Canadian bourgeois, a self-made man, aided by his Scotch and French associates, had come the happy opportunity of discovering "La Grande Mer de l'Ouest."

Alexander Mackenzie, filled with the sense of the importance of his discovery, determined to give it to the world, and spent the winter at Fort Chipewyan in preparing the material. In this he was much assisted by his cousin, Roderick McKenzie, to whom he sent the journal for revision and improvement. Early in the year 1794, the distinguished explorer left Lake Athabasca, journeyed over to Grand Portage, and a year afterward revisited his native land. He never returned to the "Upper Country," as the Athabasca region was called, but became one of the agents of the fur-traders in Montreal, never coming farther toward the North-west than to be present at the annual gatherings of the traders at Grand Portage. The veteran explorer continued in this position till the time when he crossed the Atlantic and published his well-known "Voyages from Montreal," dedicated to "His Most Sacred

Majesty George the Third." The book, while making no pretensions to literary attainment, is yet a clear, succinct, and valuable account of the fur trade and his own expeditions. It was the work which excited the interest of Lord Selkirk in Rupert's Land and which has become a recognized authority.

In 1801 this work of Alexander Mackenzie was published, and the order of knighthood was conferred upon the successful explorer. On his return to Canada, Sir Alexander engaged in strong opposition to the North-West Company and became a member of the Legislative Assembly for Huntingdon County, in Lower Canada. He lived in Scotland during the last years of his life, and died in the same year as the Earl of Selkirk, 1820. Thus passed away a man of independent mind and of the highest distinction. His name is fixed upon a region that is now coming into greater notice than ever before.

CHAPTER XVI.

A NUMBER of events conspired to make it necessary for the North-West Company to be well acquainted with the location of its forts within the limits of the territory of the United States, in some parts of which it carried on operations of trade, and to understand its relation to the Hudson's Bay Company's territory. The treaty of amity and commerce, which is usually connected with the name of John Jay, 1794, seemed to say that all British forts in United States territory were to be evacuated in two years. This threw the partners at Grand Portage into a state of excitement, inasmuch as they knew that the very place of their gathering was on the American side of the boundary line.

DAVID THOMPSON, ASTRONOMER AND SURVEYOR.

At this juncture the fitting instrument appeared at Grand Portage. This was David Thompson. This gentleman was a Londoner, educated at the Blue Coat School, in London. Trained thoroughly in mathematics and the use of astronomical instruments, he had obtained a position in the Hudson's Bay Company. In the summer of 1795, with three companions, two of them Indians, he had found his way from Hudson Bay to Lake Athabasca, and thus showed his capability as an explorer. Returning from his Western expedition, he reported to Mr. Joseph Colon, the officer in charge at York Fort, by whose orders he had gone to Athabasca, and expressed himself as willing to undertake further explorations for the Company. The answer was curt—to the effect that no more surveys could then be undertaken by the Company, however desirable. Thompson immediately decided to seek employment elsewhere in the work for which he was so well qualified. Leaving the Bay and the Company behind, attended only by two Indians, he journeyed inland and presented himself at the summer meeting of the North-West fur-traders at Grand Portage. Without hesitation they appointed him astronomer and surveyor of the North-West Company.

Astronomer Thompson's work was well mapped out for him.

(1) He was instructed to survey the forty-ninth parallel of latitude. This involved a question which had greatly perplexed the diplomatists, viz. the position of the source of the Mississippi. Many years after this date it was a question to decide which tributary is the source of the Mississippi, and to this day there is a difference of opinion on the subject, i.e. which of the lakes from which different branches spring is the true source of the river. The fact that the sources were a factor in the settling of the boundary line of this time made it necessary to have expert testimony on the question such as could be furnished by a survey by Thompson.

(2) The surveyor was to go to the Missouri and visit the ancient villages of the natives who dwelt there and who practised agriculture.

(3) In the interests of science and history, to inquire for the fossils of large animals, and to search for any monuments that might throw a light on the ancient state of the regions traversed.

(4) It was his special duty to determine the exact position of the posts of the North-West Company visited by him, and all agents and employés were instructed to render him every assistance in his work.

Astronomer Thompson only waited the departure of one of the Great Northern brigades to enter upon the duties of his new office. These departures were the events of the year, having in the eyes of the fur-traders something of the nature of a caravan for Mecca about them. Often a brigade consisted of eight canoes laden with goods and well-manned. The brigade which Thompson accompanied was made up of four canoes under trader McGillis, and was ready to start on August

9th, 1796. He had taken the observation for Grand Portage and found it to be 48 deg. (nearly) N. latitude and 89 deg. 3′ 4″ (nearly) W. longitude.

He was now ready with his instruments—a sextant of ten inches radius, with quicksilver and parallel glasses, an excellent achromatic telescope, one of the smaller kind, drawing instruments, and a thermometer, and all of these of the best make. The portage was wearily trudged, and in a few days, after a dozen shorter portages, the height of land was reached in 48 deg. N. latitude, and here begins the flow of water to Hudson Bay. It was accordingly the claim of the Hudson's Bay Company that their territory extended from this point to the Bay. At the outlet of Rainy Lake still stood a trading post, where Verandrye had founded his fort, and the position of this was determined, 48 deg. 1′ 2″ N. latitude. In this locality was also a post of the Hudson's Bay Company.

No post seems at this time to have been in use on Rainy River or Lake of the Woods by any of the trading companies, though it will be seen that the X Y Company was at this date beginning its operations. At the mouth of the Winnipeg River, however, there were two establishments, the one known as Lake Winnipeg House, or Bas de la Rivière, an important distributing point, now found to be in 50 deg. 1′ 2″ N. latitude. There was also near by it the Hudson's Bay Company post, founded in the previous year.

Thompson, being in company with his brigade, which was going to the west of Lake Manitoba, coasted along Lake Winnipeg, finding it dangerous to cross directly, and after taking this roundabout, in place of the 127 miles in a straight line, reached what is now known as the Little Saskatchewan River on the west side of Lake Winnipeg.

Going by the little Saskatchewan River through its windings and across the meadow portage, he came to Lake Winnipegoosis and, northward along its western coast, reached Swan River, the trappers' paradise. Swan River post was twelve miles up the river from its mouth, and was found to be in 52 deg 24′ N. latitude. Crossing over to the Assiniboine (Stone Indian) River, he visited several posts, the most considerable being Fort Tremblant (Poplar Fort), which some think had its name changed to Fort Alexandria in honour of Sir Alexander Mackenzie.

John McDonnell, North-West trader of this period, says:—"Fort Tremblant and the temporary posts established above it furnished most of the beaver and otter in the Red River returns, but the trade has been almost ruined since the Hudson's Bay Company entered the Assiniboine River by the way of Swan River, carrying their merchandise from one river to the other on horseback—three days' journey—who by that means, and the short distance between Swan River and their factory at York Fort, from whence they are equipped, can arrive at the *coude de l'homme* (a river bend or angle) in the Assiniboine River, a month sooner than we can return from Grand Portage, secure the fall trade, give credits to the Indians, and send them to hunt before our arrival; so that we see but few in that quarter upon our arrival."

The chief trader of this locality was Cuthbert Grant, who, as before mentioned, was a man of great influence in the fur trade.

The astronomer next went to the Fort between the Swan and Assiniboine Rivers, near the spot whore the famous Fort Pelly of the present day is situated. Taking horses, a rapid land journey was made to Belleau's Fort, lying in 53 deg. N. latitude (nearly).

The whole district is a succession of beaver meadows, and had at this time several Hudson's Bay Company posts, as already mentioned. Thompson decided to winter in this beaver country, and when the following summer had fairly sot in with good roads and blossoming prairies, he came, after journeying more than 200 miles southward, to the Qu'Appelle River post, which was at that time under a trader named Thorburn. Thompson was now fairly on the Assiniboine River, and saw it everywhere run through an agreeable country with a good soil and adapted to agriculture.

Arrived at Assiniboine House, he found it in charge of John McDonnell, brother of the well-known Miles McDonnell, who, a few years later, became Lord Selkirk's first governor on Red River.

Ensconcing himself in the comfortable quarters at Assiniboine House, Thompson wrote up in ink his journals, maps, astronomical observations, and sketches which he had taken in crayon, thus giving them more permanent form. He had now been in the employ of the North-West Company a full year, and in that time had been fully gratified by the work he had done and by the cordial reception given him in all the forts to which he had gone.

Assiniboine House, or, as he called it, Stone Indian House, was found to be a congenial spot. It was on the north side of the Assiniboine River, not far from where the Souris River empties its waters into the larger stream, though the site has been disputed.

One of the astronomer's clearly defined directions was to visit the Mandan villages on the Missouri River. He was now at the point when this could be accomplished, although the time chosen by him, just as winter was coming on, was most unsuitable. His journey reminds us of that made by Verandrye to the Mandans in 1738.

The journey was carefully prepared for. With the characteristic shrewdness of the North-West Company, it was so planned as to require little expenditure. Thompson was to be accompanied chiefly by free-traders, i.e. by men to whom certain quantities of goods would be advanced by the Company. By the profits of this trade expenses would be met. The guide and interpreter was René Jussaume (a man of very doubtful character), who had fallen into the ways of the Western Indians. He had lived for years among the Mandans, and spoke their language. Another free-trader, Hugh McCracken, an Irishman, also knew the Mandan country, while several French Canadians, with Brossman, the astronomer's servant man, made up the company. Each of the traders took a credit from Mr. McDonnell of from forty to fifty skins in goods. Ammunition, tobacco, and trinkets, to pay expenses, were provided, and Thompson was supplied with two horses, and his chief trader, Jussaume, with one. The men had their own dogs to the number of thirty, and these drew goods on small sleds. Crossing the Assiniboine, the party started south-westward, and continued their journey for thirty-three days, with the thermometer almost always below zero and reaching at times 36 deg. below. The journey was a most dangerous and trying one and covered 280 miles. Thompson found that some Hudson's Bay traders had already made flying visits to the Mandans. On his return, Thompson's itinerary was, from the Missouri till he reached the angle of the Souris River, seventy miles, where he found abundant wood and shelter, and then to the south end of Turtle Mountain, fourteen miles. Leaving Turtle Mountain, his next station was twenty-four miles distant at a point on the Souris where an outpost of Assiniboine House, known as Ash House, had been established. Another journey of forty-five miles brought the expedition back to the hospitable shelter of Mr. McDonnell at Stone Indian House. Thompson now calculated the position of this comfortable fort and found it to be 49 deg. 41' (nearly) N. latitude and 101 deg. 1' 4" (nearly) W. longitude.

The astronomer, after spending a few weeks in making up his notes and surveys, determined to go eastward and undertake the survey of the Red River. On February 26th, 1798, he started with three French Canadians and an Indian guide. Six dogs drew three sleds laden with baggage and provisions. The company soon reached the sand hills, then called the Manitou Hills, from some supposed supernatural agency in their neighbourhood. Sometimes on the ice, and at other times on the north shore of the Assiniboine to avoid the bends of the river, the party went, experiencing much difficulty from the depth of the snow. At length, after journeying ten days over the distance of 169 miles, the junction of the Assiniboine and Red River, at the point where now stands the city of Winnipeg, was reached. There was no trading post here at the time. It seems somewhat surprising that what became the chief trading centre of the company, Fort Garry, during the first half of this century should, up to the end of the former century, not have been taken possession of by any of the three competing fur companies.

Losing no time, Thompson began, on March 7th, the survey, and going southward over an unbroken trail, with the snow three feet deep, reached in seven days Pembina Post, then under the charge of a leading

French trader of the company, named Charles Chaboillez. Wearied with a journey of some sixty-four miles, which had, from the bad road, taken seven days, Thompson enjoyed the kind shelter of Pembina House for six days. This house was near the forty-ninth parallel and was one of the especial points he had been appointed to determine. He found Pembina House to be in latitude 48 deg. 58' 24" N., so that it was by a very short distance on the south side of the boundary line. Thompson marked the boundary, so that the trading post might be removed, when necessary, to the north side of the line. A few years later, the observation taken by Thompson was confirmed by Major Long on his expedition of 1823, but the final settlement of where the line falls was not made till the time of the boundary commission of 1872.

Pushing southward in March, the astronomer ascended Red River to the trading post known as Upper Red River, near where the town of Grand Forks, North Dakota, stands to-day. Here he found J. Baptiste Cadot, probably the son of the veteran master of Sault Ste. Marie, who so long clung to the flag of the Golden Lilies.

Thompson now determined to survey what had been an object of much interest, the lake which was the source of the great River Mississippi. To do this had been laid upon him in his instructions from the North-West Company. Making a detour from Grand Forks, in order to avoid the ice on the Red Lake River, he struck the upper waters of that river, and followed the banks until he reached Red Lake in what is now North-Eastern Minnesota. Leaving this lake, he made a portage of six miles to Turtle Lake, and four days later reached the point considered by him to be the source of the Mississippi. Turtle Lake, at the time of the treaty of 1783, was supposed to be further north than the north-west angle of the Lake of the Woods. This arose, Thompson tells us, from the voyageurs counting a pipe to a league, at the end of which time it was the fur-traders' custom to take a rest. Each pipe, that is, the length of time taken to smoke a pipe, however, was nearer two miles than three, so that the head waters of the Mississippi had been counted 128 miles further north than Thompson found them to be. It is to be noted, however, that the Astronomer Thompson was wrong in making Turtle Lake the source of the Mississippi. The accredited source of the Mississippi was discovered, as we shall afterwards see, in July, 1832, to be Lake Itasca, which lies about half a degree southwest of Turtle Lake. Thompson next visited Red Cedar Lake, in the direction of Lake Superior. Here he found a North-West trading house, Upper Red Cedar House, under the command of a partner, John Sayer, whose half-blood son afterward figured in Red River history. He found that Sayer and his men passed the winter on wild rice and maple sugar as their only food.

Crossing over to Sand Lake River, Mr. Thompson found a small post of the North-West Company, and, descending this stream, came to Sand Lake. By portage, reaching a small stream, a tributary of St. Louis River, he soon arrived at that river itself, with its rapids and dalles, and at length reached the North-West trading post near the mouth of the river, where it joined the Fond du Lac.

Having come to Lake Superior, the party could only obtain a dilapidated northern canoe, but with care it brought them, after making an enormous circuit and accomplishing feats involving great daring and supreme hardship, along the north shore of the lake to Grand Portage. On hearing his report of two years' work, the partners, at the annual meeting at Grand Portage, found they had made no mistake in their appointment, and gave him the highest praise.

The time had now come, after the union of the North-West Company and the X Y Company, for pushing ahead the great work in their hands and examining the vast country across the Rocky Mountains. The United Company in 1805 naturally took up what had been planned several years before, and sent David Thompson up the Saskatchewan to explore the Columbia River and examine the vast "sea of mountains" bordering on the Pacific Ocean. The other partner chosen was Simon Fraser, and his orders were to go up the Peace River, cross the Rockies, and explore the region from its northern side. We shall see how well

Fraser did his part, and meanwhile we may follow Thompson in his journey.

In 1806, we find that he crossed the Rockies and built in the following year a trading-house for the North-West Company on the Lower Columbia. Thompson called his trading post Kootenay House, and indeed his persistent use of the term "Kootenay" rather than "Columbia," which he well knew was the name of the river, is somewhat remarkable. Coming over the pass during the summer he returned to Kootenay House and wintered there in 1807-1808. During the summer of 1808, he visited possibly Grand Portage, certainly Fort Vermilion. Fort Vermilion, a short distance above the present Fort Pitt, was well down the north branch of the Saskatchewan River, and on his way to it, Thompson would pass Fort Augustus, a short distance below where Edmonton now stands, as well as Fort George.

He left Fort Vermilion in September, and by October 21st, the Saskatchewan being frozen over, he laid up canoes for the winter, and taking horses, crossed the Rocky Mountains, took to canoes on the Columbia River again, and on November 10th arrived at his fort of Kootenay House, where he wintered. On this journey, Thompson discovered Howse's Pass, which is about 52 deg. N. latitude.

In 1809, Thompson determined on extending his explorations southward on the Columbia River. A short distance south of the international boundary line, he built a post in September of that year. He seems to have spent the winter of this year in trying new routes, some of which he found impracticable, and can hardly be said to have wintered at any particular spot. In his pilgrimage, he went up the Kootenay River, which he called McGillivray's River, in honour of the famous partner, but the name has not been retained. Hastening to his post of Kootenay House, he rested a day, and travelling by means of canoes and horses, in great speed came eastward and reached Fort Augustus, eight days out from Kootenay, June 22nd, 1810. From this point he went eastward, at least as far as Rainy Lake, leaving his "little family" with his sister-in-law, a Cree woman, at Winnipeg River House.

Returning, he started on October 10th, 1810, for Athabasca. He discovered the Athabasca Pass on the "divide," and on July 3rd, 1811, started to descend the Columbia, and did so, the first white man, as far as Lewis River, from which point Lewis and Clark in 1805, having come over the Rocky Mountains, had preceded him to the sea. Near the junction of the Spokane River with the Columbia, he erected a pole and tied to it a half-sheet of paper, claiming the country north of the forks as British territory. This notice was seen by a number of the Astor employés, for Ross states that he observed it in August, with a British flag flying upon it. Thompson's name among the Indians of the coast was "Koo-Koo-Suit."

Ross Cox states that "in the month of July, 1811, Mr. David Thompson, Astronomer to the North-West Company, of which he was also a proprietor, arrived with nine men in a canoe at Astoria from the interior. This gentleman came on a voyage of discovery to the Columbia, preparatory to the North-West Company forming a settlement at the mouth of the river. He remained at Astoria until the latter end of July, when he took his departure for the interior."

Thompson was thus disappointed on finding the American company installed at the mouth of the Columbia before him, but he re-ascended the river and founded two forts on its banks at advantageous points.

Thompson left the western country with his Indian wife and children soon after this, and in Eastern Canada, in 1812-13, prepared a grand map of the country, which adorned for a number of years the banqueting-room of the bourgeois at Fort William and is now in the Government buildings at Toronto.

In 1814 he definitely left the upper country, and was employed by the Imperial Government in surveying a part of the boundary line of the United States and Canada. He also surveyed the water-courses between the Ottawa River and Georgian Bay. He lived for years at the River Raisin, near Williamstown, in Upper Canada, and was very poor. At the great age of eighty-seven, he died at Longueil. He was not appreciated as he deserved. His energy, scientific knowledge, experience, and successful work for the Company for sixteen years make him one of the most notable men of the period.

SIMON FRASER, FUR-TRADER AND EXPLORER.

As we have seen, the entrance by the northern access to the Pacific slope was confided to Simon Fraser, and we may well, after considering the exploits of David Thompson, refer to those of his colleague in the service.

Simon Fraser, one of the most daring of the fur-traders, was the son of a Scottish U. E. Loyalist, who was captured by the Americans at Burgoyne's surrender and who died in prison. The widowed mother took her infant boy to Canada, and lived near Cornwall. After going to school, the boy, who was of the Roman Catholic faith, entered the North-West Company at the age of sixteen as a clerk, and early became a bourgeois of the Company. His administrative ability led to his being appointed agent at Grand Portage in 1797. A few years afterwards, Fraser was sent to the Athabasca region, which was at that time the point aimed at by the ambitious and determined young Nor'-Westers. By way of Peace River, he undertook to make his journey to the west side of the Rocky Mountains. Leaving the bulk of his command at the Rocky Mountain portage, he pushed on with six men, and reaching the height of land, crossed to the lake, which he called McLeod's in honour of his prominent partner, Archibald Norman McLeod. Stationing three men at this point, Fraser returned to his command and wintered there.

In the spring of 1806 he passed through the mountains, and came upon a river, which he called Stuart River. John Stuart, who was at that time a clerk, was for thirty years afterwards identified with the fur trade. Stuart Lake, in British Columbia, was also called after him. On the Stuart River, Fraser built a post, which, in honour of his fatherland, he called New Caledonia, and this probably led to this great region on the west of the mountains being called New Caledonia. Stuart was left in charge of this post, and Fraser went west to a lake, which since that time has been called Fraser Lake. He returned to winter at the new fort.

Fraser's disposition to explore and his success thus far led the Company to urge their confrère to push on and descend the great River Tacoucho Tesse, down which Alexander Mackenzie had gone for some distance, and which was supposed to be the Columbia. It was this expedition which created Fraser's frame. The orders to advance had been brought to him in two canoes by two traders, Jules Maurice Quesnel and (Hugh) Faries.

Leaving behind Faries with two men in the new fort, Fraser, at the mouth of the Nechaco or Stuart River, where afterward stood Fort George, gathered his expedition, and was ready to depart on his great, we may well call it terrific, voyage, down the river which since that time has borne his name. His company consisted of Stuart, Quesnel, nineteen voyageurs, and two Indians, in four canoes. It is worthy of note that John Stuart, who was Fraser's lieutenant, was in many ways the real leader of the expedition. Having been educated in engineering, Stuart, by his scientific knowledge, was indispensable to the exploring party.

On May 22nd a start was made from the forks. We have in Masson's first volume preserved to us Simon Fraser's Journal of this remarkable voyage, starting from the Rockies down the river. The keynote to the whole expedition is given us in the seventh line of the journal. "Having proceeded about eighteen miles, we came to a strong rapid which we ran down, nearly wrecking one of our canoes against a precipice which forms the right bank of the river." A succession of rapids, overhung by enormous heights of perpendicular rocks, made it almost as difficult to portage as it would have been to risk the passage of the canoes and their loads down the boiling cauldron of the river.

Nothing can equal the interest of hearing in the explorer's own words an incident or two of the journey. On the first Wednesday of Juno he writes: "Leaving Mr. Stuart and two men at the lower end of the rapid in order to watch the motions of the natives, I returned with the other four men to the camp. Immediately on my arrival I ordered the five men out of the crews into a canoe lightly loaded, and the canoe was in a moment under way. After passing the first cascade she lost her course and was drawn into the eddy, whirled about for a considerable time, seemingly in suspense whether to sink or swim, the men having no power over her. However, she took a favourable turn, and by degrees was led from this dangerous vortex again into the stream. In this manner she continued, flying from one danger to another, until the last cascade but one, where in spite of every effort the whirlpools forced her against a low projecting rock. Upon this the men debarked, saved their own lives, and continued to save the property, but the greatest difficulty was still ahead, and to continue by water would be the way to certain destruction.

"During this distressing scene, we were on the shore looking on and anxiously concerned; seeing our poor fellows once more safe afforded us as much satisfaction as to themselves, and we hastened to their assistance; but their situation rendered our approach perilous and difficult. The bank was exceedingly high and steep, and we had to plunge our daggers at intervals into the ground to check our speed, as otherwise we were exposed to slide into the river. We cut steps in the declivity, fastened a line to the front of the canoe, with which some of the men ascended in order to haul it up, while the others supported it upon their arms. In this manner our situation was most precarious; our lives hung, as it were, upon a thread, as the failure of the line, or a false step of one of the men, might have hurled the whole of us into eternity. However, we fortunately cleared the bank before dark."

Every day brought its dangers, and the progress was very slow. Finding the navigation impossible, on the 26th Fraser says: "As for the road by land, we could scarcely make our way with even only our guns. I have been for a long period among the Rocky Mountains, but have never seen anything like this country. It is so wild that I cannot find words to describe our situation at times. We had to pass where no human being should venture; yet in those places there is a regular footpath impressed, or rather indented upon the very rocks by frequent travelling. Besides this, steps which are formed like a ladder by poles hanging to one another, crossed at certain distances with twigs, the whole suspended from the top, furnish a safe and convenient passage to the natives down these precipices; but we, who had not had the advantage of their education and experience, were often in imminent danger, when obliged to follow their example."

On the right, as the party proceeded along the river, a considerable stream emptied in, to which they gave the name Shaw's River, from one of the principal wintering partners.

Some distance down, a great river poured in from the left, making notable forks. Thinking that likely the other expedition by way of the Saskatchewan might be on the upper waters of that river at the very time, they called it Thompson River, after the worthy astronomer, and it has retained the name ever since.

But it would be a mistake to think that the difficulties were passed when the forks of the Thompson River were left behind. Travellers on the Canadian-Pacific Railway of to-day will remember the great gorge of the Fraser, and how the railway going at dizzy heights, and on strong overhanging ledges of rock, still fills the heart with fear.

On July 2nd the party reached an arm of the sea and saw the tide ebbing and flowing, showing them they were near the ocean. They, however, found the Indians at this part very troublesome. Fraser was compelled to follow the native custom, "and pretended to be in a violent passion, spoke loud, with vehement gestures, exactly in their own way, and thus peace and tranquillity were instantly restored."

The explorer was, however, greatly disappointed that he had been prevented by the turbulence of the natives from going down the arm of the sea and looking out upon the Pacific Ocean. He wished to take observations on the sea-coast. However, he got the latitude, and knowing that the Columbia is 45 deg. 20′ N., he was able to declare that the river he had followed was not the Columbia. How difficult it is to distinguish small from great actions! Here was a man making fame for all time, and the idea of the greatness of his work had not dawned upon him.

A short delay, and the party turned northward on July 4th, and with many hardships made their way up the river. On their ascent few things of note happened, the only notable event being the recognition of the fame of the second bourgeois, Jules Quesnel, by giving his name to a river flowing into the Fraser River from the east. The name is still retained, and is also given to the lake which marks the enlargement of the river. On August 6th, the party rejoined Faries and his men in the fort on Stuart Lake. The descent occupied forty-two days, and, as explorers have often found in such rivers as the Fraser, the ascent took less time than the descent. In this case, their upward journey was but of thirty-three days.

Fraser returned to the east in the next year and is found in 1811 in charge of the Red River district, two years afterward in command on the Mackenzie River, and at Fort William on Lake Superior, in 1816, when the Fort was taken by Lord Selkirk. After retiring, he lived at St. Andrews on the Ottawa and died at the advanced age of eighty-six, having been known as one of the most noted and energetic fur-traders in the history of the companies. Thus we have seen the way in which these two kings of adventure—Fraser and Thompson—a few years after Sir Alexander Mackenzie, succeeded amid extraordinary hardships in crossing to the Western Sea. The record of the five transcontinental expeditions of these early times is as follows:—

(1) Alexander Mackenzie, by the Tacouche Tesse and Bellacoola River, 1793.

(2) Lewis and Clark, the American explorers, by the Columbia River, 1805.

(3) Simon Fraser by the river that bears his name, formerly the Tacouche Tesse, 1808.

(4) David Thompson, by the Columbia River, 1811.

(5) The overland party of Astorians, by the Columbia, 1811. These expeditions shed a flood of glory on the Anglo-Saxon name and fame.

CHAPTER XVII.

FOR some years the Montreal fur companies, in their combinations and readjustments, had all the variety of the kaleidoscope. Agreements were made for a term of years, and when these had expired new leagues were formed, and in every case dissatisfied members went into opposition and kept up the heat and competition without which it is probable the fur trade would have lost, to those engaged in it, many of its charms.

In 1795 several partners had retired from the North-West Company and thrown in their lot with the famous firm that we have seen was always inclined to follow its own course—Messrs. Forsyth, Richardson and Co. For a number of years this independent Montreal firm had maintained a trade in the districts about Lake Superior. The cause of this disruption in the Company was the unpopularity, among the wintering partners especially, of the strong-willed and domineering chief in Montreal—Simon McTavish. One set of bourgeois spoke of him derisively as "Le Premier," while others with mock deference called him "Le Marquis." Sir Alexander Mackenzie had been himself a partner, had resided in the Far West, and he was regarded by all the traders in the "upper country" as their friend and advocate. Although the discontent was very great when the secession took place, yet the mere bonds of self-interest kept many within the old Company, Alexander Mackenzie most unwillingly consented to remain in the old Company, but only for three years, reserving to himself the right to retire at the end of that time.

Notwithstanding their disappointment, and possibly buoyed up with the hope of having the assistance of their former friend at a later period, the members of the X Y Company girt themselves about for the new enterprise in the next year, so that the usual date of this Company is from the year 1795. Whether it was the circumstance of its origination in dislike of "Le Premier," or whether the partners felt the need of greater activity on account of their being weaker, it must be confessed that a new era now came to the fur trade, and the opposition was carried on with a warmth much greater than had ever been known among the old companies. A casual observer can hardly help feeling that while not a member of the new Company at this date, Alexander Mackenzie was probably its active promoter behind the scenes.

The new opposition developed without delay. Striking at all the salient points, the new Company in 1797 erected its trading house at Grand Portage, somewhat more than half-a-mile from the North-West trading house and on the other side of the small stream that there falls into the Bay. A few years after, when the North-West Company moved to Kaministiquia, the X Y also erected a building within a mile of the new fort. The new Company was at some time in its history known as the New North-West Company, but was more commonly called the X Y Company. The origin of this name is accounted for as follows. On the bales which were made up for transport, it was the custom to mark the North-West Company's initials N. W. When the new Company, which was an offshoot of the old, wished to mark their bales, they simply employed the next letters of the alphabet, X Y. They are accordingly not contractions, and should not be written as such. It was the habit of members of the older Company to express their contempt for the secessionists by calling them the "Little Company" or "the Little Society." In the Athabasca country the rebellious traders were called by their opponents "Potties," probably a corruption of "Les Petits," meaning members of "La Petite Compagnie." When these names were used by the French Canadian voyageurs, the X Y Company was referred to.

However disrespectfully they may have been addressed, the traders of the new Company caused great anxiety both to the North-West

Company and to the Hudson's Bay Company, though they regarded themselves chiefly as rivals of the former. Pushing out into the country nearest their base of supplies on Lake Superior, they took hold of the Red River and Assiniboine region, as well as of the Red Lake country immediately south of and connected with it. The point where the Souris empties into the Assiniboine was occupied in the same year (1798) by the X Y Company. It had been a favourite resort for all classes of fur-traders, there having been no less than five opposing trading houses at this point four years before. No doubt the presence of the free-trading element such as McCracken and Jussaume, whom we find in the Souris region thus early, made it easier for smaller concerns to carry on a kind of business in which the great North-West Company would not care to be engaged.

Meanwhile dissension prevailed in the North-West Company. The smouldering feeling of dislike between "Le Marquis" and Alexander Mackenzie and the other fur-trading magnates broke out into a flame. As ex-Governor Masson says: "These three years were an uninterrupted succession of troubles, differences, and misunderstandings between these two opposing leaders." At the great gathering at the Grand Portage in 1799, Alexander Mackenzie warned the partners that he was about to quit the Company, and though the winterers begged him not to carry out his threat, yet he remained inexorable. The discussion reported to Mr. McTavish was very displeasing to him, and in the following year his usual letter to the gathering written from Montreal was curt and showed much feeling, he saying, "I feel hurt at the distrust and want of confidence that appeared throughout all your deliberations last season."

Alexander Mackenzie, immediately after the scene at Grand Portage, crossed over to England, published his "Voyages," and received his title. He then returned in 1801 to Canada. Flushed with the thought of his successes, he threw himself with great energy into the affairs of the opposing Company, the X Y, or, as it was also now called, that of "Sir Alexander Mackenzie and Company." If the competition had been warm before, it now rose to fever heat. The brigandage had scarcely any limit; combats of clerk with clerk, trapper with trapper, voyageur with voyageur, were common. Strong drink became, as never before or since, a chief instrument of the rival companies in dealing with the Indians.

A North-West Company trader, writing from Pembina, says: "Indians daily coming in by small parties; nearly 100 men here. I gave them fifteen kegs of mixed liquor, and the X Y gave in proportion; all drinking; I quarrelled with Little Shell, and dragged him out of the fort by the hair. Indians very troublesome, threatening to level my fort to the ground, and their chief making mischief. I had two narrow escapes from being stabbed by him; once in the hall and soon afterwards in the shop."

Such were the troubles of competition between the Companies. The new Company made a determined effort to compete also in the far-distant Peace River district. In October of this year two prominent partners of the new Company arrived with their following at the Peace River. One of these, Pierre de Rocheblave, was of a distinguished family, being the nephew of a French officer who had fought on the *Monongahela* against Braddock. The other was James Leith, who also became a prominent fur-trader in later days.

Illustrating the keenness of the trade conflict, John McDonald, of Garth, also says in 1798, writing from the Upper Saskatchewan, "We had here (Fort Augustus), besides the Hudson's Bay Company, whose fort was within a musket shot of ours, the opposition on the other side of the new concern I have already mentioned, which had assumed a powerful shape under the name of the X Y Company, at the head of which was the late John Ogilvy in Montreal, and at this establishment Mr. King, an old south trader in his prime and pride as the first among bullies."

Sir Alexander Mackenzie did wonders in the management of his Company, but the old lion at Montreal, from his mountain chateau, showed a remarkable determination, and provided as he was with great wealth, he resolved to overcome at any price the opposition which he also contemptuously called the "Little Company." In 1802, he, with the skill of a great general, reconstructed his Company. He formed a combination which was to continue for twenty years. Into this he succeeded in introducing a certain amount of new blood; those clerks who had shown ability were promoted to the position of bourgeois or partners. By this progressive and statesmanlike policy, notwithstanding the energy of the X Y Company, the old Company showed all the vigour and enthusiasm of youth.

An employé of the North-West Company, Livingston, had a few years before established a post on Slave Lake. Animated with the new spirit of his superiors, he went further north still and made a discovery of silver, but on undertaking to open trade communications with the Eskimos, the trader unfortunately lost his life.

Other expeditions were sent to the Missouri and to the sources of the South Saskatchewan; it is even said that in this direction a post was established among the fierce tribes of the Bow River, west of the present town of Calgary.

Looking out for other avenues for the wonderful store of energy in the North-West Company, the partners took into consideration the development of the vast fisheries of the St. Lawrence and the interior. Simon McTavish rented the old posts of the King—meaning by these Tadoussac, Chicoutimi, Assuapmousoin, and Mistassini, reached by way of the Saguenay; and Ile Jérémie, Godbout, Mingan, Masquaro, and several others along the north shore of the Lower St. Lawrence or the Gulf. The annual rent paid for the King's posts was 1000*l*.

But the greatest flight of the old fur king's ambition was to carry his operations into the forbidden country of the Hudson Bay itself. In furtherance of this policy, in 1803 the North-West Company sent a schooner of 150 tons to the shores of Hudson Bay to trade, and along with this an expedition was sent by land by way of St. John and Mistassini to co-operate in establishing stations on the Bay. By this movement two posts were founded, one at Charlton Island and the other at the mouth of the Moose River. Many of the partners were not in favour of these expeditions planned by the strong-headed old dictator, and the venture proved a financial loss. Simon McTavish, though comparatively a young man, now thought of retiring, and purchased the seignory of Terrebonne, proposing there to lead a life of luxury and ease, but a stronger enemy than either the X Y or Hudson's Bay Company came to break up his plans. Death summoned him away in July, 1804.

The death of Simon McTavish removed all obstacles to union between the old and new North-West Companies, and propositions were soon made to Sir Alexander Mackenzie, and his friends, which resulted in a union of the two Companies. We are fortunate in having preserved to us the agreement by which the two Companies—old and new North-West Companies—were united. The partners of the old Company were given three-quarters of the stock and those of the new one-quarter. The provisions of the agreement are numerous, but chiefly deal with necessary administration. One important clause is to the effect that no business other than the fur trade, or what is necessarily depending thereon, shall be followed by the Company. No partner of the new concern is to be allowed to have any private interests at the posts outside those of the Company. By one clause the new North-West Company is protected from any expense that might arise from Simon McTavish's immense venture on the Hudson Bay. It may be interesting to give the names of the partners of the two Companies, those who were not present, from being mostly in the interior and whose names were signed by those having powers of attorney from them, being marked Att.

NEW NORTH-WEST OR X Y COMPANY.

Alex. Mackenzie.	Thomas Forsyth, Att.
Thomas Forsyth, Att.	Late Leith, Jameson & Co.
John Richardson.	(by Trustees).
John Inglis, Att.	John Ogilvie.
James Forsyth, Att.	P. de Rocheblanc, Att.
John Mure, Att.	Alex. McKenzie, Att. (2).
John Forsyth;	John Macdonald, Att.
Alex. Elhce, Att.	James Leith, Att.
John Haldane, Att.	John Wills. Att.

OLD NORTH-WEST COMPANY.

John Finlay, Att.
Duncan Cameron, Att.
James Hughes, Att.
Alex. McKay, Att.
Hugh McGillis, Att.
Alex. Henry, Jr., Att.
John McGillivray, Att.
James McKenzie, Att.
Simon Fraser, Att.
John D. Campbell, Att.
D.Thompson, Att.
John Thompson, Att.
John Gregory.
Wm. McGillivray.
Duncan McGillivray, Att.

Wm. Hallowell.
Rod. McKenzie.
Angus Shaw, Att.
Dl. McKenzie, Att.
Wm. McKay, Att.
John McDonald, Att.
Donald McTavish, Att.
John McDonnell, Att.
Arch. N. McLeod, Att.
Alex. McDougall, Att.
Chas. Chaboillez, Alt.
John Sayer, Att.
Peter Grant, Att.
Alex. Fraser, Att.
Æneas Cameron, Att.

Anyone acquainted in the slightest degree with the early history of Canada will see in these lists the names of legislative councillors, members of Assembly, leaders in society, as well as of those who, in the twenty years following the signing of this agreement, by deeds of daring, exploration, and discovery, made the name of the North-West Company illustrious. These names represent likewise those who carried on that wearisome and disastrous conflict with the Hudson's Bay Company which in time Mould have ruined both Companies but for the happy union which took place, when the resources of each wore well-nigh exhausted.

CHAPTER XVIII.

THE union of the opposing companies from Montreal led to a great development of trade, and, as we have already seen, to important schemes of exploration.

Roderick McKenzie, the cousin of Sir Alexander, in coming down from Rainy Lake to Grand Portage, heard of a new route to Kaministiquia. We have already seen that Umfreville had found out a circuitous passage from Nepigon to Winnipeg River, but this had been considered impracticable by the fur-traders.

Accordingly, when the treaty of amity and commerce made it certain that Grand Portage had to be given up, it was regarded as a great matter when the route to Kaministiquia became known. This was discovered by Mr. Roderick McKenzie quite by accident. When coming, in 1797, to Canada on leave of absence, this trader was told by an Indian family near Rainy Lake that a little farther north there was a good route for large canoes, which was formerly used by the whites in their trading expeditions. Taking an Indian with him, McKenzie followed this course, which brought him out at the mouth of the Kaministiquia. This proved to be the old French route, for all along it traces were found of their former establishments. Strange that a route at one time so well known should be completely forgotten in forty years.

In the year 1800 the North-West Company built a fort, called the New Fort, at the mouth of the Kaministiquia, and, abandoning Grand Portage, moved their headquarters to this point in 1803. In the year after the union of the North-West and X Y Companies the name Fort

William was given to this establishment, in honour of the Hon. William McGillivray, who had become the person of greatest distinction in the united North-West Company.

As giving us a glimpse of the life of "the lords of the lakes and forests," which was led at Fort William, we have a good sketch written by a trader, Gabriel Franchère, who was a French Canadian of respectable family and began life in a business place in Montreal. At this stage, says a local writer, "the fur trade was at its apogee," and Franchère was engaged by the Astor Company and went to Astoria. Returning over the mountains, he passed Fort William. His book, written in French, has been translated into English, and is creditable to the writer, who died as late as 1856 in St. Paul, Minnesota.

Franchère says of Fort William, rather inaccurately, that it was built in 1805. This lively writer was much impressed by the trade carried on at this point, and gives the following vivid description:—

"Fort William has really the appearance of a fort from the palisade fifteen feet high, and also that of a pretty village from the number of buildings it encloses. In the middle of a spacious square stands a large building, elegantly built, though of wood, the middle door of which is raised five feet above the ground plot, and in the front of which runs a long gallery. In the centre of this building is a room about sixty feet long and thirty wide, decorated with several paintings, and some portraits in crayon of a number of the partners of the Company. It is in this room that the agents, the clerks, and the interpreters take their meals at different tables. At each extremity of the room are two small apartments for the partners."

"The back part of the house is occupied by the kitchen and sleeping apartments of the domestics. On each side of this building there is another of the same size, but lower; these are divided lengthwise by a corridor, and contain each twelve pretty sleeping-rooms. One of these houses is intended for the partners, the other for the clerks.

"On the east side of the Fort there is another house intended for the same purpose, and a large building in which furs are examined and where they are put up in tight bales by means of a press. Behind, and still on the same side, are found the lodges of the guides, another building for furs, and a powder magazine. This last building is of grey stone, and roofed in with tin. In the corner stands a kind of bastion or point of observation.

"On the west side is seen a range of buildings, some of which serve for stores and others for shops. There is one for dressing out the employés; one for fitting out canoes; one in which merchandise is retailed; another where strong drink, bread, lard, butter, and cheese are sold, and where refreshments are given out to arriving voyageurs. This refreshment consists of a white loaf, a half pound of butter, and a quart of rum. The voyageurs give to this liquor store the name 'Cantine Salope,'

"Behind is found still another row of buildings, one of which is used as an office or counting-house, a pretty square building well lighted; another serves as a store; and a third as a prison. The voyageurs give to the last the name 'Pot au beurre.' At the south-east corner is a stone shed roofed with tin. Farther back are the workshops of the carpenters, tinsmiths, blacksmiths, and their spacious courts or sheds for sheltering the canoes, repairing them, and constructing new ones.

"Near the gate of the Fort, which is to the south, are the dwelling-houses of the surgeon and resident clerk. Over the entrance gate a kind of guard-house has been built. As the river is deep enough at its entrance, the Company has had quays built along the Fort as a landing-place for the schooners kept on Lake Superior for transporting peltries, merchandise, and provisions from Fort William to Sault Ste. Marie, and *vice versa*.

"There are also on the other side of the river a number of houses, all inhabited by old French-Canadian voyageurs, worn out in the service of the North-West Company, without having become richer by it. Fort William is the principal factory of the North-West Company in the interior and a general rendezvous of the partners. The agents of Montreal and the proprietors wintering in the north nearly all assemble here every summer and receive the returns, form expeditions, and discuss the interests of their commerce.

"The employés wintering in the north spend also a portion of the summer at Fort William. They form a great encampment to the west, outside the palisades. Those who are only engaged at Montreal to go to Fort William or to Rainy Lake, and who do not winter in the North, occupy another space on the east side. The former give to the latter the name 'mangeurs de lard.' A remarkable difference is observed between the two camps, which are composed of three or four hundred men each. That of the 'mangeurs de lard' is always very dirty and that of the winterers neat and clean."

But the fur-traders were by no means merely business men. Perhaps never were there assemblages of men who feasted more heartily when the work was done. The Christmas week was a holiday, and sometimes the jollity went to a considerable excess, which was entirely to be expected when the hard life of the voyage was taken into consideration. Whether at Fort William, or in the North-West Company's house in St. Gabriel Street, Montreal, or in later day at Lachine, the festive gatherings of the Nor'-Westers were characterized by extravagance and often by hilarious mirth. The luxuries of the East and West were gathered for these occasions, and offerings to Bacchus were neither of poor quality nor limited in extent. With Scotch story and Jacobite song, intermingled with "La Claire Fontaine" or "Malbrouck s'en va," those lively songs of French Canada, the hours of evening and night passed merrily away.

At times when they had been feasting long into the morning, the traders and clerks would sit down upon the feast-room floor, when one would take the tongs, another the shovel, another the poker, and so on. They would arrange themselves in regular order, as in a boat, and, vigorously rowing, sing a song of the voyage; and loud and long till the early streaks of the east were seen would the rout continue. When the merriment reached such a height as this, ceremony was relaxed, and voyageurs, servants, and attendants were admitted to witness the wild carouse of the wine-heated partners.

We are fortunate in having the daily life of the fur-traders from the Lower St. Lawrence to the very shores of the Pacific Ocean pictured for us by the partners in the "Journals" they have left behind them. Just as the daily records of the monks and others, dreary and uninteresting as many of them at times are, commemorated the events of their time in the "Saxon Chronicle" and gave the material for history, so the journals of the bourgeois, often left unpublished for a generation or two, and the works of some of those who had influence and literary ability enough to issue their stories in the form of books, supply us with the material for reproducing their times. From such sources we intend to give a few sketches of the life of that time.

We desire to express the greatest appreciation of the work of ex-Governor Masson, who is related to the McKenzie and Chaboillez families of that period, and who has published no less than fourteen journals, sketches of the time; of the painstaking writing of an American officer, Dr. Coues, who has with great care and success edited the journals of Alexander Henry, Jr., and such remains as he could obtain of David Thompson, thus supplementing the publication by Charles Lindsey, of Toronto, of an account of Thompson. We acknowledge also the patient collection of material by Tassé in his "Canadiens de L'Ouest," as well as the interesting journals of Harmon and others, which have done us good service.

VALUABLE REMINISCENCES.

The name of McKenzie (Hon. Roderick McKenzie) was one to conjure by among the fur-traders. From the fact that there were so many well-known partners and clerks of this name arose the custom, very common in the Highland communities, of giving nicknames to distinguish them. Four of the McKenzies were "Le Rouge," "Le Blanc," "Le Borgne" (one-eyed), and "Le Picoté" (pock-marked). Sir Alexander was the most notable, and after him his cousin, the Hon. Roderick, of whom we write.

This distinguished man came out as a Highland laddie from Scotland in 1784. He at once entered the service of the fur company, and made his first journey to the North-West in the next year. His voyage from Ste. Anne, on Montreal Island, up the fur-traders' route, was taken in Gregory McLeod & Co.'s service. At Grand Portage McKenzie was initiated into the mysteries of the partners. Pushed into the North-West, he soon became prominent, and built the most notable post of the upper country, Fort Chipewyan.

On his marriage he became allied to a number of the magnates of the fur company. His wife belonged to the popular family of Chaboillez, two other daughters of which were married, one to the well-known Surveyor-General of Lower Canada, Joseph Bouchette, and another to Simon McTavish, "Le Marquis."

Roderick McKenzie was a man of some literary ability and taste. He purposed at one time writing a history of the Indians of the North-West and also of the North-West Company. In order to do this, he sent circulars to leading traders, and thus receiving a number of journals, laid the foundation of the literary store from which ex-Governor Masson prepared his book on the bourgeois.

Between him and his cousin, Sir Alexander Mackenzie, an extensive correspondence was kept up. Extracts from the letters of the distinguished partner form the burden of the "Reminiscences" published by Masson. Many of the facts have been referred to in our sketch of Sir Alexander Mackenzie's voyages.

For eight long years Roderick McKenzie remained in the Indian country, and came to Canada in 1797. Some two years afterward Sir Alexander Mackenzie left the old Company and headed the X Y Company. At that time Roderick McKenzie was chosen in the place of his cousin in the North-West Company, and this for several years caused a coolness between them.

His "Reminiscences" extend to 1829, at which time he was living in Terrebonne, in Lower Canada. He became a member of the Legislative Council in Lower Canada, and he has a number of distinguished descendants. Roderick McKenzie closes his interesting "Reminiscences" with an elaborate and valuable list of the proprietors, clerks, interpreters, &c., of the North-West Company in 1799, giving their distribution in the departments, and the salary paid each. It gives us a picture of the magnitude of the operations of the North-West Company.

TALES OF THE NORTH-WEST.

Few of the Nor'-Westers aimed at collecting and preserving the folk-lore of the natives. At the request of Roderick McKenzie, George Keith, a bourgeois who spent a great part of his life very far North, viz. in the regions of Athabasca, Mackenzie River, and Great Bear Lake, sent a series of letters extending from 1807 onward for ten years embodying tales, descriptions, and the history of the Indian tribes of his district. His first description is that of the Beaver Indians, of whom he gives a vocabulary. He writes for us a number of tales of the Beaver Indians, viz. "The Indian Hercules," "Two Lost Women." "The Flood, a Tale of the Mackenzie River," and "The Man in the Moon." One letter gives a good account of the social manners and customs of the Beaver Indians, and another a somewhat complete description of the Rocky Mountains and Mackenzie River country. Descriptions of the Filthy Lake and Grand River Indians and the Long Arrowed Indians, with a few more letters with reference to the fur trade, make up the interesting collection. George Keith may be said to have wielded the "pen of a ready writer." We give his story of

THE MAN IN THE MOON.

A Tale, or Tradition, of the Beaver Indians.

"In the primitive ages of the world, there was a man and his wife who had no children. The former was very singular in his manner of living. Being an excellent hunter, he lived entirely upon the blood of the animals he killed. This circumstance displeased his wife, who secretly determined to play him a trick. Accordingly one day the husband went out hunting, and left orders with his wife to boil some blood in a kettle, so as to be ready for supper on his return. When the time of his expected return was drawing nigh, his wife pierced a vein with an awl in her left arm and drew a copious quantity of blood, which she mixed with a greater quantity of the blood of a moose deer, that he should not discover it, and prepared the whole for her husband's supper.

"Upon his return the blood was served up to him on a bark dish; but, upon putting a spoonful to his mouth, he detected the malice of his wife, and only saying that the blood did not smell good, threw the kettle with the contents about her ears.

"Night coming on, the man went to bed and told his wife to observe the moon about midnight. After the first nap, the woman, awaking, was surprised to find that her husband was absent. She arose and made a fire, and, lifting up her eyes to the moon, was astonished to see her husband, with his dog and kettle, in the body of the moon, from which he has never descended. She bitterly lamented her misfortunes during the rest of her days, always attributing them to her malicious invention of preparing her own blood for her husband's supper."

INTERESTING AUTOBIOGRAPHY.

Among all the Nor'-Westers there was no one who had more of the Scottish pride of family than John McDonald, of Garth, claiming as he did to be descended from the lord of the isles. His father obtained him a commission in the British army, but he could not pass the examination on account of a blemish caused by an accident to his arm. The sobriquet, "Bras Croche" clung to him all his life as a fur trader.

Commended to Simon McTavish, the young man became his favourite, and in 1791 started for the fur country. He was placed under the experienced trader, Angus Shaw, and passed his first winter in the far-off Beaver River, north of the Saskatchewan. Next winter he visited the Grand Portage, and he tells us that for a couple of weeks he was feasting on the best of everything and the best of fish. Returning to the Saskatchewan, he took part in the building of Fort George on that river, whence, after wintering, the usual summer journey was made to Grand Portage. Here, he tells us, they "met the gentlemen from Montreal in goodfellowship." This life continued till 1795.

He shows us the state of feeling between the Companies. "It may not be out of the way to mention that on New Year's Day, during the customary firing of musketry, one of our opponent's bullies purposely fired his powder through my window. I, of course, got enraged, and challenged him to single combat with our guns; this was a check upon him ever after."

Remaining in the same district, by the year 1800 he had, backed as he was by powerful influence, his sister being married to Hon. William MacGillivray, become a partner in the Company. Two years afterward he speaks of old Cuthbert Grant coming to the district, but in the spring, this officer being sick, McDonald fitted up a comfortable boat with an awning, in which Grant went to the Kaministiquia, where he died.

In 1802, McDonald returned from Fort William and determined to build another fort farther up the river to meet a new tribe, the Kootenays. This was "Rocky Mountain House." Visiting Scotland in the year after, he returned to be dispatched in 1804 to English River, where he was in competition with a Hudson's Bay Company trader. In the next year he went back to the Saskatchewan, saying that, although a very dangerous department, he preferred it. Going up the south branch of the Saskatchewan, he erected the "New Chesterfield House" at the mouth of the Red Deer River, and there met again a detachment of Hudson's Bay Company people.

In 1806 he, being unwell, spent the year chiefly in Montreal, after which he was appointed to the less exacting field of Red River. One interesting note is given us as to the Red River forts. He says, "I established a fort at the junction of the Red and Assiniboine Rivers and called it 'Gibraltar,' though there was not a rock or a stone within three miles." As we shall see afterwards, the building of this fort, which was on the site of the city of Winnipeg, had taken place in the year preceding.

With his customary energy in erecting forts, he built one a distance up the Qu'Appelle River, probably Fort Esperance. While down at Fort

William in the spring, the news came to him that David Thompson was surrounded in the Rocky Mountains by Blackfoot war parties. McDonald volunteered to go to the rescue, and with thirty chosen men, after many dangers and hardships, reached Thompson in the land of the Kootenays.

McDonald was one of the traders selected to go to Britain and thence by the ship *Isaac Todd* to the mouth of the Columbia to meet the Astor Fur Company. He started in company with Hon. Edward Ellice. At Rio Janeiro McDonald shipped from the *Isaac Todd* on board the frigate *Phœbe*. On the west coast of South America they called at "Juan Fernandez, Robinson Crusoe's Island." They reached the Columbia on November 30th, 1813, and in company with trader McDougall took over Astoria in King George's name, McDonald becoming senior partner at Astoria.

In April, 1814, McDonald left for home across the mountains, by way of the Saskatchewan, and in due time arrived at Fort William. He came to Sault Ste. Marie to find the fort built by the Americans, and reached Montreal amid some dangers. The last adventure mentioned in his journal was that of meeting in Terrebonne Lord Selkirk's party who were going to the North-West to oppose the Nor'-Westers.

The veteran spent his last days in the County of Glengarry, Ontario, and died in 1860, between eighty-nine and ninety years of age. His career had been a most romantic one, and he was noted for his high spirit and courage, as well as for his ceaseless energy as a trader.

James McKenzie, brother of Hon. Roderick McKenzie, was a graphic, though somewhat irritable writer with a good style. He has left us "A Journal from the Athabasca Country," a description of the King's posts on the Lower St. Lawrence, with a journal of a jaunt through the King's posts. This fur trader joined the North-West Company.

In 1799 he was at Fort Chipewyan. His descriptions are minute accounts of his doings at his fort. He seems to have taken much interest in his men, and he gives a pathetic account of one of these trappers called "Little Labrie." Labrie had been for six days without food, and was almost frozen to death. He says: "Little Labrie's feet are still soaking in cold water, but retain their hardness. We watched him all last night; he fainted often in the course of the night, but we always brought him to life again by the help of mulled wine. Once in particular, when he found himself very weak and sick, and thought he was dying he said, 'Adieu; je m'en vais; tout mon bien a ceux qui ont soin de moi.' 10th, about twelve o'clock, Labrie was freed from all his agonies in this world." McKenzie evidently had a kind heart.

The candid writer gives us a picture of New Year's Day, January 1st, 1890. "This morning before daybreak, the men, according to custom, fired two broadsides in honour of the New Year, and then came in to be rewarded with rum, as usual. Some of them could hardly stand alone before they went away; such was the effect of the juice of the grape on their brains. After dinner, at which everyone helped themselves so plentifully that nothing remained to the dogs, they had a bowl of punch. The expenses of this day, with fourteen men and women, are: 61½ fathoms Spencer twist (tobacco), 7 flagons rum, 1 ditto wine, 1 ham, a skin's worth of dried meat, about 40 white fish, flour, sugar, &c."

McKenzie had many altercations in his trade, and seems to have been of a violent temper. He found fault with one of the X Y people, named Perroue, saying it was a shame for him to call those who came from Scotland "vachers" (cowboys). He said he did not call all, but a few of them "vachers." "I desired him to name one in the North, and told him that the one who served him as a clerk was a 'vacher,' and had the heart of a 'vacher' since he remained with him."

McKenzie has frequent accounts of drunken brawls, from which it is easy to be seen that this period of the opposition of the two Montreal Companies was one of the most dissolute in the history of the fur traders. The fur trader's violent temper often broke out against employés and Indians alike. He had an ungovernable dislike to the Indians, regarding them simply as the off-scourings of all things, and for the voyageurs and workmen of his own Company the denunciations are so strong that his violent language was regarded as "sound and fury, signifying nothing."

CHAPTER XIX.

A GOOD TRADER AND A GOOD BOOK.

To those interested in the period we are describing there is not a more attractive character than Daniel Williams Harmon, a native of Vermont, who entered the North-West Company's service in the year 1800, at the age of 22. After a number of years spent in the far West, he brought with him on a visit to New England the journal of his adventures, and this was edited and published by a Puritan minister, Daniel Haskel, of Andover, Massachusetts. Harmon and the book are both somewhat striking, though possibly neither would draw forth universal admiration. The youngest of his daughters was well known as a prominent citizen of Ottawa, and had a marked reverence for the memory of her father.

Leaving Lachine in the service of McTavish, Frobisher & Co., the young fur trader followed the usual route up the Ottawa and reached in due course Grand Portage, which he called "the general rendezvous for the fur traders." He thus describes the fort: "It is twenty-four rods by thirty, is built on the margin of the Bay, at the foot of a hill or mountain of considerable height. Within the fort there is a considerable number of dwelling-houses, shops, and stores; the houses are surrounded by palisades, which are about eighteen inches in diameter. The other fort, which stands about 200 rods from this, belongs to the X Y Company. It is only three years since they made an establishment here, and as yet they have had but little success." Harmon was appointed to follow John

McDonald, of Garth, to the Upper Saskatchewan. On the way out, however, Harmon was ordered to the Swan River district. Here he remained for four years, taking a lively interest in all the parts of a trader's life. He was much on the Assiniboine, and passed the sites of Brandon, Portage la Prairie, and Winnipeg of to-day.

In October, 1805, Harmon, having gone to the Saskatchewan, took as what was called his "country wife" a French Canadian half-breed girl, aged fourteen. He states that it was the custom of the country for the trader to take a wife from the natives, live with her in the country, and then, on leaving the country, place her and her children under the care of an honest man and give a certain amount for her support. As a matter of fact, Harmon, years after, on leaving the country, took his native spouse with him, and on Lake Champlain some of his younger children were born. There were fourteen children born to him, and his North-West wife was to her last days a handsome woman, "as straight as an arrow."

During Harmon's time Athabasca had not only the X Y Company, but also a number of forts of the Hudson's Bay Company. Cumberland House was the next place of residence of the fur trader, and at this point the Hudson's Bay Company house was in charge of Peter Fidler. Harmon's journal continues with most interesting details of the fur trade, which have the charm of liveliness and novelty. Allusions are constantly made to the leading traders, McDonald, Fraser, Thompson, Quesnel, Stuart, and others known to us in our researches. In the course of time (1810) Harmon found his way over the Rocky Mountain portage and pursued the fur trade in McLeod Lake Fort and Stuart's Lake in New Caledonia, and here we find a fort called, after him, Harmon's Fort. His description of the Indians is always graphic, giving many striking customs of the aborigines. About the end of 1813 Harmon's journal is taken up with serious religious reflections. He had been troubled with doubts as to the reality of Christianity. But after reading the Scriptures and such books as he could obtain, he tells us that a new view of things was his, and that his future life became more consistent and useful. He records us a series of the resolutions which he adopted, and they certainly indicate a high ideal on his part.

In 1816 he had really become habituated to the upper country. He gives us a glimpse of his family:—

"I now pass a short time every day, very pleasantly, in teaching my little daughter Polly to read and spell words in the English language, in which she makes good progress, though she knows not the meaning of one of them. In conversing with my children I use entirely the Cree Indian language; with their mother I more frequently employ the French. Her native tongue, however, is more familiar to her, which is the reason why our children have been taught to speak that in preference to the French language." In his journal, which at times fully shows his introspections, he gives an account of the struggle in his own mind about leaving his wife in the country, as was the custom of too many of the clerks and partners. He had instructed her in the principles of Christianity, and by these principles he was bound to her for life. After eight and a half years spent on the west side of the Rocky Mountains, Harmon arrived at Fort William, 1819, having made a journey of three thousand miles from his far-away post in New Caledonia. Montreal was soon after reached, and the journal comes to a close.

A BUSY BOURGEOIS.

We have seen the energy and ability displayed by John McDonald, of Garth, known as "Le Bras Croch." Another trader, John McDonald, is described by Ross Cox, who spent his life largely in the Rocky Mountain region. He was known as McDonald Grand. "He was 6 ft. 4 in. in height, with broad shoulders, large bushy whiskers, and red hair, which he allowed to grow for years without the use of scissors, and which sometimes, falling over his face and shoulders, gave to his countenance a wild and uncouth appearance." He had a most uncontrollable temper, and in his rage would indulge in a wild medley of Gaelic, English, French, and Indian oaths.

But a third John McDonnell was found among the fur traders. He was a brother of Miles McDonnell, Lord Selkirk's first governor of the Red River Settlement. John McDonnell was a rigid Roman Catholic, and was known as "Le Pretre" ("The Priest"), from the fact that on the voyage through the fur country he always insisted on observing the Church fasts along with his French Canadian employés. McDonnell, on leaving the service of the North-West Company, retired to Point Fortune, on the Ottawa, and there engaged in trade.

We have his journal for the years 1793-5, and it is an excellent example of what a typical fur trader's journal would be. It is minute, accurate, and very interesting. During this period he spent his time chiefly in trading up and down the Assiniboine and Red Rivers. A few extracts will show the interesting nature of his journal entries:—

Fort Esperance, Oct. 18th, 1793.—Neil McKay set out to build and winter at the Forks of the river (junction of the Qu'Appelle and Assiniboine), alongside of Mr. Peter Grant, who has made his pitch about seven leagues from here. Mr. N. McKay's effects were carried in two boats, managed by five men each. Mr. C. Grant set out for his quarters of River Tremblant, about thirty leagues from here. The dogs made a woeful howling at all the departures.

Oct. 19th.—Seventeen warriors came from the banks of the Missouri for tobacco. They slept ten nights on their way, and are emissaries from a party of Assiniboines who went to war upon the Sioux.

Oct. 20th.—The warriors traded a few skins brought upon their backs and went off ill pleased with their reception. After dark, the dogs kept up a constant barking, which induced a belief that some of the warriors were lurking about the fort for an opportunity to steal. I took a sword and pistol and went to sleep in the store. Nothing took place.

Oct. 31st.—Two of Mr. N. McKay's men came from the forts, supposing this to be All Saints' Day. Raised a flag-staff poplar, fifty feet above the ground.

Nov. 23i.—The men were in chase of a white buffalo all day, but could not get within shot of him. Faignant killed two buffalo cows. A mild day.

Nov. 30*th.*—St. Andrew's Day. Hoisted the flag in honour of the titulary saint of Scotland. A beautiful day. Expected Messrs. Peter Grant and Neil McKay to dinner. They sent excuse by Bonneau.

Dec. 2*nd.*—Sent Mr. Peter Grant a Town and Country magazine of 1790. Poitras' wife made me nine pairs of shoes (mocassins).

Jan. 1*st*, 1794.—Mr. Grant gave the men two gallons of rum and three fathoms of tobacco, by the way of New Year's gift. (It is interesting to follow McDonnell on one of his journeys down the Assiniboine.)May 1st.—Sent off the canoes early in the morning. Mr. Grant and I set out about seven. Slept at the Forks of River Qu'Appelle.

May 4*th.*—Killed four buffalo cows and two calves and camped below the Fort of Mountain à La Bosse (near Virden), about two leagues.

May 5*th.*—Arrived at Ange's River La Souris Fort (below Brandon).

May 17*th.*—Passed Fort Des Trembles and Portage La Prairie.

May 20*th.*—Arrived at the Forks Red River (present city of Winnipeg) about noon.

May 24*th.*—Arrived at the Lake (Winnipeg) at 10 a.m.

May 27*th.*—Arrived at the Sieur's Fort (Fort Alexander at the mouth of Winnipeg River).

McDonnell also gives in his journal a number of particulars about the Cree and Assiniboine Indians, describing their religion, marriages, dress, dances, and mourning. The reader is struck with the difference in the recital by different traders of the lives lived by them. The literary faculty is much more developed in some cases than in others, and John McDonnell was evidently an observing and quick-witted man. He belonged to a U. E. Loyalist Scottish family that took a good position in the affairs of early Canada.

That the first trader of the North-West whom we have described, Alexander Henry, should have been followed in the North-West fur trade by his nephew, Alexander Henry, Jr., is in itself a thing of interest; but that the younger Henry should have left us a most voluminous and entertaining journal is a much greater matter.

The copy of this journal is in the Parliamentary Library at Ottawa, and forms two large bound folio volumes of 1,642 pages. It is not the original, but is a well-approved copy made in 1824 by George Coventry, of Montreal. For many years this manuscript has been in the Parliamentary Library, and extracts have been made and printed. Recently an American writer, Dr. Coues, who has done good service in editing the notable work of Lewis and Clark, and also that of Zebulon S. Pike, has published a digest of Henry's journal and added to it very extensive notes of great value. The greatest praise is due to this author for the skill with which he has edited the journal, and all students of the period are indebted to one so well fitted to accomplish the task.

The journal opens, in 1799, with Henry on the waters of a tributary of Lake Manitoba, he having arrived from Grand Portage by the usual fur traders' route. In this place he built a trading house and spent his first winter. In the following year the trader is found on the Red River very near the forty-ninth parallel of north latitude, and is engaged in establishing a post at the mouth of the Pembina River, a tributary of Red River. At this post Henry remains until 1808, going hither and thither in trading expeditions, establishing new outposts, counter-working the rival traders of the X Y Company, and paying his visits from time to time to Grand Portage.

Henry's entries are made with singular clearness and realistic force. He recites with the utmost frankness the details of drunken debauchery among the Indians, the plots of one company to outdo the other in trading with the Indians, and the tricks of trade so common at this period in the fur trade.

A few examples of his graphic descriptions may be given. "At ten o'clock I came to the point of wood in which the fort was built, and just as I entered the gate at a gallop, to take the road that led to the gate, a gun was fired about ten yards from me, apparently by a person who lay in the long grass. My horse was startled and jumped on one side, snorting and prancing; but I kept my seat, calling out, 'Who is there?' No answer was returned. I instantly took my gun from my belt, and cocked her to fire, forgetting she was not loaded and I had no ammunition. I could still see the person running in the grass, and was disappointed in not having a shot at him. I again called out, 'Who is there?' 'C'est moi, bourgeois.' It proved to be one of my men, Charbonneau. I was vexed with him for causing me such consternation."

RED RIVER.

"*February* 28*th*, 1801.—Wolves and crows are very numerous, feeding on the buffalo carcasses that lie in every direction. I shot two buffalo cows, a calf, and two bulls, and got home after dark. I was choking with thirst, having chased the buffalo on snow-shoes in the heat of the day, when the snow so adheres that one is scarcely able to raise the feet. A draught of water was the sweetest beverage I ever tasted. An Indian brought in a calf of this year, which he found dead. It was well grown, and must have perished last night in the snow. This was thought extraordinary; they say it denotes an early spring.

"*March* 5*th*.—The buffalo have for some time been wandering in every direction. My men have raised and put their traps in order for the spring hunt, as the raccoons begin to come out of their winter quarters in the daytime, though they retire to the hollow trees at night. On the 8th it rained for four hours; fresh meat thawed. On the 9th we saw the first spring bird. Bald eagles we have seen the whole winter, but now they are numerous, feeding on the buffalo carcasses."

During the Red River period Henry made a notable journey in 1806 across the plains to the Mandans on the Missouri. Two years afterward he bids farewell to Red River and the Assiniboine, and goes to carry on trade in the Saskatchewan. While on the Saskatchewan, which was for three years, he was in charge of important forts, viz. Fort Vermilion, Terre Blanche, and the Rocky Mountain House. His energy and acquaintance with the prairie were well shown in his exploration of this great region, and the long journeys willingly undertaken by him. His account of the western prairies, especially of the Assiniboines, is complete and trustworthy. In fact, he rejoices in supplying us with the details of their lives and manners which we might well be spared.

A gap of two years from 1811 is found in Henry's journal, but it is resumed in 1813, the year in which he crosses the Rocky Mountains and is found in the party sent by the North-West Company to check the encroachments on the Columbia of the Astor Fur Company. His account of the voyage on the Pacific is regarded as valuable, and Dr. Coues says somewhat quaintly: "His work is so important a concordance that if Franchère, Cox, and Ross be regarded as the synoptical writers of Astoria, then Henry furnishes the fourth Gospel."

After the surrender of Astoria to the North-West Company and its occupation by the British, some of the Nor'-Westers returned. John McDonald, of Garth, as we have seen, crossed the mountains. In his journal occurs a significant entry: "Mr. la Rogue brings the melancholy intelligence that Messrs. D. McTavish, Alexander Henry, and five sailors were drowned on May 22nd last, in going out in a boat from Fort George to the vessel called the Isaac Todd." Ross Cox gives a circumstantial account of this sad accident, though, strange to say, he does not mention the name of Henry, while giving that of D. McTavish.

It is somewhat startling to us to find that Henry continued his journal up to the very day before his death, his last sentence being, "The weather cleared up."

A TRADER LOST FOR FORTY DAYS.

Lying before the writer is the copy of a letter of John Pritchard, of the X Y Company, written in 1805, giving an account of a forty days' adventure of a most thrilling kind. Pritchard was in charge of the X Y Fort at the mouth of the Souris River on the Assiniboine. He had on June 10th gone with one of the clerks up the River Assiniboine, intending to reach Qu'Appelle Fort, a distance of 120 miles. All went well till Montagne à la Bosse was reached, where there was a trading house. Going westward, the two traders were separated in looking for the horses. Pritchard lit fires for two days, but could attract no attention. Then he realized that he was lost. Misled by the belts of timber along the different streams, he went along the Pipestone, thinking he was going towards the Assiniboine. In this he was mistaken. Painfully he crept along the river, his strength having nearly gone. Living on frogs, two hawks, and a few other birds, he says at the end of ten days, "I perceived my body completely wasted. Nothing was left me but my bones, covered with a skin thinner than paper. I was perfectly naked, my clothes having been worn in making shoes, with which I protected my bruised and bleeding feet."

Some days after, Pritchard found a nest of small eggs and lived on them. He says, "How mortifying to mo to see the buffalo quenching their thirst in every lake near to which I slept, and geese and swans in abundance, whilst I was dying of hunger in this land of plenty, for want of wherewith to kill." After trying to make a hook and line to fish, and failing; after being tempted to lie down and give up life, he caught a hen grouse, which greatly strengthened him, as he cooked and ate it. He had now crossed the Souris River, thinking it to be the Assiniboine, and came upon a great plain where the prairie turnip (Psoralea esculenta) grew plentifully. Pushing southward, being sustained by the bulbs of this "pomme blanche," as it is called by the French voyageurs, Pritchard came at length to Whitewater Lake, near Turtle Mountain, and here found two vacant wintering houses of the fur traders. Ho now was able to identify his locality and to estimate that he was sixty miles directly south of his trading post. His feet, pierced by the spear grass (Stipa spartea), were now in a dreadful condition. He found a pair of old shoes in the vacant fort and several pairs of socks.

He determined to move northward to his fort. Soon he was met by a band of Indians, who were alarmed at his worn appearance. The natives took good care of him and carried him, at times unconscious, to his fort, which he reached after an absence of forty days. He says, "Picture to yourself a man whose bones are scraped, not an atom of flesh remaining, then over these bones a loose skin, fine as the bladder of an animal; a beard of forty days' growth, his hair full of filth and scabs. You will then have some idea of what I was." The Hudson's Bay Company officer, McKay, from the neighbouring fort, was exceedingly kind and supplied his every want.

The Cree Indians after this adventure called Pritchard the Manitou or Great Spirit. The Assiniboines called him Cheepe—or the corpse, referring to his wan appearance. For weeks after his return the miserable trader was unable to move about, but in time recovered, and lived to a good old age on the banks of the Red River.

To the last day of his life he referred to his great deliverance, and was thoroughly of the opinion that his preservation was miraculous.

ASSINIBOINE TO MISSOURI.

We are fortunate in having two very good journals of journeys made in the early years of the century from the forts at the junction of the Souris and Assiniboine River to the Missouri River. As was described in the case of David Thompson, this was a long and tedious journey, and yet it was at one time within the plans of the North-West Company to carry their trade thither. Few of the French Canadian gentlemen entered into the North-West Company. One of these, who became noted as an Indian trader, was François Antoine Larocque, brother-in-law of Quesnel, the companion of Simon Fraser. Of the same rank as himself, and associated with Mm, was a trader, Charles McKenzie, who entered the North-West Company as a clerk in 1803.

The expedition to the Mandans under these gentlemen, left Fort Assiniboine on November 11th, 1804, a party in all of seven, and provided with horses, five of which carried merchandise for trade. After the usual incidents of this trying journey, the Missouri was reached.

The notable event of this journey was the meeting with the American expedition of Lewis and Clark, then on its way to cross overland to the Pacific Ocean. Larocque in his journal gives information about this expedition. Leaving Philadelphia in 1803, the expedition, consisting of upward of forty men, had taken till October to reach the Mandans on the Missouri. The purposes of the expedition of Lewis and Clark were:—

(1) To explore the territory towards the Pacific and settle the boundary line between the British and American territories.

(2) To quiet the Indians of the Missouri by conference and the bestowment of gifts.

Larocque was somewhat annoyed by the message given him by Lewis and Clark, that no flags or medals could be given by the North-West Company to the Indians in the Missouri, inasmuch as they were American Indians. Larocque had some amusement at the continual announcement by these leaders that the Indians would be protected so long as they should behave as dutiful children to the great father, the President of the United States. In the spring the party returned, after wintering on the Missouri. In 1805, during the summer, another expedition went to the Missouri; in 1806, Charles McKenzie went in February to the Mandans, and, returning, made a second journey in the same year to the Missouri. The account given by McKenzie of the journeys of 1804-6 is an exceedingly well written one, for this leader was fond of study, and, we are told, delighted especially in the history of his native land, the highlands of Scotland.

Charles McKenzie had married an Indian woman, and became thoroughly identified with the North-West. He was fond of his native children, and stood up for their recognition on the same plane as the white children. After the union of the North-West Company and the Hudson's Bay Company, the English influence largely prevailed. Thinking that his son, who was well educated at the Red River Seminary, was not sufficiently recognized by the Company, McKenzie wrote bitterly, "It appears the present concern has stamped the Cain mark upon all born in this country. Neither education nor abilities serve them. The Honourable Company are unwilling to take natives, even as apprenticed clerks, and the favoured few they do take can never aspire to a higher status, be their education and capacity what they may."

McKenzie continued the fur trade until 1846, when he retired and settled on the Red River. His son, Hector McKenzie, now dead, was well known on the Red River, and accompanied one of the explorations to the far north.

Larocque did not continue long in the fur trade, but went to Montreal and embarked in business, in which he was very unsuccessful. He spent the last years of his life in retirement and close study, and died in the Grey nunnery in a Lower Canadian parish.

CHAPTER XX.

A DASHING FRENCH TRADER—FRANCOIS VICTOR MALHIOT.

A GAY and intelligent French lad, taken with the desire of leading the life of the traders in the "upper country" (*pays d'en haut*), at the age of fifteen deserted school and entered the North-West Company. In 1796, at the age of twenty, he was promoted to a clerkship and sent to a post in the upper part of the Red River country. On account of his inferior education he was never advanced to the charge of a post in the Company's service, but he was always noted for his courage and the great energy displayed by him in action. In 1804 Malhiot was sent to Wisconsin, where he carried on trade.

For the North-West Company there he built a fort and waged a vigorous warfare with the other traders, strong drink being one of the most ready weapons in the contest. In 1801 the trader married after the "country fashion" (*à la façon du pays*), i.e. as we have explained, he had taken an Indian woman to be his wife, with the understanding that when he retired from the fur trade, she should be left provided for as to her living, but be free to marry another.

Malhiot tired of the fur trade in 1807 and returned to Lower Canada, where he lived till his death. Malhiot's Indian wife was afterwards twice married, and one of her sons by the third marriage became a member of the Legislature in Lower Canada. A brother of Malhiot's became a colonel in the British army in India, and another brother was an influential man in his native province.

Few traders had more adventures than this French Canadian. Stationed west of Lake Superior, at Lac du Flambeau, Malhiot found himself surrounded by men of the X Y Company, and he assumed an air of great superiority in his dealings with the Indians. Two of his companions introduced him to the savages as the brother of William McGillivray, the head of the North-West Company. He says, "This thing has produced a very good effect up to the present, for they never name me otherwise than as their 'father.' I am glad to believe that they will respect me more than they otherwise would have done, and will do themselves the honour of trading with me this winter."

Speaking of the rough country through which he was passing, Malhiot says, "Of all the passages and places that I have been able to see during the thirteen years in which I travelled, this is the most frightful and unattractive. The road of the portage is truly that of heaven, for it is strait, full of obstacles, slippery places, thorns, and bogs. The men who pass it loaded, and who are obliged to carry over it bales, certainly deserve the name of 'men.'"This villainous portage is only inhabited by owls, because no other animal could find its living there, and the cries of these solitary birds are enough to frighten an angel and to intimidate a Caesar."

Malhiot maintained his dignified attitude to the Indians and held great conferences with the chiefs, always with an eye to the improvement of trade. To one he says:—

"MY FATHER,—It is with great joy that I smoke in thy pipe of peace and that I receive thy word. Our chief trader at Kaministiquia will accept it, I trust, this spring, with satisfaction, and he will send thee a mark of his friendship, if thou dost continue to do well. So I take courage! Only be as one, and look at the fort of the X Y from a distance if thou dost wish to attain to what thou desirest."

In April, 1805, the trader says, "My people have finished building my fort, and it is the prettiest of any in the Indian country. Long live the North-West Company! Honour to Malhiot!"Malhiot gives a very sad picture of the degeneracy of the trade at this time, produced by the use of strong drink in gaining the friendship of the Indians. A single example may suffice to show the state of affairs.

April 26*th*.—"The son of 'Whetstone,' brother-in-law of Chorette, came here this evening and made me a present of one otter, 15 rats, and 12 lbs. of sugar, for which I gave him 4 pots of rum. He made them drunk at Chorette's with the 'Indians,' the 'Bear,' and 'the Little Branch.' When they were well intoxicated, they cleared the house, very nearly killed Chorette, shot La Lancette, and broke open the store-house. They carried away two otters, for which I gave them more rum this morning, but without knowing they had been stolen. All this destruction occurred because Chorette had promised them more rum, and that he had not any more."

Malhiot's journal closes with the statement that after a long journey from the interior he and his party had camped in view of the island at Grand Portage.

AN IRISHMAN OF DISTINCTION.

In the conflict of the North-West, X Y, and Hudson's Bay Companies, it is interesting to come upon the life and writing of an Irishman, a man of means, who, out of love for the wilds of Lake Superior, settled down upon its shores and became a "free trader," as he was called. This was John Johnston, who came to Montreal, enjoyed the friendship of Sir Guy Carleton, the Governor of Canada, and hearing of the romantic life of the fur traders, plunged into the interior, in 1792 settled at La Pointe, on the south side of Lake Superior, and established himself as an independent trader. A gentleman of birth and education, Johnston seems to have possessed a refined and even religious spirit. Filled with high thoughts inspired by a rocky and romantic island along the shore, he named it "Contemplation Island." Determined to pass his life on the rocky but picturesque shores of Lake Superior, Johnston became friendly with the Indian people. The old story of love and marriage comes in here also. The chief of the region was Wabogish, the "White Fisher," whose power extended as far west as the Mississippi. In the wigwam of Wabogish dwelt his beautiful daughter. Her hand had been sought by many young braves, but she had refused them all. The handsome, sprightly Irishman had, however, gained her affections, and proposed to her father for her. Writing long afterward he describes her as she was when he first saw her, a year after his arrival on the shores of Lake Superior. "Wabogish or the 'White Fisher,' the chief of La Pointe, made his sugar on the skirts of a high mountain, four days' march from the entrance of the river to the south-east. His eldest daughter, a girl of fourteen, exceedingly handsome, with a cousin of hers who was two or three years older, rambling one day up the eastern side of the mountain, came to a perpendicular cliff exactly fronting the rising sun. Near the base of the cliff they found a piece of yellow metal, as they called it, about eighteen inches long, a foot broad, four inches thick and perfectly smooth. It was so heavy that they could raise it only with great difficulty. After examining it for some time, it occurred to the eldest girl that it belonged to the 'Gitche Manitou,' 'The Great Spirit,' upon which they abandoned the place with precipitation.

"As the Chippewas are not idolaters, it occurs to me that some of the southern tribes must have emigrated thus far to the North, and that the piece either of copper or of gold is part of an altar dedicated to the sun. If my conjecture is right, the slab is more probably gold—as the Mexicans have more of that metal than they have of copper."

The advances of Johnston toward chief Wabogish for marriage to his daughter were for a time resisted by the forest magnate. Afraid of the marriages made after the country fashion, he advised Johnston to return to his native country for a time. If, after a sufficient absence, his affection for his daughter should still remain strong, he would consent to their marriage. Johnston returned to Ireland, disposed of his property, and came back to Lake Superior to claim his bride.

Johnston settled at Sault Ste. Marie, where he had a "very considerable establishment with extensive plantations of corn and vegetables, a beautiful garden, a comfortable house, a good library, and carried on an important trade."

During the war of 1814 he co-operated with the British commandant, Colonel McDonald, in taking the island of Michilimackinac from the Americans. While absent, the American expedition landed at Sault Ste. Marie, and set fire to Johnston's house, stables, and other buildings, and these were burnt to the ground, his wife and children viewing the destruction of their home from the neighbouring woods.

Masson says: "A few years afterwards, Mr. Johnston once more visited his native land, accompanied by his wife and his eldest daughter, a young lady of surpassing beauty. Every inducement was offered to them to remain in the old country, the Duke and Duchess of Northumberland having even offered to adopt their daughter. They preferred, however, returning to the shores of Lake Superior, where Miss Johnston was married to Mr. Henry Schoolcraft, the United States Indian agent at Sault Ste. Marie, and the distinguished author of the 'History of the Indian Tribes of the United States.'" Mr. Johnston wrote "An Account of Lake Superior" at the request of Roderick McKenzie. This we have, but it is chiefly a geographical description of the greatest of American lakes. Johnston died at Sault Ste. Mario in 1828."

A DETERMINED TRADER OF LAKE SUPERIOR.

A most daring and impulsive Celt was Duncan Cameron. He and his family were Scottish U. E. Loyalists from the Mohawk River in New York State. As a young man he entered the fur trade, and was despatched to the region on Lake Superior to serve under Mr. Shaw, the father of Angus Shaw, of whom we have already spoken. In 1786 Cameron became a clerk and was placed in charge of the Nepigon district, an important field for his energies. Though this region was a difficult one, yet by hard work he made it remunerative to his Company. Speaking of his illness, caused by exposure, he says, in writing a letter to his friend, "I can assure you it is with great difficulty I can hold my pen, but I must tell you that the X Y sends into the Nepigon this year; therefore, should I leave my bones there, I shall go to winter."

In response to the application of Roderick McKenzie, Duncan Cameron sent a description of the Nepigon district and a journal of one of his journeys to the interior. From these we may give a few extracts. Passing over his rather full and detailed account of Saulteaux Indians of this region, we find that he speaks in a journal which is in a very damaged condition, of his visit to Osnaburgh Fort, a Hudson's Bay Company fort built in 1786, and of his decision to send a party to trade in the interior. There is abundant evidence of the great part played by strong drink at this time in the fur country.

"Cotton Shirt, a haughty Indian chief, has always been very faithful to me these several years past. He is, without exception, the best hunter in the whole department, and passes as having in consequence great influence over me. One of his elder brothers spoke next and said that he was now grown up to a man; that 'his fort,' as he calls Osnaburgh, was too far off for the winter trade; that if I left anyone here, he would come to them with winter skins; he could not live without getting drunk three or four times at least, but that I must leave a clerk to deal with him, as he was above trading with any young under-strappers. I told him that if I consented to leave a person here, I would leave one that had both sense and knowledge enough to know how to use him well, as also any other great man. This Indian had been spoiled by the H. B. people at Osnaburgh Fort, where we may consider him master. He had been invited to dine there last spring."

"This great English partisan, a few weeks ago, had his nose bit off by his son-in-law at the door of what he calls 'his fort.' He is not yet cured, and says that a great man like him must not get angry or take any revenge, especially when he stands in awe of the one who ill-used him, for there is nothing an Indian will not do rather than admit himself to be a coward."

"My canoe was very much hampered; I put a man and his wife in the small canoe and embarked in the other small canoe with my guides, after giving some liquor to the old man and his sons, who must remain here to-day to try and pack all their three canoes. We went on as well as we could against a cold head wind till the big canoe got on a stone which nearly upset her and tore a piece two feet square out of her bottom. She filled immediately and the men and goods were all in danger of going to the bottom before they reached the shore; notwithstanding their efforts, she sank in three feet of water. We hastened to get everything out of her, but my sugar and their molasses were damaged, but worse than all, my powder, which I immediately examined, was considerably damaged."

"Having decided to establish a fort, we all set to work; four men to build, one to square boards for the doors, timber for the floors, and shelves for the shops, the two others to attend the rest. . . . There are now eight Indians here, all drunk and very troublesome to my neighbour, who, I believe, is as drunk as themselves; they are all very civil to me, and so they may, for I am giving them plenty to drink, without getting anything from them as yet."

"This man (an Indian from Red Lake) tells me that the English (H. B. Co.), the X Y, and Mr. Adhemar (a free trader) were striving who would squander the most and thereby please the Indians best, but the consequence will be that the Indians will get all they want for half the value and laugh at them all, in the end. He told me that an Indian, who I know very well to have no influence on anyone but himself, got five kegs of mixt high wines to himself alone between the three houses and took 200 skins credit; that all the Indians were fifteen days without getting sober. I leave it to any rational being to judge what that Indian's skins will cost."

"Another circumstance which will tend to injure the trade very much, so long as we have the Hudson's Bay Company against us, is the premium they allow every factor or master on whatever number of skins they obtain. Those people do not care at what price they buy or whether their employés gain by them, so long as they have their premium, which sets them in opposition to one another almost as much as they are to us. The honourable Hudson's Bay Company proprietors very little knew their own interest when they first allowed this interest to their 'officers,' as they call them, as it certainly had not the desired effect, for, if it added some to their exertions, it led in a great degree to the squandering of their goods, as they are in general both needy and selfish."

PETER GRANT, THE HISTORIOGRAPHER.

While many journals and sketches were forwarded to Mr. Roderick McKenzie, none of them were of so high a character in completeness and style as that of Mr. Peter Grant on the Saulteaux Indians. Peter Grant, as quite a young man at the age of twenty, joined the North-West Company in 1784. Seven years afterward he had become a partner, had charge of Rainy Lake district, and afterward that of the Red River department. His sketch of the Indians marks him as a keen observer and a facile writer. Some of his descriptions are excellent:—

"The fruits found in this country are the wild plum, a small sort of wild cherry, wild currants of different kinds, gooseberries, strawberries, raspberries, brambleberries, blackberries, choke cherries, wild grapes, sand cherries, a delicious fruit which grows on a small shrub near sandy shores, and another blueberry, a fine fruit not larger than a currant, tasting much like a pear and growing on a small tree about the size of a willow. (No doubt the Saskatoon berry.—ED.) In the swamp you find two kinds of cranberries. Hazel nuts, but of very inferior quality, grow near the banks of the rivers and lakes. A kind of wild rice grows spontaneously in the small muddy creeks and bays."

"The North-West Company's canoes, manned with five men, carry about 3,000 lbs.; they seldom draw more than eighteen inches of water and go generally at the rate of six miles an hour in calm weather. When arrived at a portage, the bowman instantly jumps in the water to prevent the canoe from touching the bottom, while the others tie their slings to the packages in the canoe and swing them on their backs to carry over the portage. The bowman and the steersman carry their canoe, a duty from which the middle men are exempt. The whole is conducted with astonishing expedition, a necessary consequence of the enthusiasm which always attends their long and perilous voyages. It is pleasing to see them, when the weather is calm and serene, paddling in their canoes, singing in chorus their simple, melodious strains, and keeping exact time with their paddles, which effectually beguiles their labours. When they arrive at a rapid, the guide or foreman's business is to explore the waters previous to their running down with their canoes, and, according to the height of the water, they either lighten the canoe by taking out part of the cargo and carry it overland, or run down the whole load."

Speaking of the Saulteaux, Grant says, "The Saulteaux are, in general, of the common stature, well proportioned, though inclining to a slender make, which would indicate more agility than strength. Their complexion is a whitish cast of the copper colour, their hair black, long, straight, and of a very strong texture, the point of the nose rather flat, and a certain fulness in the lips, but not sufficient to spoil the appearance of the mouth. The teeth, of a beautiful ivory white, are regular, well set, and seldom fail them even in the most advanced period of life; their cheeks are high and rather prominent, their eyes black and lively, their countenance is generally pleasant, and the symmetry of their features is such as to constitute what can be called handsome faces.

"Their passions, whether of a benevolent or mischievous tendency, are always more violent than ours. I believe this has been found to be the case with all barbarous nations who never cultivate the mind; hence the cruelties imputed to savages, in general, towards their enemies. Though these people cannot be acquitted from some degree of that ferocious barbarity which characterizes the savages, they are, however, free from that deliberate cruelty which has been so often imputed to other barbarous natives. They are content to kill and scalp their enemy, and never reserve a prisoner for the refined tortures of a lingering and cruel death."

"The Saulteaux have, properly speaking, no regular system of government and but a very imperfect idea of the different ranks of society so absolutely necessary in all civilized countries. Their loading men or chief magistrates are petty chiefs, whoso dignity is hereditary, but whoso authority is confined within the narrow circle of their own particular tribe or relatives. There are no established laws to enforce obedience; all is voluntary, and yet, such is their confidence and respect for their chiefs, that instances of mutiny or disobedience to orders are very rare among them.

"As to religion, Gitche Manitou, or the 'Master of Life,' claims the first rank in their devotion. To him they attribute the creation of the heavens, of the waters, and of that portion of the earth beyond the sea from which white people come. He is also the author of life and death, taking pleasure in promoting the happiness of the virtuous, and having, likewise, the power of punishing the wicked. Wiskendjac is next in power. He is said to be the creator of all the Indian tribes, the country they inhabit and all it contains. The last of their deities is called Matchi-Manitou, or the 'Bad Spirit.' He is the author of evil, but subject to the control of the Gitche Manitou. Though he is justly held in great detestation, it is thought good policy to smooth his anger by singing and beating the drum.

"When life is gone, the body of the dead is addressed by some friend of the deceased in a long speech, in which he begs of him to take courage, and pursue his journey to the Great Meadow, observing that all his departed friends and relations are anxiously waiting to receive him, and that his surviving friends will soon follow.

"The body is then decently dressed and wrapped in a new blanket, with new shoes, garnished and painted with vermilion, on the feet. It is kept one night in the lodge, and is next day buried in the earth. After burial they either raise a pole of wood over the grave, or enclose it with a fence. At the head of the grave a small post is erected, on which they carve the particular mark of the tribe to whom the deceased belonged. The bodies of some of their most celebrated chiefs are raised upon a high scaffold, with flags flying, and the scalps of their enemies. It is customary with their warriors, at the funeral of their great men, to strike the post and relate all their martial achievements, as they do in the war dance, and their funeral ceremonies generally conclude by a feast round the grave."

Grant, in 1794, built the post on the Assiniboine at the mouth of Shell River, and five years afterward was in charge of the fort on the Rainy Lake. About the same time he erected a post, probably the first on the Red River, in the neighbourhood of the present village of St. Vincent, near 49° N. Lat., opposite Pembina. He seems to have been in the Indian country in 1804, and, settling in Lower Canada, died at Lachine in 1848, at the grand old age of eighty-four.

Thus have we sought to sketch, from their own writings, pictures of the lords of the fur trade. They were a remarkable body of men. Great as financiers, marvellous as explorers, facile as traders, bravo in their spirits, firm and yet tactful in their management of the Indians, and, except during the short period from 1800-1804, anxious for the welfare of the Red men. Looking back, we wonder at their daring and loyalty, and can well say with Washington Irving, "The feudal state of Fort William is at an end; its council chamber is silent and desolate; its banquet-hall no longer echoes to the auld world ditty; the lords of the lakes and forests have passed away."

CHAPTER XXI.

North-West and X Y Companies unite—Recalls the Homeric period—Feuds
forgotten—Men perform prodigies—The new fort re-christened—Vessel from
Michilimackinac—The old canal—Wills builds Fort Gibraltar—A lordly sway—The
"Beaver Club"—Sumptuous table—Exclusive society—"Fortitude in Distress"—
Political leaders in Lower Canada.

To the termination of the great conflict between the North-West and
the X Y Companies we have already referred. The death of Simon
McTavish removed a difficulty and served to unite the traders. The
experience and standing of the old Company and the zeal and vigour of
the new combined to inspire new hope.

Great plans were matured for meeting the opposition of the Hudson's
Bay Company and extending the trade of the Company. The
explorations of David Thompson and Simon Fraser, which, as we have
seen, produced such great results in New Caledonia, while planned
before, were now carried forward with renewed vigour, the enterprise of
the Nor'-Westers being the direct result of the union. The heroic deeds
of these explorers recall to us the adventurous times of the Homeric
period, when men performed prodigies and risked their lives for glory.
The explanation of this hearty co-operation was that the old and new
Companies were very closely allied. Brothers and cousins had been in
opposite camps, not because they disliked each other, but because their
leaders could not agree. Now the feuds were forgotten, and, with the
enthusiasm of their Celtic natures, they would attempt great things.

The "New Fort," as it had been called, at the mouth of the
Kaministiquia, was now re-christened, and the honoured name of the
chieftain McGillivray was given to this great depot—Fort William.

It became a great trading centre, and the additions required to
accommodate the increased volume of business and the greater number
of employés, were cheerfully made by the united Company.

Standing within the great solitudes of Thunder Bay, Fort William became as celebrated in the annals of the North-West Company, as York or Albany had been in the history of the Hudson's Bay Company.

A vessel came up from Lake Erie, bringing supplies, and, calling at Michilimackinac, reached the Sault Ste. Marie. Boats which had come down the canal, built to avoid the St. Mary Rapids, here met this vessel. From the St. Mary River up to Fort William a schooner carried cargoes, and increased the profits of the trade, while it protected many from the dangers of the route. The whole trade was systematized, and the trading houses, duplicated as they had been at many points, were combined, and the expenses thus greatly reduced.

As soon as the Company could fully lay its plans, it determined to take hold in earnest of the Red River district. Accordingly we see that, under instructions from John McDonald, of Garth, a bourgeois named John Wills, who, we find, had been one of the partners of the X Y Company, erected at the junction of the Red and Assiniboine Rivers, on the point of land, a fort called Fort Gibraltar. Wills was a year in building it, having under him twenty men. The stockade of this fort was made of "oak trees split in two." The wooden picketing was from twelve to fifteen feet high. The following is a list of buildings enclosed in it, with some of their dimensions. There were eight houses in all; the residence of the bourgeois, sixty-four feet in length; two houses for the servants, respectively thirty-six and twenty-eight feet long; one store thirty-two feet long; a blacksmith's shop, stable, kitchen, and an ice-house. On the top of the ice-house a watch-tower (guérite) was built. John Wills continued to live in this fort up to the time of his death a few years later. Such was the first building, so far as we know, erected on the site of the City of the Plains, and which was followed first by Fort Douglas and then by Fort Garry, the chief fort in the interior of Rupert's Land.

It was to this period in the history of the United Company that Washington Irving referred when he said: "The partners held a lordly sway over the wintry lakes and boundless forests of the Canadas almost equal to that of the East India Company over the voluptuous climes and magnificent realms of the Orient."

Some years before this, a very select organization had been formed among the fur traders in Montreal. It was known as the "Beaver Club." The conditions of the membership were very strict. They were that the candidate should have spent a period of service in the "upper country," and have obtained the unanimous vote of the members. The gatherings of the Club were very notable. At their meetings they assembled to recall the prowess of the old days, the dangers of the rapids, the miraculous deliverances accomplished by their canoe men, the disastrous accidents they had witnessed.

Their days of feasting were long remembered by the inhabitants of Montreal after the club had passed away. The sumptuous table of the Club was always open to those of rank or distinction who might visit Montreal, and the approval of the, Club gave the entry to the most exclusive society of Montreal.

Still may be met with in Montreal pieces of silverware and glassware which were formerly the property of the "Beaver Club," and even large gold medals bearing the motto, "Fortitude in Distress," used by the members of the Club on their days of celebration.

It was at this period that the power of the fur trading magnates seemed to culminate, and their natural leadership of the French Canadians being recognized in the fur trade, many of the partners became political leaders in the affairs of Lower Canada. The very success of the new Company, however, stirred up, as we shall see, opposition movements of a much more serious kind than they had ever had to meet before. Sir Alexander Mackenzie's book in 1801 had awakened much interest in Britain and now stimulated the movement by Lord Selkirk which led to the absorption of the North-West Company. The social and commercial standing of the partners started a movement in the United States which aimed at wresting from British hands the territory of New Caledonia, which the energy of the North-

West Company of explorers had taken possession of for the British crown.

It will, however, be to the glory of the North-West Company that these powerful opposition movements were mostly rendered efficient by the employment of men whom the Nor'-Westers had trained; and the methods of trade, borrowed from them by these opponents, were those continued in the after conduct of the fur trade that grew up in Rupert's Land and the Indian territories beyond.

CHAPTER XXII.

AMONG those who came to Montreal to trade with the Nor'-Westers and
to receive their hospitality was a German merchant of New York,
named John Jacob Astor. This man, who is the ancestor of the
distinguished family of Astors at the present time in New York, came
over from London to the New World and immediately began to trade in
furs. For several years Astor traded in Montreal, and shipped the furs
purchased to London, as there was a law against exporting from British
possessions. After Jay's treaty of amity and commerce (1794) this
restriction was removed, and Astor took Canadian furs to the United
States, and even exported them to China, where high prices ruled.

While Astor's ambition led him to aim at controlling the fur trade in
the United States, the fact that the western posts, such as Detroit and
Michilimackinac, had not been surrendered to the United States till
after Jay's treaty, had allowed the British traders of these and other
posts of the West to strengthen themselves. Such daring traders as
Murdoch Cameron, Dickson, Fraser, and Rolette could not be easily
beaten on the ground where they were so familiar, and where they had
gained such an ascendancy over the Indians. The Mackinaw traders
were too strong for Astor, and the hope of overcoming them through the
agency of the "American Fur Company," which he had founded in 1809,
had to be given up by him. What could not be accomplished by force
could, however, be gained by negotiation, and so two years afterward,
with the help of certain partners from among the Nor'-Westers in

Montreal, Astor brought out the Mackinaw traders (1811), and established what was called the "South-West Company."

During these same years, the St. Louis merchants organized a company to trade upon the Missouri and Nebraska Rivers. This was known as the Missouri Company, and with its 250 men it pushed its trade, until in 1808, one of its chief traders crossed the Rocky Mountains, and built a fort on the western slope. This was, however, two years afterward given up on account of the hostility of the natives. A short time after this, the Company passed out of existence, leaving the field to the enterprising merchant of New York, who, in 1810, organized his well-known "Pacific Fur Company."

During these eventful years, the resourceful Astor was, with the full knowledge of the American Government, steadily advancing toward gaining a monopoly of the fur trade of the United States. Jonathan Carver, a British officer, had, more than thirty years before this, in company with a British Member of Parliament named Whitworth, planned a route across the continent. Had not the American Revolution commenced they would have built a fort at Lake Pepin in Minnesota, gone up a tributary of the Mississippi to the West, till they could cross, as they thought would be possible, to the Missouri, and ascending it have reached the Rocky Mountain summit. At this point they expected to come upon a river, which they called the Oregon, that would take them to the Pacific Ocean.

The plan projected by Carver was actually carried out by the well-known explorers Lewis and Clark in 1804-6. Astor's penetrating mind now saw the situation clearly. He would erect a line of trading posts up the Missouri River and across the Rockies to the Columbia River on the Pacific Coast and while those on the east of the Rockies would be supplied from St. Louis, he would send ships to the mouth of the Columbia, and provide for the posts on the Pacific slope from the West. With great skill Astor made approaches to the Russian Fur Company on the Pacific Coast, offering his ships to supply their forts with all needed articles, and he thus established a good feeling between himself and the Russians.

The only other element of danger to the mind of Astor was the opposition of the North-West Company on the Pacific Coast. He knew that for years the Montreal merchants had had their eye on the region that their partner Sir Alexander Mackenzie, had discovered. Moreover, their agents, Thompson, Fraser, Stuart, and Finlay the younger, were trading beyond the summit of the Rockies in New Caledonia, but the fact that they were farther north held out some hope to Astor that an arrangement might be made with them. He accordingly broached the subject to the North-West Company and proposed a combination with them similar to that in force in the co-operation in the South-West Company, viz. that they should take a one-third interest in the Pacific Fur Company. After certain correspondence, the North-West Company declined the offer, no doubt hoping to forestall Astor in his occupation of the Columbia. They then gave orders to David Thompson to descend the Columbia, whose upper waters he had already occupied, and he would have done this had not a mutiny taken place among his men, which made his arrival at the mouth of the Columbia a few months too late.

Astor's thorough acquaintance with the North-West Company and its numerous employés stood him in good stead in his project of forming a company. After full negotiations he secured the adhesion to his scheme of a number of well-known Nor'-Westers. Prominent among these was Alexander McKay, who was Sir Alexander Mackenzie's most trusted associate in the great journey of 1793 to the Pacific Ocean. McKay had become a partner of the North-West Company, and left it to join the Pacific Fur Company. Most celebrated as being in charge of the Astor enterprise on the coast was Duncan McDougall, who also left the North-West Company to embark in Astor's undertaking. Two others, David Stuart and his nephew Robert Stuart, made the four partners of the new Company who were to embark from New York with the purpose of doubling the Cape and reaching the mouth of the Columbia.

A company of clerks and engages had been obtained in Montreal, and the party leaving Canada went in their great canoe up Lake Champlain, took it over the portage to the Hudson, and descended that river to New York. They transferred the picturesque scene so often witnessed on the Ottawa to the sleepy banks of the Hudson River, and with emblems flying, and singing songs of the voyageurs, surprised the spectators along the banks. Arrived at New York the men with bravado expressed themselves as ready to endure hardships. As Irving puts it, they declared "they could live hard, lie hard, sleep hard, eat dogs—in short, endure anything."

But these partners and men had much love for their own country and little regard to the new service into which desire for gain had led them to embark. It was found out afterwards that two of the partners had called upon the British Ambassador in New York, had revealed to him the whole scheme of Mr. Astor, and enquired whether, as British subjects, they might embark in the enterprise. The reply of the diplomat assured them of their full liberty in the matter. Astor also required of the employés that they should become naturalized citizens of the United States. They professed to have gone through the ceremony required, but it is contended that they never really did so.

The ship in which the party was to sail was the *Tonquin*, commanded by a Captain Thorn, a somewhat stern officer, with whom the fur traders had many conflicts on their outbound journey. The report having gone abroad that a British cruiser from Halifax would come down upon the *Tonquin* and arrest the Canadians on board her, led to the application being made to the United States frigate *Constitution* to give the vessel protection. On September 10th, 1810, the *Tonquin* with her convoy put out and sailed for the Southern Slain.

Notwithstanding the constant irritation between the captain and his fur trading passengers, the vessel went bravely on her way. After doubling Capo Horn on Christmas Day, they reached the Sandwich Islands in February, and after paying visits of ceremony to the king, obtained the necessary supplies of hogs, fruits, vegetables, and water from the inhabitants, and also engaged some twenty-four of the islanders, or Kanakas, as they are called, to go as employés to the Columbia.

Like a number of rollicking lads, the Nor'-Westers made very free with the natives, to the disgust of Captain Thorn. He writes:—"They sometimes dress in red coats and otherwise very fantastically, and collecting a number of ignorant natives around them, tell them they are the great chiefs of the North-West. . . . then dressing in Highland plaids and kilts, and making bargains with the natives, with presents of rum, wine, or anything that is at hand."

On February 28th the *Tonquin* set sail from the Sandwich Islands. The discontent broke out again, and the fur traders engaged in a mock mutiny, which greatly alarmed the suspicious captain. They spoke to each other in Gaelic, had long conversations, and the captain kept an ever-watchful eye upon them; but on March 22nd they arrived at the mouth of the Columbia River.

McKay and McDougall, as senior partners, disembarked, visited the village of the Chinooks, and were warmly welcomed by Comcomly, the chief of that tribe. The chief treated them hospitably and encouraged their settling in his neighbourhood. Soon they had chosen a site for their fort, and with busy hands they cut down trees, cleared away thickets, and erected a residence, stone-house, and powder magazine, which was not, however, at first surrounded with palisades. In honour of the promoter of their enterprise, they very naturally called the new settlement Astoria.

As soon as the new fort had assumed something like order, the *Tonquin*, according to the original design, was despatched up the coast to trade with the Indians for furs. Alexander McKay took charge of the trade, and sought to make the most of the honest but crusty captain. The vessel sailed on July 5th, 1811, on what proved to be a disastrous Journey.

As soon as she was gone reports began to reach the traders at Astoria that a body of white men were building a fort far up the Columbia. This was serious news, for if true it meant that the supply of furs looked for at Astoria would be cut off. An effort was made to find out the truth of the rumour, without success, but immediately after came definite information that the North-West Company agents were erecting a post at Spokane. We have already seen that this was none other than David Thompson, the emissary of the North-West Company, sent to forestall the building of Astor's fort.

Though too late to fulfil his mission, on July 15th the doughty astronomer and surveyor, in his canoe manned by eight men and having the British ensign flying, stopped in front of the new fort. Thompson was cordially received by McDougall, to the no small disgust of the other employés of the Astor Company. After waiting for eight days, Thompson, having received supplies and goods from McDougall, started on his return journey. With him journeyed up the river David Stuart, who, with eight men, was proceeding on a fur-trading expedition. Among his clerks was Alexander Ross, who has left a veracious history of the "First Settlers on the Oregon." Stuart had little confidence in Thompson, and by a device succeeded in getting him to proceed on his journey and leave him to choose his own site for a fort. Going up to within 140 miles of the Spokane River, and at the junction of the Okanagan and Columbia, Stuart erected a temporary fort to carry on his first season's trade.

In the meantime the *Tonquin* had gone on her way up the coast. The Indians were numerous, but were difficult to deal with, being impudent and greedy. A number of them had come upon the deck of the *Tonquin*, and Captain Thorn, being wearied with their slowness in bargaining and fulness of wiles, had grown impatient with the chief and had violently thrown him over the side of the ship. The Indians no doubt intended to avenge this insult. Next morning early, a multitude of canoes came about the *Tonquin* and many savages clambered upon the deck. Suddenly an attack was made upon the fur traders. Alexander McKay was one of the first to fall, being knocked down by a war club. Captain Thorn fought desperately, killing the young chief of the band,

and many others, until at last he was overcome by numbers. The remnant of the crew succeeded in getting control of the ship and, by discharging some of the deck guns, drove off the savages. Next morning the ship was all quiet as the Indians came about her. The ship's clerk, Mr. Lewis, who had been severely wounded, appeared on deck and invited them on board. Soon the whole deck was crowded by the Indians, who thought they would secure a prize. Suddenly a dreadful explosion took place. The gunpowder magazine had blown up, and Lewis and up-ward of one hundred savages were hurled into eternity. It was a fierce revenge! Four white men of the crew who had escaped in a boat were captured and terribly tortured by the maddened Indian survivors. An Indian interpreter alone was spared to return to Astoria to relate the tale of treachery and blood.

Astor's plan involved, however, the sending of another expedition overland to explore the country and lay out his projected chain of forts. In charge of this party was William P. Hunt, of Trenton, New Jersey, who had been selected by Astor, as being a native-born American, to be next to himself in authority in the Company. Hunt had no experience as a fur trader, but was a man of decision and perseverance. With him was closely associated Donald McKenzie, who had been in the service of the North-West Company, but had been induced to join in the partnership with Astor.

Hunt and McKenzie arrived in Montreal on June 10th, 1811, and engaged a number of voyageurs to accompany them. With these in a great canoe the party left the church of La Bonne Ste. Anne, on Montreal Island, and ascended the Ottawa. By the usual route Michilimackinac was reached, and here again other members of the party were enlisted. The party was also reinforced by the addition of a young Scotchman of energy and ability, Ramsay Crooks, and with him an experienced and daring Missouri trader named Robert McLellan. At Mackinaw as well as at Montreal the influence of the North-West Company was so strong that men engaged for the journey were as a rule those of the poorest quality. Thus were the difficulties of the overland party increased by the Falstaffian rabble that attended the well-chosen leaders.

The party left Mackinaw, crossed to the Mississippi, and reached St. Louis in September.

At St. Louis the explorers came into touch with the Missouri Company, of which we have spoken. The same hidden opposition that had met them in Montreal and Mackinaw was here encountered. Nothing was said, but it was difficult to get information, hard to induce voyageurs to join them, and delay after delay occurred. Near the end of October St. Louis was left behind and the Missouri ascended for 450 miles to a fort Nodowa, when the party determined to winter. During the winter Hunt returned to St. Louis and endeavoured to enlist additional men for his expedition. In this he still had the opposition of a Spaniard, Manuel de Lisa, who was the leading spirit in the Missouri Company. After some difficulty Hunt engaged an interpreter, Pierre Dorion, a drunken French half-breed, who was, however, expert and even accomplished in his work.

A start was at last made in January, and Irving tells us of the expedition meeting Daniel Boone, the famous old hunter of Kentucky, one who gloried in keeping abreast of the farthest line of the frontier, a trapper and hunter. The party went on its way ascending the river, and was accompanied by the somewhat disagreeable companion Lisa. At length they reached the country of the Anckaras, who, like the Parthians of old, seemed to live on horseback. After a council meeting the distrust of Lisa disappeared, and a bargain was struck between the Spaniard and the explorer by which he would supply them with 130 horses and take their boats in exchange. Leaving in August the party went westward, keeping south at first to avoid the Blackfeet, and then, turning northward till they reached an old trading post just beyond the summit.

The descent was now to be made to the coast, but none of them had the slightest conception of the difficulties before them. They divided themselves into four parties, under the four leaders, McKenzie,

McLellan, Hunt, and Crooks. The two former took the right bank, the two latter the left bank of the river. For three weeks they followed the rugged banks of this stream, which, from its fierceness, they spoke of as the "Mad River." Their provisions soon became exhausted and they were reduced to the dire necessity of eating the leather of their shoes. After a separation of some days the plan was struck upon by Mr. Hunt of gaining communication across the river by a boat covered with horse skin. This failed, and the unfortunate voyageur attempting to cross in it was drowned. After a time the Lewis River was reached. Trading off their horses, McKenzie's party, which was on the right bank, obtained canoes from the natives, and at length on January 18th, 1812, this party reached Astoria. Ross Cox says: "Their concave cheeks, protuberant bones, and tattered garments strongly indicated the dreadful extent of their privations; but their health appeared uninjured and their gastronomic powers unimpaired."

After the disaster of the horse-skin boat the two parties lost sight of one another. Mr. Hunt had the easier bank of the river, and, falling in with friendly Indians, he delayed for ten days and rested his wearied party. Though afterward delayed, Hunt, with his following of thirty men, one woman, and two children, arrived at Astoria, to the great delight of his companions, on February 15th, 1812.

Various accounts have been given of the journey. Those of Ross Cox and Alexander Ross are the work of actual members of the Astor Company, though not of the party which really crossed. Washington Irving's "Astoria" is regarded as a pleasing fiction, and he is very truly spoken of by Dr. Coues, the editor of Henry and Thompson's journals, in the following fashion:—"No story of travel is more familiar to the public than the tale told by Irving of this adventure, because none is more readable as a romance founded upon fact. . . . Irving plies his golden pen elastically, and from it flow wit and humour, stirring scene, and startling incident, character to the life. But he never tells us where those people went, perhaps for the simple reason that he never knew. He wafts us westward on his strong plume, and we look down on those hapless Astorians; but we might as well be ballooning for aught of exactitude we can make of this celebrated itinerary."

In October, 1811, the second party by sea left New York on the ship *Beaver*, to join the traders at the mouth of the Columbia. Ross Cox, who was one of the clerks, gives a most interesting account of the voyage and of the affairs of the Company. With him were six other cabin passengers. The ship was commanded by Captain Sowles. The voyage was on the whole a prosperous one, and Cape Horn was doubled on New Year's Day, 1812. More than a month after, the ship called at Juan Fernandez, and two months after crossed the Equator. Three weeks afterward she reached the Sandwich Islands, and on April 9th, after a further voyage, arrived at the mouth of the Columbia.

On arriving at Astoria the new-comers had many things to see and learn, but they were soon under way, preparing for their future work. There were many risks in thus venturing away from their fort. Chief Trader McDougall had indeed found the fort itself threatened after the disaster of the *Tonquin*. He had, however, boldly grappled with the case. Having few of his company to support him, he summoned the Indians to meet him. In their presence he informed them that he understood they were plotting against him, but, drawing a corked bottle from his pocket, he said: "This bottle contains small-pox. I have but to draw out the cork and at once you will be seized by the plague." They implored him to spare them and showed no more hostility.

Such recitals as this, and the sad story of the *Tonquin* related to Ross Cox and his companions, naturally increased their nervousness as to penetrating the interior.

The *Beaver* had sailed for Canton with furs, and the party of the interior was organized with three proprietors, Ramsay Crooks, Robert McLellan, and Robert Stuart, who, with eight men, were to cross the mountains to St. Louis. At the fort there remained Mr. Hunt, Duncan McDougall, B. Clapp, J. C. Halsey, and Gabriel Franchère, the last of whom wrote an excellent account in French of the Astor Company affairs.

CHAPTER XXIII.

LORD SELKIRK'S COLONY

Alexander Mackenzie's book—Lord Selkirk interested—Emigration a boon—Writes to Imperial Government—In 1802 looks to Lake Winnipeg—Benevolent project of trade—Compelled to choose Prince Edward Island—Opinions as to Hudson's Bay Company's charter—Nor'-Westers alarmed—Hudson's Bay Company's Stock— Purchases *Assiniboia*—Advertises the new colony—Religion no disqualification— Sends first colony—Troubles of the project—Arrive at York Factory—The winter— The mutiny—"Essence of Malt"—Journey inland—A second party—Third party under Archibald Macdonald—From Helmsdale—The number of colonists.

THE publication of his work by Alexander Mackenzie, entitled, "Voyages from Montreal through the Continent of North America, &c.," awakened great interest in the British Isles. Among those who were much influenced by it was Thomas, Earl of Selkirk, a young Scottish nobleman of distinguished descent and disposition. The young Earl at once thought of the wide country described as a fitting home for the poor and unsuccessful British peasantry, who, as we learn from Wordsworth, were at this time in a most distressful state.

During his college days the Earl of Selkirk had often visited the Highland glens and crofts, and though himself a Southron, he was so interested in his picturesque countrymen that he learned the Gaelic language. Not only the sad condition of Scotland, but likewise the unsettled state of Ireland, appealed to his heart and his patriotic sympathies. He came to the conclusion that emigration was the remedy for the ills of Scotland and Ireland alike.

Accordingly we find the energetic Earl writing to Lord Pelham to interest the British Government in the matter. We have before us a letter with two memorials attached. This is dated April 4th, 1802, and was kindly supplied the writer by the Colonial Office. The proposals, after showing the desirability of relieving the congested and dissatisfied population already described, go on to speak of a suitable field for the settlement of the emigrants. And this we see is the region described by Alexander Mackenzie. Lord Selkirk says: "No large tract remains unoccupied on the sea-coast of British America except barren and frozen deserts. To find a sufficient extent of good soil in a temperate climate we must go far inland. This inconvenience is not, however, an insurmountable obstacle to the prosperity of a colony, and appears to be amply compensated by other advantages that are to be found in some remote parts of the British territory. At the western extremity of Canada, upon the waters which fall into Lake Winnipeg and which in the great river of Port Nelson discharge themselves into Hudson Bay, is a country which the Indian traders represent as fertile, and of a climate far more temperate than the shores of the Atlantic under the same parallel, and not more severe than that of Germany or Poland. Here, therefore, the colonists may, with a moderate exertion of industry, be certain of a comfortable subsistence, and they may also raise some valuable objects of exportation. . . To a colony in these territories the channel of trade must be the river of Port Nelson."

It is exceedingly interesting, in view of the part afterwards played by Lord Selkirk, to read the following statement: "The greatest impediment to a colony in this quarter seems to be the Hudson's Bay Company monopoly, which the possessors cannot be expected easily to relinquish. They may, however, be amply indemnified for its abolition without any burden, perhaps even with advantage to the revenue."

The letter then goes on to state the successful trade carried on by the Canadian traders, and gives a scheme by which both the Hudson's Bay Company and the North-West Company may receive profits greater than those then enjoyed, by a plan of issuing licences, and limiting traders to particular districts.

Further, the proposal declares: "If these indefatigable Canadians were allowed the free navigation of the Hudson Bay they might, without going so far from Port Nelson as they now go from Montreal, extend their traffic from sea to sea, through the whole northern part of America, and send home more than double the value that is now derived from that region."

The matter brought up in these proposals was referred to Lord Buckinghamshire, Colonial Secretary, but failed for the time being, not because of any unsuitableness of the country, but "because the prejudices of the British people were so strong against emigration." During the next year Lord Selkirk succeeded in organizing a Highland emigration of not less than 800 souls. Not long before the starting of the ships the British Government seems to have interfered to prevent this large number being led to the region of Lake Winnipeg, and compelled Lord Selkirk to choose the more accessible shore of Prince Edward Island. After settling his colonists on the island, Lord Selkirk visited Montreal, where he was well received by the magnates of the North-West Company, and where his interest in the far West was increased by witnessing, as Astor also did about the same time, the large returns obtained by the "lords of the lakes and forests."

Years went past, and Lord Selkirk, unable to obtain the assent of the British Government to his great scheme of colonizing the interior of North America, at length determined to obtain possession of the territory wanted for his plans through the agency of the Hudson's Bay Company. About the year 1810 he began to turn his attention in earnest to the matter.

With characteristic Scottish caution he submitted the charter of the Hudson's Bay Company to the highest legal authorities in London, including the names Romilly, Holroyd, Cruise, Scarlett, and John Bell. Their clear opinion was that the Hudson's Bay Company was legally able to sell its territory and to transfer the numerous rights bestowed by the charter. They say, "We are of opinion that the grant of the soil contained in the charter is good, and that it will include all the country, the waters of which run into Hudson Bay, as ascertained by geographical observation."

Lord Selkirk, now fully satisfied that the Hudson's Bay Company was a satisfactory instrument, proceeded to obtain control of the stock of the Company.

The partners of the North-West Company learned of the steps being taken by Lord Selkirk and became greatly alarmed. They were of the opinion that the object of Lord Selkirk was to make use of his great emigration scheme to give supremacy to the Hudson's Bay Company over its rivals, and to injure the Nor'-Westers' fur trade. So far as can be seen, Lord Selkirk had no interest in the rivalry that had been going on between the Companies for more than a generation. His first aim was emigration, and this for the purpose of relieving the distress of many in the British Isles.

As showing the mind of Lord Selkirk in the matter we have before us a copy of his lordship's work on emigration published in 1805. This copy is a gift to the writer from Lady Isabella Hope, the late daughter of Lord Selkirk. In this octavo volume, upwards of 280 pages, the whole question of the state of the Highlands is ably described. Tracing the condition of the Highlanders from the Rebellion of 1745, and the necessity of emigration, Lord Selkirk refers to the demand for keeping up the Highland regiments as being less than formerly, and that the Highland proprietors had been opposed to emigration.

His patriotism was also stirred in favour of preventing the flow of British subjects to the United States, and in his desire to see the British possessions, especially in America, filled up with loyal British subjects. Ho states that in his Prince Edward Island Company in 1803 he had succeeded in securing a number from the Isle of Skye, whose friends had largely gone to North Carolina, and that others of them were from Ross, Argyle, and Inverness, and that the friends of these had chiefly gone to the United States.

After going into some detail as to the management of his Prince Edward Island Highlanders, he speaks of the success of his experiment, and gives us proof of his consuming interest in the progress and happiness of his poor fellow-countrymen. It is consequently almost beyond doubt the fact that it was his desire for carrying out his emigration scheme that led him to obtain control of the Hudson's Bay

Company, and not the desire to introduce a colony to injure the North-West trade, as charged.

There can be no doubt of Lord Selkirk's thoroughly patriotic and lofty aims. In 1808 he published a brochure of some eighty pages on "A System of National Defence." In this he shows the value of a local militia and proposes a plan for the maintenance of a sufficient force to protect Great Britain from its active enemy, Napoleon. He maintains that a Volunteer force would not be permanent; and that under any semblance of peace that establishment must immediately fall to pieces. His only dependence for the safety of the country is in a local militia.

With his plan somewhat matured, he continued in 1810 to obtain possession of stock of the Company, and succeeded in having much of it in the hands of his friends. By May, 1811, he had with his friends acquired, it is said, not less than 35,000*l.* of the total stock, 105,000*l.* sterling. A general court of the proprietors was called for May 30th, and the proposition was made by Lord Selkirk to purchase a tract of land lying in the wide expanse of Rupert's Land and on the Red River of the North, to settle, within a limited time, a large colony on their lands and to assume the expense of transport, of outlay for the settlers, of government, of protection, and of quieting the Indian title to the lands. At the meeting there was represented about 45,000*l.* worth of stock, and the vote on being taken showed the representatives of nearly 30,000*l.* of the stock to be in favour of accepting Lord Selkirk's proposal. Among those who voted with the enterprising Earl were his kinsmen, Andrew Wedderburn, Esq. (having nearly 4,500*l.* stock), William Mainwaring, the Governor Joseph Berens, Deputy-Governor John Henry Pelly, and many other well-known proprietors.

The opposition was, however, by no means insignificant, William Thwaytes, representing nearly 10,000*l.*, voted against the proposal, as did also Robert Whitehead, who held 3,000*l.* stock. The most violent opponents, however, were the Nor'-Westers who were in England at the time. Two of them had only purchased stock within forty-eight hours of the meeting. These were Alexander Mackenzie, John Inglis, and Edward Ellice, the three together representing less than 2,500*l*.

The projector of the colony having now beaten down all opposition, forthwith proceeded to carry out his great plan of colonization. His project has, of course, been greatly criticized. He has been called "a kind-hearted but visionary Scottish nobleman," and his relative, Sir James Wedderbum, spoke of him fifty years afterwards as "a remarkable man, who had the misfortune to live before his time." Certainly Lord Selkirk met with gigantic difficulties, but these were rather from the North-West Company than from any untime-liness in his emigration scheme.

Lord Selkirk soon issued the advertisement and prospectus of the new colony. He held forth the advantage to be derived from joining the colony. His policy was very comprehensive. He said: "The settlement is to be formed in a territory where religion is not the ground of any disqualification; an unreserved participation in every privilege will therefore be enjoyed by Protestant and Catholic without distinction."

The area of the new settlement was said to consist of 110,000 square miles on the Red and Assiniboine Rivers, and one of the most fertile districts of North America. The name Assiniboia was given it from the Assiniboine, and steps were taken immediately to organize a government for the embryo colony.

Active measures were then taken by the Earl of Selkirk to advance his scheme, and it was determined to send out the first colony immediately. Some years before, Lord Selkirk had carried on a correspondence with a U. E. Loyalist colonist, Miles Macdonell, formerly an officer of the King's Royal Regiment of New York, who had been given the rank of captain in the Canadian Militia. Macdonell's assistance was obtained in the new enterprise, and he was appointed by his lordship to superintend his colony at Red River.

Many incorrect statements have been made about the different bands of colonists which found their way to Red River. No loss than four parties arrived at Red River by way of York or Churchill Factories between the years 1811 and 1815. Facts connected with one of them have been naturally confused in the memories of the old settlers on Red River with what happened to other bands. In this way the author has found that representations made to him and embodied in his work on "Manitoba," published in 1882, were in several particulars incorrect. Fortunately in late years the letter-book of Captain Miles Macdonell was acquired from the Misses Macdonell of Brockville, and the voluminous correspondence of Lord Selkirk has been largely copied for the Archives at Ottawa. These letters enable us to give a clear and accurate account of the first band of colonists that found its way to the heart of the Continent and began the Red River settlement.

In the end of June, 1811, Captain Miles Macdonell found himself at Yarmouth, on the east coast of England, with a fleet of three vessels sent out by the Hudson's Bay Company for their regular trade and also to carry the first colonists. These vessels were the *Prince of Wales*, the *Eddystone*, and an old craft the *Edward and Anne*, with "old sail ropes, &c., and very badly manned." This extra vessel was evidently intended for the accommodation of the colonists. By the middle of July the little fleet had reached the Pentland Firth and were compelled to put into Stromness, when the Prince of Wales embarked a number of Orkneymen intended for the Company's service. The men of the Hudson's Bay Company at this time were largely drawn from the Orkney Islands.

Proceeding on their way the fleet made rendezvous at Stornoway, the chief town of Lewis, one of the Hebrides. Here had arrived a number of colonists or employés, some from Sligo, others from Glasgow, and others from different parts of the Highlands. Many influences were operating against the success of the colonizing expedition. It had the strenuous opposition of Sir Alexander Mackenzie, then in Britain, and the newspapers contained articles intended to discourage and dissuade people from embarking in the enterprise. Mr. Reid, collector of Customs at Stornoway, whose wife was an aunt of Sir Alexander Mackenzie, threw every impediment in the way of the project, and some of those engaged by Lord Selkirk were actually lured away by enlisting agents. A so-called "Captain" Mackenzie, denominated a "mean fellow," came alongside the *Edward and Anne*, which had some seventy-six men aboard—Glasgow men, Irish, "and a few from Orkney"—and claimed some of them as "deserters from Her Majesty's service." The demand was, however, resisted. It is no wonder that in his letter to Lord Selkirk Captain Macdonell writes, "All the men that we shall have are now embarked, but it has been an herculean task."

A prominent employ of the expedition, Mr. Moncrieff Blair, posing as a gentleman, deserted on July 25th, the day before the sailing of the vessels. A number of the deserters at Stornoway had left their effects on board, and these were disposed of by sale among the passengers. Among the officers was a Mr. Edwards, who acted as medical man of the expedition. He had his hands completely full during the voyage and returned to England with the ships. Another notable person on board was a Roman Catholic priest, known as Father Bourke. Captain Macdonell was himself a Roman Catholic, but he seems from the first to have had no confidence in the priest, who, he stated, had "come away without the leave of his bishop, who was at the time at Dublin." Father Bourke, we shall see, though carried safely to the shores of Hudson Bay, never reached the interior, but returned to Britain in the following year. After the usual incidents of "an uncommon share of boisterous, stormy, and cold weather" on the ocean, the ships entered Hudson Bay. Experiencing "a course of fine mild weather and moderate fair winds," on September 24th the fleet reached the harbour of York Factory, after a voyage of sixty-one days out from Stornoway, the *Eddystone*, which was intended to go to Churchill, not having been able to reach that Factory, coming with the other vessels to York Factory.

The late arrival of the colony on the shores of Hudson Bay made it impossible to ascend the Nelson River and roach the interior during the season of 1811. Accordingly Captain Macdonell made preparations for wintering on the Bay. York Factory would not probably have afforded sufficient accommodation for the colonists, but in addition Captain

Macdonell states in a letter to Lord Selkirk that "the factory is very ill constructed and not at all adapted for a cold country." In consequence of these considerations, Captain Macdonell at once undertook, during the fair weather of the season yet remaining, to build winter quarters on the north side of the river, at a distance of some miles from the Factory. No doubt matters of discipline entered into the plans of the leader of the colonists. In a short time very comfortable dwellings were erected, built of round logs, the front side high with a shade roof sloping to the rear a foot thick—and the group of huts was known as "Nelson encampment!"

The chief work during the earlier winter, which the captain laid on his two score men, was providing themselves with fuel, of which there was plenty, and obtaining food from the Factory, for which sledges drawn over the snow were utilized by the detachments sent on this service. The most serious difficulty was, however, a meeting, in which a dozen or more of the men became completely insubordinate, and refused to yield obedience either to Captain Macdonell or to Mr. W. H. Cook, the Governor of the Factory. Every effort was made to maintain discipline, but the men steadily held to their own way, lived apart from Macdonell, and drew their own provisions from the fort to their huts. This tended to make the winter somewhat long and disagreeable.

Captain Macdonell, being a Canadian, knew well the dangers of the dread disease of the scurvy attacking his inexperienced colonists. The men at the fort prophesied evil things in this respect for the "encampment." The captain took early steps to meet the disease, and his letters to Governor Cook always contain demands for "essence of malt," "crystallized salts of lemon," and other anti-scorbutics. Though some of his men were attacked, yet the sovereign remedy so often employed in the "lumber camps" of America, the juice of the white spruce, was applied with almost magical effect. As the winter went on, plenty of venison was received, and the health of his wintering party was in the spring much better than could have been anticipated.

After the New Year had come, all thoughts were directed to preparations for the journey of 700 miles or thereabouts to the interior.

A number of boats were required for transportation of the colonists and their effects. Captain Macdonell insisted on his boats being made after a different style from the boats commonly used at that time by the Company. His model was the flat boat, which he had seen used in the Mohawk River in the State of New York. The workmanship displayed in the making of these boats very much dissatisfied Captain Macdonell, and he constantly complained of the indolence of the workmen. In consequence of this inefficiency the cost of the boats to Lord Selkirk was very great, and drew forth the objections of the leader of the colony.

Captain Macdonell had the active assistance of Mr. Cook, the officer in charge of York, and of Mr. Auld, the Commander of Churchill, the latter having come down to York to make arrangements for the inland journey of the colonists. By July 1st, 1812, the ice had moved from the river, and the expedition started soon after on the journey to Red River. The new settlers found the route a hard and trying one with its rapids and portages. The boats, too, were heavy, and the colonists inexperienced in managing them. It was well on toward autumn when the company, numbering about seventy, reached the Red River. No special preparation had been made for the colonists, and the winter would soon be upon them. Some of the parties were given shelter in the Company fort and buildings, others in the huts of the freed men, who were married to the Indian women, and settled in the neighbourhood of the Forks, while others still found refuge in the tents of the Indian encampment in the vicinity. Governor Macdonell soon selected Point Douglas as the future centre of the colony and what is now Kildonan as the settlement. On account of the want of food the settlers were taken sixty miles south to Pembina and there, by November, a post, called Fort Daer from one of Lord Selkirk's titles, was erected for the shelter of the people and for nearness to the buffalo herds. The Governor joined the colony in a short time and retired with them early in 1813 to their settlement.

While Governor Macdonell was thus early engaged in making a beginning in the new colony, Lord Selkirk was seeking out more colonists, and sent out a small number to the New World by the Hudson's Bay Company ships. Before sailing from Stornoway the second party met with serious interruption from the collector of Customs, who, we have seen, was related to Sir Alexander Mackenzie. The number on board the ships was greater, it was claimed, than the "Dundas Act" permitted. Through the influence of Lord Selkirk the ships were allowed to proceed on their voyage. Prison fever, it is said, broke out on the voyage, so that a number died at sea, and others on the shore of Hudson Bay. A small number, not more than fifteen or twenty, reached Red River in the autumn of 1813.

During the previous winter Governor Macdonell had taken a number of the colonists to Pembina, a point sixty miles south of the Forks, where buffalo could be had, as has already been mentioned on the previous page. On returning, after the second winter, to the settlement, the colonists sowed a small quantity of wheat. They were not, however, at that time in possession of any horses or oxen and were consequently compelled to prepare the ground with the hoe.

Lord Selkirk had not been anxious in 1812 to send a large addition to his colony. In 1813 he made greater efforts, and in June sent out in the *Prince of Wales*, sailing from Orkney, a party under Mr. Archibald Macdonald, numbering some ninety-three persons. Mr. Macdonald has written an account of his voyage, and has given us a remarkably concise and clear pamphlet. Having spent the winter at Churchill, Macdonald started on April 14th with a considerable number of his party, and, coming by way of York Factory, reached Red River on June 22nd, when they were able to plant some thirty or forty bushels of potatoes. The settlers were in good spirits, having received plots of land to build houses for themselves. Governor Macdonell went northward to meet the remainder of Archibald Macdonald's party, and arrived with them late in the season.

On account of various misunderstandings between the colony and the North-West Company, which we shall relate more particularly in another chapter, 150 of the colonists were induced by a North-West officer, Duncan Cameron, to leave the country and go by a long canoe journey to Canada. The remainder, numbering about sixty persons, making up about thirteen families, were driven from the settlement, and found refuge at Norway House (Jack River) at the foot of Lake Winnipeg. An officer from Lord Selkirk, Colin Robertson, arrived in the colony to assist these settlers, but found them driven out. He followed them to Norway House, and with his twenty clerks and servants, conducted them back to Red River to their deserted homes.

While these disastrous proceedings were taking place on Red River, including the summons to Governor Macdonell to appear before the Courts of Lower Canada to answer certain charges made against him, Lord Selkirk was especially active in Great Britain, and gathered together the best band of settlers yet sent out. These were largely from the parish of Kildonan, in Sutherlandshire, Scotland. Governor Macdonell having gone east to Canada, the colony was to be placed under a new Governor, a military officer of some distinction, Robert Semple, who had travelled in different parts of the world. Governor Semple was in charge of this fourth party of colonists, who numbered about 100. With this party, hastening through his journey, Governor Semple reached his destination on Red River in the month of October, in the same year in which they had left the motherland.

Thus we have seen the arrival of those who were known as the Selkirk colonists. We recapitulate their numbers:—

In 1811, reaching Red River in 1812.   .   .   .   . 70 .   .   .
In 1812, reaching Red River in 1813.   .   .   .   . .15 or 20 .   .   .
In 1813, reaching Red River in two parties in 1814 .   .   .   .   .93 .   .   .
In 1815, reaching Red River in the same year.   .   .   .   . .100 .   .   .
Making deduction of the Irish settlers there were of the Highland colonists about .   .270 .   .   .
Less those led by the North-West Company in 1814 to Canada .   .   .   .   . .140 .   .   .
Permanent Highland settlers .   .   .   . .130 .   .   .

Of these but two remained on the banks of the Red River in 1897, George Bannerman and John Matheson, and they have both died since that time.

We shall follow the history of these colonists further; suffice it now to say that their settlement has proved the country to be one of great fertility and promise; and their early establishment no doubt prevented international complications with the United States that might have rendered the possession of Rupert's Land a matter of uncertainty to Great Britain.

CHAPTER XXIV.

TROUBLE BETWEEN THE COMPANIES

Nor'-Westers oppose the colony—Reason why—A considerable literature—
Contentions of both parties—Both in fault—Miles Macdonell's mistake—Nor' -
Wester arrogance—Duncan Cameron's ingenious plan—Stirring up the Chippewas—
Nor'-Westers warn colonists to depart—McLeod's hitherto unpublished narrative—
Vivid account of a brave defence—Chain shot from the blacksmith's smithy—Fort
Douglas begun—Settlers driven out—Governor Semple arrives—Cameron last
Governor of Fort Gibraltar—Cameron sent to Britain as a prisoner—Fort Gibraltar
captured—Fort Gibraltar decreases, Fort Douglas increases—Free traders take to
the plains—Indians favour the colonists.

To the most casual observer it must have been evident that the colony to be established by Lord Selkirk would be regarded with disfavour by the North-West Company officers. The strenuous opposition shown to it in Great Britain by Sir Alexander Mackenzie, and by all who were connected with him, showed quite clearly that it would receive little favour on the Red River.

First, it was a Hudson's Bay scheme, and would greatly advance the interests of the English trading Company. That Company would have at the very threshold of the fur country a depot, surrounded by traders and workmen, which would give them a great advantage over their rivals. Secondly, civilization and its handmaid agriculture are incompatible with the fur trade. As the settler enters, the fur-bearing animals are exterminated. A sparsely settled, almost unoccupied country, is the only hope of preserving this trade.

Thirdly, the claim of the Hudson's Bay Company under its charter was that they had the sole right to pursue the fur trade in Rupert's Land. Their traditional policy on Hudson Bay had been to drive out private trade, and to preserve their monopoly.

Fourthly, the Nor'-Westers claimed to be the lineal successors of the French traders, who, under Verandrye, had opened up the region west of Lake Superior. They long after maintained that priority of discovery and earlier possession gave them the right to claim the region in dispute as belonging to the province of Quebec, and so as being a part of Canada.

The first and second parties of settlers were so small, and seemed so little able to cope with the difficulties of their situation, that no great amount of opposition was shown. They were made, it is true, the laughing-stock of the half-breeds and Indians, for these free children of the prairies regarded the use of the hoe or other agricultural implement as beneath them. The term "Pork-eaters," applied, as we have seen, to the voyageurs east of Fort William, was freely applied to these settlers.

A considerable literature is in existence dealing with the events of this period. It is somewhat difficult, in the conflict of opinion, to reach a basis of certainty as to the facts of this contest. The Indian country is proverbial for the prevalence of rumour and misrepresentation. Moreover, prejudice and self-interest were mingled with deep passion, so that the facts are very hard to obtain.

The upholders of the colony claim that no sooner had the settlers arrived than efforts were made to stir up the Indians against them; that besides, the agents of the North-West Company had induced the Metis, or half-breeds, to disguise themselves as Indians, and that on their way to Pembina one man was robbed by these desperadoes of the gun which his father had carried at Culloden, a woman of her marriage ring, and others of various ornaments and valuable articles. There were, however, it is admitted, no specially hostile acts noticeable during the years 1812 and 1813.

The advocates of the North-West Company, on the other hand, blame the first aggression on Miles Macdonell. During the winter of 1813 and 1814 Governor Macdonell and his colonists wore occupying Fort Daer and Pembina. The supply of subsistence from the buffalo was short, food was difficult to obtain, the war with the United States was in progress and might cut off communication with Montreal, and moreover, a body of colonists was expected to arrive during the year from Great Britain. Accordingly, the Governor, on January 8th, 1814, issued a proclamation.

He claimed the territory as ceded to Lord Selkirk, and gave the description of the tract thus transferred. The proclamation then goes on to say: "And whereas the welfare of the families at present forming the settlements on the Red River within the said territory, with those on their way to it, passing the winter at York or Churchill Forts on Hudson Bay, as also those who are expected to arrive next autumn, renders it a necessary and indispensable part of my duty to provide for their support. The uncultivated state of the country, the ordinary resources derived from the buffalo, and other wild animals hunted within the territory, are not deemed more than adequate for the requisite supply; wherefore, it is hereby ordered that no persons trading in furs or provisions within the territory, for the Honourable the Hudson's Bay Company, the North-West Company, or any individual or unconnected traders whatever, shall take out any provisions, either of flesh, grain, or vegetables, procured or raised within the territory, by water or land-carriage for one twelvemonth from the date hereof; save and except what may be judged necessary for the trading parties at the present time within the territory, to carry them to their respective destinations, and who may, on due application to me, obtain licence for the same. The provisions procured and raised as above, shall be taken for the use of the colony, and that no losses may accrue to the parties concerned, they will be paid for by British bills at the customary rates, &c."

The Nor'-Westers then recalled the ceremonies with which Governor Macdonell had signalized his entrance to the country: "When he arrived he gathered his company about him, made before it some impressive ceremonies, drawn from the conjuring book of his lordship, and read to it his commission of governor or representative of Lord Selkirk; afterwards a salute was fired from the Hudson's Bay Company fort, which proclaimed his taking possession of the neighbourhood."

The Governor, however, soon gave another example of his determination to assert his authority. It had been represented to him that the North-West Company officers had no intention of obeying the proclamation, and indeed were engaged in buying up all the available supplies to prevent his getting enough for his colonists- Convinced that his opponents were engaged in thwarting his designs, the Governor sent John Spencer to seize some of the stores which had been gathered in the North-West post at the mouth of the Souris River. Spencer was unwilling to go, unless very specific instructions were given him. The Governor had, by Lord Selkirk's influence in Canada, been appointed a magistrate, and he now issued a warrant authorizing Spencer to seize the provisions in this fort.

Spencer, provided with a double escort, proceeded to the fort at the Souris, and the Nor'-Westers made no other resistance than to retire within the stockade and shut the gate of the fort. Spencer ordered his men to force an entrance with their hatchets. Afterwards, opening the store-houses, they seized six hundred skins of dried meat (pemmican) and of grease, each weighing eighty-five pounds. This booty was removed into the Hudson's Bay Company fort (Brandon House) at that place.

We have now before us the first decided action that led to the serious disturbances that followed. The question arises, Was the Governor justified in the steps taken by him? No doubt, with the legal opinion which Lord Selkirk had obtained, he considered himself thoroughly justified. The necessities of his starving people and the plea of humanity were certainly strong motives urging him to action. No doubt these considerations seemed strong, but, on the other hand, he should have remembered that the idea of law in the fur traders' country was a new thing, that the Nor'-Westers, moreover, were not prepared to credit him with purity of motive, and that they had at their disposal a force of wild Bois Brûlés ready to follow the unbridled customs of the plains. Further, even in civilized communities laws of non-intercourse, embargo, and the like, are looked upon as arbitrary and of doubtful validity. All these things should have led the Governor, ill provided as he was with the force necessary for his defence, to hesitate before taking a course likely to be disagreeable to the Nor"-Westers, who would regard it as an assertion of the claim of superiority of the Hudson's Bay

Company and of the consequent degradation of their Company, of which they were so proud.

In their writings the North-West Company take some credit for not precipitating a conflict, but state that they endured the indignity until their council at Fort William should take action in the following summer. At this council, which was interesting and full of strong feeling against their fur-trading rivals, the Nor'-Westers, under the presidency of the Hon. William McGillivray, took decided action.

In the trials that afterwards arose out of this unfortunate quarrel, John Pritchard, whose forty days' wanderings we have recorded, testified that one of the North-West agents, Mac-Kenzie, had given him the information that "the intention of the North-West Company was to seduce and inveigle away as many of the colonists and settlers at Red River as they could induce to join them; and after they should thus have diminished their means of defence, to raise the Indians of Lac Rouge, Fond du Lac, and other places, to act and destroy the settlement; and that it was also their intention to bring the Governor, Miles Macdonell, down to Montreal as a prisoner, by way of degrading the authority under which the colony was established in the eyes of the natives of that country."

Simon McGillivray, a North-West Company partner, had two years before this written from London that "Lord Selkirk must be driven to abandon his project, for his success would strike at the very existence of our trade."

Two of the most daring partners of the North-West Company were put in charge of the plan of campaign agreed on at Fort William. These were Duncan Cameron and Alexander Macdonell. The latter wrote to a friend, from one of his resting-places on his journey, "Much is expected of us. . . . so here is at them with all my heart and energy." The two partners arrived at Fort Gibraltar, situated at the forks of the Red and Assiniboine Rivers, toward the end of August. The senior partner, Macdonell, leaving Cameron at Fort Gibraltar, went westward to the

Qu'Appelle River, to return in the spring and carry out the plan agreed on.

Cameron had been busy during the winter in dealing with the settlers, and let no opportunity slip of impressing them. Knowing the fondness of Highlanders for military display, he dressed himself in a bright red coat, wore a sword, and in writing to the settlers, which he often did, signed himself, "D. Cameron, Captain, Voyageur Corps, Commanding Officer, Red River." He also posted an order at the gate of his fort purporting to be his captain's commission. Some dispute has arisen as to the validity of this authority. There seems to have been some colour for the use of this title, under authority given for enlisting an irregular corps in the upper lakes during the American War of 1812, but the legal opinion is that this had no validity in the Red River settlement.

Cameron, aiming at the destruction of the colony, began by ingratiating himself with a number of the leading settlers. Knowing the love of the Highlanders for their own language, Cameron spoke to them Gaelic in his most pleasing manner, entertained the leading colonists at his own table, and paid many attentions to their families. Promises were then made to a number of leaders to provide the people with homes in Upper Canada, to pay up wages due by the Hudson's Bay Company or Lord Selkirk, and to give a year's provisions free, provided the colony would leave the Rod River and accept the advantages offered in Canada. This plan succeeded remarkably well, and it is in sworn evidence that on three-quarters of the colony reaching Fort William, a settler, Campbell, received 100*l.*, several others 20*l.*, and so on.

Some of the best of the settlers, amounting to about one-quarter of the whole, refused all the advances of the subtle captain. Another method was taken with this class. The plan of frightening them away by the co-operation of the Cree Indians had failed, but the Bois Brûlés, or half-breeds, were a more pliant agency. These were to be employed. Cameron now (April, 1815) made a demand on Archibald Macdonald, Acting Governor, to hand over to the settlers the field pieces belonging to Lord Selkirk, on the ground that these had been used already to disturb the peace. This startling order was presented to the Governor by settler Campbell on the day on which the fortnightly issue of rations took place at the colony buildings. The settlers in favour of Cameron then broke open the store-house, and took nine pieces of ordnance and removed them to Fort Gibraltar. The Governor having arrested one of the settlers who had broken open the store-house, a number of the North-West Company clerks and servants, under orders from Cameron, broke into the Governor's house and rescued the prisoner. About this time Miles Macdonell, the Governor, returned to the settlement. A warrant had been issued for his arrest by the Nor'-Westers, but he refused for the time to acknowledge the jurisdiction of the magistrates. Cameron now spread abroad the statement that if the settlers did not deliver up the Governor, they in turn would be attacked and driven from their homes. Certain colonists were now fired at by unseen assailants.

About the middle of May, the senior partner, Alexander Macdonell, arrived from Qu'Appelle, accompanied by a band of Cree Indians. The partners hoped through these to frighten the settlers who remained obdurate, but the Indians were too astute to be led into the quarrel, and assured Governor Miles Macdonell that they were resolved not to molest the newcomers.

An effort was also made to stir up the Chippewa Indians of Sand Lake, near the west of Lake Superior. The chief of the band declared to the Indian Department of Canada that he was offered a large reward if he would declare war against the Selkirk colonists. This the Chippewas refused to do.

Early in June the lawless spirit followed by the Nor'-Westers again showed itself. A party from Fort Gibraltar went down with loaded muskets, and from a wood near the Governor's residence fired upon some of the colony employés. Mr. White, the surgeon, was nearly hit, and a ball passed close by Mr. Burke, the storekeeper. General firing then began from the wood and was returned from the house, but four of the colony servants were wounded. This expedition was under Cameron, who congratulated his followers on the result.

The demand for the surrender of the Governor, in answer to the warrant issued, was then made, and at the persuasion of the other officers of the settlement, and to avoid the loss of life and the dangers threatened against the colonists, Governor Miles Macdonell surrendered himself and was taken to Montreal for trial, though no trial ever took place.

The double plan of coaxing away all the settlers who were open to such inducement, and of then forcibly driving away the residue from the settlement, seemed likely to succeed. One hundred and thirty-four of the colonists, induced by promises of free transport, two hundred acres of land in Upper Canada, as well as in some cases by substantial gifts, deserted the colony in June (1815), along with Cameron, and arrived at Fort William on their way down the lakes at the end of July. These settlers made their way in canoes along the desolate shores of Lake Superior and Georgian Bay, and arrived at Holland Landing, in Upper Canada, on September 5th. Many of them were given land in the township of West Guillimbury, near Newmarket, and many of their descendants are there to this day.

The Nor'-Westers now continued their persecution of the remnant of the settlers. They burnt some of their houses and used threats of the most extreme kind. On June 25th, 1815, the following document was served upon the disheartened colonists:—"All settlers to retire immediately from the Red River, and no trace of a settlement to remain."

CUTHBERT GRANT.
"BOSTONNAIS PANGMAN.
"WILLIAM SHAW.
"BONHOMME MONTOUR."

The conflict resulting at this time may be said to be the first battle of the war. A fiery Highland trader, John McLeod, was in charge of the Hudson's Bay Company house at this point, and we have his account of the attack and defence, somewhat bombastic it may be, but which, so far as known to the author, has never been published before.

"In 1814-15, being in charge of the whole Red River district, I spent the winter at the Forks, at the settlement there. On June 25th, 1815, while I was in charge, a sudden attack was made by an armed band of the N.-W. party under the leadership of Alexander Maedonell (Yellow Head) and Cuthbert Grant, on the settlement and Hudson's Bay Company fort at the Forks. They numbered about seventy or eighty, well armed and on horseback. Having had some warning of it, I assumed command of both the colony and H. B. C. parties. Mustering with inferior numbers, and with only a few guns, we took a stand against them. Taking my place amongst the colonists, I fought with them. All fought bravely and kept up the fight as long as possible. Many all about me falling wounded; one mortally. Only thirteen out of our band escaped unscathed.

"The brunt of the struggle was near the H. B. C. post, close to which was our blacksmith's smithy—a log building about ten feet by ten. Being hard pressed, I thought of trying the little cannon (a three or four-pounder) lying idle in the post where it could not well be used.

"One of the settlers (Hugh McLean) went with two of my men, with his cart to fetch it, with all the cart chains he could get and some powder. Finally, we got the whole to the blacksmith's smithy, where, chopping up the chain into lengths for shot, we opened a fire of chain shot on the enemy which drove back the main body and scattered them, and saved the post from utter destruction and pillage. All the colonists' houses were, however, destroyed by fire. Houseless, wounded, and in extreme distress, they took to the boats, and, saving what they could, started for Norway House (Jack's River), declaring they would never return.

"The enemy still prowled about, determined apparently to expel, dead or alive, all of our party. All of the H. B. Company's officers and men refused to remain, except the two brave fellows in the service, viz.

Archibald Currie and James McIntosh, who, with noble Hugh McLean, joined in holding the fort in the smithy. Governor Macdonell was a prisoner.

"In their first approach the enemy appeared determined more to frighten than to kill. Their demonstration in line of battle, mounted, and in full 'war paint' and equipment was formidable, but their fire, especially at first, was desultory. Our party, numbering only about half theirs, while preserving a general line of defence, exposed itself as little as possible, but returned the enemy's fire, sharply checking the attack, and our line was never broken by them. On the contrary, when the chain-firing began, the enemy retired out of range of our artillery, but at a flank movement reached the colony houses, where they quickly and resistlessly plied the work of destruction. To their credit be it said, they took no life or property.

"Of killed, on our side, there was only poor John Warren of H. B. C. service, a worthy brave gentleman, who, taking a leading part in the battle, too fearlessly exposed himself. Of the enemy, probably, the casualties were greater, for they presented a better target, and we certainly fired to kill. From the smithy we could and did protect the trade post, but could not the buildings of the colonists, which were along the bank of the Red River, while the post faced the Assiniboine more than the Red River. Fortunately for us in the 'fort' (the smithy) the short nights were never too dark for our watch and ward.

"The colonists were allowed to take what they could of what belonged to them, and that was but little, for as yet they had neither cow nor plough, only a horse or two. There were boats and other craft enough to take them all—colonists and H. B. C. people—away, and all, save my three companions already named and myself, took ship and fled. For many days after we were under siege, living under constant peril; but unconquerable in our bullet-proof log walls, and with our terrible cannon and chain shot.

"At length the enemy retired. The post was safe, with from 800*l.*, to 1000*l.* sterling worth of attractive trade goods belonging to the

Hudson's Bay Company untouched. I was glad of this, for it enabled me to secure the services of free men about the place—French Canadians and half-breeds not in the service of the N.-W. Company—to restore matters and prepare for the future.

"I felt that we had too much at stake in the country to give it up, and had every confidence in the resources of the H. B. Company and the Earl of Selkirk to hold their own and effectually repel any future attack from our opponents.

"I found the free men about the place willing to work for me; and at once hired a force of them for building and other works in reparation of damages and in new works. So soon as I got my post in good order, I turned to save the little but precious and promising crops of the colonists, whose return I anticipated, made fences where required, and in due time cut and stacked their hay, &c.

"That done I took upon me, without order or suggestion from any quarter, to build a house for the Governor and his staff of the Hudson's Bay Company at Red River. There was no such officer at that time, nor had there ever been, but I was aware that such an appointment was contemplated.

"I selected for this purpose what I considered a suitable site at a point or sharp bend in the Red River about two miles below the Assiniboine, on a slight rise on the south side of the point—since known as Point Douglas, the family name of the Earl of Selkirk. Possibly I so christened it—I forget.

"It was of two stories; with main timbers of oak; a good substantial house; with windows of parchment in default of glass." Here ends McLeod's diary.

The Indians of the vicinity showed the colonists much sympathy, but on June 27th, after the hostile encounter, some thirteen families, comprising from forty to sixty persons, pursued their sad journey, piloted by friendly Indians, to the north end of Lake Winnipeg, where the Hudson's Bay Company post of Jack River afforded some shelter. McLeod and, as he tells us, three men only were left. These endeavoured to protect the settlers' growing crops, which this year showed great promise.

The expulsion may now be said to have been complete. The day after the departure of the expelled settlers, the colony dwellings, with the possible exception of the Governor's house, were all burnt to the ground. In July the desolate band reached Jack River House, their future being dark indeed. Deliverance was, however, coming from two directions. Colin Robertson, a Hudson's Bay Company officer, arrived from the East with twenty Canadians. On reaching the Red River settlement, he found the settlers all gone, but he followed them speedily to their rendezvous on Lake Winnipeg and returned with the refugees to their deserted homes on Red River. They were joined also by about ninety settlers from the Highlands of Scotland, who had come through to Red River in one season. The colony was now rising into promise again. A number of the demolished buildings were soon erected; the colony took heart, and under the new Governor, Robert Semple, a British officer who had come with the last party of settlers, the prospects seemed to have improved. The Governor's dwelling was strengthened, other dwellings were erected beside it, and more necessity being now seen for defence, the whole assumed a more military aspect, and took the name, after Lord Selkirk's family name, Fort Douglas.

Though a fair crop had been reaped by the returned settlers from their fields, yet the large addition to their numbers made it necessary to remove to Fort Daer, where the buffalo were plentiful. This party was under the leadership of Sheriff Alexander Macdonell, though Governor Semple was also there. The autumn saw trouble at the Forks. The report of disturbances having taken place between the Nor'-Westers and Hudson's Bay Company employés at Qu'Appelle was heard, as well as renewed threats of disturbance in the colony. Colin Robertson in October, 1815, captured Fort Gibraltar, seized Duncan Cameron, and recovered the field-pieces and other property taken by the Nor'-Westers in the preceding months. Though the capture of Cameron and his fort thus took place, and the event was speedily followed by the reinstatement of the trader on his promise to keep the peace, yet the report of the seizure led to the greatest irritation in all parts of the country where the two Companies had posts. All through the winter, threatenings of violence filled the air. The Bois Brûlés were arrogant, and, led by their faithful leader, Cuthbert Grant, looked upon themselves as the "New Nation."

Returning, after the New Year of 1816, from Fort Daer, Governor Semple saw the necessity for aggressive action. Fort Gibraltar was to become the rendezvous for a Bois Brûlés force of extermination from Qu'Appelle, Fort des Prairies (Portage la Prairie), and even from the Saskatchewan- To prevent this, Colin Robertson, under the Governor's direction, recaptured Fort Gibraltar and held Cameron as a prisoner. This event took place in March or April of 1816. The legality of this seizure was of course much discussed between the hostile parties.

It was deemed wise, however, to make a safe disposal of the prisoner Cameron. He was accordingly dispatched under the care of Colin Robertson, by way of Jack River, to York Factory, to stand his trial in England. Thus were reprisals made for the capture and removal of Miles Macdonell in the preceding year, both actions being of doubtful legality. On account of the failure of the Hudson's Bay Company ship to leave York Factory in that year, Cameron did not reach England for seventeen months, where he was immediately released.

The fall of Fort Gibraltar was soon to follow the deportation of its commandant. The matter of the dismantling of Fort Gibraltar was much discussed between Governor Semple and his lieutenant, Colin Robertson. The latter was opposed to the proposed destruction of the Nor'-Wester fort, knowing the excitement such a course would cause. However, after the departure of Robertson to Hudson Bay in charge of Cameron, the Governor carried out his purpose, and in the end of May, 1816, the buildings were pulled down. A force of some thirty men were employed, and, expecting as they did, a possible interruption from the West, the work was done in a week or a little more.

The materials were taken apart; the stockade was made into a raft, the remainder was piled upon it, and all was floated down Red River to the site of Fort Douglas. The material was then used for strengthening the fort and building new houses in it. Thus ended Fort Gibraltar. A considerable establishment it was in its time; its name was undoubtedly a misnomer so far as strength was concerned; yet it points to its origination in troublous times.

The vigorous policy carried out in regard to Fort Gibraltar was likewise shown in the district south of the Forks. As we have seen, to the south, Fort Daer had been erected, and thither, winter by winter, the settlers had gone for subsistence. Here, too, was the Nor'-Wester fort of Pembina House. During the time when Governor Semple and Colin Robertson were maturing their plans, it was determined to seize Pembina. No sooner had the news of Cameron's seizure reached Fort Daer, than Sheriff Macdonell, who was in charge, organized an expedition, took Pembina House, and its officers and inhabitants. The prisoners were sent to Fort Douglas, and were liberated on pledges of good behaviour, and the military stores were also taken to Fort Douglas. The reasons given by the colony people for this course are "self-defence and the security of the lives of the settlers." About the end of April, the settlers returned from Fort Daer, and were placed on their respective lots along the Red River.

All events now plainly pointed to armed disturbances and bloodshed. The policy of Governor Semple was too vigorous when the inflammable elements in the country were borne in mind. There was in the country a class called "Free Canadians," i.e. those French Canadian trappers and traders not connected with either Company, who obtained a precarious living for themselves, their Indian wives, and half-breed children. These, fearing trouble, betook themselves to the plains. The Indians of the vicinity seemed to have gained a liking for the colonists and their leaders. When they heard the threatenings from the West, two of the chiefs came to Governor Semple and offered the assistance of their bands. This the Governor could not accept, whereat the chiefs gave voice to their sorrow and disappointment. Governor Semple seems to have disregarded all these omens of coming trouble, and to have acted almost without common prudence. No doubt, having but lately come to the country, he failed to understand the daring character of his opponents.

CHAPTER XXV.

THE troubles between the Hudson's Bay and North-West Companies were evidently coming to a crisis. The Nor'-Westers laid their plans with skill, and determined to send one expedition from Fort William westward and another from Qu'Appelle eastward, and so crush out the opposition at Red River.

From the west the expedition was under Cuthbert Grant, and he, appealing to his fellow Metis, raised the standard of the Bois Brûlés and called his followers the "New Nation." Early in March the Bois Brûlés' leader wrote to Trader J. D. Cameron, detailing his plans and expectations. We quote from his letter: "I am now safe and sound, thank God, for I believe that it is more than Colin Robertson, or any of his suite, dare offer the least insult to any of the Bois Brûlés, although Robertson made use of some expressions which I hope he will swallow in the spring. He shall see that it is neither fifteen, thirty, nor fifty of his best horsemen that can make the Bois Brûlés bow to him. Our people at Fort Des Prairies and English River are all to be here in the spring. It is hoped that we shall come off with flying colours, and *never to see any of them again in the colonizing way in Red River*. . . . We are to remain at the Forks to pass the summer, for fear they should play us the same trick as last summer of coming back; but they shall receive a warm reception."

The details of this western expedition are well given by Lieutenant Pierre Chrysologue Pambrun, an officer of the Canadian Voltigeurs, a regiment which had distinguished itself in the late war against the United States. Pambrun had entered the service of the Hudson's Bay

Company as a trader, and been sent to the Qu'Appelle district. Having gone west to Qu'Appelle, he left that western post with five boat loads of pemmican and furs to descend the Assiniboine River to the Forks. Early in May, near the Grand Rapids, Pambrun and his party touched the shore of the river, when they were immediately surrounded by a party of Bois Brûlés and their boats and cargoes were all seized by their assailants. The pemmican was landed and the boats taken across the river. The unfortunate Pambrun was for five days kept in durance vile by Cuthbert Grant and Peter Pangman, who headed the attacking party, and the prisoner was carried back to Qu'Appelle.

While Pambrun was here as prisoner, he was frequently told by Cuthbert Grant that the half-breeds were intending in the summer to destroy the Red River settlements; their leader often reminded the Bois Brûlés of this, and they frequently sang their war songs to waken ardour for the expeditions. Captors and prisoner shortly afterward left the western fort and went down the river to Grand Rapids. Here the captured pemmican was re-embarked and the journey was resumed. Near the forks of the Qu'Appelle River a band of Indians was encamped. The Indians were summoned to meet Commander Macdonell, who spoke to them in French, though Pangman interpreted.

"MY FRIENDS AND RELATIONS,—I address you bashfully, for I have not a pipe of tobacco to give you. All our goods have been taken by the English, but we are now upon a party to drive them away. Those people have been spoiling the fair lands which belonged to you and the Bois Brûlés, and to which they have no right. They have been driving away the buffalo. You will soon be poor and miserable if the English stay. But we will drive them away if the Indians do not, for the North-West Company and the Bois Brûlés are one. If you (speaking to the chief) and some of your young men will join I shall be glad."

The chief responded coldly and gave no assistance.

Next morning the Indians departed, and the party proceeded on their journey. Pambrun was at first left behind, but in the evening was given a spare horse and overtook Grant's cavalcade at the North-West Fort near Brandon House. At the North-West Fort Pambrun saw tobacco, carpenters' tools, a quantity of furs, and other things which had been seized in the Hudson's Bay Fort, Brandon House, and been brought over as booty to the Nor'-Westers.

Resuming their journey the traders kept to their boats down the Assiniboine, while the Bois Brûlés went chiefly on horseback until they reached Portage La Prairie. Sixty miles had yet to be traversed before the Forks were reached. The Bois Brûlés now prepared their mounted force. Cuthbert Grant was Commander. Dressed in the picturesque garb of the country, the Metis now arrived with guns, pistols, lances, bows, and arrows. Pambrun remained behind with Alexander Macdonell, but was clearly led to believe that the mounted force would enter Fort Douglas and destroy the settlement. On their fleet Indian ponies these children of the prairie soon made their journey from Portage La Prairie to the Selkirk settlement.

We are indebted to the facile narrator, John Pritchard, for an account of their arrival and their attack. He states that in June, 1816, he was living at Red River, and quite looked for an attack from the western levy just described. Watch was constantly kept from the guérite of Fort Douglas for the approaching foe. The half-breeds turned aside from the Assiniboine some four miles up the River to a point a couple of miles below Fort Douglas. Governor Semple and his attendants followed them with the glass in their route across the plain. The Governor and about twenty others sallied out to meet the western party. On his way out he sent back for a piece of cannon, which was in the fort, to be brought. Soon after this the half-breeds approached Governor Semple's party in the form of a half moon. The Highland settlers had betaken themselves for protection to Fort Douglas, and in their Gaelic tongue made sad complaint.

A daring fellow named Boucher then came out of the ranks of his party, and, on horseback, approached Semple and his body-guard. He gesticulated wildly, and called out in broken English, "What do you want? What do you want?" Governor Semple answered, "What do you want?" To this Boucher replied, "We want our fort." The Governor said, "Well, go to your fort." Nothing more was said, but Governor Semple was seen to put his hand on Boucher's gun. At this juncture a shot was fired from some part of the line, and the firing became general. Many of the witnesses who saw the affair affirmed that the shot first fired was from the Bois Brûlés' line.

The attacking party were most deadly in their fire. Semple and his staff, as well as others of his party, fell to the number of twenty-two. The affair was most disastrous.

Pritchard says:—

"I did not see the Governor fall, though I saw his corpse the next day at the fort. When I saw Captain Rogers fall I expected to share his fate. As there was a French Canadian among those who surrounded me, and who had just made an end of my friend, I said, 'Lavigne, you are a Frenchman, you are a man, you are a Christian. For God's sake save my life; for God's sake try and save it. I give myself up; I am your prisoner.'"

To the appeals of Pritchard Lavigne responded, and, placing himself before his friend, defended him from the infuriated half-breeds, who would have taken his life. One Primeau wished to shoot Pritchard, saying that the Englishman had formerly killed his brother. At length they decided to spare Pritchard's life, though they called him a petit chien, told him he had not long to live, and would be overtaken on their return. It transpired that Governor Semple was not killed by the first shot that disabled him, but had his thigh-bone broken. A kind French Canadian undertook to care for the Governor, but in the fury of the fight an Indian, who was the greatest rascal in the company, shot the wounded man in the breast, and thus killed him instantly.

The Bois Brûlés, indeed, many of them, were disguised as Indians, and, painted as for the war dance, gave the war whoop, and made a hideous noise and shouting. When their victory was won they declared that their purpose was to weaken the colony and put an end to the Hudson's Bay Company opposition. Cuthbert Grant then proceeded to complete his work. He declared to Pritchard that "if Fort Douglas were not immediately given up with all the public property, instantly and without resistance, man, woman, and child would be put to death. He stated that the attack would be made upon it the same night, and if a single shot were fired, that would be the signal for the indiscriminate destruction of every soul."

This declaration of Cromwellian policy was very alarming. Pritchard believed it meant the killing of all the women and children. He remonstrated with the prairie leader, reminding him that the colonists were his father's relatives. Somewhat softened by this appeal, Grant consented to spare the lives of the settlers if all the arms and public property were given up and the colony deserted. An inventory of property was accordingly taken, and in the evening of the third day after the battle, the mournful company, for a second time, like Acadian refugees, left behind them homes and firesides and went into exile.

The joyful news was sent west by the victorious Metis. Pambrun at Portage La Prairie received news from a messenger who had hastened away to report to Macdonell the result of the attack. Hearing the account given by the courier, the trader was full of glee. He announced in French to the people who were anxiously awaiting the news, "Sacré nom de Dieu, bonnes nouvelles, vingt-deux Anglais de tués." Those present, especially Lamarre, Macdonell, and Sieveright, gave vent to their feelings boisterously.

Many of the party mounted their Indian ponies and hastened to the place of conflict; others went by water down the Assiniboine. The commander sent word ahead that the colonists were to be detained till his arrival. Pambrun, being taken part of the way by water, was delayed, and so was too late in arriving to see the colonists. Cuthbert Grant and nearly fifty of the assailing party were in the fort.

Pambrun, having obtained permission to visit Seven Oaks, the scene of the conflict, was greatly distressed by the sight. The uncovered limbs of many of the dead were above ground, and the bodies were in a mangled condition. This unfortunate affair for many a day cast a reproach upon the Nor'-Westers, although the prevailing opinion was that Grant was a brave man and conducted himself well in the engagement.

We have now to enquire as to the movements of the expedition coming westward from Fort William. The route of upwards of four hundred miles was a difficult one. Accordingly, before they reached Red River, Fort Douglas was already in the hands of the Nor'-Westers. With the expedition from Fort William came a non-commissioned officer of the De Meuron regiment, one of the Swiss bodies of mercenaries disbanded after the war of 1812-15. This was Frederick Damien Huerter. His account is circumstantial and clear. He had, as leading a military life, entered the service of the Nor'-Westers, and coming west to Lake Superior, followed the leadership of the fur trader Alexander Norman McLeod and two of the officers of his old regiment, Lieutenants Missani and Brumby.

Arriving at Fort William, a short time was given for providing the party with arms and equipment, and soon the lonely voyageurs, on this occasion in a warlike spirit, were paddling themselves over the fur traders' route in five large north canoes.

On the approach to Rainy Lake Fort, as many of the. party as were soldiers dressed in full regimentals, in order to impress upon the Indians that they had the King's authority. Strong drink and tobacco were a sufficient inducement to about twenty of the Indians to join the expedition. On the day before the fight at Seven Oaks, the party had arrived at the fort known as Bas de la Rivière, near Lake Winnipeg. Guns and two small brass field-pieces, three pounders, were put in order, and the company crossed to the mouth of the Red River, ascended to Nettley Creek, and there bivouacked, forty miles from the scene of action and two days after the skirmish. They had expected here to meet the Qu'Appelle brigade of Cuthbert Grant. No doubt this was the original plan, but the rashness of the Governor and the hot blood of the Metis had brought on the engagement, with the result we have seen.

Knowing nothing of the fight, the party started to ascend the river, and soon met seven or eight boats, laden with colonists, under the command of the sheriff of the Red River settlement. McLeod then heard of the fight, ordered the settlers ashore, examined all the papers among their baggage, and took possession of all letters, account books, and documents whatsoever. Even Governor Semple's trunks, for which there were no keys, were broken open and examined. The colonists were then set free and proceeded on their sad journey, Charles Grant being detailed to seeing them safely away.

Huerter says:—

"On the 26th I went up the river to Fort Douglas. There were many of the partners of the North-West Company with us. At Fort Douglas the brigade was received with discharges of artillery and fire-arms. The fort was under Mr. Alexander Macdonell, and there was present a great gathering of Bois Brûlés, clerks, and interpreters, as well as partners of the Company. On our arrival Archibald Norman McLeod, our leader, took the management and direction of the fort, and all made whatever they chose of the property it contained. The Bois Brûlés were entirely under the orders and control of McLeod and the partners. McLeod occupied the apartments lately belonging to Governor Semple. After my arrival I saw all the Bois Brûlés assembled in a large outer room, which had served as a mess-room for the officers of the colony.

"I rode the same day to the field of 'Seven Oaks,' where Governor Semple and so many of his people had lost their lives, in company with a number of those who had been employed on that occasion—all on horseback. At this period, scarcely a week after June 19th, I saw a number of human bodies scattered about the plain, and nearly reduced to skeletons, there being then very little flesh adhering to the bones; and I was informed on the spot that many of the bodies had been partly devoured by dogs and wolves."

There was a scene of great rejoicing the same evening at the fort, the Bois Brûlés being painted and dancing naked, after the manner of savages, to the great amusement of their masters.

On June 29th most of the partners and the northern brigade set off for the rapids at the mouth of the Saskatchewan. The departure of the grand brigade was signalized by the discharge of artillery from Fort Douglas,

The Nor'-Westers were now in the ascendant. The Bois Brûlés were naturally in a state of exultation. Their wild Indian blood was at the boiling point. Fort Douglas had been seized without opposition, and for several days the most riotous scenes took place. Threats of violence were freely indulged in against the Hudson's Bay Company, Lord Selkirk, and the colonists. As Pritchard remarks, there was nothing now for the discouraged settlers but to betake themselves for the second time to the rendezvous at the north of Lake Winnipeg, and there await deliverance at the hands of their noble patron, Lord Selkirk. The exuberance of the French half-breeds found its way into verse. We give the chanson of Pierre Falcon and the translation of it:—

CHANSON ÉCRITE PAR PIERRE FALCON.
Voulez-vous écouter chanter une chanson de vérité.
Le dix-neuf de Juin les Bois Brûlés sont arrivés
Comme des braves guerriers,
Sont arrivés à la grenouillère.
Nous avons fait trois prisonniers
Des Orcanais? Ils sont ici pour piller notre pays,
Etant sur le point de débarquer.
Deux de nos gens se sont écriés,
"Voilà l'Anglais qui vient nous attaquer."
Tous aussitot nous sommes dévirés
Pour aller les rencontrer.
J'avons cerné la bande de grenadiers;
Ils sont immobiles?—Ils sont démentés?
J'avons agi comme des gens d'honneur,
Nous envoyames un ambassadeur.
"Gouverneur, voulez-vous arreter un petit moment,
Nous voulons vous parler."
Le gouverneur, qui est enrage,
Il dit à ses soldats, "Tirez."
Le premier coup l'Anglais le tire,
L'ambassadeur a presque manque d'etre tué,
Le gouverneur se croyant l'empereur,

Il agit avec rigueur,
Le gouverneur, se croyant l'empereur,
A son malheur agit avec trop de rigueur.
Ayant vu passé les Bois Brûlés,
Il a parti pour nous épouvanter.
Il s'est trompé; il s'est bien fait tuer
Quantité de ses grenadiers.
J'avons tué presque toute son armée;
De la bande quatre de cinq se sont sauvés
Si vous aviez vu les Anglais
Et tous les Bois Brûlés après—
De butte en butte les Anglais culbutaient;
Les Bois Brûlés jetaient des cris de joie.
Qui en a composé la chanson?
C'est Pierre Falcon, le bon garcon.
Elle a été faite et composée
Sur la victoire qui nous avons gagnée.
Elle a été faite et composée.
Chantons la gloire de tous ces Bois Brûlés.

SONG WRITTEN BY PIERRE FALCON.
Come, listen to this song of truth,
A song of brave Bois Brûlés,
Who at Frog Plain took three captives,
Strangers come to rob our country.
Where dismounting there to rest us,
A cry is raised, "The English!
They are coming to attack us."
So we hasten forth to meet them.
I looked upon their army,
They are motionless and downcast;
So, as honour would incline us,
We desire with them to parley.
But their leader, moved with anger,
Gives the word to fire upon us;
And imperiously repeats it,
Bushing on to his destruction.
Having seen us pass his stronghold,
He has thought to strike with terror

The Bois Brûlés.—Ah! mistaken,
Many of his soldiers perish.
But a few escaped the slaughter,
Rushing from the field of battle;
Oh, to see the English fleeing!
Oh, the shouts of their pursuers!
Who has sung this song of triumph?
The good Pierre Falcon has composed it,
That his praise of these Bois Brûlés
Might be evermore recorded.

CHAPTER XXVI.

THE sad story of the beleaguered and excited colonists reached the ears of Lord Selkirk through his agents. The trouble threatening his settlers determined the energetic founder to visit Canada for himself, and, if possible, the infant colony. Accordingly, late in the year 1815, in company with his family—consisting of the Countess, his son, and two daughters—he reached Montreal. The news of the first dispersion of the colonists, their flight to Norway House, and the further threatenings of the Bois Brûlés, arrived about the time of their coming to Now York. Lord Selkirk hastened on to Montreal, but it was too late in the season, being about the end of October, to penetrate to the interior.

He must winter in Montreal. He was here in the very midst of the enemy. With energy, characteristic of the man, he brought the matter of protection of his colony urgently before the Government of Lower Canada. In a British colony surely the rights of property of a British subject would be protected, and surely the safety of hundreds of loyal people could not be trifled with. As we shall see in a later chapter, the high-minded nobleman counted without his host; he had but to live a few years in the New World of that day to find how skilfully the forms of law can be adapted to carry out illegal objects and shield law-breakers.

As early as February of that year (1815), dreading the threatenings even then made by the North-West Company, he had represented to Lord Bathurst, the British Secretary of State, the urgent necessity of an armed force, not necessarily very numerous, being sent to the Red River settlement to maintain order in the colony. Now, after the outrageous proceedings of the summer of 1815 and the arrival of the dreary intelligence from Red River, Lord Selkirk again brings the matter before the authorities, this time before Sir Gordon Drummond, Governor of Lower Canada, and encloses a full account of the facts as to the expulsion of the settlers from their homes, and of the many acts of violence perpetrated at Red River.

Nothing being gained in this way, his Lordship determined to undertake an expedition himself, as soon as it could be organized, and carry assistance to his persecuted people, who, he knew, had been gathered together by Colin Robertson, and to whom he had sent as Governor, Mr. Semple, in whom he reposed great confidence. We have seen that during the winter of 1815-16, peace and a certain degree of confidence prevailed among the settlers, more than half of whom were spending their first winter in the country. Fort Douglas was regarded as strong enough to resist a considerable attack, and the presence of Governor Semple, a military officer, was thought a guarantee for the protection of the people. During the winter, however, Lord Selkirk learned enough to assure him that the danger was not over—that, indeed, a more determined attack than ever would be made as soon as the next season should open. He had been sworn in as a Justice of the Peace in Upper Canada and for the Indian territories; he had obtained for his personal protection from the Governor the promise of a sergeant and six men of the British army stationed in Canada, but this was not sufficient.

He undertook a plan of placing upon his own land in the colony a number of persons as settlers who could be called upon in case of emergency, as had been the intention in the case of the Highland colonists, to whom muskets had been furnished. The close of the Napoleonic wars had left a large number of the soldiers engaged in these wars out of employment, the British Government having been compelled to reduce the size of the army. During the Napoleonic wars a number of soldiers of adventure from Switzerland and Italy, captured by Britain in Spain, entered her service and were useful troops. Two of these regiments, one named "De Meuron," and the other "Watteville," had been sent to Canada to assist in the war against the United States. This war being now over also, orders came to Sir Gordon Drummond to disband the two regiments in May, 1815. The former of the regiments was at the time stationed at Montreal, the latter at Kingston.

From these bodies of men Lord Selkirk undertook to provide his colony with settlers willing to defend it. The enemies of Lord Selkirk have been very free in their expression of opinion as to the worthlessness of these soldiers and their unfitness as settlers. It is worthy of notice, however, that the Nor'-Westers did not scruple to use Messrs. Missani and Brumby, as well as Reinhard and Huerter of the same corps, to carry out their own purposes. The following order, given by Sir John Coape Sherbrooke, effectually disposes of such a calumny:—

"Quebec, July 26th, 1816.

"In parting with the regiments 'De Meuron' and 'Watte-ville,' both of which corps his Excellency has had the good fortune of having under his command in other parts of the world, Sir John Sherbrooke desires Lieutenant-Colonel De Meuron and Lieutenant-Colonel May, and the officers and men of these corps will accept his congratulations on having, by their conduct in the Canadas, maintained the reputation which they have deservedly acquired by their former services. His Excellency can have no hesitation in saying that his Majesty's service in these provinces has derived important advantages during the late war from the steadiness, discipline, and efficiency of those corps."

J. HARVEY, Lieutenant-Colonel, D.A.G."

Testimony to the same effect is given by the officer in command of the garrison of Malta, on their leaving that island to come to Canada.

These men afforded the material for Lord Selkirk's purpose, viz. to till the soil and protect the colony. Like a wise man, however, he made character the ground of engagement in the case of all whom he took. To those who came to terms with him he agreed to give a sufficient portion of land, agricultural implements, and as wages for working the boats on the voyage eight dollars a month. It was further agreed that should any choose to leave Red River on reaching it, they should be taken back by his Lordship free of expense.

Early in June, 1816, four officers and about eighty men of the "De Meurons" left Montreal in Lord Selkirk's employ and proceeded westward to Kingston. Here twenty more of the "Watteville" regiment joined their company. Thence the expedition, made up by the addition of one hundred and thirty canoe-men, pushed on to York (Toronto), and from York northward to Lake Simcoe and Georgian Bay.

Across this Bay and Lake Huron they passed rapidly on to Sault Ste. Marie, Lord Selkirk leaving the expedition before reaching that place to go to Drummond's Isle, which was the last British garrison in Upper Canada, and at which point he was to receive the sergeant and six men granted for his personal protection by the Governor of Canada. At Drum-mond's Island a council was held with Kawtawabetay, an Ojibeway chief, by the Indian Department, Lieut.-Colonel Maule, of the 104th Regiment, presiding. Kawtawabetay there informed the council that in the spring of 1815 two North-West traders, McKenzie and Morrison, told him that they would give him and his people all the goods or merchandise and rum that they had at Fort William, Leach Lake, and Sand Lake, if he, the said Kawtawabetay, and his people would make and declare war against the settlers in Red River. On being asked by the chief whether this was at the request of the "great chiefs" at Montreal or Quebec, McKenzie and Morrison said it was solely from the North-West Company's agents, who wished the settlement destroyed, as it was an annoyance to them. The chief further stated that the last spring (1816), whilst at Fond Du Lac Superior, a Nor'-Wester agent (Grant) offered him two kegs of rum and two carrots of tobacco if he would send some of his young men in search of certain persons employed in taking despatches to the Red River, pillage these bearers of despatches of the letters and papers, and kill them should they make any resistance. The chief stated he had refused to have anything to do with those offers. On being asked in the council by Lord Selkirk, who was present, as to the feelings of the Indians towards the settlers at Red

River, he said that at the commencement of the Red River settlement some of the Indians did not like it, but at present they are all glad of its being settled.

Lord Selkirk soon hastened on and overtook his expedition at Sault Ste. Marie, now consisting of two hundred and fifty men all told, and these being maintained at his private expense. They immediately proceeded westward, intending to go to the extreme point of Lake Superior, near where the town of Duluth now stands, and where the name Fond du Lac is still retained. The expedition would then have gone north-westward through what is now Minnesota to Red Lake, from which point a descent could have been made by boat, through Red Lake River and Red River to the very settlement itself. This route would have avoided the Nor'-Westers altogether.

Westward bound, the party had little more than left Sault Ste. Marie, during the last week of July, when they were met on Lake Superior by two canoes, in one of which was Miles Macdonell, former Governor of Red River, who brought the sad intelligence of the second destruction of the colony and of the murder of Governor Semple and his attendants. His Lordship was thrown into the deepest despair. The thought of his Governor killed, wholesale murder committed, the poor settlers led by him from the Highland homes, where life at least was safe, to endure such fear and privation, was indeed a sore trial. To any one less moved by the spirit of philanthropy, it must have been a serious disappointment, but to one feeling so thorough a sympathy for the suffering and who was himself the very soul of honour, it was a crushing blow.

He resolved to change his course and to go to Fort William, the headquarters of the Nor'-Westers. He now determined to act in his office as magistrate, and sought to induce two gentlemen of Sault Ste. Marie, Messrs. Ermatinger and Askin, both magistrates, to accompany him in that capacity. They were unable to go. Compelled to proceed alone, he writes from Sault Ste. Marie, on July 29th, to Sir John Sherbrooke, and after speaking of his failure to induce the two gentlemen mentioned by him to go, says, "I am therefore reduced to the alternative of acting alone, or of allowing an audacious crime to pass unpunished. In these circumstances I cannot doubt that it is my duty to act, though I am not without apprehension that the law may be openly resisted by a set of people who have been accustomed to consider force as the only true criterion of right."

One would have said, on looking at the matter dispassionately, that the Governor-General, with a military force so far west as Drummond Isle in Georgian Bay, would have taken immediate steps to bring to justice the offenders.

Governor Sherbrooke seems to have felt himself powerless, for he says in a despatch to Lord Bathurst, "I beg leave to call your Lordship's serious attention to the forcible and, I fear, too just description given by the Earl of Selkirk of the state of the Red River territory. I leave to your Lordship to judge whether a banditti such as he describes will yield to the influence, or be intimidated by the menaces of distant authority." It may be well afterwards to contrast this statement of the Governor's with subsequent despatches. It must not be forgotten that while "the banditti" was pursuing its course of violence in the far-off territory, and, as has been stated, thoroughly under the direction and encouragement of the North-West Company partners, the leading members of this Company, who held, many of them, high places in society and in the Government in Montreal, were posing as the lovers of peace and order, and were lamenting over the excesses of the Indians and Bois Brûlés. By this course they were enabled to thwart any really effective measures towards restoring peace at the far-away "seat of war."

The action of the North-West Company may be judged from the following extracts from a letter of the Hon. John Richardson, one of the partners, and likewise a member of the executive council of Lower Canada, addressed to Governor Sherbrooke. He says on August 17th, 1816: "It is with much concern that I have to mention that blood has been shed at the Red River to an extent greatly to be deplored; but it is consolatory to those interested in the North-West Company to find that none of their traders or people were concerned, or at the time within a hundred miles of the scene of contest." What a commentary on such a statement are the stories of Pambrun and Huerter, given in a previous chapter! What a cold-blooded statement after all the plottings and schemes of the whole winter before the attack! What a heartless falsehood as regards the Indians, who, under so great temptations, refused to be partners in so bloody an enterprise!

The resolution of Lord Selkirk to go to Fort William in the capacity of a magistrate was one involving, as he well knew, many perils. He was not, however, the man to shrink from a daring enterprise having once undertaken it.

To Fort William, then, with the prospect of meeting several hundreds of the desperate men of the North-West Company, Lord Selkirk made his way. So confident was he in the rectitude of his purpose and in the justice of his cause, that he pushed forward, and without the slightest hesitation encamped upon the Kaministiquia, on the south side of the river, in sight of Fort William. The expedition arrived on August 12th. A demand was at once made on the officers of the North-West Company for the release of a number of persons who had been captured at Red River after the destruction of the colony and been brought to Fort William, The Nor'-Westers denied having arrested these persons, and to give colour to this assertion immediately sent them over to Lord Selkirk's encampment.

On the 13th and following days of the month of August, the depositions of a number of persons were taken before his Lordship as a justice of the peace. The depositions related to the guilt of the several Nor'-Wester partners, their destroying the settlement, entering and removing property from Fort Douglas, and the like; and were made by Pambrun, Lavigne, Nolin, Blondoau, Brisbois, and others. It was made so clear to Lord Selkirk that the partners were guilty of inciting the attacks on the colony and of approving the outrages committed, that he determined to arrest a number of the leaders. This was done by regular process—by warrants served on Mr. McGillivray, Kenneth McKenzie,

Simon Fraser, and others, but these prisoners were allowed to remain in Fort William.

In one case, that of a partner named John McDonald, resistance having been offered, the constables called for the aid of a party of the De Meurons, who had crossed over from the encampment with them in their boats. The leaving of the prisoners with their liberty in Fort William, however, gave the opportunity for conspiracy; and it was represented to Lord Selkirk that Fort William would be used for the purposes of resistance, and that the prisoners arrested would be released. The facts leading to this belief were that a canoe, laden with arms, had left the fort at night; that eight barrels of gunpowder had been secreted in a thicket, and that these had been taken from the magazine; while some forty stand of arms, fresh-loaded, had been found in a barn among some hay. These indications proved that an attempt was about to be made to resist the execution of the law, and accordingly the prisoners were placed in one building and closely guarded, while Lord Selkirk's encampment was removed across the river and pitched in front of the fort to prevent any surprise.

A further examination of the prisoners took place, and their criminality being so evident, they were sent to York, Upper Canada, Three canoes, well manned and containing the prisoners, left the fort on August 18th, under the charge of Lieutenant Fauche, one of the De Meuron officers. The journey down the lakes was marred by a most unfortunate accident. One of the canoes was upset some fifteen miles from Sault Ste. Marie. This was caused by the sudden rise in the wind. The affair was purely accidental, and there were drowned one of the prisoners, named McKenzie, a sergeant and a man of the De Meurons, and six Indians. The prisoners were taken to Montreal and admitted to bail. The course taken by Lord Selkirk at Fort William has been severely criticized, and became, indeed, the subject of subsequent legal proceedings. One of the Nor'-Wester apologists stated to Governor Sherbrooke "that the mode of proceeding under Lord Selkirk's orders resembled nothing British, and exceeded even the military despotism of the French in Holland."

No doubt it would have been better had Lord Selkirk obtained other magistrates to take part in the proceedings at Fort William, but we have seen he did try this and failed. Had it been possible to have had the arrests effected without the appearance of force made by the De Meurons, it would have been more agreeable to our ideas of ordinary legal proceedings; but it must be remembered he was dealing with those called by a high authority "a banditti." Could Fort William have been left in the hands of its possessors, it would have been better; but then there was clear evidence that the Nor'-Westers intended violence. To have left Fort William in their possession would have been suicidal. It would probably have been better that Lord Selkirk should not have stopped the canoes going into the interior with North-West merchandise, but to have allowed them to proceed was only to have assisted his enemies—the enemies, moreover, of law and order. Thousands of pounds' worth of his property stolen from Fort Douglas by the agents of the North-West Company, and the fullest evidence in the depositions made before him that this was in pursuance of a plan devised by the Company and deliberately carried out! Several hundreds of lawless voyageurs and unscrupulous partners ready to use violence in the wild region of Lake Superior, where, during fifty years preceding, they had committed numerous acts of bloodshed, and had never been called to account! The worrying reflection that homeless settlers and helpless women and children were crying, in some region then unknown to him, for his assistance, after their wanton dispersion by their enemies from their homes on the banks of Red River! All these things were sufficient to nerve to action one of far less generous impulses than Lord Selkirk.

Is it at all surprising that his Lordship did not act with all the calmness and scrupulous care of a judge on the bench, who, under favourable circumstances, feels himself strong in his consciousness of safety, supported by the myriad officers of the law, and surrounded by the insignia of justice? The justification of his course, even if it be interpreted adversely, is, that in a state of violence, to preserve the person is a preliminary to the settlement of other questions of personal right. One thing at least is to Lord Selkirk's credit, that, as soon as possible, he handed over the law-breakers to be dealt with by the Canadian Courts, where, however, unfortunately, another divinity presided than the blind goddess of justice.

Let us now see where we are in our story. Lord Selkirk is at Fort William. The Nor'-Wester partners have been sent to the East. It is near the end of August, and the state of affairs at Fort William does not allow the founder to pass on to his colony for the winter. He is surrounded by his De Meuron settlers. During the months of autumn the expedition is engaged in laying in supplies for the approaching winter, and opening up roads toward the Red River country. The season was spent in the usual manner of the Lake Superior country, shut out from the rest of the world. The winter over, Lord Selkirk started on May 1st, 1817, for Red River, accompanied by his body-guard. The De Meurons had preceded him in the month of March, and, reaching the interior, restored order.

The colonizer arrived at his colony in the last week of June, and saw, for the first time, the land of his dreams for the preceding fifteen years. In order to restore peace, he endeavoured to carry out the terms of the proclamation issued by the Government of Canada, that all property taken during the troubles should be restored to its original owners. This restitution was made to a certain extent, though much that had been taken from Fort Douglas was never recovered. The settlers were brought back from their refuge at Norway House, and the settlement was again organized. The colonists long after related, with great satisfaction, how Lord Selkirk cheered them by his presence. After their return to their despoiled homesteads a gathering of the settlers took place, and a full consideration of all their affairs was had in their patron's presence.

This gathering was at the spot where the church and burying-ground of St. John's are now found. "Here," said his Lordship, pointing to lot number four, on which they stood, "here you shall build your church; and that lot," said he, pointing to lot number three across the little stream called Parsonage Creek, "is for the school." The people then reminded his Lordship that he had promised them a minister, who should follow them to their adopted country. This he at once acknowledged, saying, "Selkirk never forfeited his word;" while he promised to give the matter attention as soon as practicable. In addition, Lord Selkirk gave a document stating that, "in consideration of the hardships which the settlers had suffered, in consequence of the lawless conduct of the North-West Company, his intention was to grant gratuitously the twenty-four lots which had been occupied to those of the settlers who had made improvements on their lands before they were driven away from them in the previous year."

Before the dispersion of this public gathering of the people, the founder gave the name, at the request of the colonists, to their settlement. The name given by him to this first parish in Rupert's Land was that of Kildonan, from their old home in the valley of Helmsdale, in Sutherlandshire, Scotland. In more fully organizing the colony, his Lordship ordered a complete survey to be made of the land, and steps to be taken towards laying out roads, building bridges, erecting mills, &c.

It will be remembered, as already stated, that at the inception of the colony scheme, in 1811, the Nor'-Westers had threatened the hostility of the Indians. It may be mentioned as a strange fact that, to this day, it is a trick of the Bois Brûlés, taking their cue from the Nor'-Westers, when making any demand, to threaten the Government with the wrath of the Indians, over whom they profess to exercise a control. We have already seen that the Nor'-Westers' boast as to their influence over the Indians was empty. In the publications of the Nor'-Westers of 1816-20 a speech is sometimes set forth of an Indian chief, "Grandes Oreilles," breathing forth threatenings against the infant settlement. It is worthy of notice that even this resource is swept away by the author of the speech, a

Nor'-Wester trader, confessing that he had manufactured the speech and "Grandes Oreilles" had never spoken it.

Within throe weeks of his arrival at Red River Lord Selkirk carried out his promise of making a treaty with the Indians. All the Indians were most willing to do this, as on many occasions during the troubles they had, by giving early information as to the movements of the Nor'-Westers, and by other means, shown their sympathy and feeling toward the settlers. The object of the treaty was simply to do what has since been done all over the north-west territories—to extinguish the Indian title. The treaty is signed alike by Ojibeway, Cree, and Assiniboine chiefs, the last mentioned being a tribe generally considered to belong to the Sioux stock. Lord Selkirk afterwards made a treaty, on leaving the Red River, with the other Sioux nations inhabiting his territory. The chiefs were met at Red River by his Lordship, and those whose names are attached to the treaty are, giving their French names in some cases as shorter than the Indian, Le Sonent, Robe Noire, Peguis, L'Homme Noir, and Grandes Oreilles. His Lordship seems to have had a most conciliatory and attractive manner. It is worth while closing this chapter by giving extracts from the speeches of these Indian chiefs, taken down at the grand council at which Lord Selkirk smoked the pipe of peace with the assembled warriors.

Peguis, the Saulteaux chief, always the fast friend of the colonists, said, "When the English settlers first came here we received them with joy. It was not our fault if even the stumps of the brushwood were too rough for their feet; but misfortunes have since overtaken them. Evil-disposed men came here, calling themselves great chiefs, sent from our Great Father across the big lake, but we believe they were only traders, pretending to be great chiefs on purpose to deceive us. They misled the young men who are near us (a small party of Bois Brûlés encamped in the neighbourhood), and employed them to shed the blood of your children and to drive away the settlers from this river. We do not acknowledge these men as an independent tribe. They have sprung up here and there like mushrooms and we know them not.

"At the first arrival of the settlers we were frequently solicited by the North-West Company to frighten them away; but we were pleased to see that our Great Father had sent some of his white children to live among us, and we refused to do or say anything against them. The traders even demanded our calumets, and desired to commit our sentiments to paper, that they might send to our Great Father; but we refused to acknowledge the speeches which they wished to put into our mouths. We are informed that they have told a tale that it was the Indians who drove away and murdered the children of our Great Father, but it is a falsehood.

"As soon as I saw the mischief that happened I went to Lake Winnipeg with a few friends to wait for news from the English, but I could meet none. We have reasons to be friends of the colony. When there were only traders here we could not get a blanket, or a piece of cloth, without furs to give in exchange. Our country is now almost destitute of furs, so that we were often in want; from the people of the colony we get blankets and cloth for the meat we procure them. The country abounds with meat, which we can obtain, but to obtain furs is difficult."

Next, L'Homme Noir, a chief of the Asiniboines, who had come from a long distance, addressing Lord Selkirk, particularly declares, "we were often harassed with solicitations to assist the Bois Brûlés in what they have done against your children, but we always refused. We are sure you must have had much trouble to come here. We have often been told you were our enemy; but we have to-day the happiness to hear from your own mouth the words of a true friend. We receive the present you give us with great pleasure and thankfulness."

After this, Robe Noire, an Ojibeway chief, spoke in like terms; when the veritable Grandes Oreilles, to whose spurious war speech we have already referred, said as follows:—"I am happy to see here our own father. Clouds have overwhelmed me. I was a long time in doubt and difficulty, but now I begin to see clearly.

"We have reason to be happy this day. We know the dangers you must have encountered to come so far. The truth you have spoken pleases us. We thank you for the present you give us. There seems an end to our distress, and it is you who have relieved us.

"When our young men are drunk they are mad; they know not what they say or what they do; but this must not be attended to; they mean no harm."

Long after, Selkirk was remembered and beloved by these Indian tribes, who spoke of him as the "Silver Chief."

So much for the founder's work in his colony in 1817. His affairs urgently required attention elsewhere. In the language of a writer of the period, "having thus restored order, infused confidence in the people, and given a certain aid to their activity, Lord Selkirk took his final leave of the colony." With a guide and a few attendants he journeyed southward, passing through the country of the warlike Sioux, with whom he made peace.

The writer had at one time in his possession a note-book with, in Lord Selkirk's writing, an itinerary of his journey from Red River Colony, in which familiar names, such as Rivière Sale, Rivière Aux Gratias, Pembina, and the like, appear with their distances in leagues. Among other memoranda is one, "lost on the Prairie," and the distance in leagues estimated as lost by the misadventure. Every traveller over the Manitoba prairie will take a feeling interest in that entry.

Passing through the Mississippi country, he seems to have proceeded eastward to Washington; he next appears in Albany, and hastens back to Upper Canada, without even visiting his family in Montreal, though he had been absent from them for upwards of a year. In Upper Canada his presence was urgently needed to meet the artful machinations of his enemies.

CHAPTER XXVII.

British law disgraced—Governor Sherbrooke's distress—A Commission decided on—Few unbiassed Canadians—Colonel Coltman chosen—Over ice and snow—Alarming rumours—The Prince Regent's order—Coltman at Red River—The Earl submissive—The Commissioner's report admirable—The celebrated Reinhart case—Disturbing lawsuits—Justice perverted—A storehouse of facts—Sympathy of Sir Walter Scott—Lord Selkirk's death—Tomb at Orthes, in France.

THE state of things in Rupert's Land in 1816 was a disgrace to British institutions. That subjects of the realm, divided into two parties, should be virtually carrying on war against each other on British soil, was simply intolerable. Not only was force being used, but warrants were being issued and the forms of law employed on both sides to carry out the selfish ends of each party. An impartial historian cannot but say that both parties were chargeable with grievous wrong.

Sir John Coape Sherbrooke, Governor-General of Canada, felt very keenly the shameful situation, and yet the difficulties of transport and the remote distance of the interior where the conflict was taking place made interference almost impossible. He was in constant communication with Lord Bathurst, the Imperial Colonial Secretary.

Governor Sherbrooke's difficulties were, however, more than those of distance. The influence of the North-West Company in Canada was supreme, and public sentiment simply reflected the views of the traders. The plan of sending a commission to the interior to stop hostilities and examine the conflicting statements which were constantly coming to the Governor, seemed the most feasible; but with his sense of British fair-play, Governor Sherbrooke knew he could find no one suitable to recommend.

At last, driven to take some action, Sir John named Mr. W. B. Coltman, a merchant of Quebec and a lieutenant-colonel in the Militia, a man accustomed to Government matters, and one who bore a good reputation for fairness and justice. With this Commissioner, who did not enter on his task with much alacrity, was associated Major Fletcher, a man of good legal qualifications.

The Commissioners were instructed to proceed immediately to the North-West. They were invested with the power of magistrates, and were authorized to make a thorough investigation into the troubles which were disturbing the country. "You are particularly," say the instructions, "to apply yourselves to mediate between the contending parties in the aforesaid territories; to remove, as far as possible, all causes of dissension between them; to take all legal measures to prevent the recurrence of those violences which have already so unhappily disturbed the public peace; and generally to enforce and establish, within the territory where you shall be, the influence and authority of the laws."

Various accidents prevented the Commissioners from leaving for the Indian country as soon as had been expected. They did not reach York (Toronto) till November 23rd, and on their arriving on the shores of Lake Huron they found the lake frozen over and impassable. They could do nothing themselves other than return to York, but they succeeded in fitting out an expedition under North-Western auspices to find its way over the ice and snow to Fort William, carrying the revocation of all the commissions of magistrates west of Sault Ste. Marie and the news of the new appointments in their stead. Reports during the winter continued to be of a disquieting kind, and as the spring drew nigh, preparations were made for sending up the Commissioners with a small armed force.

The gravity of the situation may be judged from the steps taken by the Imperial Government and the instructions sent out by the authority of George, the Prince Regent, to Governor Sherbrooke to issue a proclamation in his name calling on all parties to desist from hostilities, and requiring all military officers or men employed by any of the parties to immediately retire from such service. All property, including forts or trading stations, was to be immediately restored to the rightful owners, and any impediment or blockade preventing transport to be at once removed.

It is worthy of note that the proclamation and instructions given had the desired effect. Coltman and his fellow Commissioner left in May for the field of their operations, accompanied by forty men of the 37th Regiment as a bodyguard. On arriving at Sault Ste. Marie, Commissioner Coltman, after waiting two or three weeks, hastened on to Fort William, leaving Fletcher and the troops to follow him. On July 2nd he wrote from the mouth of the River Winnipeg, stating that his presence had no doubt tended to preserve peace in the North-West, and that in two days he would see Lord Selkirk in his own Fort Douglas at Red River.

Three days after the despatch of this letter, Commissioner Coltman arrived at Red River. He immediately grappled with the difficulties and met them with much success. The news of Lord Selkirk's actions had all arrived at Montreal through the North-West sources, so that both in Quebec and London a strong prejudice had sprung up against his Lordship. Colonel Coltman found, however, that Lord Selkirk had been much misrepresented. The illegal seizures he had made at Fort William were dictated only by prudence in dealing with what he considered a daring and treacherous enemy. He had submitted to the ordinance recalling magistrates' commissions immediately on receiving it. Colonel Coltman was so impressed with Lord Selkirk's reasonableness and good faith that he recommended that the legal charges made against him should not be proceeded with.

Colonel Coltman then started on his return journey, and wrote that he had stopped at the mouth of the Winnipeg River for the purpose of investigating the conspiracy, in which he states he fears the North-West Company had been implicated, to destroy the Selkirk settlement. The energetic Commissioner returned to Quebec in November of that year. Governor Sherbrooke had the satisfaction of reporting to Lord Bathurst the return of Mr. Coltman from his mission to the Indian territories, and "that the general result of his exertions bad been so far successful, that he had restored a degree of tranquillity there which promises to continue during the winter."

Colonel Coltman's report, of about one hundred folio pages, is an admirable one. His summary of the causes and events of the great struggle between the Companies is well arranged and clearly stated. The writer, in an earlier work, strongly took up Lord Selkirk's view of the case, and criticised Colt-man. Subsequent investigations and calmer reflection have led him to the conclusion that while Lord Selkirk was in the right and exhibited a high and noble character, yet the provoking circumstances came from both directions, and Colonel Coltman's account seems fairly impartial.

The cessation of hostilities brought about by the influence of Colonel Coltman did not, however, bring a state of peace. The conflict was transferred to the Courts of Lower and Upper Canada, these having been given power some time before by the Imperial Parliament to deal with cases in the Indian territories.

A *cause célèbre* was that of the trial of Charles Reinhart, an employé of the North-West Company, who had been a sergeant in the disbanded De Meuron Regiment. Having gone to the North-West, he was during the troubles given charge of a Hudson's Bay Company official named Owen Keveny, against whom it was urged that he had maltreated a servant of the North-West Company. In bringing Keveny down from Lake Winnipeg to Rat Portage, it was brought against Reinhart that at a place called the Falls of the River Winnipeg, he had brutally killed the prisoner under his charge. While Lord Selkirk was at Fort William, Reinhart arrived at that point and made a voluntary confession before his Lordship as a magistrate. This case was afterwards tried at Quebec and gave rise to an argument as to the jurisdiction of the Court, viz. whether the point where the murder occurred on the River Winnipeg was in Upper Canada, Lower Canada, or the Indian territories. Though Reinhart was found guilty, sentence was not carried out, probably on account of the uncertainty of jurisdiction. The Reinhart case became an important precedent in settling the boundary line of Upper Canada, and also in dealing with the troubles arising out of the Riel rebellion of 1869.

In the year after Colonel Coltman's return, numerous cases were referred to the Courts, all these arising out of the violence at Red River. Colonel Coltman had bound Lord Selkirk, though only accused of an offence amounting to a misdemeanour, in the large sum of 6,000*l.* and under two sureties of 3,000*l.* each—in all 12,000*l.* Mr. Gale, Lord Selkirk's legal adviser, called attention to the illegality of this proceeding, but all to no effect.

After Lord Selkirk had settled up his affairs with his colonists, he journeyed south from the Red River to St. Louis in the Western States, and then went eastward to Albany in New York, whence he appeared in Sandwich in Upper Canada, the circuit town where information had been laid. Here he found four accusations made against him by the North-West Company. These were: (1) Having stolen eighty-three muskets at Fort William; (2) Having riotously entered Fort William, August 13th; (3) Assault and false imprisonment of Deputy-Sheriff Smith; (4) Resistance to legal warrant.

On these matters being taken up, the first charge was so contradictory that the magistrates dismissed it; but the other three could not be dealt with on account of the absence of witnesses, and so bail was accepted from Lord Selkirk of 350*l.* for his appearance. When Lord Selkirk presented himself at Montreal to answer to the charges for which Colonel Coltman's heavy bail had bound him, the Court admitted it had no jurisdiction, but with singular high-handedness bound Lord Selkirk to appear in Upper Canada under the same bail.

In Montreal in May, 1818, an action was brought before Chief Justice Monk and Justice Bowen against Colin Robertson and four others, charging them with riotously destroying Fort Gibraltar, the Nor'-Wester fort. A number of witnesses were called, including Miles Macdonell, John Pritchard, Auguste Cadot, and others. A verdict of not guilty was rendered.

In September of the same year a charge was laid against Lord Selkirk and others of a conspiracy to ruin the trade of the North-West Company. This was before the celebrated Chief Justice Powell. The grand jury refused to give the Chief Justice an answer in the case. The Court was summarily adjourned, and legislation was introduced at the next meeting of the Legislature of Upper Canada to remedy defects in the Act in order that the case might be tried. Afterward the cases were taken up in York, and Deputy-Sheriff Smith was given a verdict against Lord Selkirk for 500*l.*, and McKenzie, a North-West partner, a verdict of 1,500*l.* for false imprisonment at Fort William. The general impression has always prevailed there that the whole procedure in these cases against Lord Selkirk was high-handed and unjust, though it is quite possible that Lord Selkirk had exceeded his powers in the troubled state of affairs at Fort William.

On his Lordship's side charges were also brought in October, 1818. In the full Court Chief Justice Powell and Justices Campbell and Boulter presided. The most notable of these cases was against Cuthbert Grant, Boucher, and sixteen others as either principals or accessories in the murder of Robert Semple on June 19th, 1816. A few days later, in the same month, a slightly different charge was brought against six of the North-West partners in connection with the murder of Governor Semple. Upwards of three hundred pages of evidence gave a minute and complete account of the affair of Seven Oaks and of the whole conflict as found in a volume of Canadian trials. In these two cases a verdict of not guilty was also rendered.

Two other trials, one by Lord Selkirk's party against Paul I Brown for robbery of a blanket and a gun, and the other against John Cooper and Hugh Bannerman for stealing a cannon in a dwelling-house of Lord Selkirk, were also carried through, with in both cases a verdict of not guilty. The evidence in these cases was printed by both parties, with foot-notes, giving a colour to each side concerned of a more favourable kind.

So much for this most disheartening controversy. It would I be idle to say that Lord Selkirk was faultless; but as we dispassionately read the accounts of the trials, and consider that while Lord Selkirk was friendless in Canada, the North-West Company had enormous influence, we cannot resist the conclusion that advantage was taken of his Lordship, and that justice was not done. It is true that, in the majority of cases, the conclusion was reached that it was impossible to precisely place the blame on either side; but we cannot be surprised that Lord Selkirk, harassed and discouraged by the difficulties of his colony and his treatment in the courts of Upper Canada and Lower Canada, should write as he did in October, 1818, to the Duke of Richmond, the new Governor-General of Canada:—

"To contend alone and unsupported, not only against a powerful association of individuals, but also against all those whose official duty it should have been to arrest them in the prosecution of their crimes, was at the best an arduous task; and, however confident one might be of the intrinsic strength of his cause, it was impossible to feel a very sanguine expectation that this alone would be sufficient to bear him up against the swollen tide of corruption which threatened to overwhelm him. He knew that in persevering under existing circumstances he must necessarily submit to a heavy sacrifice of personal comfort, incur an expense of ruinous amount, and possibly render himself the object of harassing and relentless persecution."

Though Lord Selkirk crossed the Atlantic in 1818, yet the sounds of the judicial battle through which he had passed were still in his ears. In June his friend, Sir James Montgomery, brought the matter before the British House of Commons, moving for all the official papers in the case. The motion was carried, and the Blue Book containing this matter is a storehouse where we may find the chief facts of this long and heart-breaking struggle recorded.

In June, 1818, we find in a copy of a letter in the possession of the writer, written by Sir Walter Scott, a reference to the very poor health of his Lordship. Worn out and heart-broken by his trials, Lord Selkirk did not rally, but in the course of a few months died at Pau, in the South of France, April, 1820. His Countess and daughters had accompanied him to Montreal on his Canadian visit, and they were now with him to soothe his dying hours and to see him laid to rest in the Protestant cemetery of Orthes.

Though he was engaged in a difficult undertaking in seeking so early in the century to establish a colony on the Red River, and though it has been common to represent him as being half a century before his time, yet we cannot resist the conclusion that he was an honourable, patriotic, and far-seeing man, and that the burden of right in this grand conflict was on his side.

CHAPTER XXVIII.

THE skirmish of Seven Oaks was the most notable event that ever occurred on the prairies of Rupert's Land or in the limits of the fur country. It was the crisis which indicated the determination of the Company, whose years were numbered by a century and a half, to hold its own in a great contest, and of the pluck of a British nobleman to show the "*perfervidum in-genium Scotorum*" and unflinchingly to meet either in arms or legal conflict the fur-trading oligarchy of that time in Canada. It represented, too, the fierce courage and desperate resource of the traders of the great Canadian Company, who, we have seen, were called by Washington Irving "the lords of the lakes and forests."

It was also the *dénouement* which led the Old and the New Worlds' fur companies, despite the heat of passion and their warmth of sentiment, to make a peace which saved both from impending destruction.

It led, moreover, to the sealing up for half a century of Rupert's Land to all energetic projects and influx of population, and allowed Sir George Simpson to build up for the time being the empire of the buffalo, the beaver, and the fox, instead of developing a home of industry.

Crises such as this develop character and draw out the powers of men who would otherwise waste their sweetness on the desert air. The shock of meeting of two such great bodies as the Hudson's Bay Company and the North-West Company enabled men to show courage, loyalty, honest indignation, decision of character, shrewdness, diplomatic skill, and great endurance. These are the elements of human character. It is ever worth while to examine the motives, features of action, and ends aimed at by men under the trying circumstances of such a conflict. At the risk of some repetition we give sketches of the lives of several of the leading persons concerned.

THE EARL OF SELKIRK.

Chief, certainly, of the actors who appeared on this stage was Lord Selkirk. Born to the best traditions of the Scottish nobility, Thomas Douglas belonged to the Angus-Selkirk family, which represented the Douglases of Border story, one of whom boasted that no ancestor of his had for ten generations died within chambers. Lord Daer, as his title then was, had studied at Edinburgh University, was an intimate friend of Sir Walter Scott, and though a Lowlander, had formed a great attachment for the Highlanders and had learned their language. He was, moreover, of most active mind, broad sympathies, and generous impulses. At the age of thirty years, having become Earl of Selkirk, he sought to take part in assisting the social condition of Britain, which was suffering greatly from the Napoleonic wars. He took a large colony of Highlanders to Prince Edward Island, acquired land in Upper Canada and also in New York State, and then, solely for the purpose of helping on his emigration project, entered on the gigantic undertaking of gaining control of the Hudson's Bay Company. In all these things he succeeded. We have seen the conflicts into which he was led and the manly way in which he conducted himself.

We do not say he made no mistakes. We frankly admit that he went beyond the ordinary powers of a magistrate's commission at Fort William. But we believe his aim was good. Ho was convinced that the Nor'-Westers had no legal right to the Hudson's Bay Company lands over which they traded. He believed them to be unscrupulous and dangerous, and his course was taken to meet the exigency of the case. It must be remembered his responsibility was a great one. His Highland and Irish colonists at Red River were helpless; he was their only defence; no British law was present at Red River to help them. They were regarded as intruders, as enemies of the fur trade, and he felt that loyalty and right compelled him to act as he did.

No doubt it seemed to the Canadian traders—who considered themselves as the successors of the French who, more than three-quarters of a century before, had established forts at what was called the post of the Western Sea—a high-handed and even foolhardy thing to bring his colony by way of Hudson Bay, and to plant them down at the forks on Red River, in a remote and probably unsuccessful colony. However, in the main the legal right was with his Lordship. The popular feeling in Canada toward Lord Selkirk was far from being a pure one, and a fair-minded person can hardly refrain from saying it was an interested and selfish one.

Certainly, as we see him, Lord Selkirk was a high-minded, generous, far-seeing, adventurous, courageous, and honourable man. We may admit that his opinion of the North-West Company opponents was a prejudiced and often unjust one. But we linger on the picture of his Lordship returning from Montreal with his Countess, their two young daughters, the one afterward Lady Isabella Hope, and the other Lady Katherine Wigram, with the young boy who grew up to be the last Earl of Selkirk; we think of him worried by the lawsuits and penalties of which we have spoken, going home to meet the British Government somewhat prejudiced against him as having been a personage in what they considered a dangerous *émeute*: we follow him passing over to France, attended by his family, and dying in a foreign land—and we are compelled to say, how often does the world persecute its benefactors and leave its greatest uncrowned. The Protestant cemetery at Orthes contains the bones of one who, under other circumstances, might have been crowned with laurel.

GOVERNOR MILES MACDONELL.

Engaged by Lord Selkirk to lead his first company and superintend the planting of his colony, Capt. Miles Macdonell found himself thrust into a position of danger and responsibility as local governor at Red River. He was a man with a considerable experience. Of Highland origin, he had with his father, John Macdonell, called "Scotas," from his residence in Scotland, settled in the valley of the Mohawk River, on the estates of Sir William Johnson, in New York State. The estates of Sir William were a hotbed of loyalism, and here was enlisted by his son, Sir John Johnson, under the authority of the British Government, at the time of the American Revolution, the well-known King's Royal Regiment of New York, familiarly known as the "Royal Greens." The older Macdonell was a captain in this regiment, and Miles, as a boy of fifteen, was commissioned as ensign. Afterward the young Macdonell returned to Scotland, where he married, and again came to Canada. Following a military career, he was engaged by Lord Selkirk shortly before the war of 1812 to lead his colony to the Red River. We have seen how faithfully, both at York Factory and the Red River, he served his Lordship. The chief point in dispute in connection with Governor Macdonell is whether the embargo against the export of supplies from Red River in 1814 was legal or not. If it was not, then on him rests much of the responsibility for the troubles which ensued. The seizure of pemmican, belonging to the North-West Company, at the mouth of the Souris River, seems to have been high-handed. Undoubtedly Miles Macdonell believed it to be necessary for the support of the settlers in the country. His life was one of constant worry after this event. Reprisals began between the parties. These at length ended in Miles Macdonell being seized by the North-West Company agents on June 22nd, 1815, and taken as a prisoner to Fort William, and thence to Montreal. Macdonell lived upon the Ottawa till the time of his death in 1828.

He was a man of good mind and seemingly honest intentions. His military education and experience probably gave him the habits of regularity and decision which led to the statement made of him by the Hon. William McGillivray, "that he conducted himself like a Turkish bashaw." The justification of Governor Macdonell seems to be that the Nor'-Westers had determined early in the history of the colony to destroy it, so that the charges made against the Governor wee merely an advantage taken of disputed points. Capt. Macdonell's management at York Factory was certainly judicious, and there seems but the one debatable point in his administration of Red River, and that was the proclamation of January 8th, 1814.

DUNCAN CAMERON.

One of the most notable leaders on the Nor'-Wester side was Duncan Cameron, who has the distinction of being the last commanding officer of Fort Gibraltar. Like Miles Macdonell, Duncan Cameron was the son of a Highland U. E. Loyalist, who had been settled on the Hudson in New York State. He entered the North-West Company in 1785 and fourteen years after was in charge of Nepigon district, as we have seen. He gained much distinction for his company by his daring and skilful management of the plan to induce the Selkirk settlers to leave Red River and settle in Upper Canada. Coming from the meeting of the Nor'-Westes in Grand Portage, in 1814 Cameron took up his abode in Fort Gibraltar, and according to the story of his opponents did so with much pomp and circumstance. Miles Macdonell says:—"Mr. Duncan Cameron arrived at Red River, sporting a suit of military uniform, gave himself out as captain in his Majesty's service, and acting by the King's authority for Sir George Prevost." Every well-informed person looked upon this as a self-created appointment, at most a North-West trick; but it had a very considerable effect upon the lower class of people.

In regard to this the writer in his work on "Manitoba," London, 1882, took up strong ground against Cameron. The calming influence of years, and the contention which has been advanced that there was some ground for Cameron claiming the commission in the "Voyageur Corps" which he formerly held, has led the writer to modify his opinion somewhat as to Cameron.

Cameron succeeded in leading away about three-quarters of the colony. This he was appointed to do and he seems to have done it faithfully. The means by which he appealed to the Highland colonists may have been less dignified than might have been desired, yet his warm Highland nature attracted his own countrymen in the settlement, and they probably needed little persuasion to escape from their hardships to what was to them the promised land of Upper Canada.

In the following year (1816), as already stated, Cameron was in command of Fort Gibraltar, and it was determined by Governor Semple to destroy the North-West fort and bring its material down the river to supplement the colony establishment, Fort Douglas. Before this was done the same treatment that was given to Governor Macdonell by the Nor'-Westers in arresting him was meted out to Cameron. He was seized by Colin Robertson and carried away to York Factory, to be taken as a prisoner to England. This high-handed proceeding was objectionable on several grounds. The Imperial Parliament had transferred the right of dealing with offences committed in Rupert's Land to the Courts of Canada, so that Robertson's action was clearly *ultra vires*. Moreover, if the Hudson's Bay Company under its charter exercised authority, it is questionable whether that gave the right to send a prisoner to Britain for trial, the more that no definite charge was laid against Cameron. Certainly Cameron had reason to complain of great injustice in this arrest. Taking him all in all, he was a hot, impulsive Highland leader of men, persuasive and adroit, and did not hesitate to adopt the means lying nearest to attain his purpose. The fact that from 1823 to 1828, after he had left the Company's service, he represented the County of Glengarry in the Upper Canadian Legislature, shows that those who knew him best had a favourable opinion about this last commander of Fort Gibraltar. Fort Gibraltar was never rebuilt, its place and almost its very site under the United Company being taken by the original Fort Garry. Sir Roderick Cameron, of New York, who has been connected with the Australian trade, was a son of Duncan Cameron, and still survives.

The skirmish of Seven Oaks brought into view a fact that had hardly made itself known before, viz., that a new race, the Metis, or half-breed children of the fur traders and employés by Indian women, were becoming a guild or body able to exert its influence and beginning to realize its power.

Of this rising and somewhat dangerous body a young Scottish half-breed, Cuthbert Grant, had risen to sudden prominence as the leader. His father, of the same name, had been a famous North-West trader, and was looked upon as the special guardian of the Upper Assiniboine and Swan River district. He had died in 1799, but influential as he had been, the son became from circumstances much more so. The North-West Company knew that the Scottish courage and endurance would stand them in good stead, and his Indian blood would give him a great following in the country. Educated in Montreal, he was fitted to be the leader of his countrymen. His dash and enthusiasm were his leading characteristics. When the war party came down from Qu'Appelle and Portage La Prairie, young Cuthbert Grant was its natural leader. When the fight took place he was well to the front in the *mêlee*, and it is generally argued that his influence was exerted toward saving the wounded and preventing acts of barbarity, such as savage races are prone to when the passions are aroused. On the night of June 19th, when the victory had come to his party, Cuthbert Grant took possession of Fort Douglas, and the night was one for revelry exceeding what his Highland forbears had ever seen, or equal to any exultation of the Red man in his hour of triumph.

In after years, when peace had been restored, Cuthbert Grant settled in the neighbourhood of White Horse Plains, a region twenty miles west of Red River on the Assiniboine, and here became an influential man. He was the leader of the hunt against the buffalo, on which every year the adventurous young men went to bring back their winter supply of food. In order that this might be properly managed, to protect life in a dangerous sport and to preserve the buffalo from wanton destruction, strict rules were agreed on and penalties attached to their breach. The officer appointed by the Council of Assiniboia to carry out these laws was called the "Warden of the Plains." This office Cuthbert Grant filled. Of the fifteen members of the Council of Assiniboia, Grant was one, and he largely reflected the opinion of the French half-breed population of the Red River settlement. He was the hero of the plain hunters, and the native bards never ceased to sing his praises. His case is a remarkable example of the power that native representatives obtain among mixed communities.

JOHN PRITCHARD.

The name of John Pritchard carries us back on the Red River to the beginning of the century—to a time even before the coming of the Selkirk colony. His descendants to the fourth generation are still found in Manitoba and are well known. He was born in 1777 in a small village in Shropshire, England, and received his education in the famous Grammar School of Shrewsbury. Early in the century he emigrated to Montreal. At that time the ferment among the fur traders was great. The old North-West Company of Montreal had split into sections, and to the new Company, or X Y Company, young Pritchard was attached. We first hear of him at the mouth of the Souris River in 1805, and shortly after in charge of one of the forts at that point where the Souris River empties into the Assiniboine.

We have already given the incident of Pritchard being lost on the prairie for forty days. Pritchard does not seem to have taken kindly to the United North-West Company, for at the time of the Seven Oaks affair we find him as one of the garrison occupying Fort Douglas, although he represents himself as being a settler on the Red River.

After the skirmish of Seven Oaks Pritchard sought to escape with the other settlers to the north of Lake Winnipeg, but was made prisoner by the North-West Company's agents and taken to Fort William. Thence he went east to Montreal and gave evidence in connection with the trials arising out of the Red River troubles. Pritchard was a capable and ready man. His evidence is clear and well expressed. He had much facility in doing business, and had a smooth, diplomatic manner that stood him in good stead in troublous times.

Pritchard afterwards entered Lord Selkirk's service and as his agent went over to London. Returning to the Red River settlement, he married among the people of Kildonan, and lived not far from the Kildonan Church, on the east side of the river. A number of his letters have been printed, which show that he took a lively interest in the affairs of the settlement, especially in its religious concerns. It is not, then, remarkable that among his descendants there should be no less than seven clergymen of the Church of England. It is interesting to know that the Hudson's Bay Company voted him about 1833 a gratuity of 25*l.* in consideration of valuable services rendered by him to education, and especially in the establishment of Sunday schools and day schools. This man, whose life was a chronicle of the history of the settlement, passed away in 1856 and was buried in St. John's Churchyard.

PIERRE FALCON, THE RHYMESTER.

Among the wild rout of the Nor'-Westers at the skirmish of Seven Oaks was a young French half-breed, whose father was a French Canadian engaged in the fur trade, and his mother an Indian woman from the Missouri country. The young combatant had been born in 1793, at Elbow Fort, in the Swan River district. Taken as a child to Canada, young Pierre lived for a time at Laprairie, and at the age of fifteen returned with his father to the Red River, and with him engaged in the service of the North-West Company. What part Falcon took in the affair at Seven Oaks we are not told, except that he behaved bravely, and saw Governor Semple killed.

Pierre Falcon was, however, the bard or poet of his people. This characteristic of Falcon is quite remarkable, considered in connection with the time and circumstances. That a man who was unable to read or write should have been able to describe the striking events of his time in verso is certainly a notable thing. He never tires singing in different times and metres the valour of the Bois Brûlés at Seven Oaks.

Voulez-vous écouter chanter
Une chanson do vérité?
Le dix-neuf Juin, la bande des Bois Brûlés
Sont arrivés comme des braves guerriers."

Then with French gaiety and verve he gives an account of the attack on the Orkneymen, as he calls them, and recites the Governor's action and his death. Falcon finishes up the chanson with a wild hurrah of triumph—

"Les Bois Brûlés jetaient des cris de joie."

The lively spirit of the rhymester broke out in song upon all the principal events which agitated the people of the settlement. Joseph Tasse, to whom we are chiefly indebted in this sketch, says of him, "all his compositions are not of the same interest, but they are sung by our voyageurs to the measured stroke of the oar, on the most distant rivers and lakes of the North-West. The echoes of the Assiniboine, the Mackenzie, and Hudson Bay will long repeat them."

The excitable spirit of the rhymer never left him. At the time of the Riel rebellion (1869-70) Falcon was still alive, and though between seventy and eighty years of age, he wished to march off with his gun to the fray, declaring that "while the enemy would be occupied in killing him his friends would be able to give hard and well-directed blows to the."

For about half a century he lived on the White Horse Plains, twenty miles or more up the Assiniboine from Winnipeg, and became an influential man in the neighbourhood. His mercurial disposition seems to have become more settled than in his fiery youth, for though unlettered, he was made a justice of the peace.

His verse-making was, of course, of a very simple and unfinished kind. One of his constant fashions was to end it with a declaration that it was made by Falcon, the singer of his people."

> Qui en a fait la chanson?
> Un poète de canton;
> Au bout de la chanson
> Nous vous le nommerons.
> Un jour étant à table,
> A boire et à chanter,
> A chanter tout au long
> La nouvelle chanson.
> Amis, buvons, trinquons,
> Saluons la chanson
> De Pierriche Falcon,
> Ce faiseur de chanson."

The last line being often varied to

> "Pierre Falcon, le bon garcon."

CHAPTER XXIX.

Both Companies in danger—Edward Ellice, a mediator—George Simpson, the man of destiny—Old feuds buried—Gatherings at Norway House—Governor Simpson's skill—His marvellous energy—Reform in trade—Morality low—A famous canoe voyage—Salutes fired—Pompous ceremony at Norway House—Strains of the bagpipe—Across the Rocky Mountains—Fort Vancouver visited—Great executive ability—The governor knighted—Sir George goes around the world—Troubles of a book—Meets the Russians—Estimate of Sir George.

AFFAIRS in Rupert's Land had now reached their worst and had begun to mend, the strong hand of British law had made itself felt, and hostilities had ceased from Fort William to far-off Qu'Appelle and to the farther distant Mackenzie River. The feeling of antagonism was, however, stirring in the bosoms of both parties. The death of Lord Selkirk in France brought the opposing fur traders closer together, and largely through the influence of Hon. Edward Ellice, a prominent Nor'-Wester, a reconciliation between the hostile Companies took place and a union was formed on March 26th, 1821, under the name of the Hudson's Bay Company.

The affairs of both Companies had been brought to the verge of destruction by the conflicts, and the greatest satisfaction prevailed both in England and Canada at the union. The prospect now was that the stability of the English Company and the energy of the Canadian combination would result in a great development of the fur trade.

As is so often the case, the man for the occasion also appeared. This was not an experienced man, not a man long trained in the fur trade, not oven a man who had done more than spend the winter in the fur country at Lake Athabasca. He was simply a young clerk, who had approved himself in the London Hudson's Bay Company office to Andrew Colville, a relation of the Earl of Selkirk. He was thus free from the prejudices of either party and young enough to be adaptable in the new state of things. This man was George Simpson, a native of Ross-shire, in Scotland. He was short of stature, but strong, vigorous, and observing. He was noted for an ease and affability of manner that stood him in good stead all through his forty years of experience as chief officer of the Hudson's Bay Company. He became a noted traveller, and made the canoe voyage from Montreal to the interior many times. For many years the Nor'-Westers, as we have seen, held their annual gathering at Grand Portage on Lake Superior, and it was to this place that the chief officers had annually resorted. The new element of the English Company coming in from Hudson Bay now made a change necessary. Accordingly, Norway House on Lake Winnipeg became the new centre, and for many years the annual gathering of the Company leaders in the active trade took place here. The writer has had the privilege of perusing the minutes of some of these gatherings, which were held shortly after Governor Simpson was appointed. These are valuable as showing the work done by the young Governor and his method of dealing with difficulties.

While it has always been said that Governor Simpson was dictatorial and overbearing, it will be seen that at this stage he was conciliatory and considerate. He acted like the chairman of a representative body of men called together to consult over their affairs, the members having equal rights. On June 23rd, 1823, one of his first meetings was held at Norway House. Reports were given in detail from the various posts and districts in turn. Bow River, at the foot of the Rocky Mountains, was reported as abandoned; from the Upper Red River, it was stated that on account of prairie fires the buffalo were few, and that the wild Assiniboines had betaken themselves to the Saskatchewan to enjoy its plenty.

From Lower Red River came the news that the attempt to prevent the natives trading in furs had been carried rather too far. Furs belonging to a petty trader, Laronde, had been seized, confiscated, and sent to Hudson Bay- It was learned that Laronde had not been duly aware of the new regulations, and it was ordered that compensation be made to him. This was done, and he and his family were fully satisfied. The Catholic Mission at Pembina had been moved down to the Forks, where now St. Boniface stands, and the desire was expressed that the traders should withdraw their trade as much as possible from the south side of the United States' boundary line.

The reports from the Selkirk settlement were of a favourable kind. The Sioux, who had come from their land of the Dakotas to meet Lord Selkirk, were not encouraged to make any further visits. The Selkirk colony was said to be very prosperous, and it is stated that it was the intention of the new Company soon to take over the property belonging to Lord Selkirk in the colony.

Some conflicts had arisen in the Lac La Pluie (Rainy Lake) district, and these were soothed and settled. Reference is made to the fact that Grand Portage having been found to be on United States' territory, new arrangements had been made for avoiding collision with the Americans.

Reports were even given in of prosperous trade in the far-distant Columbia, and steps were taken at various points to reduce the number of posts, the union of the Companies having made this possible.

In all these proceedings, there may be seen the influence of the diplomatic and shrewd young Governor doing away with difficulties and making plans for the extension of a successful trade in the future. It was not surprising that the Council invested Governor Simpson with power to act during the adjournment.

Sometimes at Moose Factory, now at York, then at Norway House, and again at Red River, the energetic Governor paid his visits. He was noted for the imperious and impetuous haste with which he drove his voyageurs through the lonely wilds. For years a story was prevalent in the Red River country that a stalwart French voyageur, who was a favourite with the Governor, was once, in crossing the Lake of the Woods, so irritated by the Governor's unreasonable urging, that he seized his tormentor, who was small in stature, by the shoulders, and dipped him into the lake, giving vent to his feelings in an emphatic French oath.

The Governor knew how to attach his people to himself, and he gathered around him in the course of his career of forty years a large number of men most devoted to the interests of the Company. His visits to Fort Garry on the Red River were always notable. He was approachable to the humblest, and listened to many a complaint and grievance with apparent sympathy and great patience. He had many of the arts of the courtier along with his indomitable will.

At another of his gatherings at Norway House with the traders in 1823 we have records of the greatest interest. The canoe had been the favourite craft of the Nor'-Westers, but he now introduced boats and effected a saving of one-third in wages, and he himself superintended the sending of an expedition of four boats with twenty men by way of Nelson River from York Factory to far distant Athabasca. He was quick to see those who were the most profitable as workmen for the Company. On one occasion he gives his estimate as follows: "Canadians (i.e., French Canadians) preferable to Orkneymen. Orkneymen less expensive, but slow. Less physical strength and spirits. Obstinate if brought young into the service. Scotch and Irish, when numerous, quarrelsome, independent, and mutinous."

At this time it was determined to give up the practice of bestowing presents upon the Indians. It was found better to pay them liberally for their pelts, making them some advances for clothing.

The minutes state at this time that there was little progress in the moral and religious instruction of the Indians. The excessive use of spirits, which still continued, was now checked; the quantity given in 1822 and 1823 was reduced one-half and the strength of the spirits lowered. Missionaries could not be employed with success, on account of the small number of Indians at any one point. The only hope seemed to be to have schools at Red River and to remove the children from their parents to these. Many difficulties, arising from the objections of the parents, were, however, sure to come in the way.

Evidences were not wanting of chief factors being somewhat alienated from the Governor, but those dissatisfied were promptly invited to the Council and their coolness removed. In carrying out discipline among the men some difficulty was experienced, as the long conflicts between the Companies had greatly demoralized the employés. One plan suggested was that offenders should be fined and the fines vested in a charitable fund. It was found that this would only do for Europeans. "A blow was better for a Canadian," and though this was highly reprobated, it was justified by experience.

At a meeting at York Factory instructions were given to Chief Factor Stuart on Lake Superior to complete and launch a new vessel much larger than the Discovery, then afloat. Captain Bayfield, R.N., the British officer surveying the lakes, wintered at this time with his crew at Fort William, and the work of surveying the lakes promised to take him three summers.

The following entry, September 5th, 1823, shows the considerate way in which the Governor sought the advice of his Council:—"Governor Simpson requested permission to visit England. If granted, will hold himself ready to return to Canada in 1825 and proceed by express canoe in time to make arrangements for the season." At the same date, 1823, a step in advance was taken in having a permanent and representative council to regulate the affairs of Red River Settlement. The entry reads, "Captain Robert Parker Pelly, Governor of Assiniboia, Rev. Mr. West, Rev. Mr. Jones, Mr. Logan added to the council. Jacob Corrigal, chief trader, appointed sheriff, vice Andrew Stewart, deceased. Rev. Mr. Jones appointed chaplain at a salary of 100l. during absence of Mr. West. He will officiate at Red River."

There lies before the writer a work entitled "Peace River; a Canoe Voyage from the Hudson Bay to the Pacific." It was written by Archibald Macdonald and annotated between forty and fifty years after by Malcolm McLeod, of Ottawa. It gives a graphic account of the state maintained by Governor Simpson and his method of appealing to the imagination of the Indians and Company servants alike. The journey was made from ocean to ocean, the point of departure being York Factory, on Hudson Bay, and the destination Fort Vancouver, on the Columbia River. In addition to Macdonald, Governor Simpson took with him Dr. Hamlyn as medical adviser, and in two light canoes, provided with nine men each, the party went with extraordinary speed along the waterways which had already been the scenes of many a picturesque and even sanguinary spectacle.

Fourteen chief officers—factors and traders—and as many more clerks were summoned on July 12th, 1828, to give a send-off to the important party. As the pageant passed up Hayes River, loud cheers were given and a salute of seven guns by the garrison. The voyageurs then struck up one of the famous chansons by which they beguiled the lonely waterways, and with their dashing paddles, hastened away to the interior.

So well provided an expedition, with its tents for camping, suitable utensils for the camp fire, arms to meet any danger, provisions including wine for the gentlemen, and spirits for the voyageurs, was not long in ascending the watercourses to Norway House, where the outlet of Lake Winnipeg was reached.

The arrival at Norway House was signalized by much pomp. The residents of the fort were on the qui vive for the important visitor. The Union Jack, with its magic letters "H. B. C," floated from the tall flagstaff of Norway pine, erected on Signal Hill. Indians from their neighbouring haunts were present in large numbers, and the lordly Red men, at their best when "en fete," were accompanied by bevies of their dusky mates, who looked with admiring gaze on the "Kitche Okema" who was arriving.

The party had prepared for the occasion. They had, before reaching the fort, landed and put themselves in proper trim and paid as much attention to their toilets as circumstances would permit. Fully ready, they resumed their journey, and with flashing paddles speeded through the deep rocky gorge, quickly turned the point, and from the gaudily painted canoe of the Governor with high prow, where sat the French Canadian guide, who for the time commanded, there pealed forth the strains of the bagpipes, while from the second canoe was heard the sound of the chief factor's bugle. As the canoes came near the shore, the soft and lively notes fell on the ear of "La Claire Fontaine" from the lively voyageurs. Altogether, it was a scene very impressive to the quiet residents of the post.

The time of the Governor was very fully occupied at each stopping-place. A personal examination and inspection of each post, of its officers and employés, buildings, books, trade, and prospects was made with "greatest thoroughness." Fond as the Governor was of pomp, when the pageant was passed, then he was a man of iron will and keenest observation. His correspondence at each resting-place was great, and he was said to be able to do the work of three men, though twelve years after the date of the present journey he became affected with partial blindness.

Fort Chipewyan had always maintained its pre-eminence as an important depot of the fur trade. The travelling emperor of the fur traders was captured by its picturesque position as well as by its historic memories. Here he found William McGillivray, with whose name the fur traders conjured, and under invitation from the Governor the former Nor'-Wester and his family joined the party in crossing the Rockies. The waving of flags, firing of guns, shouting of the Indians and employés, and the sound of singing and bagpipe made the arrival and departure as notable as it had been at Norway House.

A little more than a month after they had left York Factory the indomitable travellers entered Peace River, in order to cross the Rocky Mountains. Fort Vermilion, Fort Dunvegan, St. John, all had their objects of interest for the party, but one of the chief was that it was a scarce year, and at Dunvegan, as well as at Fort McLeod across the mountains, there was not enough of food at hand to supply the visitors. Cases of dispute were settled by the Governor, who presided with the air of a chief justice. Caution and advice were given in the most impressive fashion, after the manner of a father confessor, to the Indians, fault being found with their revelries and the scenes of violence which naturally followed from these.

From McLeod to Fort St. James the journey was made by land. Thus the crest of the Rocky Mountains was crossed, the voyageurs packing on their shoulders the impedimenta, and horses being provided for the gentlemen of the party. This was the difficult portage which so often tried the traders. Fort St. James, it will be remembered, was at Lake Stuart, where Fraser started on his notable journey down the Fraser River. It was the chief place and emporium of New Caledonia. The entry is thus described: "Unfurling the British ensign, it was given to the guide, who marched first. After him came the band, consisting of buglers and bagpipers. Next came the Governor, mounted, and behind him Hamlyn and Macdonald also on horses. Twenty men loaded like beasts of burden, formed the line; after them a loaded horse; and finally, McGillivray with his wife and family brought up the rear."

Thus arranged, the imposing body was put in motion. Passing over a gentle elevation, they came in full view of the fort, when the bugle sounded, a gun was fired, and the bagpipes struck up the famous march of the clans, "Si coma leum codagh na sha" ("If you will it, war"). Trader Douglas, who was in charge of the fort, replied with small ordnance and guns, after which he advanced and received the distinguished visitors in front of the fort.

Passing on, by September 24th the party came to Fort Alexandria, four days down the Fraser, and reached Kamloops, the junction of the North and South Thompson. At every point of importance, the Governor took occasion to assemble the natives and employés, and gave them good advice, "exhorting them to honesty, frugality, temperance," finishing his prelections with a gift of tobacco or some commodity appreciated by them. Running rapids, exposed to continual danger, but fortunate in their many escapes, they reached Fort Langley, near the mouth of the Fraser River, two days less than three months from the time of their starting from York Factory. From this point, Governor Simpson made his way to Fort Vancouver on the Columbia, then the chief post on the Pacific Coast, and in the following year returned over the mountains, satisfied that he had gained much knowledge and that he had impressed himself on trader, engagé, and Indian chief alike.

With marvellous energy, the Governor-in-Chief, as he was called, covered the vast territory committed to his care. Establishments in unnecessary and unremunerative places were cut down or closed. Governor Simpson, while in some respects fond of the "show and circumstance" which an old and honourable Company could afford, was nevertheless a keen business man, and never forgot that he was the head of a Company whose object was trade. It cannot be denied that the personal element entered largely into his administration. He had his favourites among the traders, he was not above petty revenges upon those who thwarted his plans, and his decisions were sometimes harsh and tyrannical, but his long experience, extending over forty years, was marked on the whole by most successful administration and by a restoration of the prestige of the Company, so nearly destroyed at the time of the union.

In the year 1839, when the Colonial Office was engaged in settling up the Canadian rebellion which a blundering colonial system had brought upon both Lower and Upper Canada, the British Government sought to strengthen itself among those who had loyally stood by British influence. Governor Simpson and the whole staff of the Hudson's Bay Company had been intensely loyal, and it was most natural and right that the young Queen Victoria, who had lately assumed the reins of power, should dispense such a favour as that of knighthood on the doughty leader of the fur traders. Sir George Simpson worthily bore the honours bestowed upon him by his Sovereign, and in 1841 undertook a voyage round the world, crossing, as he did so, Rupert's Land and the territories in his rapid march. Two portly volumes containing an itinerary of the voyage, filling nine hundred pages, appeared some five years after this journey was completed. This work is given in the first person as a recital by the Governor of what he saw and passed through. Internal evidence, however, as well as local tradition on the Red River, shows another hand to have been concerned in giving it a literary form. It is reported that the moulding agent in style and arrangement was Judge Thom, the industrious and strong-minded recorder of the Red River Settlement.

The work is dedicated to the directors of the Hudson's Bay Company. These were nine in number, and their names are nearly all well known in connection with the trade of this period. Sir John Henry Pelly, long famous for his leadership; Andrew Colville, Deputy-Governor, who, by family connection with Lord Selkirk, long held an important place; Benjamin Harrison; John Halkett, another kinsman of Lord Selkirk; H. H. Berens; A. Chapman, M.P.; Edward Ellice, M.P., a chief agent in the Union and a most famous trader; the Earl of Selkirk, the son of the founder; and R. Weynton. The names of almost all these traders will be found commemorated in forts and trading-posts throughout Rupert's Land.

Leaving London, March 3rd, 1841, the Governor called at Halifax, but disembarked at Boston, went by land to Montreal, and navigation being open on May 4th on the St. Lawrence, he and his party started and soon reached Ste. Anne, on Montreal Island. The evidence of the humour of Sir George's editor, who knew Montreal well, is seen in his referring to Moore's "Canadian Boat Song," in saying, "At Ste. Anne's Rapid, on the Ottawa, we neither sang our evening hymn nor bribed the Lady Patroness with shirts, caps, &c., for a propitious journey; but proceeded." Following the old canoe route, Georgian Bay and Lake Superior were soon passed over, though on the latter lake the expedition was delayed about a week by the ice, and here too Sir George met the sad news of the unfortunate death of his kinsman, Thomas Simpson, of whom we shall speak more fully in connection with Arctic exploration. Taking the route from Fort William by Kaministiquia, the travellers hastened over the course by way of Rainy Lake and River and Lake of the Woods. In referring to Rainy River the somewhat inflated style of the editor makes Sir George speak without the caution which every fur trader was directed to cultivate in revealing the resources of the fur country. A decade afterwards Mr. Roebuck, before the Committee of the House of Commons, "heckled" Sir George over this fulsome passage. The passage is: "From the very brink of the river (Rainy River) there rises a gentle slope of greenwood, crowned in many places with a plentiful growth of birch, poplar, beech, elm, and oak. Is it too much for the eye of philanthropy to discern, through the vista of futurity, this noble stream, connecting, as it does, the fertile shores of two spacious lakes, with crowded steamboats on its bosom and populous towns on its borders?"

Following the usual route by River Winnipeg, Lake Winnipeg, and Red River, Fort Garry was soon reached, and here the Governor somewhat changed his plans. He determined to cross the prairies by light conveyances, and accordingly on July 3rd, at five in the morning, with his fellow-travellers, with only six men, three horses, and one light cart, the Emperor of the Plains left Fort Garry under a salute and with the shouting of the spectators, as he started on his journey to skirt the winding Assiniboine River.

A thousand miles over the prairie in July is one of the most cheery and delightsome journeys that can be made. The prairie flowers abound, their colours have not yet taken on the full blaze of yellow to be seen a month later, and the mosquitoes have largely passed away on the prairies. The weather, though somewhat warm, is very rarely oppressive on the plains, where a breeze may always be felt. This long journey the party made with most reckless speed—doing it in three weeks, and arriving at Edmonton House, to be received by the firing of guns and the presence of nine native chiefs of the Blackfeet, Piegans, Sarcees, and Bloods, dressed in their grandest clothes and decorated with scalp locks. "They implored me," says the Governor, "to grant their horses might always be swift, that the buffalo might instantly abound, and that their wives might live long and look young."

Four days sufficed at Edmonton on the North Saskatchewan to provide the travellers with forty-five fresh horses. They speedily passed up the Saskatchewan River, meeting bands of hostile Sarcees, using supplies of pemmican, and soon catching their first view of the white peaks of the Rocky Mountains. Deep muskegs and dense jungles were often encountered, but all were overcome by the skill and energy of the expert fur trader Row and their guide. Through clouds of mosquitoes they advanced until the sublime mountain scenery was beheld whenever it was not obscured with the smoke arising from the fires through this region, which was suffering from a very dry season. At length Fort Colville, on the Columbia River, was gained after nearly one thousand miles from Edmonton; and this journey, much of it mountain travelling, had averaged forty miles a day. The party from Fort Garry had been travelling constantly for six weeks and five days, and they had averaged eleven and a half hours a day in the saddle. The weather had been charming, with a steady cloudless sky, the winds were light, the nights cool, and the only thing to be lamented was the appearance of the whole party, who, with tattered garments and crownless hats, entered the fort.

Embarking below the Chaudiere Falls of the Columbia, the company took boats, worked by six oars each, and the Mater being high they were able to make one hundred, and even more miles a day, in due course reaching Fort Vancouver.

At Fort Vancouver Governor Simpson met Trader Douglas— afterward Sir James Douglas. He accompanied the party, which now took horses and crossed country by a four days' journey to Fort Nisqually. Here on the shore of Puget Sound lay the ship *Beaver*, and embarking on her the party went on their journey to Sitka, the chief place in Alaska, whence the Governor exchanged dignified courtesies with the Russian Governor Etholin, and enjoyed the hospitality of his "pretty and lady-like" wife. In addition, Governor Simpson examined into the Company's operations (the Hudson's Bay Company had obtained exclusive licence of this sleepy Alaska for twenty years longer), and found the trade to be 10,000 fur seals, 1000 sea otters, 12,000 beaver, 2500 land otters,------foxes and martins, 20,000 sea-horse teeth.

The return journey was made, the *Beaver* calling, as she came down the coast, at Forts Stikine, Simpson, and McLoughlin. In due course Fort Vancouver was reached again. Sir George's journey to San

Francisco, thence to Sandwich Islands, again direct to Alaska, and then westward to Siberia, and over the long journey through Siberia on to St. Petersburg, we have no special need to describe in connection with our subject. The great traveller reached Britain, having journeyed round the globe in the manner we have seen, in nineteen months and twenty-six days.

Enough has been shown of Sir George's career, his administration, method of travel, and management, to bring before us the character of the man. At times he was accompanied on his voyages to more accessible points by Lady Simpson, and her name is seen in the post of Fort Frances on Rainy River and in Lake Frances on the upper waters of the Liard River, discovered and named by Chief Factor Robert Campbell. Sir George lived at Lachine, near Montreal, where so many retired Hudson's Bay Company men have spent the sunset of their days. He took an interest in business projects in Montreal, held stock at one time in the Allan Line of steamships, and was regarded as a leader in business and affairs in Montreal. He passed away in 1860. Sir E. W. Watkin, in his work, "Recollections of Canada and the States," gives a letter from Governor Dallas, who succeeded Sir George, in which reference is made to "the late Sir George Simpson, who for a number of years past lived at his ease at Lachine, and attended more apparently to his own affairs than to those of the Company." Whether this is a true statement, or simply the biassed view of Dallas, who was rather rash and inconsiderate, it is hard for us to decide.

Governor Simpson lifted the fur trade out of the depth into which it had fallen, harmonised the hostile elements of the two Companies, reduced order out of chaos in the interior, helped, as we shall see, various expeditions for the exploration of Rupert's Land, and though, as tradition goes and as his journey around the world shows, he never escaped from the witchery of a pretty face, yet the business concerns of the Company were certainly such as to gain the approbation of the financial   world.

CHAPTER XXX.

IT was an empire that Governor Simpson established in the solitudes of Rupert's Land. The chaos which had resulted from the disastrous conflict of the Companies was by this Napoleon of the fur trade reduced to order. Men who had been in arms against one another—Macdonell against Macdonell, McLeod against McLeod—learned to work together and gathered around the same Council Board. The trade was put upon a paying basis, the Indians were encouraged, and under a peaceful rule the better life of the traders began to grow up.

It is true this social life was in many respects unique. The trading posts were often hundreds of miles apart, being scattered over the area from Labrador to New Caledonia. Still, during the summer, brigades of traders carried communications from post to post, and once or twice in winter the swift-speeding dog-trains hastened for hundreds of miles with letters and despatches over the icy wastes. There grew up during the well-nigh forty years of George Simpson's governorship a comradeship of a very strong and influential kind.

Leading posts like York Factory on Hudson Bay, Fort Garry in the Red River settlement, Fort Simpson on the Mackenzie River, and Fort Victoria on the Pacific Coast, were not only business centres, but kept alive a Hudson's Bay Company sentiment which those who have not met it can hardly understand. Letters were written according to the good old style. Not mere telegraphic summaries and business orders as at the present day, but real news-letters—necessary and all the more valuable because there were no newspapers in the land. The historian of to-day finds himself led back to a very remarkable and interesting social life as he reads the collection of traders' letters and hears the tales of retired factors and officers. Specimens and condensed statements from these materials may help us to picture the life of the period.

QUEER OLD PETER FIDLER.

Traditions have come down from this period of men who were far from being commonplace in their lives and habits. Among the most peculiar and interesting of these was an English trader, Peter Fidler, who for forty years played his part among the trying events preceding Governor Simpson's time, and closed his career in the year after the union of the Companies. The quaint old trader, Peter Fidler, is said to have belonged to the town of Bolsover, in the County of Derby, England, and was born August 16th, 1769. From his own statement we know that he kept a diary in the service of the Company beginning in 1791, from which it is inferred that he arrived in Rupert's Land about that time and was then engaged in the fur trade. Eight years afterwards he was at Green Lake, in the Saskatchewan district, and about the same time in Isle à la Crosse. In this region he came into active competition with the North-West Company traders, and became a most strenuous upholder of the claims of the Hudson's Bay Company.

Promoted on account of his administrative ability, he is found in the early years of the new century at Cumberland House, the oldest post of the Company in the interior. His length of service at the time of the establishment of the Selkirk colony being above twenty years, he was entrusted with the conduct of one of the parties of settlers from Hudson Bay to Red River.

In his will, a copy of which lies before the writer, it is made quite evident that Fidler was a man of education, and he left his collection of five hundred books to be the nucleus of a library which was afterwards absorbed into the Red River library, and of which volumes are to be seen in Winnipeg to this day.

But Fidler was very much more than a mere fur trader. He is called in his will "Surveyor" and trader for the Honourable Hudson's Bay Company. He was stated to have made the boundary survey of the district of Assiniboia, the limits of which have been already referred to in the chapter on Lord Selkirk. He also surveyed the lots for the Selkirk settlers, in what was at that time the parish of Kildonan. The plan of the Selkirk settlement made by him may be found in Amos's Trials and in the Blue Book of 1819, and this proved to be of great value in the troublesome lawsuits arising out of the disputes between the fur companies. The plan itself states that the lots were established in 1814; and we find them to be thirty-six in number.

About the same time Fidler was placed in charge of the Red River district, and it is said that the traders and clerks found him somewhat arbitrary and headstrong. As the troubles were coming on, and Governor Semple had taken command of the Red River Company's fort and colony, Fidler was placed in charge of Brandon House, then a considerable Hudson's Bay Company Fort. He gives an account of the hostilities between the Companies there and of the seizure of arms. He continues actively engaged in the Company's service, and from his will being made at Norway House, this would seem to have been his headquarters, although in the official statement of the administration of his effects he is stated to be "late of York Factory."

Mr. Justice Archer Martin, in his useful book, "Hudson's Bay Company's Land Tenure," gives us an interesting letter of Alexander McLean to Peter Fidler, dated 1821. This is the time of the Union of the Hudson's Bay Company and the North-West Company. In the letter mention is made of the departure for New York of (Mr. Nicholas) Garry, a gentleman of the honourable committee, and of Mr. Simon McGillivray, one of the North-West Company. We have spoken elsewhere of Mr. Garry's visit, and a few years afterward Fort Garry was named after this officer.

The chief interest to us, however, centres in Fidler's eccentric will. We give a synopsis of it:—

(1) He requests that he may be buried at the colony of Red River should he die in that vicinity.

(2) He directs that his journals, covering twenty-five or thirty years, also four or five vellum bound books, being a fair copy of the narrative of his journeys, as well as astronomical and meteorological and thermometrical observations, also his manuscript maps, be given to the committee of the Honourable Hudson's Bay Company.

(3) The books already mentioned making up his library, his printed maps, two sets of twelve-inch globes, a large achromatic telescope, Wilson's microscope, and a brass sextant, a barometer, and all his thermometers were to be taken by the Governor of the Red River colony and kept in Government hands for the general good of the Selkirk colonists.

(4) Cattle, swine, and poultry, which he had purchased for one hundred pounds from John Wills, of the North-West Company, the builder of Fort Gibraltar, were to be left for the solo use of the colony, and if any of his children were to ask for a pair of the aforesaid animals or fowls their request was to be granted.

(5) To his Indian wife, Mary Fidler, he bequeathed fifteen pounds a year for life to be paid to her in goods from the Hudson's Bay Company store, to be charged against his interest account in the hands of the Company.

(6) The will required further that of all the rest of the money belonging to him, in the hands of the Hudson's Bay Company or the Bank of England, as well as the legacy left him by his Uncle Jasper Fidler and other moneys due him, the interest be divided among his children according to their needs.

(7) After the interest of Fidler's money had been divided among his children till the youngest child Peter should come of age, the testator makes the following remarkable disposal of the residue: "All my money in the funds and other personal property after the youngest child has attained twenty-one years of age, to be placed in the public funds, and the interest annually due to be added to the capital and continue so

until August 16th, 1969 (I being born on that day two hundred years before), when the whole amount of the principal and interest so accumulated I will and desire to be then placed at the disposal of the next male child heir in direct descent from my son Peter Fidler" or to the next-of-kin. He leaves his "Copyhold land and new house situated in the town of Bolsover, in the county of Derby," after the death of Mary Fidler, the mother of the testator, to be given to his youngest son, Peter Fidler.

This will was dated on August 16th, 1821, and Fidler died in the following year. The executors nominated were the Governor of the Hudson's Bay Company, the Governor of the Selkirk settlement, and the secretary of the Hudson's Bay Company.

Some time after the death of this peculiar man, John Henry Pelly, Governor-in-Chief of the Hudson's Bay Company, Donald McKenzie, Governor of the Selkirk settlement, and William Smith, Secretary of the Hudson's Bay Company, renounced the probate and execution of the will, and in October, 1827, "Thomas Fidler," his natural and lawful son, was appointed by the court to administer the will.

A considerable amount of interest in this will has been shown by the descendants of Peter Fidler, a number of whom still live in the province of Manitoba, on the banks of the Red and Assiniboine Rivers. Lawyers have from time to time been appointed to seek out the residue, which, under the will, ought to be in process of accumulation till 1969, but no trace of it can be found in Hudson's Bay Company or Bank of England accounts, though diligent search has been made.

STUBBORN JOHN MCLEOD.

John McLeod has already figured in our story. Coming out with Lord Selkirk's first party from the Island of Lewis, as one of the "twelve or thirteen young gentleman clerks," he, as we have seen, gave a good account of himself in the "imminent and deadly breach," when he defended the Hudson's Bay Company encampment at the Forks against the fierce Nor'-Westers. His journal account of that struggle we found to be well told, even exciting. It further gives a picture of the fur trader's life, as seen with British eyes and by one of Hudson's Bay Company sympathies.

He met at the Forks, immediately on his arrival, three chiefs of the Nor'-Westers. One of these was John Wills, who, as an old X Y trader, had joined the Nor'-Westers and shortly after built Fort Gibraltar. A second of the trio was Benjamin Frobisher, of the celebrated Montreal firm of that name, who perished miserably; and the last was Alexander Macdonell, who was commonly known as "Yellow Head," and afterward became the "Grasshopper Governor."

McLeod vividly describes the scene on his arrival, when the Hudson's Bay Company, as represented by trader William Hillier, formally transferred to Miles Macdonell, Lord Selkirk's agent, the grant of land and the privileges pertaining thereto. The ceremony was performed in the presence of the settlers and other spectators. McLeod quaintly relates that the three bourgeois mentioned were present on his invitation, but Wills would not allow his men to witness the transaction, which consisted of reading over the concession and handing it to Macdonell. Hugh Henney, the local officer in charge of the Hudson's Bay Company affairs, then read over the concession in French for the benefit of the voyageurs and free traders.

McLeod relates a misadventure of irascible Peter Fidler in dealing with a trader, Pangman, who afterwards figured in Red River affairs. After Henney had taken part in the formal cession, he departed, leaving McLeod and Pangman in charge of the Hudson's Bay Company interests at the Forks. McLeod states that prior to this time (1813), the Hudson's Bay Com-pany "had no house at this place" thus disposing of a local tradition that there was a Hudson Bay trading post at the Forks before Lord Selkirk's time. McLeod, however, proceeded immediately to build "a good snug house." This was ready before the return of the fall craft (trade), and it was this house that McLeod so valiantly defended in the following year.

During the summer McLeod found Pangman very useful in meeting the opposition of the North-West Company traders. Peter Pangman was a German who had come from the United States, and was hence called "Bostonnais Pangman," the title Bostonnais being used in the fur-trading country for an American. Fidler, who had charge of the district for the Hudson's Bay Company, refused to give the equipment promised by Henney to Pangman. McLeod speaks of the supreme blunder of thus losing, for the sake of a few pounds, the service of so capable a man as Pangman. Pangman left the Hudson's Bay Company service, joined the Nor'-Westers, and was ever after one of the most bitter opponents of the older Company. After many a hostile blow dealt to his opponents, Pangman retired to Canada, where he bought the Seigniory of Lachenaie, and his son was an influential public man in Lower Canada, Hon. John Pangman.

Events of interest rapidly followed one another at the time of the troubles. After the fierce onset at the Forks had been met by McLeod, he was honoured by being sent 500 miles south-westward by his senior officer, Colin Robertson, with horses, carts, and goods, to trade with the Indians on the plains. This daring journey he accomplished with only three men—"an Orkneyman and two Irishmen." In early winter he had returned to Pembina, where he was to meet the newly-appointed Governor, Robert Semple. McLeod states that Semple was appointed under the resolution of the Board of Directors in London on May 19th, 1811, first Governor of Assiniboia. From this we are led to think that Miles Macdonell was Lord Selkirk's agent only, and was Governor by courtesy, though this was not the case.

The unsettled state of the country along the boundary line is shown in a frightful massacre spoken of by McLeod. On a journey down the Red River, McLeod had spent a night near Christmas time in a camp of the Saulteaux Indians. He had taken part in their festivities and passed the night in their tents. He was horrified to hear a few days after at Pembina that a band of Sioux had, on the night of the feast, fallen upon the camp of Saulteaux, which was composed of thirty-six warriors, and that all but three of those making up the camp had been brutally killed in a night attack. On his return to his post McLeod passed the scene of the terrible massacre, and he says he saw "the thirty-three slain bodies scalped, the knives and arrows and all that had touched their flesh being left there."

McLeod was noted for his energy in building posts. Ho erected an establishment on Turtle River; and in the year after built a trading house beyond Lake Winnipeg, at the place where Oxford House afterward stood.

McLeod, being possessed of courage and energy, was sent west to Saskatchewan, where, having wintered in the district with traders Bird and Pruden, and faced many dangers and hardships, he returned to Red River and was among those arrested by the Nor'-Westers. He was sent to Montreal, where, after some delay, the charge against him was summarily dismissed. He was, while there, summoned as a witness in the case against Reinhart in Quebec.

In Montreal McLeod was rejoiced to meet Lady Selkirk, the wife of his patron, from whom he received tokens of confidence and respect.

The trader had a hand in the important movement by which Lord Selkirk provided for his French and German dependents on the Red River, who belonged to the Roman Catholic faith, the ordinances of religion. As we shall see, Lord Selkirk secured, according to his promise, the two priests Provencher and Dumoulin, and with them sent out a considerable number of French Canadians to Red River.

McLeod's account of his part in the matter is as follows:—"On my way between Montreal and Quebec, I took occasion, with the help of the good Roman Catholic priests, Dumoulin of Three Rivers, and Provencher of Montreal, to beat up recruits for the Hudson's Bay Company service and the colony among the French Canadians. On the opening of navigation about May 1st, I started, in charge with a brigade of seven large canoes, and with about forty Canadians, some with their families, headed by my two good friends the priests—the first missionaries in the north since the time of the French before the conquest. Without any loss or difficulty, I conducted the whole through to Norway House, whence in due course they were taken in boats and schooner to Red River. At this place we had a navy on the lake, but lately under the command of Lieutenant Holt, one of the victims of 1816. Holt had been of the Swedish navy."

At Norway House McLeod's well-known ability and trustworthiness led to his appointment to the far West, "and from this time forth his field was northward to the Arctic." He had the distinguished honour of establishing a permanent highway, by a line of suitable forts and trade establishments to the Peace River region. While in charge of his post he had the pleasure of entertaining Franklin (the noble Sir John) on his first Arctic land expedition, and afterwards at Norway House saw the same distinguished traveller on his second journey to the interior of the North land.

After the union of the Companies, McLeod, now raised to the position of Chief Trader, was the first officer of the old Hudson's Bay Company to be sent across the Rocky Mountains to take charge of the district in New Caledonia. Among the restless and vindictive natives of that region he continued for many years with a good measure of success, and ended up a career of thirty-seven years as a successful trader and thorough defender of the name and fame of the Hudson's Bay Company, by retiring to spend the remainder of his days, as so many of the traders did, upon the Ottawa River.

WILLARD FERDINAND WENTZEL'S DISLIKES AND THE NEW RÉGIME.

Wentzel was a Norwegian who had entered the North-West Company in 1799, and spent most of his time in Athabasca and Mackenzie River districts, where he passed the hard life of a "winterer" in the northern department. He was intelligent, but a mimic—and this troublesome cleverness prevented his promotion in the Company. He co-operated with Franklin the explorer in his journey to the Arctic Ocean. Wentzel was a musician—according to Franklin "an excellent musician." This talent of his brightened the long and dreary hours of life and contributed to keep all cheerful around him. A collection of the voyageur songs made by him is in existence, but they are somewhat gross. Wentzel married a Montagnais Indian woman, by whom he had two children. One of them lived on the Red River and built the St. Norbert Roman Catholic Church in 1855. From Wentzel's letters we quote extracts showing the state of feeling at the time of the union of the fur companies in 1821 and for a few years afterwards.

March 20*th*, 1821.—"In Athabasca, affairs seem to revive; the natives are beginning to be subjected by the rivalship in trade that has been carried on so long, and are heartily desirous of seeing themselves once more in peaceable times, which makes the proverb true that says, 'Too much of a good thing is good for nothing.' Besides, the Hudson's Bay Company have apparently realized the extravagance of their measures; last autumn they came into the department with fifteen canoes only, containing each about fifteen pieces. Mr. Simpson (afterward Sir George), a gentleman from England last spring, superintends their business. His being a stranger, and reputedly a gentlemanly man, will not create much alarm, nor do I presume him formidable as an Indian trader. Indeed, Mr. Leith, who manages the concerns of the North-West Company in Athabasca, has been so liberally supplied with men and goods that it will be almost wonderful if the opposition can make good a subsistence during the winter. Fort Chipewyan alone has an equipment of no less than seventy men, enough to crush their rivals." (Editor's note.—Another year saw Simpson Governor of the United Company.)

April 10*th*, 1823.—"Necessity rather than persuasion, however, influenced me to remain; my means for future support are too slender for me to give up my employment, but the late revolution in the affairs of the country (the coalition of the Hudson's Bay Company with the North-West Company in 1821) now obliges me to leave it the ensuing year, as the advantages and prospects are too discouraging to hold forth a probability of clearing one penny for future support. Salaries do not exceed one hundred pounds sterling, out of which clerks must purchase every necessity, even tobacco, and the prices of goods at the Bay are at the rate of one hundred and fifty or three hundred per cent. on prime cost, therefore I shall take this opportunity of humbly requesting your advice how to settle my little earnings, which do not much exceed five hundred pounds, to the best advantage."

March 1st, 1824.—"Respecting the concerns of the North-West (country), little occurs that can be interesting to Canada. Furs have lost a great deal of their former value in Europe, and many of the chief factors and traders would willingly compound for their shares with the Company for one thousand five hundred pounds, in order to retire from a country which has become disgusting and irksome to all classes. Still, the returns are not altogether unprofitable; but debts, disappointments, and age seem to oppress everyone alike. *Engagés'* prices are now reduced to twenty-five pounds annually to a boute (foreman), and twenty pounds to middlemen, without equipment or any perquisites whatever. In fact, no class enjoys the gratuity of an equipment. Besides, the committee at home insist upon being paid for families residing in posts and belonging to partners, clerks, or men, at the rate of two shillings for every woman and child over fourteen years of age, one shilling for every child under that age. This is complained of as a grievance by all parties, and must eventually become very hard on some who have large families to support. In short, the North-West is now beginning to be ruled with a rod of iron." (Evidently Wentzel is not an admirer of the new régime.)

FINLAY'S SEARCH FOR FUR.

The name of Finlay was a famous one among the traders. As we have seen, James Finlay was one of the first to leave Montreal, and penetrate among the tribes of Indians, in search of fur, to the far distant Saskatchewan. His son James was a trader, and served in the firm of Gregory, McLeod & Co. As was not uncommon, these traders had children by the Indian women, having a "country marriage," as it was called. As the result of these there was connected with the Finlay family a half-breed named Jaceo, or Jacko Finlay, who took his part in exploration in the Rocky Mountains in company with David Thompson. Besides these, there was a well-known trader, John Finlay, who is often difficult to separate from the other traders of the name.

The writer has lying before him a manuscript, never hitherto published, entitled "A Voyage of Discovery from the Rocky Mountain Portage in Peace River, to the Sources of Finlay's Branch, and North-Westward: Summer, 1824." This is certified by Chief Factor McDougall, to-day of Prince Albert, to be the journal of John Finlay. As it illustrates the methods by which the fur country was opened, we give a few extracts.

May 13*th*.—"Rainy weather. In the evening, left Rocky Mountain Portage establishment. Crossed over to the portage and encamped for the night. . . . The expedition people are as follows: six effective canoe men, Joseph Le Guard, Antoine Perreault (bowman), Joseph Cunnayer, J. B. Tourangeau, J. M. Bouche, and Louis Olsen (middleman), M. McDonald, Manson, and myself, besides Le Prise, and wife, in all ten persons. Le Prise is in the double capacity of hunter and interpreter."

Finlay speaks of "The existing troubles in this quarter caused by the murderers of our people at St. John's, roving about free and, it is said, menacing all; but as this is an exploratory voyage, and the principal motive to ascertain the existence of beaver in the country we are bound for, we shall do our best to accomplish the intentions of the voyage."

17*th*.—"Encamped at the hill at the little lake on the top of the hills at the west side of the Portage, Mr. M. shot a large fowl of the grouse kind, larger than the black heath cock in Scotland. Found some dried salmon in exchange with Mr. Stunt for pemmican—a meal for his men, and this year he seems independent of the Peace River, at least as far as Dunvegan: they have nothing in provisions at the Portage."

Finlay is very much in the habit of describing the rock formations seen on his voyage. His descriptions are not very valuable, for he says, "I am not qualified to give a scientific description of the different species and genera of the different substances composing the strata of the Rocky Mountains."

22*nd May*.—"In this valley, about four miles before us right south, Finlay's branch comes in on the right: a mile and a half below Finlay's branch made a portage of five hundred paces. At a rapid here we found the Canny cache (a hiding place for valuables); said to be some beaver in it of last year's hunt."

23rd.—"Met a band of Indians, who told us they were going up the small river—(evidently this had been named after the elder Finlay, as this instances its familiarity)—on the left, to pass the summer, and a little before another river on the right; that there were some beavers in it, but not so many as the one they were to pass the summer in."

24th.—"To-day some tracks of the reindeer, mountain sheep and goats, but the old slave (hunter) has killed nothing but a fowl or beaver now and then."

25th.—"I have never seen in any part of the country such luxuriance of wood as hereabout, the valley to near the tops of the mountains on both sides covered with thick, strong, dark-green branching pines. We see a good many beaver and some fowl, game (bustards), and duck, but kill few."

Finlay declares to the slave, the hunter of his party, his intention to go up the large branch of the Finlay. "This is a disappointment to him as well as to the people, who have indulged their imaginations on this route falling on the Liard River, teeming in beaver and large animals."

7th June.—"This afternoon we have seen a great deal of beaver work, and killed some bustards and Canadian grey geese; we have seen no swans, and the ducks, with few exceptions, are shabby."

Finlay gives a statement of his journey made so far, thus:—

Rocky Mountain Portage to entrance of Finlay's Branch.	6	days..
To Deserter's Portage .	4	."
To Large Branch .	5	."
To Point Du Mouton.	4	."
To end of Portage .	4	."
To Fishing Lakes.	3	."
	26	days.

FINLAY GIVES HIS VIEWS AS TO A "BEAVER COUNTRY."

"In some of the large rivers coming into Finlay's branch, where soft ground with wood, eligible for beaver, had been accumulated, beaver were to be found. Otherwise, except such places as here and here, the whole country is one continued mountain valley of rock and stone, and can by no means come under the denomination of a beaver country, in the common acceptation of the word, on the waters of the Hudson's Bay and Mackenzie River."

June 15th.—"Very fine warm weather; huge masses of snow falling down from the mountains with a noise resembling thunder. Those snow déboules seem irresistible, shivering the trees to atoms, carrying all clean before them, forming ruins as if the Tower of Babel or the Pyramids of Egypt had been thrown down from their foundations."

June 29th.—"Made a good fishery to-day: 7 trout, 12 carp, 1 small white fish, like those at McLeod's lake in Western Caledonia."

Finlay closes his journal of seventy-five closely-written quarto pages at the lake high in the mountains, where he saw a river rising. This lake we see from the map to be the source of the Liard River.

A TRUSTED TRADER AND HIS FRIENDS.

Not very long ago it was the good fortune of the writer to be in Edinburgh. He was talking to his friend, a well-known Writer to the Signet. The conversation turned on the old fur-trading days, and in a short time author and lawyer found themselves four stories high, in a garret, examining boxes, packages, and effects of James Hargrave and his son Joseph, who as fur traders, father and son, had occupied posts in the Hudson's Bay Company service extending from 1820 to 1892.

Several cases were filled with copies of a book entitled "Red River," published by the younger Hargrave in 1871. Other boxes enclosed the library of father and son. Two canvas bags contained many pounds of new farthings, which, by some strange mischance, had found their way to the Hudson Bay and had been returned as useless. Miscellaneous articles of no value to the searchers lay about, but in one large valise were many bundles of letters. These were done up in the most careful manner. The packages were carefully tied with red tape, and each, securely sealed with three black ominous seals, emphasized the effect of the directions written on them, in some cases "to be opened only by my son," in others, "to be opened only by my children." After some delay the permission of the heirs was obtained, and the packages were opened and examined.

They were all letters written between 1821 and 1859 by fur-trading friends to James Hargrave, who had carefully preserved them, folded, docketed, and arranged them, and who had, in the last years of his life at "Burnside House," his residence at Brockville, Canada, kept the large correspondence as the "apple of his eye." The vast majority of the letters, numbering many hundreds in all, had been addressed to York Factory. For most of his life Hargrave had been in charge of York Factory, on Hudson Bay. York Factory was during the greater part of this fur trader's life, as it had been for more than a century before his time, the port of entry to which goods brought by ship from Britain had been borne to the interior of Rupert's Land, and also the port from which the ships had carried their precious cargoes of furs to the mother country. James Hargrave had thus become the trusted correspondent of governor and merchant, of bishop and clergyman, of medical man and educationist. He was emphatically a middleman, a sort of Janus, looking with one face to the London merchants and with the other to the dwellers in Rupert's Land.

But Hargrave was also a letter-writer, and a receiver of many news letters and friendly letters, a man who enjoyed conversation, and when this could not be had with his friends *tête-à-tête*, his social chats were carried on by means of letters, many months and even years apart. By degrees he rose in the service. From the first a friend of the emperor-governor, he has the good wishes of his friends expressed for his first rise to the post of chief trader, which he gained in 1833, and by-and-bye came his next well-deserved promotion to be chief factor in 1844.

Along with all these letters was a book handsomely bound for keeping accounts and private memoranda. This book shows James

Hargrave to have been a most methodical and painstaking man. In it is contained a list of all the promotions to official positions of commissioned officers for nearly forty years, from the Atlantic to the Pacific. Here also is an account of his investments, and the satisfactory statement that, during his nearly forty years of service, his shares of the profits, investments, and re-investments of what he did not use, allowed him to retire from active service with, as the result of his labour, about 8,700*l*.

The writer has sought to glean from the hundreds of letters in the Edinburgh garret what is interesting in the life of Rupert's Land, so far as is shown in the writing and acting of this old fur trader and his friends.

Many of the letters are from Governor Simpson. These letters of the Governor are chiefly written from Red River or Norway House—the former the "Fur Traders' Paradise," the latter the meeting-place of the Council, held once a year to decide all matters of business. Occasionally a letter of the Governor's is from Bas de la Rivière (i.e. the mouth of the Winnipeg River), written by that energetic officer, as might be said, "on the wing," and in a few cases from London, England, whither frequently Governor Simpson crossed on the business of the Company.

Governor Simpson's remarks as to society in Red River, 1831, are keen and amusing:—"As yet we have had one fete, which was honoured by the presence of all the elegance and dignity of the place from his Reverence of Juliopolis (Bishop Provencher) down to friend Cook, who (the latter) was as grave and sober as a bishop. . . . By-the-bye, we have got a very 'rum' fellow of a doctor here now: the strangest compound of skill, simplicity, selfishness, extravagance, musical taste, and want of courtesy, I ever fell in with. The people are living on the fat of the earth, in short, Red River is a perfect land of Canaan as far as good cheer goes. . . . Do me the favour to pick out a couple pounds of choice snuff for me and send them by Mr. Miles."

A short time after this, Governor Simpson, writing, says, speaking of the completion of St. John's Church, afterward the Cathedral Church, and referring to the discontent of the Selkirk settlers, with which he had small sympathy, "We have got into the new church, which is really a splendid edifice for Red River, and the people are less clamorous about a Gaelic minister than they were." The good Governor had his pleasant fling at the claim made by the Highlanders to have their private stills when he says, "And about whiskey they say not one word, now that rum is so cheap, and good strong 'heavy wet' in general use." Speaking of one of the chief officers who was off duty, the Governor says "Chief Factor Charles is like a fish out of water, having no musquash to count, nor Chipewyans to trade with; he is as brisk and active as a boy, and instead of showing any disposition to retire, wishes to volunteer to put a finishing hand to the as yet fruitless attempt at discovering the North-West passage."

Governor Simpson knows well the art of flattery, and his skill in managing his large force of Company officers and men is well seen. He states to Hargrave that he once predicted at the board that the traders of York Factory would yet have a seat at the Board. This, he stated, gave mortal offence to some members, but he was to bear the prediction in mind. He compliments him on sending the best-written letter that he has received for a long time, and we find that in the following year Hargrave was made Chief Trader. This was the occasion for numerous congratulations from his friends Archdeacon Cochrane of Red River, Trader Sieveright, and others.

The news of the time was common subject of discussion between the traders in their letters. Governor Simpson gave an account of the outbreak of cholera in the eastern states and provinces, and traces in a very graphic way its dangerous approach towards Rupert's Land. Up to August, 1832, fifteen hundred people had died in Montreal. The pestilence had reached Mackinaw, and two hundred of the steamboat passengers were carried off, and some near Sault Ste. Marie. "God grant," says the Governor, "it may not penetrate further into our wilds, but the chances are decidedly against us."

That the Hudson's Bay Company officers were not traders only is made abundantly evident. In one of his letters, Governor Simpson states that their countryman, Sir Walter Scott, has just passed away, he thanks Hargrave for sending him copies of *Blackwood's Magazine*, and orders are often given for fresh and timely books. A little earlier we find the minute interest which the fur traders took in public events in a letter from Chief Factor John Stuart, after whom Stuart's Lake, in New Caledonia, was named. He speaks to Hargrave of the continuation of Southey's "History of the War of the Peninsula" not being published, and we know from other sources that this History fell still-born, but Stuart goes on to say that he had sent for Col. Napier's "History of the Peninsular War." "Napier's politics," says Stuart, "are different, and we shall see whether it is the radical or a laurel (Southey was poet laureate) that deserves the palm." These examples but illustrate what all close observers notice, that the officers of the Hudson's Bay Company not only read to purpose, but maintained a keen outlook for the best and most finished contemporary literature. Much additional evidence might be supplied on this point.

All through Governor Simpson's letters there is a strain of sympathy for the people of the Company that is very beautiful. These show that instead of being a hard and tyrannical man, the Governor had a tender heart. In one of his letters he expresses sympathy for Trader Heron, who had met misfortune. He speaks of his great anxiety for a serious trouble that had arisen in Rev. Mr. Jones's school at Red River, and hopes that it may not injure education; he laments at considerable length over Mr. J. S. McTavish's unfortunate accident. Having heard of Hargrave's long illness he sends a letter of warm sympathy, and this in the midst of a flying visit, and in London in the following year pays every attention by giving kind, hospitable invitations to Hargrave to enjoy the society of himself and Lady Simpson.

The racy letters of Governor Simpson are by no means more interesting than those of many others of Hargrave's friends. Ordinary business letters sometimes seem to have a humorous turn about them even fifty years after they were written. The Roman Catholic Bishop Provencher (Bishop of Juliopolis *in partibus infidelium*) affords an example of this. He writes in great distress to Hargrave as to the loss of a cask of white wine (*une barrique de vin blanc*). He had expected it by the York boats sent down by the great Red River merchant, Andrew McDermott. . . . The cask had not arrived. The good Bishop cannot understand it, but presumes, as it is December when he writes, that it will come in the spring. The Bishop's last remark is open to a double meaning, when he says, "Leave it as it is, for he will take it without putting it in barrels."

The Bishop in a more important matter addresses Governor Simpson, and the Governor forwards his letter to York Factory. In this Bishop Provencher thanks him for giving a voyage in the canoes, from Red River to Montreal, to Priest Harper, and for bringing up Sub-Deacon Poiré, a "young man of talent." He also gives hearty thanks for a passage, granted by the Governor on the fur traders' route from the St. Lawrence, to two stonemasons. "I commence," he said, "to dig the foundation of my church to-morrow." He asks for a passage down and up for members of his ecclesiastical staff. He wants from York Factory forty or fifty hoes for Mr. Belcour to use in teaching the Indians to cultivate potatoes and Indian corn, and he naively remarks, "while thus engaged, he will at the same time cultivate their spirits and their hearts by the preaching of the Word of God." The eye for business is seen in the Bishop's final remark that he thinks "that the shoes from the Bay will cost much less than those made by the smiths at Red River."

Archdeacon Cochrane, a man of gigantic form and of amazing *bonhomie*, who has been called the "founder of the Church of England on Red River," writes several interesting letters. Beginning with business he drifts into a friendly talk. One of his letters deals with the supplies for the school he had opened (1831) at St. Andrew's, Red River, another sings the praises of his new church at the rapids; "It is an elegant little church, pewed for three hundred and forty people, and finished in the neatest manner it could be for Red River. The ceiling is an arc of an ellipse, painted light blue. The moulding and pulpit brown; the jambs and sashes of the windows white."

A little of the inner working of the fur-trading system in the predominance of Scottish influence is exhibited by Archdeacon Cochrane in one letter to Hargrave. Recurring to Hargrave's promotion to the chief tradership, not yet bestowed, the old clergyman quaintly says, "Are you likely to get another feather in your cap? I begin to think that your name will have to be changed into MacArgrave. A 'mac' before your name would produce a greater effect than all the rest of your merits put together. Can't you demonstrate that you are one of the descendants of one of the great clans?"

Among the correspondence is a neat little note to Hargrave (1826) from Rev. David Jones, the Archdeacon's predecessor, written at Red River, asking his company to a family dinner on the next Monday, at 2 p.m.; and a delicate missive from Acting-Governor Bulger, of Red River, asking Hargrave to accept a small quantity of snuff.

Among Hargrave's correspondents are such notable fur traders as Cuthbert Grant, the leader of the Bois Brûlés, who had settled down on White Horse Plains, on the Assiniboine River, and was the famous captain of the buffalo hunters; and William Conolly, the daring Chief Factor of New Caledonia. Events in Fort Churchill are well described in the extensive correspondence of J. G. McTavish, long stationed there; and good Governors Finlayson and McMillan of Red River are well represented; as well as Alexander Ross, the historian of the Rod River affairs. A full account of the wanderings from York Factory to the far distant Pacific slope of Mr. George Barnston, who afterwards was well known in business circles as a resident of Montreal, could be gathered, did time permit, from a most regular correspondence with Hargrave.

Probably the man most after the York Chief Factor's own heart was a good letter writer, John Sieveright, who early became Chief Trader and afterwards Chief Factor in 1846. Sieveright had become acquainted with Hargrave at Sault Ste. Marie. Afterwards he was removed to Fort

Coulonge on the Upper Ottawa, but he still kept up his interest in Hargrave and the affairs of Rupert's Land. Sieveright has a play of humour and pleasant banter that was very agreeable to Hargrave. He rallies him about an old acquaintance, the handsome daughter of Fur Trader Johnston, of Sault Ste. Marie, who, it will be remembered, married an Indian princess. He has a great faculty of using what other correspondents write to him, in making up very readable and well written letters to his friends.

For many years Sieveright was at Fort Coulonge, and thus was in touch with the Hudson's Bay Company house at Lachine, the centre of the fur trade on this continent. Every year he paid a visit to headquarters, and had an advantage over the distant traders on the Saskatchewan, Mackenzie, and Nelson Rivers. He, however, seemed always to envy them their lot. Writing of Fort Coulonge, he gives us a picture of the fur trader's life: "This place has the advantage of being so near the civilized world as to allow us to hear now and then what is going on in it; but no society or amusement to help pass the time away. In consequence I cannot help reading a great deal too much—injurious at any time of life—particularly so when on the wrong side of fifty. I have been lately reading John Galt's 'Southernan,' not much to be admired. His characters are mostly all caricatures. If place will be allowed in paper trunk, I shall put that work and 'Laurie Todd' in for your acceptance."

CHAPTER XXXI.

MONTREAL, to-day the chief city of Canada, was, after the union of the Companies, the centre of the fur trade in the New World. The old Nor'-Wester influence centred on the St. Lawrence, and while the final court of appeal met in London, the forces that gave energy and effect to the decrees of the London Board acted from Montreal. At Lachine, above the rapids, nine miles from the city, lived Governor Simpson, and many retired traders looked upon Lachine as the Mecca of the fur trade. Even before the days of the Lachine Canal, which was built to avoid the rapids, it is said the pushing traders had taken advantage of the little River St. Pierre, which falls into the St. Lawrence, and had made a deep cutting from it up which they dragged their boats to Lachine. To the hardy French voyageurs, accustomed to "portage" their cargoes up steep cliffs, it was no hardship to use the improvised canal and reach Lachine at the head of the rapids.

Accordingly, Lachine became the port of departure for the voyageurs on their long journeys up the Ottawa, and on to the distant fur country. Heavy canoes carrying four tons of merchandise were built for the freight, and light canoes, some times manned with ten or twelve men, took the officers at great speed along the route. The canoes were marvels of durability. Made of thin but tough sheets of birch bark, securely gummed along the seams with pitch, they were so strong, and yet so light, that the Indians thought them an object of wonder, and said they were the gift of the Manitou.

The voyageurs were a hardy class of men, trained from boyhood to the use of the paddle. Many of them were Iroquois Indians—pure or with an admixture of white blood. But the French Canadians, too, became noted for their expert management of the canoe, and were favourites of Sir George Simpson. Like all sailors, the voyageurs felt the day of their departure a day of fate. Very often they sought to drown their sorrows in the flowing bowl, and it was the trick of the commander to prevent this by keeping the exact time of the departure a secret, filling up the time of the voyageurs with plenty to do and leaving on very short notice. However, as the cargo was well-nigh shipped, wives, daughters, children, and sweethearts too, of the departing canoe men began to linger about the docks, and so were ready to bid their sad farewells.

In the governor's or chief factor's brigade each voyageur wore a feather in his cap, and if the wind permitted it a British ensign was hoisted on each light canoe. Farewells were soon over. Cheers filled the air from those left behind, and out from Lachine up Lake St. Louis, an enlargement of the St. Lawrence, the brigade of canoes were soon to shoot on their long voyage. No sooner had "le maitre" found his cargo afloat, his officers and visitors safely seated, than he gave the cheery word to start, when the men broke out with a "chanson de voyage." Perhaps it was the story of the "Three Fairy Ducks," with its chorus so lively in French, but so prosaic, even in the hands of the poetic McLennan, when translated into English as the "Rolling Ball":—

> "Derrière chez nous, il y a un étang
> (Behind the manor lies the mere),
>   En roulant ma boule. (Chorus.)
> Trois beaux canards s'en vont baignant.)
> (Three ducks bathe in its waters clear.)
>   En roulant ma boule.
> Rouli, roulant, ma boule roulant,
> En roulant, ma boule roulant,
>   En roulant ma boule."

And now the paddles strike with accustomed dash. The voyageurs are excited with the prospect of the voyage, all scenes of home swim before their eyes, and the chorister leads off with his story of the prince (fils du roi) drawing near the lake, and with his magic gun cruelly sighting the black duck, but killing the white one. With falling voices the swinging men of the canoe relate how from the snow-white drake his

> "Life blood falls in rubies bright,
> His diamond eyes have lost their light,
> His plumes go floating east and west,
> And form at last a soldier's bed.
>   En roulant ma boule
> (Sweet refuge for the wanderer's head),
>   En roulant ma boule,
> Rouli, roulant, ma boule roulant,
> En roulant ma boule roulant,
>   En roulant ma boule."

As the brigade hies on its way, to the right is the purplish brown water of the Ottawa, and on the left the green tinge of the St. Lawrence, till suddenly turning around the western extremity of the Island of Montreal, the boiling waters of the mouth of the Ottawa are before the voyageurs. Since 1816 there has been a canal by which the canoes avoid these rapids, but before that time all men and officers disembarked and the goods were taken by portage around the foaming waters.

And now the village of Ste. Anne's is reached, a sacred place to the departing voyageurs, and here at the old warehouse the canoes are moored. Among the group of pretty Canadian houses stands out the Gothic church with its spire so dear an object to the canoe men. The superstitious voyageurs relate that old Bréboeuf, who had gone as priest with the early French explorers, had been badly injured on the portage by the fall of earth and stones upon him. The attendance possible for him was small, and he had laid himself down to die on the spot where stands the church. He prayed to Ste. Anne, the sailors' guardian, and on her appearing to him he promised to build a church if he survived. Of course, say the voyageurs, with a merry twinkle of the eye, he recovered and kept his word. At the shrine of "la bonne Ste. Anne" the voyageur made his vow of devotion, asked for protection on his voyage, and left such gift as he could to the patron saint.

Coming up and down the river at this point the voyageurs often sang the song:—

> "Dans mon chemin j'ai rencontré
> Deux cavaliers très bien montés;"

with the refrain to every verse:—

> "A l'ombre d'un bois je m'en vais jouer,
> A l'ombre d'un bois je m'en vais jouer."
> ("Under the shady tree I go to play.")

It is said that it was when struck with the movement and rhythm of this French chanson that Thomas Moore, the Irish poet, on his visit to Canada, while on its inland waters, wrote the "Canadian Boat Song," and made celebrated the good Ste. Anne of the voyageurs. Whether in the first lines he succeeded in imitating the original or not, his musical notes are agreeable:—

> "Faintly as tolls the evening chime,
> Our voices keep tune and our oars keep time."

Certainly the refrain has more of the spirit of the boatman's song:—

> "Row, brothers, row; the stream runs fast,
> The rapids are near and the daylight's past."

The true colouring of the scene is reflected in

> "We'll sing at Ste. Anne;"

and—

> "Uttawa's tide, this trembling moon,
> Shall see us float over thy surges soon."

Ste. Anne really had a high distinction among all the resting-places on the fur trader's route. It was the last point in the departure from Montreal Island. Religion and sentiment for a hundred years had consecrated it, and a short distance above it, on an eminence overlooking the narrows—the real mouth of the Ottawa—was a venerable ruin, now overgrown with ivy and young trees, "Chateau brillant," a castle speaking of border foray and Indian warfare generations ago.

If the party was a distinguished one there was often a priest included, and he, as soon as the brigade was fairly off and the party had settled down to the motion, reverently removing his hat, sounded forth a loud invocation to the Deity and to a long train of male and female saints, in a loud and full voice, while all the men at the end of each versicle made response, "Qu'il me bénisse." This done, he called for a song. None of the many songs of France would be more likely at this stage than the favourite and most beloved of all French Canadian songs, "A la Claire Fontaine."

The leader in solo would ring out the verse—

> "A la claire fontaine,
> M'en allent promener,
> J'ai trouve l'eau si belle,
> Que je m'y sois baigné."
> ("Unto the crystal fountain,
> For pleasure did I stray;
> So fair I found the waters,
> My limbs in them I lay.")

Then in full chorus all would unite, followed verse by verse. Most touching of all would be the address to the nightingale—

> "Chantez, rossignol, chantez,
> Toi qui as le coeur gai;
> Tu as le coeur à rire,
> Moi, je l'ai à pleurer."
> ("Sing, nightingale, keep singing,
> Thou hast a heart so gay;
> Thou hast a heart so merry,
> While mine is sorrow's prey.")

The most beautiful of all, the chorus, is again repeated, and is, as translated by Lighthall:—

> "Long is it I have loved thee,
> Thee shall I love alway,
>   My dearest;
> Long is it I have loved thee,
> Thee shall I love alway."

The brigade swept on up the Lake of Two Mountains, and though the work was hard, yet the spirit and exhilaration of the way kept up the hearts of the voyageurs and officers, and as one song was ended, another was begun and carried through. Now it was the rollicking chanson, "C'est la Belle Françoise," then the tender "La Violette Dandine," and when inspiration was needed, that song of perennial interest, "Malbrouck s'en va-t-en guerre."

A distance up the Ottawa, however, the scenery changes, and the river is interrupted by three embarrassing rapids. At Carillon, opposite to which was Port Fortune, a great resort for retired fur traders, the labours began, and so these rapids, Carillon, Long Sault, and Chute au Blondeau, now avoided by canals, were in the old days passed by portage with infinite toil. Up the river to the great Chaudière, where the City of Ottawa now stands, they cheerfully rowed, and after another great portage the Upper Ottawa was faced.

The most dangerous and exacting part of the great river was the well-known section where two long islands, the lower the Calumet, and the Allumette block the stream, and fierce rapids are to be encountered. This was the piece de resistance of the canoe-men's experience. Around it their superstitions clustered. On the shores were many crosses erected to mark the death, in the boiling surges beside the portage, of many comrades who had perished here. Between the two islands on the north side of the river, the Hudson's Bay Company had founded Fort Coulonge, used as a depot or refuge in case of accident. No wonder the region, with "Deep River" above, leading on to the sombre narrows of

"Hell Gate" further up the stream, appealed to the fear and imagination of the voyageurs.

Ballad and story had grown round the boiling flood of the Calumet. As early as the time of Champlain, the story goes that an educated and daring Frenchman named Cadieux had settled here, and taken as his wife one of the dusky Ottawas. The prowling Iroquois attacked his dwelling. Cadieux and one Indian held the enemy at bay, and firing from different points led them to believe that the stronghold was well manned. In the meantime, the spouse of Cadieux and a few Indians launched their canoes into the boiling waters and escaped. From pool to pool the canoe was whirled, but in its course the Indians saw before them a female figure, in misty robes, leading them as protectress. The Christian spouse said it was the "bonne Ste. Anne," who led them out of danger and saved them. The Iroquois gave up the siege. Cadieux's companion had been killed, and the surviving settler himself perished from exhaustion in the forest. Beside him, tradition says, was found his death-song, and this "Lament de Cadieux," with its touching and attractive strain, the voyageurs sang when they faced the dangers of the foaming currents of the Upper Ottawa.

The whole route, with its rapids, whirlpools, and deceptive currents, came to be surrounded, especially in superstitious minds, with an air of dangerous mystery. A traveller tells us that a prominent fur trader pointed out to him the very spot where his father had been swept under the eddy and drowned. The camp-fire stories were largely the accounts of disasters and accidents on the long and dangerous way. As such a story was told on the edge of a shadowy forest the voyageurs were filled with dread. The story of the Wendigo was an alarming one. No crew would push on after the sun was set, lest they should see this apparition.

Some said he was a spirit condemned to wander to and fro in the earth on account of crimes committed, others believed the Wendigo was a desperate outcast, who had tasted human flesh, and prowled about at night, seeking in camping-places of the traders a victim. Tales were told of unlucky trappers who had disappeared in the woods and had never been heard of again. The story of the Wendigo made the camping-place to be surrounded with a sombre interest to the traders.

Unbelievers in this mysterious ogre freely declared that it was but a partner's story told to prevent the voyageurs delaying on their journey, and to hinder them from wandering to lonely spots by the rapids to fish or hunt. One of the old writers spoke of the enemy of the voyageurs—

> "Il se nourrit des corps des pauvres voyageurs,
> Des malheureux passants et des navigateurs."
> ("He feeds on the bodies of unfortunate men of the river, of
> unlucky travellers, and of the mariners.")

Impressed by the sombre memories of this fur traders' route, a traveller in the light canoes in fur-trading days, Dr. Bigsby, relates that he had a great surprise when, picking his way along a rocky portage, he "suddenly stumbled upon a young lady sitting alone under a bush in a green riding habit and white beaver bonnet." The impressionable doctor looked upon this forest sylph and doubted whether she was

> "One of those fairy shepherds and shepherdesses
> Who hereabouts live on simplicity and watercresses."

After confused explanations on the part of both, the lady was found to be an Ermatinger, daughter of the well-known trader of Saulte Ste. Marie, who with his party was then at the other end of the portage.

We may now, with the privilege accorded the writer, omit the hardships of hundreds of miles of painful journeying, and waft the party of the voyageurs, whose fortunes we have been following, up to the head of the west branch of the Ottawa, across the Vaz portages, and down a little stream into Lake Nipissing, where there was an old-time fort of the Nor'-Westers, named La Ronde. Across Lake Nipissing, down the French River, and over the Georgian Bay with its beautiful scenery, the voyageurs' brigade at length reached the River St. Mary, soon to rest at the famous old fort of Sault Ste. Marie. Sault Ste. Marie was the home of the Ermatingers, to which the fairy shepherdess belonged.

The Ermatinger family, whose name so continually associates itself with Sault Ste. Marie, affords a fine example of energy and influence. Shortly after the conquest of Canada by Wolfe, a Swiss merchant came from the United States and made Canada his home. One of his sons, George Ermatinger, journeyed westward to the territory now making up Michigan, and, finding his way to Sault Ste. Marie, married, engaged in the fur trade, and died there.

Still more noted than his brother, Charles Oaks Ermatinger, going westward from Montreal, also made Sault Ste. Marie his homo. A man of great courage and local influence in the war of 1812, the younger brother commanded a company of volunteers in the expedition from Fort St. Joseph, which succeeded that summer in capturing Michilimackinac. His fur-trading establishment at Sault Ste. Marie was situated on the south side of the river, opposite the rapids. When this territory was taken possession of by the troops of the United States in 1822, the fur trader's premises at Sault Ste. Marie were seized and became the American fort. For some years after this seizure trader Ermatinger had a serious dispute with the United States Government about his property, but finally received compensation. True to the Ermatinger disposition, the trader then withdrew to the Canadian side, retained his British connection, and carried on trade at Sault Ste. Marie, Drummond Island, and elsewhere.

A resident of Sault Ste. Marie informs the writer that the family of Ermatinger about that place is now a very numerous one, "related to almost all the families, both white and red." Very early in the century (1814), a passing trader named Franchère arrived from the west country at the time that the American troops devastated Sault Ste. Marie. Charles Ermatinger then had his buildings on the Canadian side of the river, not far from the houses and stores of the North-West Company, which had been burnt down by the American troops. Ermatinger at the time was living on the south side of the river temporarily in a house of old trader Nolin, whose family, the traveller tells us, consisted of "three half-breed boys and as many girls, one of whom was passably pretty." Ermatinger had just erected a grist mill, and was then building a stone house "very elegant." To this home the young lady overtaken by Dr. Bigsby on the canoe route belonged. Of the two nephews of the doughty old trader of Sault Ste. Marie, Charles and Francis Ermatinger, who were prominent in the fur trade, more anon.

The dashing rapids of the St. Mary River are the natural feature which has made the place celebrated. The exciting feat of "running the rapids" is accomplished by all distinguished visitors to the place. John Busheau, or some other dusky canoe-man, with unerring paddle, conducts the shrinking tourist to within a yard of the boiling cauldron, and sweeps down through the spray and splash, as his passenger heaves a sigh of relief.

The obstruction made by the rapids to the navigation of the river, which is the artery connecting the trade of Lakes Huron and Superior, early occupied the thought of the fur traders. A century ago, during the conflict of the North-West Company and the X Y, the portage past the rapids was a subject of grave dispute. Ardent appeals were made to the Government to settle the matter. The X Y Company forced a road through the disputed river frontage, while the North-West Company used a canal half a mile long, on which was built a lock; and at the foot of the canal a good wharf and storehouse had been constructed. This waterway, built at the beginning of the century and capable of carrying loaded canoes and considerable boats, was a remarkable proof of the energy and skill of the fur traders.

The river and rapids of St. Mary past, the joyful voyageurs hastened to skirt the great lake of Superior, on whoso shores their destination lay. Deep and cold, Lake Superior, when stirred by angry winds, became the grave of many a voyageur. Few that fell into its icy embrace escaped. Its rocky shores were the death of many a swift canoe, and its weird legends were those of the Inini-Wudjoo, the great giant, or of the hungry heron that devoured the unwary. Cautiously along its shores Jean Baptiste crept to Michipicoten, then to the Pic, and on to Nepigon, places where trading posts marked the nerve centres of the fur trade.

At length, rounding Thunder Cape, Fort William was reached, the goal of the "mangeur de lard" or Montreal voyageur. Around the walls of the fort the great encampment was made. The River Kaministiquia was gay with canoes; the East and West met in rivalry—the wild couriers of the West and the patient boatmen of the East. In sight of the fort stood, up the river, McKay Mountain, around which tradition had woven fancies and tales. Its terraced heights suggest man's work, but it is to this day in a state of nature. Here in the days of conflict, when the opposing trappers and hunters went on their expeditions, old Trader McKay ascended, followed them with his keen eye in their meanderings, and circumvented them in their plans.

The days of waiting, unloading, loading, feasting, and contending being over, the Montreal voyageurs turned their faces homeward, and with flags afloat, paddled away, now cheerfully singing sweet "Alouette."

> "Ma mignonette, embrassez-moi.
> Nenni, Monsieur, je n'oserais,
> Car si mon papa le savait."
> (My darling, smile on me.
> No! No! good sir, I do not dare,
> My dear papa would know! would know!)
> "But who would tell papa?"
> "The birds on the forest tree."
> "Ils parlent francais, latin aussi,
> Hélas! que le monde est malin
> D'apprendre aux oiseaux le latin."
> ("They speak French and Latin too,
> Alas! the world is very bad
> To tell its tales to the naughty birds.")

Bon voyage! Bon voyage, mos voyageurs!

CHAPTER XXXII.

EXPLORERS IN THE FAR NORTH

The North-West Passage again—Lieut. John Franklin's land expedition—Two lonely winters—Hearne's mistake corrected—Franklin's second journey—Arctic sea coast explored—Franklin knighted—Captain John Ross by sea—Discovers magnetic pole— Magnetic needle nearly perpendicular—Back seeks for Ross—Dease and Simpson sent by Hudson's Bay Company to explore—Sir John in *Erebus* and *Terror*—The Paleocrystic Sea—Franklin never returns—Lady Franklin's devotion—The historic search—Dr. Rae secures relics—Captain McClintock finds the cairn and written record—Advantages of the search.

THE British people were ever on the alert to have their famous sea captains explore new seas, especially in the line of the discovery of the North-West Passage. From the time of Dobbs, the discomfiture of that bitter enemy of the Hudson's Bay Company had checked the advance in following up the explorations of Davis and Baffin, whose names had become fixed on the icy sea channels of the North.

Captain Phipps, afterwards Lord Mulgrave, had been the last of the great captains who had taken part in the spasm of north-west interest set agoing by Dobbs. Two generations of men had passed when, in 1817, the quest for the North-West Passage was taken up by Captain William Scoresby. Scoresby advanced a fresh argument in favour of a new effort to attain this long-harboured dream of the English captains. He maintained that a change had taken place in the seasons, and the position of the ice was such as probably to allow a successful voyage to be made from Baffin's Bay to Behring Strait.

Sir John Barrow with great energy advocated the project of a new expedition, and Captain John Ross and Edward Parry were despatched to the northern seas. Parry's second expedition enabled him to discover Fury and Hecla Strait, to pass through Lancaster Strait, and to name the continuation of it Barrow Strait, after the great patron of northern exploration.

Meanwhile John Franklin was despatched to cross the plains of Rupert's Land to forward Arctic enterprise. This notable man has left us an heritage of undying interest in connection with this movement. A native of Lincolnshire, a capable and trusted naval officer, who had fought with Nelson at Copenhagen, who had gone on an Arctic voyage to Spitzbergen, and had seen much service elsewhere, he was appointed to command the overland expedition through Rupert's Land to the Arctic Sea, while Lieutenant Parry sought, as we have seen, the passage with two vessels by way of Lancaster Sound.

Accompanied by a surgeon—Dr. Richardson—two midshipmen, Back and Hood, and a few Orkneymen, Lieutenant Franklin embarked from England for Hudson Bay in June, 1819. Wintering for the first season on the Saskatchewan, the party were indebted to the Hudson's Bay Company for supplies, and reached Fort Chipewyan in about a year from the time of their departure from England. The second winter was spent by the expedition on the famous barren grounds of the Arctic slope. Their fort was called Fort Enterprise, and the party obtained a living chiefly from the game and fish of the region. In the following summer the Franklin party descended the Coppermine River to the Arctic Sea. Here Hearne's mistake of four degrees in the latitude was corrected and the latitude of the mouth of the Coppermine River fixed at 67° 48′ N. Having explored the coast of the Arctic Sea eastward for six degrees to Cape Turnagain and suffered great hardships, the survivors of the party made their return journey, and reached Britain after three years' absence. Franklin was given the rank of captain and covered with social and literary honours.

Three years after his return to England, Captain Franklin and his old companions went upon their second journey through Rupert's Land. Having reached Fort Chipewyan, they continued the journey northward, and the winter was spent at their erection known as Fort Franklin, on Great Bear Lake. Here the party divided, one portion under Franklin going down the Mackenzie to the sea, and coasting westward to Return Reef, hoping to reach Captain Cook's icy cape of 1778. In this they failed. Dr. Richardson led the other party down the Mackenzie River to its mouth, and then, going eastward, reached the mouth of the Coppermine, which he ascended. By September both parties had gained their rendezvous, Fort Franklin, and it was found that unitedly they had traced the coast line of the Arctic Sea through thirty-seven degrees of longitude. On the return of the successful adventurer, after an absence of two years, to England, he was knighted and received the highest scientific honours.

CAPTAIN JOHN ROSS BY SEA.

When the British people become roused upon a subject, failure seems but to whet the public mind for new enterprise and greater effort. The North-West Passage was now regarded as a possibility. After the coast of the Arctic Ocean had been traced by the Franklin-Richardson expedition, to reach this shore by a passage from Parry's Fury and Hecla Strait seemed feasible.

Two years after the return of Franklin from his second overland journey, an expedition was fitted out by a wealthy distiller, Sheriff Felix Booth, and the ship, the Victory, provided by him, was placed under the command of Captain John Ross, who had already gained reputation in exploring Baffin's Bay. Captain Ross was ably seconded in his expedition by his nephew, Captain James Ross. Going by Baffin's Bay and through Lancaster Sound, Prince Regent's Inlet led Ross southward between Cockburn Island and Somerset North, into an open sea called after his patron, Gulf of Boothia, on the west side of which he named the newly-discovered land Boothia Felix. He even discovered the land to the west of Boothia, calling it King William Land. His ship became embedded in the ice. After four winters in the Arctic regions he was rescued by a whaler in Barrow Strait.

One of the most notable events in this voyage of Ross's was his discovery of the North Magnetic Pole on the west side of Boothia Felix. During his second winter (1831) Captain Ross determined to gratify his ambition to be the discoverer of the point where the magnetic needle stands vertically, as showing the centre of terrestrial magnetism for the northern hemisphere.

After four or five days' overland journey, with a trying headwind from the north-west, he reached the sought-for point on June 1st. We deem it only just to state the discovery in the words of the veteran explorer himself:—

"The land at this place is very low near the coast, but it rises into ridges of fifty or sixty feet high about a mile inland. We could have wished that a place so important had possessed more of mark or note. It was scarcely censurable to regret that there was not a mountain to indicate a spot to which so much interest must ever be attached; and I could even have pardoned any one among us who had been so romantic or absurd as to expect that the magnetic pole was an object as conspicuous and mysterious as the fabled mountain of Sinbad, that it was even a mountain of iron, or a magnet as large as Mont Blanc. But Nature had here erected no monument to denote the spot which she had chosen as the centre of one of her great and dark powers; and where we could do little ourselves towards this end, it was our business to submit, and to be content in noting in mathematical numbers and signs, as with things of far more importance in the terrestrial system, what we could ill distinguish in any other manner."

The necessary observations were immediately commenced, and they were continued throughout this and the greater part of the following day. . . . The amount of the dip, as indicated by my dipping-needle, was 89° 59', being thus within one minute of the vertical; while the proximity at least of this pole, if not its actual existence where we stood, was further confirmed by the action, or rather by the total inaction, of several horizontal needles then in my possession. ... There was not one which showed the slightest effort to move from the position in which it was placed."

As soon as I had satisfied my own mind on this subject, I made known to the party this gratifying result of all our joint labours; and it was then that, amidst mutual congratulations, we fixed the British flag on the spot, and took possession of the North Magnetic Pole and its adjoining territory, in the name of Great Britain and King William the Fourth. We had abundance of material for building in the fragments of limestone that covered the beach; and we therefore erected a cairn of some magnitude, under which we buried a canister containing a record of the interesting fact, only regretting that we had not the means of constructing a pyramid of more importance and of strength sufficient to withstand the assaults of time and of the Esquimaux. Had it been a pyramid as large as that of Cheops I am not quite sure that it would have done more than satisfy our ambition under the feelings of that exciting day. The latitude of this spot is 70° 5′ 17″ and its longitude 96° 46′ 45″.

Thus much for the magnetic pole. This pole is almost directly north of the city of Winnipeg, and within less than twenty degrees of it. One of Lady Franklin's captains—Captain Kennedy, who resided at Red River—elaborated a great scheme for tapping the central supply of electricity of the magnetic pole, and developing it from Winnipeg as a source of power.

SIR GEORGE BACK, THE EXPLORER.

In the third year of Captain Ross's expedition his protracted absence became a matter of public discussion in Britain. Dr. Richardson, who had been one of Franklin's followers, offered to take charge of an overland expedition in search of Ross, but his proposition was not accepted. Mr. Ross, a brother of Sir John and father of Captain James Ross, was anxious to find an officer who would take charge of a relief expedition, and the British Government favoured the enterprise. Captain George Back, one of the midshipmen who had accompanied Franklin, was favourably regarded for the important position.

The Hudson's Bay Company was in sympathy with the exploration of its Arctic possessions and gave every assistance to the project. Nicholas Garry, the Deputy-Governor of the Company, ably supported it; and the British Government at last gave its consent to grant two thousand pounds, provided the Hudson's Bay Company would furnish, according to its promise, the supplies and canoes free of charge, and that Captain Ross's friends would contribute three thousand pounds.

Captain Back cordially accepted the offer to command the expedition, and his orders from the Government were to find Captain Ross, or any survivors or survivor of his party; and, "subordinate to this, to direct his attention to mapping what remains unknown of the coasts which he was to visit, and make such other scientific observations as his leisure would admit."

In 1833 Captain Back crossed the Atlantic, accompanied by a surgeon, Dr. Richard King, and at Montreal obtained a party of four regulars of the Royal Artillery. Pushing on by the usual route, he reached Lake Winnipeg, and thence by light canoe arrived at Fort Resolution on Great Slave Lake in August. He wintered at Fort Reliance, near the east end of Great Slave Lake, which was established by Roderick McLeod, a Hudson's Bay Company officer, who had received orders to assist the expedition. Before leaving this point a message arrived from England that Captain Ross was safe. Notwithstanding this news, in June of the following year Back and his party crossed the country to Artillery Lake, and drew their boats and baggage in a most toilsome manner over the ice of this and three other lakes, till the Great Fish River was reached and its difficult descent begun.

On July 30th the party encamped at Cape Beaufort, a prominent point of the inlet of the Arctic Ocean into which the Great Fish River empties. The expedition again descended the river and returned to England, where it was well received, and Captain Back was knighted for his pluck and perseverance. An expedition under Back in the next year, to go by ship to Wager Bay and then to cross by portage the narrow strip of land to the Gulf of Boothia, was a failure, and the party with difficulty reached Britain again.

A HUDSON'S BAY COMPANY EXPEDITION—DEASE AND SIMPSON.

Dr. Richard King, who had been Back's assistant and surgeon, now endeavoured to organize an expedition to the Arctic Ocean by way of

Lake Athabasca and through a chain of lakes leading to the Great Fish River. This project received no backing from the British Government or from the Hudson's Bay Company. The Company now undertook to carry out an expedition of its own. The reasons of this are stated to have been—(1) The interest of the British public in the effort to connect the discoveries of Captains Back and Ross; (2) They are said to have desired a renewal of their expiring lease for twenty-one years of the trade of the Indian territories; (3) The fact was being pointed out, as in former years, that their charter required the Company to carry on exploration.

In 1836 the Hudson's Bay Company in London decided to carrying out the expedition, and gave instructions to Governor Simpson to organize and despatch it. At Norway House, at the meeting of the Governor and officers of that year, steps were taken to explore the Arctic Coast. An experienced Hudson's Bay Company officer, Peter Warren Dease, and with him an ardent young man, Thomas Simpson, a relation of the Governor, was placed in charge.

The party, after various preparations, including a course of mathematics and astronomy received by Thomas Simpson at Red River, made its departure, and Fort Chipewyan was reached in February, where the remainder of the winter was spent. As soon as navigation opened, the descent of the Mackenzie River was made to the mouth. The party then coasting westward on the Arctic Ocean, passed Franklin's "Return Reef," reached Boat Extreme, and Simpson made a foot journey thence to Cape Barrow.

Having returned to the mouth of the Mackenzie River, the Great Bear Lake, where Fort Confidence had been erected by the advance guard of the party, was reached.

The winter was passed at this point, and in the following spring the expedition descended the Copper-mine River, and coasting eastward along the Polar Sea, reached Cape Turnagain in August. Returning and ascending the Coppermine for a distance, the party halted, and Simpson made a land journey eastward to new territory which he called Victoria Land, and erected a pillar of stones, taking possession of the country, "in the name of the Honourable Company, and for the Queen of Great Britain." Their painful course was then retraced to Fort Confidence, where the second winter was spent.

On the opening of spring, the Company descended to the coast to carry on their work. Going eastward, they, after much difficulty, reached new ground, passed Dease's Strait, and discovered Cape Britannia.

Taking two years to return, Simpson arrived at Fort Garry, and disappointed at not receiving further instructions, he joined a freight party about to cross the plains to St. Paul, Minnesota. While on the way he was killed, either by his half-breed companions or by his own hand. His body was brought back to Fort Garry, and is buried at St. John's cemetery.

The Hudson's Bay Company thus made an earnest effort to explore the coast, and through its agents, Dease and Simpson, may be said to have been reasonably successful.

THE SEARCH FOR FRANKLIN.

After the return of Sir John Franklin from his second overland expedition in Rupert's Land, Sir John was given the honourable position of Lieutenant-Governor of Tasmania, and on his coming again to England, was asked by the Admiralty to undertake a sea voyage for the purpose of finding his way from Lancaster Sound to Behring's Strait.

Sir John accepted the trust, and his popularity led to the offer of numerous volunteers, who were willing to undertake the hazards of the journey. Two excellent vessels, the *Erebus* and *Terror*, well fitted out for the journey, were provided, and his expedition started with the most glowing hopes of success, on May 19th, 1845. Many people in Britain were quite convinced that the expectation of a north-west passage was now to be realized.

We know now only too well the barrier which lay in Franklin's way. Almost directly north-east of the mouth of Fish River, which Back and Simpson had both found, there lies a vast mass of ice, which can neither move toward Behring's Strait on account of the shallow opening there, or to Baffin's Bay on account of the narrow and tortuous winding of the channels. This, called by Sir George Nares the Paleocrystic Sea, we are now aware bars the progress of any ship. Franklin had gone down on the west side of North Somerset and Boothia, and coming against the vast barrier of the Paleo-crystic Sea, had been able to go no further.

Two years after the departure of the expedition from which so much was expected, there were still no tidings. Preparations were made for an expedition to rescue the adventurers, and in 1848 the first party of relief sailed.

For the next eleven years the energy and spirit and liberality of the British public were something unexampled in the annals of public sympathy. Regardless of cost or hazard, not less than fifteen expeditions were sent out by England and the United States on their sad quest. Lady Franklin, with a heroism and skill past all praise, kept the eye of the nation steadily on her loss, and sacrificed her private fortune in the work of rescue. We are not called upon to give the details of these expeditions, but may refer to a few notable points.

The Hudson's Bay Company at once undertook a journey by land in quest of the unfortunate navigator. Dr. Richardson, who had gone on Franklin's first expedition, along with a well-known Hudson's Bay Company officer, Dr. Rae, scoured the coast of the Arctic Sea, from the mouth of the Mackenzie to that of the Coppermine River. For two years more, Dr. Rae continued the search, and in the fourth year (1851) this facile traveller, by a long sledge journey in spring and boat voyage in summer, examined the shores of Wollaston and Victoria Land.

A notable expedition took place in the sending out by Lady Franklin herself of the *Prince Albert* schooner, under Captain Kennedy, who afterwards made his home in the Red River settlement. His second in command was Lieutenant Bellot, of the French Navy, who was a plucky and shrewd explorer, and who, on a long sledge journey, discovered the Strait which bears his name between North Somerset and Boothia.

The names of McClure, Austin, Collinson, Sir Edmund Belcher, and Kellett stand out in bold relief in the efforts—fruitless in this case—made to recover traces of the unfortunate expedition.

The first to come upon remains of the Franklin expedition was Dr. John Rae, who, we have seen, had thoroughly examined the coast along the Arctic Ocean. The writer well remembers meeting Dr. Rae many years after in the city of Winnipeg and hearing his story.

Rae was a lithe, active, enterprising man. In 1853, he announced that the drawback in former expeditions had been the custom of carrying a great stock of provisions and useless impedimenta, and so under Hudson's Bay Company auspices he undertook to go with gun and fishing tackle up the west coast of Hudson Bay. This he did, ascended Chesterfield Inlet, and wintered with eight men at Repulse Bay.

In the next season he made a remarkable journey of fifty-six days, and succeeded in connecting the discoveries of Captain James Ross with those of Dease and Simpson, proving King William Land to be an island. Rae discovered on this journey plate and silver decorations among the Eskimos, which they admitted had belonged to the Franklin party. Dr. Rae was awarded a part of the twenty thousand pounds reward offered by the Imperial Government.

The British people could not, however, be satisfied until something more was done, and Lady Franklin, with marvellous self-devotion, gave the last of her available means to add to the public subscription for the purchase and fitting out of the little yacht Fox, which, under Captain Leopold McClintock, sailed from Aberdeen in 1857. Having in less than two years reached Bellot Strait, McClintock's party was divided into three sledging expeditions. One of them, under Captain McClintock, was very successful, obtaining relics of the lost Franklin and his party and finding a cairn which contained an authoritative record of the fortunes of the company for three years. Sir John had died a year before this record was written. Captain McClintock was knighted for his successful effort and the worst was now at last known.

The attempt of Sir John and the efforts to find him reflect the highest honour on the British people. And not only sentiment, but reason was satisfied. As had been said, "the catastrophe of Sir John Franklin's expedition led to seven thousand miles of coast line being discovered, and to a vast extent of unknown country being explored, securing very considerable additions to geographical knowledge. Much attention was also given to the collection of information, and the scientific results of the various search expeditions were considerable."

CHAPTER XXXIII.

THE Treaty of Paris was an example of magnanimity on the part of
Great Britain to the United States, her wayward Transatlantic child,
who refused to recognize her authority. It is now clearly shown that
Lord Shelbourne, the English Premier, desired to promote good feeling
between mother and daughter as nations. Accordingly the boundary
line west of Lake Superior gave over a wide region where British
traders had numerous establishments, and where their occupation
should have counted for possession.

In the treaty of amity and commerce, eleven years afterward, it was
agreed that a line drawn from Lake of the Woods overland to the source
of Mississippi should be the boundary. But, alas! the sources of the
Mississippi for fifty years afterward proved as difficult a problem as the
source of the Nile. In the first decade of this century it was impossible
to draw the southern line of Rupert's Land. The United States during
this period evinced some anxiety in regard to this boundary, and, as we
shall see, a number of expeditions were despatched to explore the
country. The sources of the Mississippi naturally afforded much interest
to the Government at Washington, even though the convention of
London of 1818 had settled the 49 deg. N. as the boundary.

The region west of the Mississippi, which was known as Louisiana,
extended northward to the British possessions, having been transferred
by Spain to the United States in 1803. A number of expeditions to the

marches or boundary land claim a short notice from us, as being bound up with the history and interests of the Hudson's Bay Company.

LEWIS AND CLARKE'S EXPEDITION.

Of these, a notable and interesting voyage was that of Captains Meriwether Lewis and William Clarke, of the United States army. This expedition consisted of nearly fifty men—soldiers, volunteers, adventurers, and servants. Being a Government expedition, it was well provided with stores, Indian presents, weapons, and other necessary articles of travel. Leaving Wood River, near St. Louis, the party started up the Missouri in three boats, and were accompanied by two horses along the bank of the River to bring them game or to hunt in case of scarcity. After many adventures the expedition, which began its journey on May 14th, 1804, reached the headquarters of the Mandan Indians on the Missouri on October 26th.

The Mandans, or, as they have been called, the White Bearded Sioux, were at this time a large and most interesting people. Less copper-coloured than the other Indians, agricultural in habit, pottery makers, and dwelling in houses partly sunk in the earth, their trade was sought from different directions. We have seen already that Verandrye first reached them; that David Thompson, the astronomer of the North-West Company, visited them; that Harmon and others, North-West traders, met them; that fur traders from the Assiniboine came to them; that even the Hudson's Bay Company had penetrated to their borders. The Mandans themselves journeyed north to the Assiniboine and carried Indian corn, which they grew, to Rupert's Land to exchange for merchandise. The Mandan trail can still be pointed out in Manitoba.

A fur trader, Hugh McCracken, met Lewis and Clarke at this point, and we read, "That he set out on November 1st on his return to the British fort and factory on the Assiniboine River, about one hundred and fifty miles from this place. He took a letter from Captain Lewis to the North-West Company, enclosing a copy of the passport granted by the British Minister in the United States."

This shows the uncertainty as to the boundary line, the leaders of the expedition having provided themselves with this permission in case of need.

In dealing with the Mandans, Captain Lewis gave them presents, and "told them that they had heard of the British trader, Mr. Laroche, having attempted to distribute medals and flags among them; but that these emblems could not be received from any other than the American nation, without incurring the displeasure of their Great Father, 'the President.' On December 1st the party was visited by a trader, Henderson, who came from the Hudson's Bay Company. He had been about eight days on his route in a direction nearly south, and brought with him tobacco, beads, and other merchandise to trade for furs, and a few guns which were to be exchanged for horses. On December 17th Hugh Harvey and two companions arrived at the camp, having come in six days from the British establishment on the Assiniboine, with a letter from Mr. Charles Chaboillez, one of the North-West Company, who, with much politeness, offered to render us any service in his power."

With the expedition of Lewis and Clarke we have little more to do. It successfully crossed from the sources of the Missouri, over the Rocky Mountains to the Columbia, descended it to the mouth, and returned by nearly the same route, reaching the mouth of the Missouri in 1806.

The expedition of Lewis and Clarke has become the most celebrated of the American transcontinental ventures. Its early presence at the mouth of the Columbia River gave strength to the claim of the United States for that region; it was virtually a taking possession of the whole country from the Mississippi to the Pacific Ocean; it had a picturesqueness and an interest that appealed to the national mind, and the melancholy death of Captain Lewis, who, in 1809, when the American Government refused to fulfil its engagements with him, blew out his brains, lends an impressiveness to what was really a great and successful undertaking.

The source or sources of the Mississippi was, as we have seen, an important matter in settling the boundary line between the possessions of Great Britain and the United States. The matter having occupied the authorities at Washington, Zebulon M. Pike, a lieutenant of the United States army, was sent to examine the country upon the Upper Mississippi and to maintain the interests of the Government in that quarter. Leaving St. Louis on August 9th, 1805, he ascended the "Father of Waters," and reached Prairie du Chien in September. Here he was met by the well-known free-traders who carried on the fur trade in this region. Their names were Fisher, Frazer and Woods. These men were in the habit of working largely in harmony with the North-West Company traders, and, on account of their British origin, were objects of suspicion to the United States authorities. Pushing on among the Indians, by the help of French Canadian interpreters, he came to Lake Pepin. On the shores of this lake Pike met Murdoch Cameron, the principal British free-trader on the upper Minnesota River. Cameron was a shrewd and daring Scotchman, noted for his generosity and faithfulness. He was received with distinction by Pike, and the trader as shown by his grave, pointed out many years afterward on the banks of the Minnesota, was in every way worthy of the attention. Shortly after this, Pike passed near where the city of St. Paul, Minn., stands to-day, the encampment of J. B. Faribault, a French Canadian free-trader of note, whose name is now borne by an important town south of St. Paul. Pike held a council with the Dakota Indians, and purchased from them a considerable amount of land for military purposes, for which the Senate paid them the sum of two thousand dollars. Pike seems to have cautioned the Dakotas or Sioux to beware of the influence of the English, saying, "I think the traders who come from Canada are bad birds among the Chippeways, and instigate them to make war upon their red brothers, the Sioux."

About the end of October, unable to proceed further up the Mississippi on account of ice, Pike built a blockhouse, which he enclosed with pickets, and there spent the most severe part of the winter.

At his post early in December he was visited by Robert Dickson, a British fur trader, described by Neill as "a red-haired Scotchman, of strong intellect, good family, and ardent attachment to the crown of England, who was at the head of the Indian trade in Minnesota." Pike himself speaks of Dickson as a "gentleman of general commercial knowledge and of open, frank manners." Explanations took place between the Government agent and the trader as to the excessive use of spirits by the Indians.

On December 10th Pike started on a journey northward in sleds, taking a canoe with him for use so soon as the river should open. When Pike arrived near Red Cedar Lake, he was met by four Chippewa Indians, a Frenchman, and one of the North-West traders, named Grant. Going with Grant to his establishment on the shores of the lake, Pike tells us, "When we came in sight of the house I observed the flag of Great Britain flying. I felt indignant, and cannot say what my feelings would have excited me to had Grant not told mo that it belonged to the Indians."

On February 1st Pike reached Leech Lake, which he considered to be the main source of the Mississippi. He crossed the lake twelve miles to the establishment of the North-West Company, which was in charge of a well-known North-West trader, Hugh McGillies. While he was treated with civility, it is plain from his cautions to McGillies and his bearing to him, that he was jealous of the influence which British traders were then exercising in Minnesota.

Having made a treaty with the Chippewa Indians of Rod Lake, Pike's work was largely accomplished, and in April he departed from this region, whore he had shown great energy and tact, to give in his report after a voyage of some nine months.

A most melancholy interest attaches to this gentlemanly and much-respected officer of the United States. In the war of 1812-15, Pike, then made a general, was killed at the taking of York (Toronto), in Upper Canada, by the explosion of the magazine of the fort evacuated by General Sheaffe. Pike, as leader on this Mississippi expedition, as commanding an expedition on the Rio Grande, where he was captured by the Spaniards, and as a brave soldier, has handed down an honourable name and fame.

LONG AND KEATING.

The successful journey of Lewis and Clarke, as well as the somewhat useful expedition of Lieutenant Pike, led the United States Government to send in 1823 an expedition to the northern boundary line 49 deg. N., which had been settled a few years before. In charge of this was Major Stephen H. Long. He was accompanied by a scientific corps consisting of Thomas Say, zoologist and antiquary; Samuel Seymour, landscape painter and designer; and William H. Keating, mineralogist and geologist, who also acted as historian of the expedition.

Leaving Philadelphia in April, the company passed overland to Prairie du Chien on the Mississippi, ascended this river, and going up its branch, the Minnesota, reached the town of Mendota in the month of July. A well-known French half-breed, Joseph Renville, acted as guide, and several others joined the party at this point. After journeying up the Minnesota River, partly by canoe, and partly by the use of horses, they reached in thirteen days Big Stone Lake, which is considered to be the source of the river. Following up the bed of a dried-up stream for three miles, they found Lake Traverse, the source of the Red River, and reached Pembina Village, a collection of fifty or sixty log huts inhabited by half-breeds, numbering about three hundred and fifty. We have already seen how the North-West and Hudson's Bay Companies had posts at this place, and that it had been visited regularly by the Selkirk settlers as being in proximity to the open plains where buffalo could be obtained. On the day after Long's arrival he saw the return of the buffalo hunters from the chase. The procession consisted of one hundred and fifteen carts, each loaded with about eight hundred pounds of the pressed buffalo meat. There were three hundred persons, including the women. The number of horses was about two hundred. Twenty hunters, mounted on their best steeds, rode abreast, giving a salute as they passed the encampment of the expedition.

One of Major Long's objects in making his journey was to ascertain the point where the parallel of 49 deg. N. crossed the Red River. For four days observations were taken and a flagstaff planted a short distance south of the 49th parallel. The space to the boundary line was measured off, and an oak post fixed on it, having on the north side the letters G. B., and on the south side U. S. This post was kept up and was seen by the writer in 1871. In 1872, a joint expedition of British and American engineers took observations and found Long's point virtually correct. They surveyed the line of 49 deg. eastward to Lake of the Woods and westward to the Rocky Mountains. Posts were erected at short distances along the boundary line, many of them of iron, with the words on them, "Convention of London, 1818."

His work at Pembina having been accomplished, Major Long gave up, on account of the low country to be passed, the thought of following the boundary line eastward to the Lake of the Woods. He sold his horses and took canoes down the river to the Hudson's Bay Company at Fort Garry, where he was much interested in the northern civilization as well as in the settlers who had Fort Douglas as their centre.

It was August 17th when Long's expedition left Fort Douglas and went down the Red River. It took but two days to reach the mouth of the river and cross Lake Winnipeg to Fort Alexander at the mouth of the Winnipeg River. Six days more brought the swift canoe-men up the river to Lake of the Woods. At the falls of Rainy River was the Hudson's Bay Company establishment, then under the charge of fur trader McGillivray. On the opposite side of the river was the fort of the American Fur Company. Following the old route, they reached Grand Portage, September 12th, and thence the expedition returned to the East. Major Long's expedition was a well-conducted and successful enterprise. Its members were of the highest respectability, and the two volumes written by Secretary Keating have the charm of real adventure about them.

When Major Long was leaving Fort Snelling, on the Mississippi, to go upon the expedition we have just described, an erratic but energetic and clever Italian, named J. C. Beltrami, asked to be allowed to accompany him. This aspiring but wayward man has left us a book, consisting of letters addressed to Madame la Comtesse Compagoni, a lady of rank in Florence, which is very interesting. On starting he wrote, "My first intention, that of going in search of the real source of the Mississippi, was always before my eyes."

Beltrami, while clever, seems to have been a man of insufferable conceit. On the journey to Big Stone Lake and thence along the river, in the buffalo hunts, in conferences with the Sioux, the Italian adventurer awakened the resentment of the commander of the expedition, who refused to allow him to accompany his party further. This proved rather favourable to the purpose of Beltrami, who, with a half-breed guide and Chippewa Indians, started to go eastward, having a mule and a dog train as means of transport. After a few days' journey the guide left him, returning with the mule and dog train to Pembina. Next his Indian guide deserted him, fearing the Sioux, and Beltrami was left to make his way in a canoe up the river to Red Lake. Inexperienced in the management of a birch bark canoe, Beltrami was upset, but he at length proceeded along the bank and shallows of the river, dragging the canoe with a tow line after him, and arrived in miserable plight at Red Lake.

Here he engaged a guide and interpreter, and writes that he went "where no white man had previously travelled." He was now on the highway to renown. He was taken from point to point on the many lakes of Northern Minnesota, and affixed names to them. On August 20th, 1823, he went over several portages, led by his guide to Turtle Lake, which was to him a source of wonder, as he saw it from the flow of waters south to the Gulf of Mexico, north to the Frozen Sea, east to the Atlantic, and west toward the Pacific Ocean.

His own words are: "A vast platform crosses this distinguished supreme elevation, and, what is more astonishing, in the midst of it rises a lake. How is this lake formed ? Whence do its waters proceed? This lake has no issue! And my eyes, which are not deficient in sharpness, cannot discover in the whole extent of the clearest and widest horizon any land which rises above it. All places around it are, on the contrary, considerably lower."

Beltrami then went to examine the surrounding country, and found the lake, to which he gave the name of Lake Julia, to be bottomless. This lake he pronounces to be the source of the Mississippi River. This opinion was published abroad and accepted by some, but later explorations proved him to be wrong. A small lake to the south-west, afterwards found to be the true source, was described to him by his guide as Lac La Biche, and he placed this on his chart as "Doe Lake," the west source of the Mississippi. It is a curious fact that Lake Julia was the same lake surveyed twenty-five years before by astronomer Thompson.

After further explorations, Beltrami returned to Fort Snelling, near St. Paul, Minn., being clothed in Indian garments, with a piece of bark for a hat.

The intrepid explorer found his way to New Orleans, where he published "La Découverté des Sources du Mississippi." Though the work was criticized with some severity, yet Beltrami, on his arrival at London in 1827, published "A Pilgrimage in Europe and America" in two volumes, which are the source of our information. The county in Minnesota, which includes both Julia and Doe Lakes, is appropriately called Beltrami County.

CASS AND SCHOOLCRAFT.

Lewis Cass, of New Hampshire was appointed Governor of Michigan in 1813. Six years after this he addressed the Secretary of War in Washington, proposing an expedition to and through Lake Superior, and to the sources of the Mississippi. It was planned for an examination of the principal features of the North-West tributary to Lake Superior and the Mississippi River. This was sanctioned in 1820, and the expedition embarked in May of that year at Detroit, Michigan, Henry Schoolcraft being mineralogist, and Captain D. B. Douglas topographer and astronomer.

The expedition, after much contrary weather, reached Sault Ste. Marie, and the Governor, after much difficulty, here negotiated a treaty with the Indians. Going by way of the Fond du Lac, the party entered the St. Louis River, and made a tiresome portage to Sandy Lake station. This fur-trading post the party left in July, and ascended the Upper Mississippi to the Upper Cedar Lake, the name of which was changed to Lake Cassina, and afterwards Cass Lake. From the Indians Governor Cass learned that Lac La Biche—some fifty miles further on—was the true source of the river, but he was deterred by their accounts of the lowness of the water and the fierceness of the current from attempting the journey any further- The expedition ingloriously retired from the project, going down to St. Anthony Falls, ascending the Wisconsin River, and thence down Fox River. The Governor himself in September arrived in Detroit, having crossed the Southern Peninsula of Michigan on horseback.

Hon. J. W. Brown says: "When Governor Cass abandoned his purpose to ascend the Mississippi to its source, he was within an easy distance, comparatively speaking, of the goal sought for. Less timidity had often been displayed in canoe voyages, even in the face of low water, and an O-z-a-win-dib or a Keg-wed-zis-sag, Indian guides, would have easily won the battle of the day for Governor Cass."

SCHOOLCRAFT AT LENGTH SUCCEEDS.

Henry Rowe Schoolcraft, of good family, was born in New York State, and was educated in that State and in Vermont. His first expedition was in company with De Witt Clinton in a journey to Missouri and Arkansas. On his return he published two treatises which gave him some reputation as an explorer and scientist. We have already spoken of the part taken by him in the expedition of Governor Cass. He received after this the appointment of "Superintendent of Indian Affairs" at Sault Ste. Marie, and to this we are indebted for the treasury of Indian lore published in four large quarto volumes, from which Longfellow obtained his tale of "Hiawatha," In 1830 Schoolcraft received orders from Washington, ostensibly for conference with the Indians, but in reality to determine the source of the Mississippi. The Rev. W. T. Boutwell, representing a Board of Missions, accompanied the expedition.

Lac La Biche was already known to exist, and to this Schoolcraft pointed his expedition. On their journey outward Schoolcraft suddenly one day asked Boutwell the Greek and Latin names for the headwaters or true source of a river. Mr. Boutwell could not recall the Greek, but gave the two Latin words—*veritas* (truth) and *caput* (head). These were written on a slip of paper, and Mr. Schoolcraft struck out the first and last three letters, and announced to Boutwell that "Itasca shall be the name." It is true that Schoolcraft wrote a stanza in which he says, "By fair Itasca shed," seemingly referring to an Indian maiden. Boutwell, however, always maintained his story of the name, and this is supported by the fact that the word was never heard in the Ojibeway mythology.

The party followed the same route as that taken by Governor Cass on his journey, reaching Cass Lake on July 10th, 1832. Taking the advice of Ozawinder, a Chippewa Indian, they followed up their journey in birch bark canoes, went up the smaller fork of the Mississippi, and then by portage reached the eastern extremity of La Biche or Itasca Lake.

The party landed on the island in the lake which has since been known as Schoolcraft Island, and here raised their flag. After exploring the shores of the lake, he returned to Cass Lake, and, full of pride of his discovery, journeyed home to Sault Ste. Marie. On the map drawn to illustrate Schoolcraft's inland journey occurs, beside the lake of his discovery, the legend, "Itasca Lake, the source of the Mississippi River;

length from Gulf of Mexico, 3,160 miles; elevation, 1,500 ft. Reached July 13th, 1832."

CHAPTER XXXIV.

THE vast area of Rupert's Land and the adjoining Indian territories have always had a fascination for the British imagination; and not alone its wide extent, but its being a fur traders' paradise, and in consequence largely a "terra incognita," has led adventurous spirits to desire to explore it.

Just as Sir John Mandeville's expedition to the unknown regions of Asia in the fourteenth century has appealed to the hardy and brave sons of Britain from that early day; and in later times the famous ride of Colonel Burnaby to Khiva in our own generation has led Central Asia to be viewed as a land of mystery; so the plains of Rupert's Land, with the reputed Chinese wall thrown around them by the Hudson's Bay Company's monopoly, have been a favourite resort for the traveller, the mighty hunter, and the scientist.

It is true no succeeding records of adventure can have the interest for us that gathers around those of the intrepid Verandrye, the mysterious Hearne, or the heroic Alexander Mackenzie, whose journeys we have already described, yet many daring adventurers who have gone on scientific or exploratory expeditions, or who have travelled the wide expanse for sport or for mere curiosity, may claim our attention.

The discovery of the magnetic pole by Sir John Ross, and the continued interest in the problems connected with the Arctic Sea, the romance of the North land, and the dream of a North-West Passage, led to the desire to have a scientific survey of the wide expanse of Rupert's Land. The matter was brought to the notice of the Royal Society by Major, afterwards General Sir Edward Sabine, a noted student of magnetism. Sir John Herschell, the leading light on the subject of physics, succeeded in inducing the Society to pronounce a favourable opinion on the project, and the strong influence of the Royal Society, under the presidency of the Marquis of Northampton, induced the Lords of the Treasury to meet the estimated expenses, nine hundred and ten pounds, with the understanding that, as stated by the President, gratuitous canoe conveyance would be provided by the Hudson's Bay Company in the territories belonging to them.

Lieutenant, afterwards General Sir Henry Lefroy, a young artillery officer, was selected to go upon the journey. A circu lar letter was sent to the Hudson's Bay Company posts by Governor Simpson, directing that every assistance should be given to the survey. Lefroy, having wintered in Montreal, was given a passage on May 1st, 1842, on the canoes for the North-West. Passing up the Ottawa and along the fur traders' route, he soon reached Sault Ste. Marie and Fort William; magnetic observations, accurate observations of latitude and longitude being made at the Hudson's Bay Company posts along the route. Kakabeka Falls and the various points along the Kaministiquia route were examined, and exchanging the "canot de maître" for the "canot de Nord," by way of Lake of the Woods and Lake Winnipeg, the observer arrived at Fort Garry on June 29th, having found Sir George Simpson at Lower Fort Garry.

After a close examination of the Red River Valley and some geological observations on the west side of Lake Winnipeg, Lefroy made his way to Norway House, and then by the watercourses, four hundred miles, to York Factory. Having done good work on the Bay, he made the return journey to Norway House, and on August 22nd, Cumberland House on the Saskatchewan was gained. Here he adopted the latitude and longitude taken by Franklin's two land expeditions, and here took seven independent observations of variation and dip of the magnetic needle.

Now striking energetically northward, and stopping long enough at the posts to take the necessary observations, the explorer arrived at Fort Chipewyan on September 23rd. It was twelve years since the dwellers on Lake Athabasca had been visited by any traveller from the south, and Lefroy's voyageurs, as they completed their three thousand miles of journey, decked out in their best apparel, made the echoes of the lake resound with their gay chansons. Lefroy wintered in the fort, where the winter months were enjoyed in the well-selected library of the Company and the new experiences of the fur trader's life, while his voyageurs went away to support themselves at a fishing station on the lake.

The summer of 1843 was spent in a round of thirteen hundred and forty miles, going from Lake Athabasca, up the Peace River to Fort Dunvegan, then by way of Lower Slave Lake to Edmonton, and down the Saskatchewan to Cumberland. Lefroy claims that no scientific traveller had visited the Peace River since the time of Alexander Mackenzie, fifty-five years before. Unfortunately, Lefroy's notes of this journey and some of his best observations were lost in his return through the United States, and could not be replaced.

In March, 1844, Lieutenant Lefroy left Lake Athabasca, and travelled on snow shoes to Fort Resolution on Great Slave Lake, and thence to Fort Simpson, four hundred and fifty miles, having his instruments for observation borne on dog sleds. This journey was made in nineteen days. Waiting at the Fort till May, he accomplished the descent of the Mackenzie River after the breaking up of the ice, and reached Fort Good Hope. The return journey to Fort Resolution was made at a very rapid rate, and the route thence to Lake Athabasca was followed. The diary ends June 30th, 1844.

At the close of the expedition some misunderstanding arose as to the settlement of the accounts. The Hudson's Bay Company had promised to give "gratuitous canoe conveyance." The original plan of the journey was, however, much changed, and Lieutenant Lefroy was a much greater expense to the Company than had been expected. A bill of upwards of twelve hundred pounds was rendered by the Hudson's Bay Company to the Royal Society. After certain explanations and negotiations a compromise of eight hundred and fifty pounds was agreed on, and this was paid by the Treasury Department to the Company.

The work done by Lieutenant Lefroy was of the most accurate and valuable kind. His name is remembered as that of one of the most trustworthy of the explorers of the plains of Rupert's Land and the North, and is commemorated by Fort Lefroy in the Rocky Mountains. It is true his evidence, recorded in the Blue Book of 1857, was somewhat disappointing, but his errors were those of judgment, not of prejudice or intention.

PALLISER AND HECTOR.

The approach of the time when the twenty-one years' lease of the Indian territories granted by the Imperial Parliament to the Hudson's Bay Company was drawing near a close in 1857, when the Committee of the House of Commons met in February of this year to consider the matter. A vast mass of evidence was taken, and the consideration of the Blue Book containing this will afford us material for a very interesting chapter. The interest in the matter, and the necessity for obtaining expert information, led the Imperial Government to organize an expedition under Captain John Palliser, R.N.A., of the Royal Engineers. With Captain Palliser, who was to go up the Canadian lakes to the interior, was associated Lieutenant Blakiston, R.N., who received orders to proceed by ship to York Factory and meet the main expedition at some point in Rupert's Land. The geologist of the expedition was James Hector, M.D. (Edin.). J. W. Sullivan was secretary and M. E. Bourgeau, botanist.

After the usual incidents of an ocean voyage, some difficulty with the Customs authorities in New York arose as to the entry of astronomical instruments, which was happily overcome, and after a long journey by way of Detroit, Sault Ste. Marie was reached, where Palliser found two birch bark canoes and sixteen voyageurs awaiting him, as provided by the Hudson's Bay Company. Sir George Simpson had lately passed this point. Journeying along the fur traders' route, the explorers found themselves expected at Fort Frances, on Rainy River.

Here a deputation of Indians waited upon them, and the old chief discoursed thus: "I do not ask for presents, although I am poor and my people are hungry, but I know you have come straight from the Great Country, and we know that no men from that country ever came to us and lied. I want you to declare to us truthfully what the Great Queen of your country intends to do to us when she will take the country from the fur company's people. All around me I see the smoke of the white men to rise. The 'Long Knives' (the Americans) are trading with our neighbours for their lands and they are cheating them and deceiving them. Now, we will not sell nor part with our lands."

Having reached Fort Garry, Captain Palliser divided his party, sending one section west, and himself going south to the boundary line with the other. Going west from Pembina, Palliser reached the French half-breed settlement of St. Joseph (St. Jo.), and some days afterwards Turtle Mountain. Thence he hurried across country to Fort Ellice to meet the other portion of his expedition.

While the tired horses rested here he made an excursion of a notable kind to the South-West. This was to the "Roches Percées" on the Souris River. This is a famous spot, noted for the presence of Tertiary sandstone exposures, which have weathered into the most fantastic shapes. It is a sacred spot of the Indians. Here, as at the "Red Pipestone Quarry," described by Longfellow, and not more than one hundred and fifty miles distant from it, Sioux, Assiniboines, and Crees meet in peace. Though war may prevail elsewhere, this spot is by mutual agreement kept as neutral. At this point Palliser saw a great camp of Assiniboines.

Returning from this side excursion, the Captain resumed his command, and having obtained McKay, the Hudson's Bay Company officer at Fort Ellice, with Governor Christie's permission, set off by way of Qu'Appelle Lakes for the elbow of the Saskatchewan.

On the South Saskatchewan Palliser came to the "heart of the buffalo country." The whole region as far as the eye could reach was covered with the buffalo in bands varying from hundreds to thousands. So vast were the herds, that he began to have serious apprehensions for his horses, as "the grass was eaten to the earth, as if the place had been devastated by locusts."

Crossing the Saskatchewan the explorers went northward to Fort Carlton on the north branch, where the party wintered while Captain Palliser returned to Canada, paying 65*l.* to a Red River trader to drive him five hundred and twenty miles from Fort Garry to Crow Wing, the nearest Minnesota settlement. Palliser's horse, for which he had bargained, was killed at Pembina, and he walked the four hundred and fifty miles of the journey, which was made with painful slowness by the struggling horses and sleds of the traders.

In June of the following year Palliser left Fort Carlton, part of his command going to the Red Deer River, the other part to visit Fort Pitt and Edmonton House. From Edmonton the explorer reports that during the summer, his men had succeeded in finding a pass through the Rocky Mountains, one not only practicable for horses, but which, with but little expense, could be rendered available for carts also.

He also states the passes discovered by him to be:—

(1) Kananaskis Pass and Vermilion Pass;

(2) Lake Pass and Beaver Foot Pass;

(3) Little Fork Pass;

(4) Kicking Horse Pass—six in all, which, with the North Kootenay (on British territory), make up seven known passes.

Having wintered at Edmonton, he satisfied himself that this region so far north and west is a good agricultural region, that the Saskatchewan region compares favourably with that of the Red River

Valley, that the rule of the country should be given over by the Hudson's Bay Company to the general Government, and that a railway could be built easily from the Red River to the eastern foot of the Rocky Mountains.

Orders having reached Palliser to proceed, he undertook, in the summer of 1859, a journey across the Rocky Mountains, following in part the old Hudson's Bay Company trail. On St. Andrew's Day, the party arrived at the Hudson's Bay Company post at Vancouver on the Columbia, and was welcomed by Mr. Graham, the officer in charge.

Taking steamer down the Columbia with his assistant Sullivan, Captain Palliser went to Victoria, a Hudson's Bay Company establishment on Vancouver Island, whither they were followed by Dr. Hector. Journeying south-west to San Francisco, he returned, via Isthmus of Panama, to New York and England.

The expedition was one of the best organized, best managed, and most successful that visited Rupert's Land. The report is a sensible, well-balanced, minute, and reliable account of the country passed over.

HIND AND DAWSON'S EXPLORATION.

In the same year that Palliser's expedition was despatched by the British Government to examine the resources and characteristics of Rupert's Land, a party was sent by the Canadian Government with similar ends in view, but more especially to examine the routes and means of access by which the prairies of the North-West might be reached from Lake Superior.

The staff of the party was as follows: George Gladman, director; Professor Henry Youle Hind, geologist; W. H. E. Napier, engineer; S. J. Dawson, surveyor. These, along with several foremen, twelve Caughnawaga Iroquois, from near Lachine, and twelve Ojibeway Indians from Fort William, made up a stirring canoe party of forty-four persons.

In July, 1857, the expedition left Toronto, went by land to Collingwood on Lake Huron, embarked there on the steamer *Collingwood*, and passing by Sault St. Marie, reached on August 1st

Fort William at the mouth of the Kaministiquia. Mr. John McIntyre, the officer of the Hudson's Bay Company in charge of Fort William, has given to the writer an account of the arrival of the party there with their great supply canoes, trading outfit, and apparatus, piled up high on the steamer's deck—a great contrast to the scanty but probably more efficient means of transport found on a Hudson's Bay Company trading journey. The party in due time went forward over the usual fur traders' route, which we have so often described, and arrived at Fort Garry early in September.

As the object of the expedition was to spy out the land, the Red River settlement, now grown to considerable size, afforded the explorers an interesting field for study. Simple though the conditions of life were, yet the fact that six or seven thousands of human beings were gaining a livelihood and were possessed of a number of the amenities of life, made its impress on the visitors, and Hind's chapters VI. to X. of his first volume are taken up with a general account of the settlement, the banks of the Red River, statistics of population, administration of justice, trade, occupations of the people, missions, education, and agriculture at Red River.

Having arrived at the settlement, the leaders devised plans for overtaking their work. The approach of winter made it impossible to plan expeditions over the plains to any profit. Mr. Gladman returned by canoe to Lake Superior early in September, Napier and his assistants took up their abode among the better class of English-speaking half-breeds between the upper and lower forts on the banks of the Red River. Mr. Dawson found shelter among his Roman Catholic co-religionists half a mile from Fort Garry. Ho and his party were to be engaged during the winter between Red River and the Lake of the Woods, along the route afterwards called the Dawson Road, while Hind followed his party up the western bank of Red River to Pembina, and his own account is that there was of them "all told, five gentlemen, five half-breeds, six saddle horses, and five carts, to which were respectively attached four poor horses and one refractory mule."

This party was returning to Canada, going by way of Crow Wing, thence by stage coach to St. Paul, on the Mississippi, then by rail unbroken to Toronto, which was reached after an absence of three and a half months.

The next season Hind was placed in charge of the expedition, and with new assistants went up the lakes in May, leading them by the long-deserted route of Grand Portage instead of by Kaministiquia. The journey from Lake Superior to Fort Garry was made in about twenty-one days. On their arrival at Red River the party found that Mr. Dawson had gone on an exploring tour to the Saskatchewan. Having organized his expedition Hind now went up the Assiniboine to Fort Ellice. The Qu'Appelle Valley was then explored, and the lake reached from which two streamlets flow, one into the Qu'Appelle and thence to the Assiniboine, the other into the Saskatchewan. Descending the Saskatchewan, at the mouth of which the Grand Rapids impressed the party, they made the journey thence up Lake Winnipeg and Red River to the place of departure. The tour was a most interesting one, having occupied all the summer. Hind was a close observer, was most skilful in working with the Hudson's Bay Company and its officers, and he gained an excellent view of the most fertile parts of the country. His estimate of it on the whole has been wonderfully borne out by succeeding years of experience and investigation.

MILTON AND CHEADLE.

The world at large, after Hind's expedition and the publication of his interesting observations, began to know more of the fur traders' land and showed more interest in it. In the years succeeding Hind's expedition a number of enterprising Canadians reached Fort Garry by way of St. Paul, Minn., and took up their abode in the country. A daring band of nearly 200 Canadians, drawn by the gold fever, started in 1862, on an overland journey to Cariboo; but many of them perished by the way. Three other well-known expeditions deserve notice.

The first of these was in 1862 by Viscount Milton and Dr. Cheadle. Coming from England by way of Minnesota to Fort Garry, they stopped at Red River settlement, and by conveyance crossed the prairies in their first season as far as Fort Carlton on the North Saskatchewan, and wintered there. The season was enjoyable, and in spring the explorers ascended the Saskatchewan to Edmonton, and then, by way of the Yellow Head Pass, crossed the Rocky Mountains. Their descent down the Thompson River was a most difficult one. The explorers were nearly lost through starvation, and on their arrival by way of Fraser River at Victoria their appearance was most distressing and their condition most pitiable. A few years ago, in company with a party of members of the British Association, Dr. Cheadle visited Winnipeg, and at a banquet in the city expressed to the writer his surprise that the former state of scarcity of food even on Red River had been so changed into the evident plenty which Manitoba now enjoys. Milton and Cheadle's "The North-West Passage by Land" is a most enjoyable book.

CAPTAIN BUTLER.

In the early months of the year 1870, when Red River -settlement was under the hand of the rebel Louis Riel, a tall, distinguished-looking stranger descended the Red River in the steamer *International*. News had been sent by a courier on horseback to the rebel chief that a dangerous stranger was approaching. The stalwart Irish visitor was Captain W. F. Butler, of H. M. 69th Regiment of Foot. As the *International* neared Fort Garry, Butler, with a well-known resident of Red River settlement, sprang upon the river-bank from the steamer in the dark as she turned into the Assiniboine River.

He escaped to the lower part of the settlement, but the knowledge that he had a letter from the Roman Catholic Archbishop Taché led to the rebel chief sending for and promising him a safe-conduct. Butler came and inspected the fort, and again departed to Lake Winnipeg, River Winnipeg, and Lake of the Woods, where he accomplished his real mission, in telling to General Wolseley, of the relief expedition coming to drive away the rebels, the state of matters in the Red River.

Captain Butler then went west, crossed country to the Saskatchewan, descended the river, and in winter came through, by snow-shoe and dog train, over Lakes Winnipegoosis and Manitoba to the east, and then to Europe.

Love of adventure brought Captain Butler back to the North-West. In 1872 he journeyed through the former fur traders' land, reaching Lake Athabasca in March, 1873. Ascending the Peace River, he arrived in Northern British Columbia in May. Through three hundred and fifty miles of the dense forests of New Caledonia he toiled to reach Quesnel, on the Fraser, four hundred miles north of Victoria, British Columbia, where he in due time landed.

Captain Butler has left a graphic, perhaps somewhat embellished, account of his travels in the books, "Great Lone Land" and "Wild North Land." The central figure of his first book is the faithful horse "Blackie" and of the second the Eskimo dog "Cerf-Vola." The appreciative reader feels, however, especially in the latter, the spirit and power of Milton's and Cheadle's "North-West Passage by Land" everywhere in these descriptive works.

FLEMING AND GRANT.

Third of these expeditions was that undertaken in 1872, under the leadership of Sandford Fleming, which has been chronicled in the work "Ocean to Ocean," by Rev. Principal Grant. The writer saw this expedition at Winnipeg in the summer of its arrival. It came for the purpose of crossing the plains, as a preliminary survey for a railway. The party came up the lakes, and by boat and portage over the traders' route, and the Dawson Road from Lake of the Woods to Red River, and halted near Fort Garry. Going westward, they for the most part followed the path of Milton and Cheadle. Fort Carlton and then Edmonton House were reached, and the Yellow Head Pass was followed to the North Thompson River. The forks of the river at Kamloops were passed, and then the canoe way down the Fraser to the sea was taken. The return journey was made by way of San Francisco. The expedition did much to open the way for Canadian emigration and to keep before the minds of Canadians the necessity for a waggon road across the Rocky Mountains and for a railway from ocean to ocean as soon as possible. Dr. Grant's conclusion was: "We know that we have a great North-West, a country like old Canada—not suited for lotus-eaters to live in, but fitted to rear a healthy and hardy race."

CHAPTER XXXV.

1817-1846

Chiefly Scottish and French settlers—Many hardships—Grasshoppers—Yellow Head—"Gouverneur Sauterelle"—Swiss settlers—Remarkable parchment—Captain Bulger, a military governor—Indian troubles—Donald Mackenzie, a fur trader, governor—Many projects fail—The flood—Plenty follows—Social condition—Lower Fort built—Upper Fort Garry—Council of Assiniboia—The settlement organized— Duncan Finlayson governor—English farmers—Governor Christie—Serious epidemic—A regiment of regulars—The unfortunate major—The people restless.

THE cessation of hostilities between the rival Companies afforded an opportunity to Lord Selkirk's settlement to proceed with its development. To the scared and harassed settlers it gave the prospects of peace under their Governor, Alexander Macdonell, who had been in the fur trade, but took charge of the settlement after the departure of Miles Macdonell. The state of affairs was far from promising. The population of Scottish and Irish settlers was less than two hundred. There were a hundred or thereabout of De Meurons, brought up by Lord Selkirk, and a number of French voyageurs, free traders or "freemen" as opposed to *engagés*, and those who, with their half-breed families, had begun to assemble about the forks and to take up holdings for themselves. For the last mentioned, the hunt, fishing, and the fur trade afforded a living; but as to the settlers and De Meurons, Providence seemed to favour them but little more than the hostile Nor'-Westers had done.

The settlers were chiefly men who were unacquainted with farming, and they had few implements, no cattle or horses, and the hoe and spade were their only means of fitting the soil for the small quantity of grain supplied them for sowing. Other means of employment or livelihood there were none. In 1818 the crops of the settlers were devoured by an incursion of locusts. On several occasions clouds of these destructive insects have visited Red River, and their ravages are not only serious, but they paralyze all effort on the part of the husbandmen. The description given by the prophet Joel was precisely reproduced on the banks of the Red River, "the land is as the Garden of Eden before them, and behind them is a desolate wilderness; yea, and nothing shall escape them." There was no resource for the settlers but to betake themselves to Pembina to seek the buffalo. In the next year they sowed their scanty seed, but the young "grass-hoppers," as they were called, rose from the eggs deposited in the previous year, and while the wheat was in the blade, cleared it from the fields more thoroughly than any reaper could have done. This scourge continued till the spring of 1821, when the locusts disappeared suddenly, and the crop of that year was a bountiful one.

During these years the colony was understood to be under the personal ownership of Lord Selkirk. He regarded himself as responsible, as lord paramount of the district, for the safety and support of the colonists. In the first year of the settlement he had sent out supplies of food, clothing, implements, arms, and ammunition; a store-house had been erected; and this continued during these years to be supplied with what was needed. It was the Governor's duty to regulate the distribution of these stores and to keep account of them as advances to the several settlers, and of the interest charged upon such advances. Whilst the store was a boon, even a necessity, to the settlers, it was also an instrument of oppression. Alexander Macdonell was called "Gouverneur Sauterelle" ("Grasshopper Governor"), the significant statement being made by Ross "that he was so nicknamed because he proved as great a destroyer within doors as the grasshoppers in the fields." He seems, moreover, to have been an extravagant official, being surrounded by a coterie of kindred spirits, who lived in "one prolonged scene of debauchery."

With the departure of the grasshoppers from the country departed also the unpopular and unfaithful Governor. It was only on the visit of Mr. Halkett, one of Lord Selkirk's executors, that Macdonell's course of "false entries, erroneous statements, and over-charges" was discovered, and the accounts of the settlers adjusted to give them their rights. The disgraceful reign of Governor Macdonell was brought to a close none too soon.

During the period of Governor Macdonell's rule a number of important events had taken place. The union of the two rival Companies was accomplished. Clergy, both Roman Catholic and of the Church of England, had arrived in the colony. A farm had been begun by the Colony officers on the banks of the Assiniboine, and the name of Hayfield Farm was borne by it. Perhaps the most notable event was the arrival at Red River of a number of Swiss settlers. These were brought out by Colonel May, late of the De Watteville regiment. A native of Berne, he had come to Canada, but not to Red River.

The Swiss were in many ways an element of interest. Crossing the ocean by Hudson's Bay Company's ships they arrived at York Factory in August, 1821, and were borne in the Company's York boats to their destination. Gathered, as they had been, from the towns and villages of Switzerland, and being chiefly "watch and clock makers, pastry cooks, and musicians," they were ill-suited for such a new settlement as that of Red River, where they must become agriculturists. They seem to have been honest and orderly people, though very poor.

It will be remembered that the De Meurons had come as soldiers; they were chiefly, therefore, unmarried men. The arrival of the Swiss, with their handsome sons and daughters, produced a flutter of excitement in the wifeless De Meuron cabins along Gorman Creek. The result is described in the words of a most trustworthy eye-witness of what took place: "No sooner had the Swiss emigrants arrived than many of the Germans, who had come to the settlement a few years ago from Canada and had houses, presented themselves in search of a wife, and having fixed their attachment with acceptance, they received those families in which was their choice into their habitations. Those who had no daughters to afford this introduction were obliged to pitch their tents along the banks of the river and outside the stockades of the fort, till they removed to Pembina in the better prospects of provisions for the winter." The whole affair was a repetition of the old Sabine story.

In connection with these De Meurons and Swiss, it may be interesting to mention a remarkable parchment agreement which the writer has perused. It is eleven feet long, and one and a half feet wide, containing the signatures of forty-nine settlers, of which twenty-five are those of De Meurons or Swiss, the remainder being of Highlanders and Norwegians. Among these names are Bender, Lubrevo, Quiluby, Bendowitz, Kralic, Wassloisky, Joli, Jankosky, Wachter, Lassota, Laidece, Warcklur, Krusel, Jolicoeur, Maquet, and Lalonde.

This agreement binds the Earl of Selkirk or his agents not to engage in the sale of spirituous liquors or the fur trade, but to provide facilities for transport of goods from and into the country, and at moderate rates. The settlers are bound to keep up roads, to support a clergyman, and to provide for defence. The document is not only a curiosity, but historically valuable. There is no date upon it, but the date is fixed by the signatures, viz. "for the Buffalo Wool Company, John Pritchard." That Company, we know, began, and as we shall see afterwards, failed in the years 1821 and 1822. This, accordingly, is the date of the document marking the era of the fusion of the Hudson's Bay Company and the Nor'-Westers.

The De Meurons and Swiss never took kindly to Red River. So early as 1822, after wintering at Pembina, a number of them, instead of turning their faces toward Fort Garry, went up the Red River into Minnesota, and took up farms where St. Paul now stands, on the Mississippi. They were the first settlers there. Among their names are those of Garvas, Pierrie, Louis Massey, and that of Perry, men who became very rich in herds in the early days of Minnesota.

On the removal of Governor Macdonell, Captain A. Bulger was, in June, 1822, installed as Governor of Assiniboia. His rule only lasted one year and proved troublous, though he was a high-minded and capable official. There lies before the writer, "Papers Referring to Red River," consisting chiefly of a long letter published by the Captain in India, written in 1822 to Andrew Colville, one of the executors of Lord Selkirk.

One of his chief troubles was the opposition given him by the Hudson's Bay Company officer Clarke, who was in charge of their establishment at the Forks. Every effort was put forth by Clarke to make Bulger's position uncomfortable, and the opposition drove the Captain away.

Bulger also had a worrying experience with Peguis, the chief of the Indians on the Lower Red River. Though Peguis and the other chiefs had made a treaty with Lord Selkirk and ceded certain lands to his Lordship, they now, with the fickleness of children, repented of their bargain and sought additional payment for the concession. Bulger's military manner, however, overcame the chief, and twenty-five lashes administered to an Indian who had attempted violence had a sobering effect upon the Red man.

Governor Bulger expresses himself very freely on the character of the De Meuron settlers. He says: "It is quite absurd to suppose they will ever prove peaceable and industrious settlers. The only charm that Red River possesses in their eyes, and, I may say, in the eyes of almost all the settlers, is the colony stores. Their demands are insatiable, and when refused, their insolence extreme. United as they are among themselves, and ferocious in their dispositions, nothing can be done against them." It is but fair, however, to state that the Captain had a low opinion both of the Hudson's Bay Company's officers and of the French Canadian freemen.

Governor Bulger, on retiring, made the following suggestions, which show the evils which he thought needed a remedy, viz. "to got courts and magistrates nominated by the King; to get a company of troops sent out to support the magistrates and keep the natives in order; to circulate money; to find a market for the surplus grain; to let it be determined whether the council at York Factory are justified in preventing the settlers from buying moose or deer skin for clothing and provisions." The Governor's closing words are, "if these things cannot be done, it is my sincere advice to you to spend no more of Lord Selkirk's money upon Red River."

Governor Bulger was succeeded by Robert Pelly, who was the brother of Sir J. H. Pelly, the Governor of the Company in London- It seems to have been about this time that the executors of Lord Selkirk, while not divesting themselves of their Red River possessions, yet in order to avoid the unseemly conflicts seen in Bulger's time, entrusted the administration of their affairs to the Company's officers at Red River. We have seen in a former chapter the appointment of the committee to manage these Red River affairs at Norway House council.

After two years Pelly retired, and Donald McKenzie, a fur trader who had taken part in the stirring events of Astoria, to which we have referred, became Governor.

The discontent of the settlers, and the wish to advance the colony, led the Company for a number of years after the union of the Companies to try various projects for the development of the colony. Though the recital of these gives a melancholy picture of failure, yet it shows a heartiness and willingness on the part of the Company to do the best for the settlers, albeit there was in every case bad management.

Immediately after the union of the two fur Companies in 1821, a company to manufacture cloth from buffalo wool was started. This, of course, was a mad scheme, but there was a clamour that work should be found for the hungry immigrants. The Company began operations, and every one was to become rich. $10,000 of money raised in shares was deposited in the Hudson's Bay Company's hands as the bankers of the "Buffalo Wool Company," machinery was obtained, and the people largely gave up agriculture to engage in killing buffalo and collecting buffalo skins. Trade was to be the philosopher's stone. In 1822 the bubble burst. It cost $12.50 to manufacture a yard of buffalo wool cloth on Red River, and the cloth only sold for $1.10 a yard in London. The Hudson's Bay Company advanced $12,500 beyond the amount deposited, and a few years afterwards was under the necessity of forgiving the debt. The Hudson's Bay Company had thus its lesson in encouraging the settlers.

The money distributed to the settlers through this Company, however, bought cattle for them, several hundred cattle having been brought from Illinois that year. A model farm for the benefit of the settlers was next undertaken. Buildings, implements, and also a mansion, costing $3,000, for the manager, were provided. A few years of mismanagement and extravagance brought this experiment to an end also, and the founders were $10,000 out of pocket. Such was another scheme to encourage the settlers.

Driven to another effort by the discontent of the people, Governor Simpson tried another model farm. At a fine spot on the Assiniboine, farm dwellings, barns, yards, and stables were erected and fields enclosed, well-bred cattle were imported, also horses. The farm was well stocked with implements. Mismanagement, however, again brought its usual result, and after six years the trial was given up, there having been a loss to the Company of $17,500.

Nothing daunted, the Red River settlers started the "Assiniboine Wool Company," but as it fell through upon the first demand for payment of the stock, it hurt nobody, and ended, according to the proverb, with "much cry and little wool."

Another enterprise was next begun by Governor Simpson, "The Flax and Hemp Company," but though the farmers grew a plentiful quantity of these, the undertaking failed, and the crop rotted on the fields. A more likely scheme for the encouragement of the settlers was now set on foot by the Governor, viz. a new sheep speculation. Sheep were purchased in Missouri, and after a journey of nearly fifteen hundred miles, only two hundred and fifty sheep out of the original fourteen hundred survived the hardships of the way.

A tallow company is said to have swallowed up from $3,000 to $5,000 for the Hudson's Bay Company, and a good deal of money was spent in opening up a road to Hudson Bay. Thus was enterprise after enterprise undertaken by the Company, largely for the good of the settlers. If ever an honest effort was made to advance an isolated and difficult colony, it was in these schemes begun by the Hudson's Bay Company here.

The most startling event during the rule of Governor Mackenzie was the Red River flood in 1826. The winter of this year had been severe, and a great snowfall gave promise of a wet and dangerous spring. The snow had largely cleared away, when, early in the month of May, the waters began rising with surprising rapidity. The banks of the rivers were soon unable to contain the floods, and once on the prairie level the waters spread for miles east and west in a great lake. The water rose several feet in the houses of the settlers. When the wind blew the waves dashed over the roofs. Buildings were undermined and some were floated away. The settlers were compelled to leave their homes, and took flight to the heights of Stony Mountain, Little Mountain, Bird's Hill, and other elevations. For weeks the flood continued, but at last, on its receding, the homeless settlers returned to their battered and damaged houses, much disheartened. The crops, however, were sown, though late, and a fair harvest was gathered in that unpromising year.

The flood was the last straw that broke the back of the endurance of De Meurons and Swiss colonists. They almost all withdrew from the country and became settlers in Minnesota and other States of the American Union. Either from pride or real dislike, the Selkirk settlers declared that they were well rid of these discontented and turbulent foreigners.

The year of the flood seems to have introduced an era of plenty, for the people rebuilt their houses, cultivated their fields, received full returns for their labour, and were enabled to pay off their debts and improve their buildings. During Governor McKenzie's regime at the time of the flood, the population of the Red River settlement had reached fifteen hundred.

After this, though the colony lost by desertions, as we have seen, yet it continued to gain by the addition of retiring Hudson's Bay Company officers and servants, who took up land as allowed by the Company in strips along the river after the Lower Canadian fashion, for which they paid small sums. There were in many cases no deeds, simply the registration of the name in the Company's register. A man sold his lot for a horse, and it was a matter of chance whether the registration of the change in the lot took place or not. This was certainly a mode of transferring land free enough to suit an English Radical or even Henry George. The land reached as far out from the river as could be seen by looking under a horse, say two miles, and back of this was the limitless prairie, which became a species of common where all could cut hay and where herds could run unconfined. Wood, water, and hay were the necessaries of a Red River settler's life; to cut poplar rails for his fences in spring and burn the dried rails in the following winter was quite the authorized thing. There was no inducement to grow surplus grain, as each settler could only get a market for eight bushels of wheat from the Hudson's Bay Company. It could not be exported. Pemmican from the plains was easy to get; the habits of the people were simple; their wants were few; and while the condition of Red River settlement was far from being that of an Arcadia, want was absent and the people were becoming satisfied.

To Governor McKenzie, who ruled well for eight years, credit is due largely for the peace and progress of the period. Alexander Ross, who came from the Rocky Mountains to Red River in 1825, is the chronicler of this period, and it is with amusement we read his gleeful account of the erection of the first stone building, small though it was, on the banks of Red River. Lime had been burnt from the limestone, found abundantly along the lower part of the Red River, during the time of Governor Bulger. It was in 1830 that the Hudson's Bay Company built a small powder magazine of stone, near Fort Garry. This was the beginning of solid architecture in the settlement.

In the following year the Hudson's Bay Company, evidently encouraged by the thrift and contentment of the people, began the erection of a very notable and important group of buildings some nineteen miles down the river from the forks. This was called Lower Fort Garry. It was built on the solid rock, and was, and is to this day, surrounded by a massive stone wall. Various reasons have been advanced for the building of this, the first permanent fort so far from the old centre of trade, and of the old associations at the "forks." Some have said it was done to place it among the English people, as the French settlers were becoming turbulent; some that it was at the head of navigation from Lake Winnipeg, being north of the St. Andrew's rapids; and some maintained that the site was chosen as having been far above the high water during the year of flood, when Fort Douglas and Upper Fort Garry had been surrounded. The motive will probably never be known; but for a time it was the residence of the Governor of Rupert's Land when he was in the country, and was the seat of government. Four years afterwards, when Alexander Christie had replaced Mr. Donald McKenzie as local governor, Fort Garry or Upper Fort Garry was begun in 1835 at the forks, but on higher ground than the original Fort Garry of 1821, which had been erected after the union of the Companies.

This fort continued the centre of business, government, education, and public affairs for more than three decades and was the nucleus of the City of Winnipeg. Sold in the year 1882, the fort was demolished, and the front gate, now owned by the city, is all that remains of this historic group of buildings. The destruction of the fort was an act of vandalism, reflecting on the sordid man who purchased it from the Hudson's Bay Company.

In Governor Christie's time the necessity was recognized of having a form of government somewhat less patriarchal than the individual rule of the local governor had been. Accordingly, the Council of Assiniboia was appointed by the Hudson's Bay Company, the president being Sir George Simpson, the Governor of Rupert's Land, and with him fourteen councillors. It may be of interest to give the names of the members of this first Council. Besides the president there were: Alexander Christie, Governor of the Colony; Rev. D. T. Jones, Chaplain H. B. C.; Right Rev. Bishop Provencher; Rev. William Cochrane, Assistant Chaplain; James Bird, formerly Chief Factor, H. B. C.; James Sutherland, Esq.; W. H.

Cook, Esq.; John Pritchard, Esq.; Robert Logan, Esq.; Sheriff Alex. Ross; John McCallum, Coroner; John Bunn, Medical Adviser; Cuthbert Grant, Esq., Warden of the Plains; Andrew McDermott, Merchant.

It is generally conceded, however, that the Council did not satisfy the public aspirations. The president and councillors were all declared either sinecurists or paid servants of the Company. The mass of the people complained at not being represented. It was, however, a step very much in advance of what had been, although there was a suspicion in the public mind that it had something of the form of popular government without the substance.

At the first meeting of the Council a number of measures were passed. To preserve order a volunteer corps of sixty men was organized, with a small annual allowance per man. Of this body, Sheriff Ross was commander. The settlement was divided into four districts, over each of which a Justice of the Peace was appointed, who held quarterly courts in their several jurisdictions. At this court small actions only were tried, and the presiding magistrate was allowed to refer any case of exceptional difficulty to the court of Governor and Council. This higher court sat quarterly also. In larger civil cases and in criminal cases the law required a jury to be called. A jail and court-house were erected outside the walls of Fort Garry. To meet the expense involved under the new institutions a tax of 7½ per cent. duty was levied on imports and a like duty on exports. The Hudson's Bay Company also agreed to contribute three hundred pounds a year in aid of public works throughout the settlement.

The year 1839 was notable in the history of the colony. A new Governor, Duncan Finlayson, was appointed, and steps were taken also to improve the judicial system which had been introduced. An appointment was made of the first recorder for Red River settlement. The new appointee was a young Scottish lawyer from Montreal, named Adam Thorn. He had been a journalist in Montreal, was of an ardent and somewhat aggressive disposition, but was a man of ability and broad reading. Judge Thorn was, however, a Company officer, and as such there was an antecedent suspicion of him in the public mind. It was pointed out that he was not independent, receiving his appointment and his salary of seven hundred pounds from the Company. In Montreal he had been known as a determined loyalist in the late Papineau rebellion, and the French people regarded him as hostile to their race.

The population of the settlement continued to increase. In the last year of Governor Finlayson's rule, twenty families of Lincolnshire farmers and labourers came to the country to assist with their knowledge of agriculture. After five years' rule Governor Finlayson retired from office, and was succeeded for a short time by his old predecessor, Mr. Alexander Christie.

A serious epidemic visited the Red River in the year 1846. Ross describes it in the following graphic way: "In January the influenza raged, and in May the measles broke out; but neither of these visitations proved fatal. At length in June a bloody flux began its ravages first among the Indians, and others among the whites; like the great cry in Egypt, 'There was not a house where there was not one dead.' On Red River there was not a smiling face on 'a summer's day.' From June 18th to August 2nd, the deaths averaged seven a day, or three Hundred and twenty-one in all, being one out of every sixteen of our population. Of these one-sixth were Indians, two-thirds half-breeds, and the remainder white. On one occasion thirteen burials were proceeding at once."

During this year also the Oregon question, with which we shall afterwards deal, threatened war between Great Britain and the United States. The policy of the British Government is, on the first appearance of trouble, to prepare for hostilities. Accordingly the 6th Royal Regiment of Foot, with sappers and artillery, in all five hundred strong, was hurried out under Colonel Crofton to defend the colony. Colonel Crofton took the place of Alexander Christie as Governor. The addition of this body of military to the colony gave picturesqueness to the hitherto monotonous life of Red River. A market for produce and the circulation of a large sum of money marked their stay on Red River. The turbulent spirits who had made much trouble were now silenced, or betook themselves to a safe place across the boundary line.

CHAPTER XXXVI.

THE great prairies of Rupert's Land and their intersecting rivers afforded the means for the unique and picturesque life of the prairie hunters and traders. The frozen, snowy plains and lakes were crossed in winter by the serviceable sledge drawn by Eskimo dogs, familiarly called "Eskies" or "Huskies." When summer had come, the lakes and rivers of the prairies, formerly skimmed by canoes, during the fifty years from the union of the Companies till the transfer of Rupert's Land to Canada, were for freight and even rapid transit crossed and followed by York and other boats. The transport of furs and other freight across the prairies was accomplished by the use of carts—entirely of wood—drawn by Indian ponies, or by oxen in harness, while the most picturesque feature of the prairie life of Red River was the departure of the brigade of carts with the hunters and their families on a great expedition for the exciting chase of the buffalo. These salient points of the prairie life of the last half-century of fur-trading life we may with profit depict.

SLEDGE AND PACKET.

Under the regime established by Governor Simpson, the communication with the interior was reduced to a system. The great winter event at Red River was the leaving of the North-West packet about December 10th. By this agency every post in the northern department was reached. Sledges and snowshoes were the means by which this was accomplished. The sledge or tobogan was drawn by three or four "Huskies," gaily comparisoned; and with these neatly harnessed dogs covered with bells, the traveller or the load of valuables was hurried across the pathless snowy wastes of the plains or over the ice of the frozen lakes and rivers. The dogs carried their freight of fish on which they lived, each being fed only at the close of his day's work, and his allowance one fish.

The winter packet was almost entirely confined to the transport of letters and a few newspapers. During Sir George Simpson's time an annual file of the *Montreal Gazette* was sent to each post, and to some of the larger places came a year's file of the London *Times.* A box was fastened on the back part of the sledge, and this was packed with the important missives so prized when the journey was ended.

Going at the rate of forty or more miles a day with the precious freight, the party with their sledges camped in the shelter of a clump of trees or bushes, and built their camp fire; then each in his blankets, often joined by the favourite dog as a companion for heat, sought rest on the couch of spruce or willow boughs for the night with the thermometer often at 30 deg. or 40 deg. below zero F.

The winter packet ran from Fort Garry to Norway House, a distance of 350 miles. At this point the packet was all rearranged, a part of the freight being carried eastward to Hudson Bay, the other portion up the Saskatchewan to the western and northern forts. The party which had taken the packet to Norway House, at that point received the packages from Hudson Bay and with them returned to Fort Garry. The western mail from Norway House was taken by another sledge party up the Saskatchewan River, and leaving parcels at posts along the route, reached its rendezvous at Carlton House. The return party from that point received the mail from the North, and hastened to Fort Garry by way of Swan River district, distributing its treasures to the posts it passed and reaching Fort Garry usually about the end of February.

At Carlton a party of runners from Edmonton and the Upper Saskatchewan made rendezvous, deposited their packages, received the outgoing mail, and returned to their homes. Some of the matter collected from the Upper Saskatchewan and that brought, as we have seen, by the inland packet from Fort Garry was taken by a new set of runners to Mackenzie River, and Athabasca. Thus at Carlton there met three parties, viz. from Fort Garry, Edmonton, and Athabasca. Each brought a packet and received another back in return. The return packet from Carlton to Fort Garry, arriving in February, took up the accumulated material, went with it to Norway House, the place whence they had started in December, thus carrying the "Red River spring packet," and at Norway House it was met by another express, known as the "York Factory spring packet," which had just arrived. The runners on these various packets underwent great exposure, but they were fleet and athletic and knew how to act to the best advantage in storm and danger. They added a picturesque interest to the lonely life of the ice-bound post as they arrived at it, delivered their message, and again departed.

KEEL AND CANOE.

The transition from winter to spring is a very rapid one on the plains of Rupert's Land. The ice upon the rivers and lakes becomes honey-combed and disappears very soon. The rebound from the icy torpor of winter to the active life of the season that combines spring and summer is marvellous. No sooner were the waterways open in the fur-trading days than freight was hurried from one part of the country to another by moans of inland or York boats.

These boats, it will be remembered, were introduced by Governor Simpson, who found them more safe and economical than the canoe generally in use before his time.

Each of these boats could carry three or four tons of freight, and was manned by nine men, one of them being steersman, the remainder, men for the oar. Four to eight of these craft made up a brigade, and the skill and rapidity with which these boats could be loaded or unloaded, carried past a portage or decharge, guided through rapids or over considerable stretches of the lakes, was the pride of their Indian or half-breed tripsmen, as they were called, or the admiration of the officers dashing past them in their speedy canoes.

The route from York Factory to Fort Garry being a long and continuous waterway, was a favourite course for the York boat brigade. Many of the settlers of the Red River settlement became well-to-do by commanding brigades of boats and carrying freight for the Company. In the earlier days of Governor Simpson the great part of the furs from the interior were carried to Fort Garry or the Grand Portage, at the mouth of the Saskatchewan, and thence past Norway House to Hudson Bay. From York Factory a load of general merchandise was brought back, which had been cargo in the Company's ship from the Thames to York. Lake Winnipeg is generally clear of ice early in June, and the first brigade would then start with its seven or eight boats laden to the gunwales with furs; a week after, the second brigade was under way, and thus, at intervals to keep clear of each other in crossing the portages, the catch of the past season was carried out. The return with full supplies for the settlers was earnestly looked for, and the voyage both ways, including stoppages, took some nine weeks.

Far up into the interior the goods in bales were taken. One of the best known routes was that of what was called, "The Portage Brigade." This ran from Lake Winnipeg up the Saskatchewan northward, past Cumberland House and Ile a la Crosse to Methy Portage, otherwise known as Portage la Loche, where the waters part, on one side going to Hudson's Bay, on the other flowing to the Arctic Sea. The trip made from Fort Garry to Portage la Loche and return occupied about four months. At Portage la Loche the brigade from the Mackenzie River arrived in time to meet that from the south, and was itself soon in motion, carrying its year's supply of trading articles for the Far North, not even leaving out Peel's River and the Yukon.

The frequent transhipments required in these long and dangerous routes led to the secure packing of bales, of about one hundred pounds each, each of them being called an "inland piece." Seventy-five made up the cargo of a York boat. The skill with which these boats could be laden was surprising. A good half-breed crew of nine men was able to load a boat and pack the pieces securely in five minutes.

The boat's crew was under the command of the steersman, who sat on a raised platform in the stern of the boat. At the portages it was the part of the steersman to raise each piece from the ground and place two of them on the back of each tripsman, to be held in place by the "portage strap" on the forehead. It will be seen that the position of the captain was no sinecure. One of the eight tripsmen was known as "bows-man." In running rapids he stood at the bow, and with a light pole directed the boat, giving information by word and sign to the steersman. The position of less responsibility though great toil was that of the "middlemen," or rowers. When a breeze blew, a sail hoisted in the boat lightened their labours. The captain or steersman of each boat was responsible to the "guide," who, as a commander of the brigade, was a man of much experience, and consequently held a position of some importance. Such were the means of transport over the vast water system of Rupert's Land up to the year 1869, although some years before that time transport by land to St. Paul in Minnesota had reached large proportions. Since the date named, railway and steamboat have directed trade into new channels, for even Mackenzie River now has a Hudson's Bay Company steamboat.

CART AND CAYUSE.

The lakes and rivers were not sufficient to carry on the trade of the country. Accordingly, land transport became a necessity. If the Ojibeway Indians found the birch bark canoe and the snowshoe so useful that they assigned their origin to the Manitou, then certainly it was a happy thought when the famous Rod River cart was similarly evolved. These two-wheeled vehicles are entirely of wood, without any iron whatever.

The wheels are large, being five feet in diameter, and are three inches thick. The felloes are fastened to one another by tongues of wood, and pressure in revolving keeps them from falling apart. The hubs are thick and very strong. The axles are wood alone, and even the lynch pins are wooden. A light box frame, tightened by wooden pegs, is fastened by the same agency and poised upon the axle. The price of a cart in Red River of old was two pounds.

The harness for the horse which drew the cart was made of roughly-tanned ox hide, which was locally known as "shagganappe." The name "shagganappe" has in later years been transferred to the small-sized horse used, which is thus called a "shagganappe pony."

The carts were drawn by single ponies, or in some cases by stalwart oxen. These oxen were harnessed and wore a collar, not the barbarous yoke which the ox has borne from time immemorial. The ox in harness has a swing of majesty as he goes upon his journey. The Indian pony, with a load of four or five hundred pounds in a cart behind him, will go at a measured jog-trot fifty or sixty miles a day. Heavy freighting carts made a journey of about twenty miles a day, the load being about eight hundred pounds.

A train of carts of great length was sometimes made to go upon some long expedition, or for protection from the thievish or hostile bands of Indians. A brigade consisted of ten carts, under the charge of three men. Five or six more brigades were joined in one train, and this was placed under the charge of a guide, who was vested with much authority. He rode on horseback forward, marshalling his forces, including the management of the spare horses or oxen, which often amounted to twenty per cent. of the number of those drawing the carts. The stopping-places, chosen for good grass and a plentiful supply of water, the time of halting, the management of brigades, and all the details of a considerable camp were under the care of this officer-in-chief.

One of the most notable cart trails and freighting roads on the prairies was that from Fort Garry to St. Paul, Minnesota. This was an excellent road, on the west side of the Red River, through Dakota territory for some two hundred miles, and then, by crossing the Red River into Minnesota, the road led for two hundred and fifty miles down to St. Paul. The writer, who came shortly after the close of the fifty years we are describing, can testify to the excellence of this road over the level prairies. At the period when the Sioux Indians were in revolt and the massacre of the whites took place in 1862, this route was dangerous, and the road, though not so smooth and not so dry, was followed on the east side of the Red River.

Every season about three hundred carts, employing one hundred men, departed from Fort Garry to go upon the "tip," as it was called, to St. Paul, or in later times to St. Cloud, when the railway had reached that place. The visit of this band coming from the north, with their wooden carts, "shag-ganappe" ponies, and harnessed oxen, bringing huge bales of precious furs, awakened great interest in St. Paul. The late J. W. Taylor, who for about a quarter of a century held the position of American Consul at Winnipeg, and who, on account of his interest in the North-West prairies, bore the name of "Saskatchewan Taylor," was wont to describe most graphically the advent, as he saw it, of this strange expedition, coming, like a Midianitish caravan in the East, to trade at the central mart. On Sundays they encamped near St. Paul. There was the greatest decorum and order in camp; their religious demeanour, their honest and well-to-do appearance, and their peaceful disposition were an oasis in the desert of the wild and reckless inhabitants of early Minnesota.

Another notable route for carts was that westward from Fort Garry by way of Fort Ellice to Carlton House, a distance of some five hundred miles. It will be remembered that it was by this route that Governor Simpson in early days, Palliser, Milton, and Cheadle found their way to the West. In later days the route was extended to Edmonton House, a thousand miles in all. It was a whole summer's work to make the trip to Edmonton and return.

On the Hudson's Bay Company reserve of five hundred acres around Fort Garry was a wide camping-ground for the "trippers" and traders. Day after day was fixed for the departure, but still the traders lingered. After much leave-taking, the great train started. It was a sight to be remembered. The gaily-comparisoned horses, the hasty farewells, the hurry of women and children, the multitude of dogs, the balky horses, the subduing and harnessing and attaching of the restless ponies, all made it a picturesque day. The train in motion appealed not only to the eye, but to the ear as well, the wooden axles creaked, and the creaking of a train with every cart contributing its dismal share, could be heard more than a mile away. In the Far-West the early traders used the cayuse, or Indian pony, and "travoie," for transporting burdens long distances. The "travoie" consisted of two stout poles fastened together over the back of the horse, and dragging their lower ends upon the ground. Great loads—almost inconceivable, indeed—were thus carried across the pathless prairies. The Red River cart and the Indian cayuse were the product of the needs of the prairies.

PLAIN HUNTERS AND THE BUFFALO.

A generation had passed since the founding of the Selkirk settlement, and the little handful of Scottish settlers had become a community of five thousand. This growth had not been brought about by immigration, nor by natural increase, but by what may be called a process of accretion. Throughout the whole of Rupert's Land and adjoining territories the employés of the Company, whether from Lower Canada or from the Orkney Islands, as well as the clerks and officers of the country, had intermarried with the Indian women of the tribes.

When the trader or Company's servant had gained a competence suited to his ideas, he thought it right to retire from the active fur trade and float down the rivers to the settlement, which the first Governor of Manitoba called the "Paradise of Red River." Here the hunter or officer procured a strip of land from the Company, on it erected a house for the shelter of his "dusky race," and engaged in agriculture, though his former life largely unfitted him for this occupation. In this way, four-fifths of the population of the settlement were half-breeds, with their own traditions, sensibilities, and prejudices—the one part of them speaking French with a dash of Cree mixed with it, the other English which, too, had the form of a Red River patois.

We have seen that tripping and hunting gave a livelihood to some, if not the great majority, but these occupations unfitted men for following the plough. In addition there was no market for produce, so that agriculture did not in general thrive. One of the favourite features of Red River, which fitted in thoroughly with the roving traditions of the large part of the population, was the annual buffalo hunt, which, for those who engaged in it, occupied a great portion of the summer.

We have the personal reminiscences of the hunt by Alexander Ross, sometime sheriff of Assiniboia, which, as being lively and graphic, are worthy of being reproduced.

Ross says: "Buffalo hunting here, like bear baiting in India, has become a popular and favourite amusement among all classes; and Red River, in consequence, has been brought into some degree of notice by the presence of strangers from foreign countries. We are now occasionally visited by men of science as well as men of pleasure. The war road of the savage and the solitary haunt of the bear have of late been resorted to by the florist, the botanist, and the geologist; nor is it uncommon nowadays to see officers of the Guards, knights, baronets, and some of the higher nobility of England and other countries coursing their steeds over the boundless plains and enjoying the pleasures of the chase among the half-breeds and savages of the country. Distinction of rank is, of course, out of the question, and at the close of the adventurous day all squat down in merry mood together, enjoying the social freedom of equality round Nature's table and the novel treat of a fresh buffalo steak served up in the style of the country, that is to say, roasted on a forked stick before the fire; a keen appetite their only sauce, cold water their only beverage. Looking at this assemblage through the medium of the imagination, the mind is led back to the chivalric period of former days, when chiefs and vassals took counsel together. . . .

"With the earliest dawn of spring the hunters are in motion like bees, and the colony in a state of confusion, from their going to and fro, in order to raise the wind and prepare themselves for the fascinating enjoyments of hunting. It is now that the Company, the farmers, the petty traders are all beset by their incessant and irresistible importunities. The plain mania brings everything else to a stand. One wants a horse, another an axe, a third a cart; they want ammunition, they want clothing, they want provisions; and though people refuse one or two they cannot deny a whole population, for, indeed, over-much obstinacy would not be unattended with risk. Thus the settlers are reluctantly dragged into profligate speculation.

"The plain hunters, finding they can get whatever they want without ready money, are led into ruinous extravagances; but the evil of the long credit system does not end here. . . . So many temptations, so many attractions are held out to the thoughtless and giddy, so fascinating is the sweet air of freedom, that even the offspring of the Europeans, as well as natives, are often induced to cast off their habits of industry and leave their comfortable homes to try their fortunes in the plains.

The practical result of all this may be stated in a few words. After the expedition starts there is not a man-servant or maidservant to be found in the colony. At any season but seedtime and harvest-time, the settlement is literally swarming with idlers; but at these urgent periods money cannot procure them."

The actual money value expended on one trip, estimating also their lost time, is as follows:—

1210	carts (in 1840).	£1815
620	hunters (two months) at 1s. a day.	1860
600	women (two months) at 9d.	1460
360	boys and girls (two months) at 4d.	360
403	buffalo runners (horses) at 15l.	6045
655	cart horses at 8l.	6240
586	draught oxen at 6l.	23516
Guns, gunpowder, knives, axes, harness, camp equipage, and utensils (estimate approaching)		3700
	Say	£24,000

"From Fort Garry, June 15th, 1840, the cavalcade and followers went crowding on to the public road, and thence, stretching from point to point, till the third day in the evening, when they reached Pembina (sixty miles south of Fort Garry), the great rendezvous on such occasions. When the hunters leave the settlement it enjoys that relief which a person feels on recovering from a long and painful sickness. Here, on a level plain, the whole patriarchal camp squatted down like pilgrims on a journey to the Holy Land in ancient days, only not quite so devout, for neither scrip nor staff were consecrated for the occasion. Here the roll was called and general muster taken, when they numbered on this occasion 1,630 souls; and hero the rules and regulations for the journey were finally settled. The officials for the trip were named and installed into office, and all without the aid of writing materials.

"The camp occupied as much ground as a modern city, and was formed in a circle. All the carts were placed side by side, the trams outward. Within this line of circumvallation, the tents were placed in double, treble rows, at one end, the animals at the other, in front of the tents. This is the order in all dangerous places, but where no danger is apprehended, the animals are kept on the outside. Thus the carts formed a strong barrier, not only for securing the people and their animals within, but as a place of shelter and defence against an attack of the enemy from without."

In 1820 the number of carts assembled for the first trip was							540
" 1825	"	"	"	"	"	"	680
" 1825	"	"	"	"	"	"	680
" 1825	"	"	"	"	"	"	680
" 1825	"	"	"	"	"	"	680

"There is another appendage belonging to the expedition, and these are not always the least noisy, viz. the dogs or camp followers. On the present occasion they numbered no fewer than 542. In deep snow, where horses cannot conveniently be used, dogs are very serviceable animals to the hunters in these parts. The half-breed, dressed in his wolf costume, tackles two or three sturdy curs into a flat sled, throws himself on it at full length, and gets among the buffalo unperceived. Here the bow and arrow play their part to prevent noise. And here the skilful hunter kills as many as he pleases, and returns to camp without disturbing the band.

"But now to the camp again—the largest of the kind, perhaps, in the world. The first step was to hold a council for the nomination of chiefs or officers for conducting the expedition. Ten captains were named, the senior on this occasion being Jean Baptiste Wilkie, an English half-breed, brought up among the French, a man of good sound sense and long experience, and withal a fine, bold-looking, and discreet fellow, a second Nimrod in his way.

"Besides being captain, in common with the others, he was styled the great war chief or head of the camp, and on all public occasions he occupied the place of president. All articles of property found without an owner were carried to him and he disposed of them by a crier, who went round the camp every evening, were it only an awl. Each captain had ten soldiers under his orders, in much the same way as policemen are subject to the magistrate. Ten guides were likewise appointed, and here we may remark that people in a rude state of society, unable either to read or write, are generally partial to the number ten. Their duties were to guide the camp each in his turn—that is day about—during the expedition. The camp flag belongs to the guide of the day; he is therefore standard bearer in virtue of his office.

"The hoisting of the flag every morning is the signal for raising camp. Half an hour is the full time allowed to prepare for the march; but if anyone is sick or their animals have strayed, notice is sent to the guide, who halts till all is made right. From the time the flag is hoisted, however, till the hour of camping arrives it is never taken down. The flag taken down is a signal for encamping. While it is up the guide is chief of the expedition. Captains are subject to him, and the soldiers of the day are his messengers; he commands all. The moment the flag is lowered his functions cease, and the captains and soldiers' duties commence. They point out the order of the camp, and every cart as it arrives moves to its appointed place. This business usually occupies about the same time as raising camp in the morning; for everything moves with the regularity of clockwork."

All being ready to leave Pembina, the captains and other chief men hold another council and lay down the rules to be observed during the expedition. Those made on the present occasion were:—

(1) No buffalo to be run on the Sabbath day.

(2) No party to fork off, lag behind, or go before, without permission.

(3) No person or party to run buffalo before the general order.

(4) Every captain with his men in turn to patrol the camp and keep guard.

(5) For the first trespass against these laws, the offender to have his saddle and bridle cut up.

(6) For the second offence the coat to be taken off the offender's back and to be cut up.

(7) For the third offence the offender to be flogged.

(8) Any person convicted of theft, even to the value of a sinew, to be brought to the middle of the camp, and the crier to call out his or her name three times, adding the word "Thief" at each time.

On the 21st the start was made, and the picturesque line of march soon stretched to the length of some five or six miles in the direction of south-west towards Cote à Pique. At 2 p.m. the flag was struck, as a signal for resting the animals. After a short interval it was hoisted again, and in a few minutes the whole line was in motion, and continued the route till five or six o'clock in the evening, when the flag was hauled down as a signal to encamp for the night. Distance travelled, twenty miles.

"The camp being formed, all the leading men, officials, and others assembled, as the general custom is, on some rising ground or eminence outside the ring, and there squatted themselves down, tailor-like, on the grass in a sort of council, each having his gun, his smoking bag in his hand, and his pipe in his mouth. In this situation the occurrences of the day were discussed, and the line of march for the morrow agreed upon. This little meeting was full of interest, and the fact struck me very forcibly that there is happiness and pleasure in the society of the most illiterate men, sympathetically if not intellectually inclined, as well as among the learned, and I must say I found less selfishness and more liberality among these ordinary men than I had been accustomed to find in higher circles. Their conversation was free, practical, and interesting, and the time passed on more agreeably than could be expected among such people, till we touched on politics.

"Of late years the field of chase has been far from Pembina, and the hunters do not so much as know in what direction they may find the buffalo, as those animals frequently shift their ground. It is a mere leap in the dark, whether at the outset the expedition takes the right or the wrong road; and their luck in the chase, of course, depends materially on the choice they make. The year of our narrative they travelled a south-west or middle course, being the one generally preferred, since it leads past most of the rivers near their sources, where they are easily crossed. The only inconvenience attending this choice is the scarcity of wood, which in a warm season is but a secondary consideration.

"Not to dwell on the ordinary routine of each day's journey, it was the ninth day from Pembina before we reached the Cheyenne River, distant only about 150 miles, and as yet we had not seen a single band of buffalo. On July 3rd, our nineteenth day from the settlement, and at a distance of little more than 250 miles, we came in sight of our destined hunting grounds, and on the day following we had our first buffalo race. Our array in the field must have been a grand and imposing one to those who had never seen the like before. No less than 400 huntsmen, all mounted, and anxiously waiting for the word 'Start!' took up their position in a line at one end of the camp, while Captain Wilkie, with his spyglass at his eye, surveyed the buffalo, examined the ground, and issued his orders. At eight o'clock the whole cavalcade broke ground, and made for the buffalo; first at a slow trot, then at a gallop, and lastly at full speed. Their advance was over a dead level, the plain having no hollow or shelter of any kind to conceal their approach. We need not answer any queries as to the feeling and anxiety of the camp on such an occasion. When the horsemen started the cattle might have been a mile and a half ahead, but they had approached to within four or five hundred yards before the bulls curved their tails or pawed the ground. In a moment more the herd took flight, and horse and rider are presently seen bursting in among them. Shots are heard, and all is smoke, dash, and hurry. The fattest are first singled out for slaughter, and in less time than we have occupied with the description, a thousand carcases strew the plain.

"The moment the animals take to flight the best runners dart forward in advance. At this moment a good horse is invaluable to his owner, for out of the 400 on this occasion, not above fifty got the first chance of the fat cows. A good horse and an experienced rider will select and kill from ten to twelve animals at one heat, while inferior horses are contented with two or three. But much depends on the nature of the ground. On this occasion the surface was rocky, and full of badger holes. Twenty-three horses and riders were at one moment sprawling on the ground. One horse, gored by a bull, was killed on the spot, two men disabled by the fall. One rider broke his shoulder blade; another burst his gun and lost throe of his fingers by the accident; and a third was struck on the knee by an exhausted ball. These accidents will not be thought over-numerous considering the result; for in the evening no less than. 1,375 buffalo tongues wore brought into camp.

"The rider of a good horse seldom fires till within three or four yards of his object, and never misses. And, what is admirable in point of training, the moment the shot is fired his steed springs on one side to avoid stumbling over the animal, whereas an awkward and shy horse will not approach within ten or fifteen yards, consequently the rider has often to fire at random and not infrequently misses. Many of them, however, will fire at double that distance and make sure of every shot. The mouth is always full of balls; they load and fire at the gallop, and but seldom drop a mark, although some do to designate the animal.

"Of all the operations which mark the hunter's life and are essential to his ultimate success, the most perplexing, perhaps, is that of finding out and identifying the animals he kills during a race. Imagine 400 horsemen entering at full speed a herd of some thousands of buffalo, all in rapid motion. Riders in clouds of dust and volumes of smoke which darken the air, crossing and recrossing each other in every direction; shots on the right, on the left, behind, before, here, there, two, three, a dozen at a time, everywhere in close succession, at the same moment. Horses stumbling, riders falling, dead and wounded animals tumbling here and there, one over the other; and this zigzag and bewildering melée continued for an hour or more together in wild confusion. And yet, from practice, so keen is the eye, so correct the judgment, that after getting to the end of the race, he can not only toll the number of animals which he had shot down, but the position in which each lies—on the right or on the left side—the spot where the shot hit, and the direction of the ball; and also retrace his way, step by step, through the whole race and recognize every animal he had the fortune to kill, without the least hesitation or difficulty. To divine how this is accomplished bewilders the imagination.

"The main party arrived on the return journey at Pembina on August 17th, after a journey of two months and two days. In due time the settlement was reached, and the trip being a successful one, the returns on this occasion may be taken as a fair annual average. An approximation to the truth is all we can arrive at, however. Our estimate is nine hundred pounds weight of buffalo meat per cart, a thousand being considered the full load, which gives one million and eighty-nine thousand pounds in all, or something more than two hundred pounds weight for each individual, old and young, in the settlement. As soon as the expedition arrived, the Hudson's Bay Company, according to usual custom, issued a notice that it would take a certain specified quantity of provisions, not from each fellow that had been on the plains, but from each old and recognized hunter. The established price at this period for the three kinds over head, fat, pemmican, and dried meat, was two pence a pound. This was then the Company's standard price; but there is generally a market for all the fat they bring. During the years 1839, 1840, and 1841, the Company expended five thousand pounds on the purchase of plain provisions, of which the hunters got last year the sum of twelve hundred pounds, being rather more money than all the agricultural class obtained for their produce in the same year. It will be remembered that the Company's demand affords the only regular market or outlet in the Colony, and, as a matter of course, it is the first supplied."

CHAPTER XXXVII.

LIFE ON THE SHORES OF HUDSON BAY AND LABRADOR

The bleak shores unprogressive—Now as at the beginning—York Factory—
Description of Ballantyne—The weather—Summer comes with a rush—Picking up
subsistence—The Indian trade—Inhospitable Labrador—Establishment of Ungava
Bay—McLean at Fort Chimo—Herds of cariboo—Eskimo crafts—"Shadowy
Tartarus"—The king's domains—Mingan—Mackenzie—The Gulf settlements—The
Moravians—Their four missions—Rigolette, the chief trading post—A school for
developing character—Chief Factor Donald A. Smith—Journeys along the coast—A
barren shore.

LIFE on the shores of Hudson Bay is as unchangeable as the shores and
scenery of the coast are monotonous. The swampy, treeless flats that
surround the Bay simply change from the frozen, snow-clad expanse
which stretches as far as the eye can see in winter, to the summer green
of the unending grey willows and stunted shrubs that cover the swampy
shores. For a few open months the green prevails, and then nature for
eight months assumes her winding sheet of icy snow.

For two hundred and fifty years life has been as unvarying on these
wastes as travellers tell us are the manners and customs of living of the
Bedouins on their rocky Araby. No log shanties give way in a generation
to the settler's house, and then to the comfortable, well-built stone or
brick dwelling, which the fertile parts of America so readily permit. The
accounts of McLean, Rae, Ryerson, and Ballantyne of the middle of the
nineteenth century are precisely those of Robson, Ellis, or Hearne of the
eighteenth century, or indeed practically those of the early years of the
Company in the seventeenth century.

The ships sail from Gravesend on the Thames with the same
ceremonies, with the visit and dinner of the committee of the directors,
the "great guns," as the sailors call them, as they have done for two
centuries and a quarter, from the days of Zachariah Gillam and Pierre
Esprit Radisson. No more settlement is now seen on Hudson Bay than
in the early time, unless it be in the dwellings of the Christianized and
civilized swampy Crees and in the mission houses around which the

Indians have gathered. York Factory, up to the middle of the nineteenth century, retained its supremacy. However, at times, Fort Churchill, with its well-built walls and formidable bastions, may have disputed this primacy, yet York Factory was the depot for the interior almost uninterruptedly. To it came the goods for the northern department, by way in a single season of the vessel the *Prince Rupert*, the successor of a long line of *Prince Rupert's*, from the first one of 1680, or of its companions, the *Prince Albert* or the *Prince of Wales*. By these, the furs from the Far North found their way, as at the first, to the Company's house in London.

York Factory is a large square of some six acres, lying along Hayes River, and shut in by high stockades. The houses are all wooden, and on account of the swampy soil are raised up to escape the water of the spring-time floods. At a point of advantage, a lofty platform was erected to serve as a "lookout" to watch for the coming ship, the great annual event of the slow-passing lives of the occupants of the post. The flag-staff, on which, as is the custom at all Hudson's Bay Company posts, the ensign with the magic letters H. B. C. floats, speaks at once of many an old tradition and of great achievements.

Ballantyne in his lively style speaks of his two years at the post, and describes the life of a young Hudson's Bay Company officer. The chief factor, to the eye of the young clerk, represents success achieved and is the embodiment of authority, which, on account of the isolation of the posts and the absence of all law, is absolute and unquestioned. York Factory, being a depot, has a considerable staff, chiefly young men, who live in the bachelors' hall. Here dwell the surgeon, accountant, postmaster, half a dozen clerks, and others.

In winter, Ballantyne says, days, if not weeks, passed without the arrival of a visitor, unless it were a post from the interior, or some Cree trader of the neighbourhood, or some hungry Indian seeking food. The cold was the chief feature of remark and consideration. At times the spirit thermometer indicated 65 deg. below zero, and the uselessness of the mercury thermometer was then shown by a pot of quicksilver being made into bullets and remaining solid. Every precaution was taken to erect strong buildings, which had double windows and double doors, and yet in the very severe weather, water contained in a vessel has been known to freeze in a room where a stove red hot was doing its best. It is worthy of notice, however, that even in Arctic regions, a week or ten days is as long as such severe weather continues, and mild intervals come regularly.

On the Bay the coming of spring is looked for with great expectation, and when it does come, about the middle of May, it sets in with a "rush;" the sap rises in the shrubs and bushes, the buds burst out, the rivers are freed from ice, and indeed, so rapid and complete is the change, that it may be said there are only two seasons—summer and winter—in these latitudes.

As summer progresses the fare of dried geese, thousands of which are stored away for winter use, of dried fish and the white ptarmigan and wood partridge that linger about the bushes and are shot for food, is superseded by the arrival of myriads of ducks and geese and the use of the fresh fish of the Bay. In many of the posts the food throughout the whole year is entirely flesh diet, and not a pound of farinaceous food is obtainable. This leads to an enormous consumption of the meat diet in order to supply a sufficient amount of nourishment. An employé will sometimes eat two whole geese at a meal.

In Dr. Rae's celebrated expedition from Fort Churchill, north along the shore of Hudson Bay, on his search for Sir John Franklin, the amount of supplies taken was entirely inadequate for his party for the long period of twenty-seven months, being indeed only enough for four months' full rations. In Rae's instructions from Sir George Simpson it is said, "For the remaining part of your men you cannot fail to find subsistence, animated as you are and they are by a determination to fulfil your mission at the cost of danger, fatigue, and privation. Whenever the natives can live, I can have no fears with respect to you, more particularly as you will have the advantage of the Eskimos, not merely in your actual supplies, but also in the means of recruiting and renewing them."

The old forts still remained in addition to the two depot posts, York and Moose Factory, there being Churchill, Severn, Rupert's House, Fort George, and Albany—and the life in then all of the stereotyped description which we have pictured. Besides the preparation in summer of supplies for the long winter, the only variety was the arrival of Indians with furs from the interior. The trade is carried on by means of well-known standards called the "castor" or "beaver." The Indian hands his furs over to the trader, who sorts them into different lots. The value is counted up at so many—say fifty—castors. The Indian then receives fifty small bits of wood, and with these proceeds to buy guns, knives, blankets, cloth, beads, or trinkets, never stopping till his castors are all exhausted. The castor rarely exceeds two shillings in value.

While resembling in its general features the life on the Bay, the conduct of the fur trader on the shore of Labrador and throughout the Labrador Peninsula is much more trying and laborious than around the Bay. The inhospitable climate, the heavy snows, the rocky, dangerous shore, and the scarcity in some parts of animal life, long prevented the fur companies from venturing upon this forbidding coast.

The northern part of Labrador is inhabited by Eskimos; further south are tribes of swampy Crees. Between the Eskimos and Indians deadly feuds long prevailed. The most cruel and bloody raids were made upon the timid Eskimos, as was done on the Coppermine when Hearne went on his famous | expedition.

McLean states that it was through the publication of a pamphlet by the Moravian missionaries of Labrador, which I declared that "the country produced excellent furs," that the Hudson's Bay Company was led to establish trading posts in Northern Labrador. The stirring story of "Ungava," written by Ballantyne, gives what is no doubt in the main a correct account of the establishment of the far northern post called "Fort Chimo," on Ungava Bay.

The expedition left Moose Factory in 1831, and after escaping the dangers of floating ice, fierce storms, and an unknown coast, erected the fort several miles up the river running into Ungava Bay. The story recalls the finding out, no doubt somewhat after the manner of the famous boys' book, "The Swiss Family Robinson," the trout and salmon of the waters, the walrus of the sea, and the deer of the mountain valleys, but the picture is not probably overdrawn. The building of Fort Chimo is plainly described by one who was familiar with the exploration and life of the fur country; the picture of the tremendous snowstorm and its overwhelming drifts is not an unlikely one for this coast, which, since the day of Cortcreal, has been the terror of navigators.

McLean, a somewhat fretful and biassed writer, though certainly not lacking in a clear and lively style, gives an account of his being sent, in 1837, to take charge of the district of North Labrador for the Company. On leaving York Factory in August the brig encountered much ice, although it escaped the mishaps which overtook almost all small vessels on the Bay. The steep cliffs of the island of Akpatok, which stands before Ungava Bay, were very nearly run upon in the dark, and much difficulty was experienced in ascending the Ungava, or South River, to Fort Chimo.

The trader's orders from Governor Simpson were to push outposts into the interior of Labrador, to support his men on the resources of the country, and to open communication with Esquimaux Bay, on the Labrador coast, and thus, by means of the rivers, to establish an inland route of intercommunication between the two inlets. McLean made a most determined attempt to establish the desired route, but after innumerable hardships to himself and his company, retired, after nearly four months' efforts, to Fort Chimo, and sent a message to his superior officer that the proposed line of communication was impracticable.

McLean gives an account of the arrival of a herd of three hundred reindeer or cariboo, and of the whole of them being captured in a "pound," as is done in the case of the buffalo. The trader was also visited by Eskimos from the north side of Hudson Strait, who had crossed the rough and dangerous passage on "a raft formed of pieces of driftwood picked up along the shore." The object of their visit was to obtain wood for making canoes. The trader states that the fact of these people having crossed "Hudson's Strait on so rude and frail a conveyance" strongly corroborates the opinion that America was originally peopled from Asia by way of Behring's Strait.

It became more and more evident, however, that the Ungava trade could not be profitably continued. Great expense was incurred in supplying Ungava Bay by sea; the country was poor and barren, and the pertinacity of the Eskimos in adhering to their sealskin dresses made the trade in fabrics, which was profitable among the Indians, an impossibility at Ungava. McLean continued his explorations and was somewhat successful in opening the sought-for route by way of the Grand River, and, returning to Fort Chimo, wintered there. Having been promoted by Sir George Simpson, McLean obtained leave to visit Britain, and before going received word from the directors of the Company that his recommendation to abandon Ungava Bay had been accepted, and that the ship would call at that point and remove the people and property to Esquimaux Bay. McLean, in speaking of the weather of Hudson Straits during the month of January (1842), gives expression to his strong dislike by saying, "At this period I have neither seen, read, nor heard of any locality under heaven that can offer a more cheerless abode to civilized man than Ungava."

Referring also to the fog that so abounds at this point as well as at the posts around Hudson Bay, the discontented trader says: "If Pluto should leave his own gloomy mansion *in tenebris Tartari*, he might take up his abode here, and gain or lose but little by the exchange."

But the enterprising fur-traders were not to be deterred by the iron-bound coast, or foggy shores, or dangerous life of any part of the peninsula of Labrador. Early in the century, while the Hudson's Bay Company were penetrating southward from the eastern shore of Hudson Bay, which had by a kind of anomaly been called the "East

Main," the North-West Company were occupying the north shore of the St. Lawrence and met their rivals at the head waters of the Saguenay.

The district of which Tadousac was the centre had from the earliest coming of the French been noted for its furs. That district all the way down to the west end of the island of Anti-costi was known as the "King's Domains." The last parish was called Murray Bay, from General Murray, the first British governor of Quebec, who had disposed of the district, which furnished beef and butter for the King, to two of his officers, Captains Nairn and Fraser.

The North-West Company, in the first decade of the nineteenth century, had leased this district, which along with the Seigniory of Mingan that lay still further down the Gulf of St. Lawrence, was long known as the "King's Posts." Beyond the Seigniory of Mingan, a writer of the period mentioned states that the Labrador coast had been left unappropriated, and was a common to which all nations at peace with England might resort, unmolested, for furs, oil, cod-fish, and salmon.

A well-known trader, James McKenzie, after returning from the Athabasca region, made, in 1808, a canoe journey through the domains of the King, and left a journal, with his description of the rocky country and its inhabitants. He pictures strongly the one-eyed chief of Mingan and Father Labrosse, the Nestor for twenty-five years of the King's posts, who was priest, doctor, and poet for the region. McKenzie's voyage chiefly inclined him to speculate as to the origin and religion of the natives, while his description of the inland Indians and their social life is interesting. His account of the manners and customs of the Montagners or Shore Indians was more detailed than that of the Nascapees, or Indians of the interior, and he supplies us with an extensive vocabulary of their language.

McKenzie gives a good description of the Saguenay River, of Chicoutimi, and Lake St. John, and of the ruins of a Jesuit establishment which had flourished during the French regime. Whilst the bell and many implements had been dug up from the scene of desolation, the plum and apple trees of their garden were found bearing fruit. From the poor neglected fort of Assuapmousoin McKenzie returned, since the fort of Mistassini could only be reached by a further journey of ninety leagues. This North-West post was built at the end of Lake Mistassini, while the Hudson's Bay Company Fort, called Birch Point, was erected four days' journey further on toward East Main House.

Leaving the Saguenay, McKenzie followed the coast of the St. Lawrence, passing by Portneuf, with its beautiful chapel, "good enough for His Holiness the Pope to occupy," after which—the best of the King's posts for furs—Ile Jérémie was reached, with its buildings and chapels on a high eminence. Irregularly built Godbout was soon in view, and the Seven Islands Fort was then come upon. Mingan was the post of which McKenzie was most enamoured. Its fine harbour and pretty chapel drew his special attention. The "Man River" was famous for its fisheries, while Masquaro, the next port, was celebrated for the supply of beavers and martins in its vicinity. The salmon entering the river in the district are stated to be worthy of note, and the traveller and his company returned to Quebec, the return voyage being two hundred leagues.

Since the time of McKenzie the fur trade has been pushed along the formerly unoccupied coast of Labrador. Even before that time the far northern coast had been taken up by a brave band of Moravians, who supported themselves by trade, and at the same time did Christian work among the Eskimos. Their movement merits notice. As early as 1749 a brave Hollander pilot named Erhardt, stimulated by reading the famous book of Henry Ellis on the North-West Passage, made an effort to form a settlement on the Labrador coast. He lost his life among the deceitful Eskimos.

Years afterward, Count Zinzendorf made application to the Hudson's Bay Company to be allowed to send Moravian missionaries to the different Hudson's Bay Company posts. The union of trader and missionary in the Moravian cult made the Company unwilling to grant this request. After various preparations the Moravians took up unoccupied ground on the Labrador coast, in 56 deg. 36′ N., where they found plenty of wood, runlets of sparkling water and a good anchorage. They erected a stone marked G.R. III., 1770, for the King, and another with the inscription V.F. (Unitas fratrum), the name of their sect.

Their first settlement was called Nain, and it was soon followed by another thirty miles up the coast known as "Okkak," Thirty miles south of Nain they found remains of the unfortunate movement first made by the Society, and here they established a mission, calling it "Hopedale." When they had become accustomed to the coast, they showed still more of the adventurous spirit and founded their most northerly post of Hebron, well nigh up to the dreaded "Ungava Bay." A community of upwards of eleven hundred Christian Eskimos has resulted from the fervour and self-denial of these humble but faithful missionaries. Their courage and determination stand well beside that of the daring fur traders.

The Hudson's Bay Company was not satisfied with Mingan as their farthest outward point. In 1832 and 1834, Captain Bayfield, R.N., surveyed the Labrador coast. In due time the Company pushed on to the inlet known as Hamilton Inlet or Esquimaux Bay, on the north side of which the fort grew up, know as Rigolette. Hero a farm is maintained stocked with "Cattle, sheep, pigs and hens," and the place is the depot of the Hudson's Bay Company and of the general trade of the coast. Farther up two other sub-posts are found, viz., Aillik, and on the opposite side of the Inlet Kaipokok. The St. Lawrence and Labrador posts of the Hudson's Bay Company have been among the most difficult and trying of those in any part where the Company carries on its vast operations from Atlantic to Pacific. This Labrador region has been a noble school for the development of the firmness, determination, skill, and faithfulness characteristic of both the officers and men of the Hudson's Bay Company.

Most notable of the officers of the first rank who have conducted the fur trade in Labrador is Lord Strathcona and Mount Royal, the present Governor of the Company. Coming out at eighteen, Donald Alexander

Smith, a well-educated Scottish lad, related to Peter and Cuthbert Grant, and the brothers John and James Stuart, prominent officers, whose deeds in the North-West Company are still remembered, the future Governor began his career. Young Smith, on arriving at Montreal (1838), was despatched to Moose Factory, and for more than thirty years was in the service, in the region of Hudson Bay and Labrador. Rising to the rank of chief trader, after fourteen years of laborious service he reached in ten years more the acme of desire of every aspirant in the Company, the rank of chief factor. His years on the coast of Labrador, at Rigolette, and its subordinate stations were most laborious. The writer has had the privilege from time to time of hearing his tales, of the long journey along the frozen coast, of camping on frozen islands, without shelter, of storm-staid journeys rivalling the recitals of Ballantyne at Fort Chimo, of cold receptions by the Moravians, and of the doubtful hospitalities of both Indians and Eskimos. Every statement of Cortereal, Gilbert, or Cabot of the inhospitable shore is corroborated by this successful officer, who has lived for thirty years since leaving Labrador to fill a high place in the affairs both of Canada and the Empire. One of his faithful subordinates on this barren coast was Chief Factor P. W. Bell, who gained a good reputation for courage and faithfulness, not only in Labrador, but on the barren shore of Lake Superior. The latter returned to Labrador after his western experience, and retired from the charge of the Labrador posts a few years ago. It is to the credit of the Hudson's Bay Company that it has been able to secure men of such calibre and standing to man even its most difficult and unattractive stations.

CHAPTER XXXVIII.

ATHABASCA, MACKENZIE RIVER, AND THE YUKON

(The map on should be consulted while this chapter is being read.)

LESS than twenty years after the conquest of Canada by the British, the traders heard of the Lake Athabasca and Mackenzie River district. The region rapidly rose into notice, until it reached the zenith as the fur traders' paradise, a position it has held till the present time.

As we have seen, Samuel Hearne, the Hudson's Bay Company adventurer—the Mungo Park of the North—first of white men, touched, on his way to the Coppermine, Lake Athapuscow, now thought to have been Great Slave Lake.

It was the good fortune, however, of the North-West Company to take possession of this region first for trade.

LAKE AND RIVER ATHABASCA.

The daring Montreal traders, who had seized upon the Saskatchewan and pushed on to Lake Ile à la Crosse, having a surplus of merchandise in the year 1778, despatched one of their agents to Lake Athabasca, and "took seisin" of the country. As already stated, the man selected was the daring and afterwards violent trader Peter Pond. On the River Athabasca, some thirty miles south of the Lake, Pond built the first Indian trading post of the region, which, however, after a few years was abandoned and never afterwards rebuilt.

Less than ten years after this pioneer led the way, a fort was built on the south side of Lake Athabasca, at a point a few miles east of the entrance of the river. To this, borrowing the name of the Indian nation of the district, was given the name Fort Chipewyan. This old fort became celebrated as the starting-place of the great expedition of Alexander Mackenzie, when he discovered the river that bears his name and the Polar Sea into which it empties. At this historic fort also, Roderick McKenzie, cousin of the explorer, founded the famous "Athabasca Library," for the use of the officers of the Company in the northern posts, and in its treasures Lieutenant Lefroy informs us he revelled during his winter stay.

At the beginning of the century the X Y Company aggressively invaded the Athabasca region, and built a fort a mile north of Fort Chipewyan, near the site of the present Roman Catholic Mission of the Nativity.

As the conflict between the North-West and Hudson's Bay Companies waxed warm, the former Company, no doubt for the purpose of being more favourably situated for carrying on the trade with the Mackenzie River, removed their fort on Lake Athasbaca to the commanding promontory near the exit of Slave River from the lake. Renewed and often enlarged, Fort Chipewyan has until recently remained the greatest depot of the north country.

THE HUDSON'S BAY COMPANY AROUSED.

The fierceness of the struggle for the fur trade may be seen in the fact that the Hudson's Bay Company (1815) with vigour took up a site on an island in front of Fort Chipewyan and built Fort Wedderburn, at no greater distance than a single mile, and though it was not their first appearance on the lake, yet they threw themselves in considerable force into the contest, numbering, under John Clark, afterward Chief Factor, ten clerks, a hundred men, and fourteen large canoes loaded with supplies. Many misfortunes befell the new venture of the Company. A writer of the time says, "No less than fifteen men, one woman, and several children perished by starvation. They built four trade posts on the Peace River (lower) and elsewhere in the autumn; but not one of them was able to weather out the following winter. All were obliged to come to terms with their opponents to save the party from utter destruction. That year the Athabasca trade of the North-West Company was four hundred packs against only five in all secured by the Hudson's Bay Company.

Three years afterward the old Company, with British pluck, again appeared on this lake, having nineteen loaded canoes. Trader Clark was now accompanied by the doughty leader, Colin Robertson, whose prowess we have already seen in the Red River conflict.

It will be remembered that in the year before the union of the Companies, George Simpson, the young clerk, arrived on Lake Athabasca with fifteen loaded canoes. He was chiefly found at Fort Wedderburn and a short distance up the Peace River. It is not certain that the prospective Governor ever visited Slave Lake to the north. He gives, however, the following vivid summary of his winter's experience in Athabasca: "At some seasons both whites and Indians live in wasteful abundance on venison, buffalo meat, fish, and game of all kinds, while at other times they are reduced to the last degree of hunger, often passing several days without food. In the year 1820 our provisions fell short at the establishment, and on two or three occasions I went for two or three whole days and nights without having a single morsel to swallow, but then again, I was one of a party of eleven men and one woman which discussed at one sitting meal no less than three ducks and twenty-two geese!" This winter's knowledge was of great value to the man afterwards called to be the arbiter of destiny of many a hard-pressed trader.

Other forts are mentioned as having been established by both Companies at different points on the Athabasca River, but their period of duration was short. In some cases these abandoned forts have been followed by new forts, in recent times, on the same sites.

THE PEACE RIVER.

Soon after the arrival of the first traders in the Athabasca district, the fame of the Peace River—the Indian "Unjijah," a mighty stream, whose waters empty into the river flowing from Lake Athabasca—rose among the adventurers. An enterprising French Canadian trader, named Boyer, pushed up the stream and near a small tributary—Red River—established the first post of this great artery, which flows from the West, through the Rocky Mountains. Long abandoned, this post has in late years been re-established.

The Peace River has ever had a strange fascination for trader and tourist, and a few years after Boyer's establishment became known, a trading house was built above the "Chutes" of the river. This was afterwards moved some distance up stream and became the well-known Fort Vermilion. This fort has remained till the present day.

Farther still up the Peace River, where the Smoky River makes its forks, a fort was erected whose stores and dwelling-houses were on a larger scale than those of the mother establishment of Fort Chipewyan, having had stockaded walls; a good powder magazine, and a good well of water. This fort for a time was known as McLeod's Fort, but in the course of events its site was abandoned. Fort Dunvegan, famous to later travellers, was first built on the south side of the river, and was the head-quarters of the Beaver Indians, from whom the North-West Company received a formal gift of the site. The present fort is on the opposite side of the Peace River.

It will be remembered, however, that it was from the post -at the mouth of Smoky River that Alexander Mackenzie, having wintered, started on his great journey to the Pacific. In later years the Hudson's Bay Company has maintained a fort at this point as an outpost of Dunvegan.

Early in the century we find allusions to the fact that the catch of beaver was, from over-hunting, declining in the Peace River country, and that, in consequence, the North-West Company had been compelled to give up several of their forts. Around Fort St. John's a tragic interest gathers. John McLean, in his "Notes of a Twenty-five Years' Service," speaks of reaching on his journey—1833—the "tenantless fort," where some years before a massacre had taken place. It had been determined by the Hudson's Bay Company to remove the fort to Rocky Mountain Portage. The tribe of Tsekanies, to whom the fort was tributary, took this as an insult. At the time of removal the officer in charge, Mr. Hughes, had sent off a part of his men with effects of the fort intended for the new post. Hughes was shot down on the riverside by the Indians. The party of boatmen, on returning, "altogether unconscious of the fate that awaited them, came paddling towards the landing-place, singing a voyageur's song, and just as the canoe touched the shore, a volley of bullets was discharged at them, which silenced them for ever. They were all killed on the spot." An expedition was organized by the traders to avenge the foul murder, but more peaceful counsels prevailed. Most of the fugitives paid the penalty of their guilt by being starved to death. The deserted fort was some twenty miles below the present Fort St. John's. The present fort was built in the latter half of the century, and its outpost of Hudson's Hope, together with the trade station at Battle River, below Dunvegan, was erected about a generation ago.

GREAT SLAVE LAKE.

The extension of the fur trade to Great Slave Lake dates back to within seven years after the advent of Peter Pond on the Athabasca River. The famous trader, Cuthbert Grant, father of the "Warden of the Plains," who figured in the Seven Oaks fight, led the way, and with him a Frenchman, Laurent Loroux. Reaching this great lake, these ardent explorers built a trading post on Slave River, near its mouth. A short time afterwards the traders moved their first post to Moose Deer Island, a few miles from the old site, and here the North-West Company remained until the time of the union of the Companies. The impulse of union led to the construction of a new establishment on the site chosen by the Hudson's Bay Company for the erection of their post some six years before. The new post was called Fort Resolution, and was on the mainland two miles or more from the island. This post marked the extreme limit of the operations of the Hudson's Bay Company up to the time of the union.

When Alexander Mackenzie determined to make his first great voyage, he started from Fort Chipewyan and bravely pushing out into the unknown wilds, left Great Slave Lake and explored the river that bears his name. Here he promised the tribe of the Yellow Knife Indians to establish a post among them in the next year. The promise was kept to the letter. The new post, built at the mouth of the Yellow Knife River, was called Fort Providence. It was afterwards removed to a large island in the north arm of the lake, and to this the name Fort Rae, in honour of the celebrated Arctic explorer, John Rae, was given. Near this new station there has been for years a Roman Catholic Mission. It was from the neighbourhood of these forts on the lake that Captain Franklin set out to build his temporary station, Fort Enterprise, one hundred miles from his base of supplies. Fort Rae has remained since the time of its erection a place of some importance. It formed the centre of the northern operations of Captain Dawson, R.A., on his expedition for circumpolar observation in recent times.

After the Hudson's Bay Company had transferred Rupert's Land to Canada, a new post was opened on the Slave River, midway between Athabasca and Great Slave Lake. It was called Fort Smith, in honour of Chief Commissioner Donald A., Smith, now Lord Strathcona and Mount Royal. Near the site of Fort Smith are the dangerous Noyé Raids of Slave River, where Grant and Leroux, on their voyage to Great Slave Lake, lost a canoe and five of its occupants. From Fort Smith southward to Smith Landing a waggon or cart road has been in use up to the present time. Now this is to be converted into a tramway.

MACKENZIE RIVER.

Northward the course of the fur traders' empire has continually made its way. Leaving Great Slave Lake four years before the close of the eighteenth century, along the course of Alexander Mackenzie's earlier exploration, Duncan Livingston, a North-West Company trader, built the first fort on the river eighty miles north of the lake. Three years later the trader, his three French-Canadian voyageurs and Indian interpreter, were basely killed by the Eskimos on the Lower Mackenzie River. A year or two afterward a party of fur traders, under John Clark, started on an expedition of exploration and retaliation down the river, but again the fury of the Eskimos was roused. In truth, had it not been for a storm of fair wind which favoured them, the traders would not have escaped with their lives.

Very early in the present century, Fort Simpson, the former and present head-quarters of the extensive Mackenzie River district, was built, and very soon after its establishment the prominent trader, and afterwards Chief Factor, George Keith, is found in charge of it. It is still the great trading and Church of England Mission centre of the vast region reaching to the Arctic Sea.

During the first half of the century, Big Island, at the point whore the Mackenzie River leaves Great Slave Lake, was, on account of its good supply of white fish, the wintering station for the supernumerary district servants of the Hudson's Bay Company. Though this point is still visited for fishing in the autumn, yet in later years the trade of this post has been transferred to another built near the Roman Catholic Mission at Fort Providence, forty miles farther down the river. On Hay River, near the point of departure of the Mackenzie River from the lake, several forts have been built from time to time and abandoned, among them a Fort George referred to by the old traders. The eastern end of the lake, known as Fond du Lac, became celebrated, as we have already seen, in connection with the Arctic explorers, Sir George Back and Dr. Richard King, for here they built Fort Reliance and wintered, going in the spring to explore the Great Fish River. In after years, on account of the district being the resort for the herds of cariboo, Fort Reliance was rebuilt, and was for a time kept up as an outpost of Fort Resolution for collecting furs and "country provisions." It may be re-occupied soon on account of the discoveries of gold and copper in the region.

Journeying down the Mackenzie River, we learn that there was a fur traders' post of the Montreal merchants sixty miles north of Fort

Simpson. In all probability this was but one of several posts that were from time to time occupied in that locality. At the beginning of the century the North-West Company pushed on further north, and had a trading post on the shore of Great Bear Lake, but almost immediately on its erection they were met here by their rivals, the X Y Company. At this point, reached by going up the Bear River from its junction with the Mackenzie on the south-west arm of the lake, Chief Factor Peter Dease built Fort Franklin for the use of the great Arctic explorer, after whom he named the fort.

FORT NORMAN, ON THE MACKENZIE.

To explore new ground was a burning desire in the breasts of the Nor'-Westers. Immediately in the year of their reunion with the X Y Company, the united North-West Company established a post on the Mackenzie River, sixty miles north of the mouth of Bear River. Indeed, the mouth of Bear River on the Mackenzie seems to have suggested itself as a suitable point for a post to be built, for in 1810 Fort Norman had been first placed there. For some reason the post was moved thirty or forty miles higher up the river, but a jam of ice having occurred in the spring of 1851, the fort was mainly swept away by the high water, though the occupants and all the goods were saved. In the same year the mouth of the Bear River came into favour again, and Fort Norman was built at that point. After this time the fort was moved once or twice, but was finally placed in its present commanding position. It was in quite recent times that, under Chief Factor Camsell's direction, a station half-way between Fort Norman and Fort Simpson was fixed and the name of Fort Wrigley given to it.

FORT GOOD HOPE.

Not only did the impulse of union between the North-West and X Y Companies reach Bear River, but in the same year, at a point on the Mackenzie River beyond the high perpendicular cliffs known as "The Ramparts," some two hundred miles further north than Fort Norman, was Fort Good Hope erected. Here it remained for nearly a score of years as the farthest north outpost of the fur trade, but after the union of the North-West and Hudson's Bay Companies it was moved a hundred miles southward on the river and erected on Manitoulin Island. After some years (1836) an ice jam of a serious kind took place, and though the inmates escaped in a York boat, yet the fort was completely destroyed by the rushing waters of the angry Mackenzie. The fort was soon rebuilt, but in its present beautiful situation on the eastern bank of the river, opposite the old site on Manitoulin Island.

During Governor Simpson's time the extension of trade took place toward the mouth of the Mackenzie River. A trader, John Bell, who not only faced the hardships of the region within the Arctic Circle, but also gained a good name in connection with Sir John Richardson's expedition in search of Franklin, built the first post on Peel's River, which runs into the delta of Mackenzie River. Bell, in 1846, descended the Rat River, and first of British explorers set eyes on the Lower Yukon.

In the following year the Hudson's Bay Company established La Pierre's House in the heart of the Rocky Mountains toward the Arctic Sea, and Chief Trader Murray built and occupied the first Fort Yukon. This fort the Hudson's Bay Company held for twenty-two years, until the territory of Alaska passed into the hands of the people of the United States. Rampart House was built by the Hudson's Bay Company within British territory. Both Rampart House and La Pierre's House were abandoned a few years ago as unprofitable. A similar fate befell Fort Anderson, two degrees north of the Arctic Circle, built for the Eastern Eskimos on the Anderson River, discovered in 1857 by Chief Factor R. MacFarlane, a few years before the transfer of the territory of the Hudson's Bay Company to Canada. No doubt the withdrawal from Fort Anderson was hastened by the terribly fatal epidemic of scarlatina which prevailed all over the Mackenzie River district in the autumn and early winter of 1865. More than eleven hundred Indians and Eskimos, out of the four thousand estimated population, perished. The loss of the hunters caused by this disease, and the difficulties of overland transport, led to the abandonment of this out-of-the-way post.

THE LIARD RIVER.

The conflict of the North-West and X Y Companies led to the most extraordinary exploration that Rupert's Land and the Indian territories have witnessed. At the time when the Mackenzie River, at the beginning of the century, was being searched and occupied, a fort known as The Forks was established at the junction of the Liard and Mackenzie Rivers. This fort, called, after the union of the Hudson's Bay and North-West Companies, Fort Simson, became the base of operations for the exploration of the Liard River. We have followed the course of trade by which the Mackenzie itself was placed under tribute; it may be well also to look at the occupation of the Liard, the most rapid and terrible of all the great eastern streams that dash down from the heart of the Rocky Mountains.

The first post to be established on this stream was Fort Liard, not far below the junction of the western with the east branch of the river. There was an old fort between Fort Liard and Fort Simpson, but Fort Liard, which is still occupied by the Hudson's Bay Company, began almost with the century, and a few years afterwards was under the experienced trader, George Keith. Probably, at an equally early date, Fort Nelson, on the eastern branch of the river, was established. In the second decade of the century, Alexander Henry, the officer in charge, and all of his people were murdered by the Indians. The post was for many years abandoned, but was rebuilt in 1865, and is still a trading post.

It was probably shortly after the union of the North-West and Hudson's Bay Companies that Fort Halkett, far up the western branch of the river, was erected. After forty or fifty years of occupation, Fort Halkett was abandoned, but a small post called Toad River was built some time afterward, half way between its site and that of Fort Liard. In 1834, Chief Trader John M. McLeod, not the McLeod whose journal we have quoted, pushed up past the dangerous rapids and boiling whirlpools, and among rugged cliffs and precipices of the Rocky

Mountains, discovered Dease River and Dease Lake from which the river flows.

Robert Campbell, an intrepid Scottish officer of the Hudson's Bay Company, in 1838, succeeded in doing what his predecessors had been unable to accomplish, viz. to establish a trading-post on Dease Lake. In the summer of the same year Campbell crossed to the Pacific Slope and reached the head waters of the Stikine River.

In opening his new post Campbell awakened the hostility of the coast Indians. He and his men became so reduced in supplies that they subsisted for some time on the skin thongs of their moccasins and snow shoes and on the parchment windows of their huts, boiled to supply the one meal a day which kept them alive. In the end Campbell was compelled to leave his station on the Dease Lake, and the fort was burnt by the Indians.

DISCOVERY OF THE UPPER YUKON.

Under orders from Governor Simpson, Campbell, in 1840, undertook the exploration that has made his name famous. This was to ascend the northern branch of the wild and dangerous Liard River. For this purpose he left the mountain post, Fort Halkett, and passing through the groat gorge arrived at Lake Francos, where he gave the promontory which divides the lake the name "Simpson's Tower." Leaving the Lake and ascending one of its tributaries, called by him Finlayson's River, he reached the interesting reservoir of Finlayson's Lake, of which, at high water, one part of the sheet runs west to the Pacific Ocean and the other to the Arctic Sea. With seven trusty companions he crossed the height of land and saw the high cliffs of the splendid river, which he called "Pelly Banks," in honour of the then London Governor of the Company. The Company would have called it Campbell's River, but the explorer refused the honour. Going down the stream a few miles on a raft, Campbell then turned back, and reached Fort Halkett after an absence of four months.

Highly complimented by Governor Simpson, Campbell, under orders, in the next year built a fort at Lake Frances, and in a short time another establishment at Pelly Banks. Descending the river, the explorer met at the junction of the Lewis and Pelly Banks a band of Indians, who would not allow him to proceed further, and indeed plotted to destroy him and his men. Eight years after his discovery of Pelly Banks, Campbell started on his great expedition, which was crowned with success. Reaching again the junction of the Pelly and Lewis Rivers, he erected a post, naming it Fort Selkirk, although it was long locally known as Campbell's Fort. Two years after the building of Fort Selkirk, Campbell, journeying in all from the height of land for twelve hundred miles, reached Fort Yukon, where, as we have seen, Trader Murray was in charge. Making a circuit around by the Porcupine River and ascending the Mackenzie River, Campbell surprised his friends at Fort Simpson by coming up the river to Fort Simpson.

In 1852, a thievish band of coast Indians called the Chilkats plundered Fort Selkirk and shortly afterward destroyed it. Its ruins remain to this day, and the site is now taken up by the Canadian Government as a station on the way to the Yukon gold-fields.

Campbell went home to London, mapped out with the aid of Arrowsmith the country he had found, and gave names to its rivers and other features. A few years ago an officer of the United States army, Lieutenant Schwatka, sought to rob Campbell of his fame, and attempted to rename the important points of the region. Campbell's merit and modesty entitle him to the highest recognition.

The trading posts of the great region we are describing have been variously grouped into districts. Previous to the union of the North-West and Hudson's Bay Companies, from Athabasca north and west was known as the "Athabasca-Mackenzie Department," their returns all being kept in one account. This northern department was long under the superintendency of Chief Factor Edward Smith.

A new district was, some time after the transfer of the Indian territories to Canada, formed and named "Peace River." The management has changed from time to time, Fort Dunvegan, for example, for a period the head-quarters of the Peace River district, having lost its pre-eminence and been transferred to be under the chief officer on Lesser Slave Lake.

The vast inland water stretches of which we have spoken have been the chief means of communication throughout the whole country. Without these there could have been little fur trade. The distances are bewildering. The writer remembers seeing Bishop Bompas, who had left the far distant Fort Yukon to go to England, and who by canoe, York boat, dog train, snow shoe, and waggon, had been nine months on the journey before he reached Winnipeg.

The first northern inland steamer in these remote retreats was the *Graham* (1882), built by the Company at Fort Chipewyan on Lake Athabasca, by Captain John M. Smith. Three years later the same captain built the screw-propeller *Wrigley*, at Fort Smith, on the Slave River; and a few years afterward, this indefatigable builder launched at Athabasca landing the stern-wheeler *Athabasca*, for the water stretches of the Upper Athabasca River.

How remarkable the record of adventure, trade, rivalry, bloodshed, hardship, and successful effort, from the time, more than a century ago, when Peter Pond started out on his seemingly desperate undertaking!

CHAPTER XXXIX.

THE great exploration early in the century secured the Pacific Slope very largely to the North-West Company. Several of their most energetic agents, as the names of the rivers running into the Pacific Ocean show, had made a deep impression on the region even as far south as the mouth of the Columbia River. On the union of the North-West and Hudson's Bay Companies, Governor Simpson threw as much energy into the development of trade in the country on the western side of the Rocky Mountains as if he had been a thorough-going Nor'-Wester.

In his administration from ocean to ocean he divided the trading territory into four departments, viz. Montreal, the Southern, the Northern, and the Western. In each of these there were four factors, and these were, in the Western or Rocky Mountain department, subject to one chief. Under the chief factor the gradation was chief trader, chief clerk, apprenticed clerk, postmaster, interpreter, voyageur, and labourer.

This fuller organization and the cessation of strife resulted in a great increase of the trade of the Hudson's Bay Company on the coast as well as the east side of the Rocky Mountains. The old fort of Astoria, which was afterwards known as Fort George, was found too far from the mountains for the convenience of the fur traders. Accordingly in 1824-5, a new fort was erected on the north side of the Columbia River, six miles above its junction with the Willamette River. The new fort was called Fort Vancouver, and was built on a prairie slope about one mile back from the river, but it was afterwards moved nearer the river bank.

The new site was very convenient for carrying on the overland traffic to Puget Sound. This fort was occupied for twenty-three years, until international difficulties rendered its removal necessary.

Fort Vancouver was of considerable size, its stockade measuring 750 ft. in length and 600 ft. in breadth. The Governor's residence, Bachelor's Hall, and numerous other buildings made up a considerable establishment. About the fort a farm was under cultivation to the extent of fifteen hundred acres, and a large number of cattle, sheep, and horses were bred upon it and supplied the trade carried on with the Russians in the Far North.

Farther up the Columbia River, where the Walla Walla River emptied in, a fort was constructed in 1818. The material for this fort was brought a considerable distance, and being in the neighbourhood of troublesome tribes of Indians, care was taken to make the fort strong and defensible.

Still further up the Columbia River and near the mountains, an important post, Fort Colville, was built. This fort became the depot for all the trade done on the Columbia River; and from this point the brigade which had been organized at Fort Vancouver made its last call before undertaking the steep mountain climb which was necessary in order that by the middle of March it might reach Norway House and be reported at the great summer meeting of the fur traders' council there. This task needed a trusty leader, and for many years Chief Factor, afterward Sir James, Douglas became the man on whom Governor and Council depended to do this service.

The mention of the name of James Douglas brings before us the greatest and most notable man developed by the fur trade of the Pacific slope. The history of this leader was for fifty years after the coalition of the Companies in 1821, the history of the Hudson's Bay Company on the Pacific.

Born near the beginning of the century, a scion of the noble house of Douglas, young Douglas emigrated to Canada, entered the North-West Company, learned French as if by magic, and though little more than a lad, at once had heavy responsibilities thrown upon him. He was enterprising and determined, with a judicious mixture of prudence. He had capital business talents and an adaptability that stood him in good stead in dealing with Indians. The veteran Chief Factor, McLoughlin, who had served his term in the Nor'-Wester service about Lake Superior and Lake Nepigon, was appointed to the charge of the Pacific or Western District. He discerned the genius of his young subordinate, and with the permission of the directors in London, after a short interval, took Douglas west of the mountains to the scene of his future successes. The friendship . between these chiefs of the Pacific Coast was thus early begun, and they together did much to mould the British interests on the Pacific Coast into a comely shape.

While McLoughlin crossed at once to the Columbia and took charge of Fort Vancouver, he directed Douglas to go north to New Caledonia, or what is now Northern British Columbia, to learn the details of the fur trade of the mountains. Douglas threw himself heartily into every part of his work. He not only learned the Indian languages, and used them to advantage in the advancement of the fur trade, but studied successfully the physical features of the country and became an authority on the Pacific Slope which proved of greatest value to the Company and the country for many a day.

Douglas had as his head-quarters Fort St. James, near the outlet of Stuart Lake, i.e. just west of the summit of the Rocky Mountains. He determined to enforce law and do away with the disorder which prevailed in the district. An Indian, who some time before had murdered one of the servants of the Hudson's Bay Company, had been allowed to go at large. Judgment being long deferred, the murderer thought himself likely to be unmolested, and visited Stuart Lake. Douglas, learning of his presence, with a weak garrison seized the criminal and visited vengeance on him. The Indians were incensed, but knowing that they had to deal with a doughty Douglas, employed stratagem in their reprisals. The old chief came very humbly to the fort and, knocking at the gate, was given admittance. He talked the affair over with Douglas, and the matter seemed in a fair way to be settled when another knock was heard at the gate. The chief stated that it was his brother who sought to be admitted. The gate was opened, when in rushed the whole of the Nisqually tribe. McLean vividly describes the scene which ensued: "The men of the fort were overpowered ere they had time to stand on their defence. Douglas, however, seized a wall-piece that was mounted in the hall, and was about to discharge it on the crowd that was pouring in upon him, when the chief seized him by the hands and held him fast. For an instant his life was in the utmost peril, surrounded by thirty or forty Indians, their knives drawn, and brandishing them over his head with frantic gestures, and calling out to the chief, "Shall we strike? Shall we strike?"

The chief hesitated, and at this critical moment the interpreter's wife (daughter of an old trader, James McDougall) stepped forward, and by her presence of mind saved him and the establishment.

"Observing one of the inferior chiefs, who had always professed the greatest friendship for the whites, standing in the crowd, she addressed herself to him, exclaiming, 'What! you a friend of the whites, and not say a word in their behalf at such a time as this! Speak! You know the murderer deserved to die; according to your own laws the deed was just; it is blood for blood. The white men are not dogs; they love their own kindred as well as you; why should they not avenge their murder?'

The moment the heroine's voice was heard the tumult subsided; her boldness struck the savages with awe. The chief she addressed, acting on her suggestion, interfered, and being seconded by the old chief, who had no serious intention of injuring the whites, and was satisfied with showing them that they were fairly in his power, Douglas and his men were sot at liberty, and an amicable conference having taken place, the Indians departed much elated with the issue of their enterprise.

Douglas spent his four years in the interior in a most interesting and energetic life. The experience there gained was invaluable in his after career as a fur trader. In 1826, at Bear Lake, at the head of a branch of the River Skeena, he built a fort, which he named Fort Connolly, in honour of his superior officer, the chief of the Pacific department. Other forts in this region date their origin to Douglas's short stay in this part of the mountains. Douglas also had an "affair of the heart" while at Fort St. James. Young and impressionable, he fell in love with Nellie, the daughter of Mr. Connolly, a young "daughter of the country," aged sixteen. She became his wife and survived him as Lady Douglas.

His life of adventure in the Rocky Mountains came to an end by the summons of Chief Factor McLoughlin to appear at Fort Vancouver, the chief point of the Company's trade on the Pacific slope. In two years more the rising young officer became chief trader, and three years afterward he had reached the high dignity of chief factor. His chief work was to establish forts, superintend the trade in its different departments, and inspect the forts at least annually. His vigilance and energy were surprising. He became so noted that it was said of him: "He was one of the most enterprising and inquisitive of men, famous for his intimate acquaintance with every service of the coast."

Though James Douglas rose by well marked tokens of leadership to the chief place on the Pacific Coast, yet the men associated with him were a worthy and able band. His friend, Chief Factor Dr. John McLoughlin, who had been his patron, was a man of excellent ability. McLoughlin was of a sympathetic and friendly disposition, and took an interest in the settlement of the fertile valley of the Columbia. His course seems to have been disapproved of by the London Committee of the Company, and his place was given to Douglas, after which he spent his life in Oregon. His work and influence cannot, however, be disregarded. He passed through many adventures and dangers. He was fond of show, and had a manner which might well recommend him to Sir George Simpson, Governor-in-chief.

From a trader's journal we learn: "McLoughlin and his suite would sometimes accompany the south-bound expeditions from Fort Vancouver, in regal state, for fifty or one hundred miles up the Willamette, when he would dismiss them with his blessing and return to the fort. He did not often travel, and seldom far; but on these occasions he indulged his men rather than himself in some little variety. . . . It pleased Mrs. McLoughlin thus to break the monotony of her fort life. Upon a gaily-caparisoned steed, with silver trappings and strings of bells on bridle reins and saddle skirt, sat the lady of Fort Vancouver, herself arrayed in brilliant colours and wearing a smile which might cause to blush and hang its head the broadest, warmest, and most fragrant sunflower. By her side, also gorgeously attired, rode her lord, king of the Columbia, and every inch a king, attended by a train of trappers, under a chief trader, each upon his best behaviour."

But a group of men, notable and competent, gathered around these two leaders of the fur trade on the Pacific Coast. These comprised Roderick Finlayson, John Work, A. C. Anderson, W. F. Tolmie, John Tod, S. Black, and others. These men, in charge of important posts, were local magnates, and really, gathered together in council, determined the policy of the Company along the whole coast.

In 1827 the spirit of extension of the trading operations took possession of the Hudson's Bay Company. In that year the officers at Fort Vancouver saw arrive from the Thames the schooner *Cadboro*, seventy-two tons burthen. She became as celebrated on the Pacific Coast as any prominent fur trader could have become. It was said of this good ship, "She saw buried every human body brought by her from England, save one, John Spence, ship carpenter." Her arrival at this time was the occasion for an expedition to occupy the Lower Fraser with a trading post. John McMillan commanded the expedition of twenty-five men. Leaving Fort Vancouver in boats, and, after descending the Columbia for a distance, crossing the country to Pugot's Sound, they met the *Cadboro*, which had gone upon her route. Transported to the mouth of the Fraser River, which empties into the Gulf of Georgia, they, with some difficulty, ascended the river and planted Fort Langley, where in the first season of trade a fair quantity of beaver was purchased, and a good supply of deer and elk meat was brought in by the hunters. The founding of Fort Langley meant virtually the taking hold of what we now know as the mainland of British Columbia.

The reaching out in trade was not favoured by the Indians of the Columbia. Two years after the founding of Fort Langley, a Hudson's Bay Company ship from London, the *William and Ann*, was wrecked at the mouth of the Columbia River. The survivors were murdered by the Indians, and the cargo was seized and secreted by the savage wreckers. Chief Factor McLoughlin sent to the Indians, demanding the restoration of the stolen articles. An old broom was all that was brought to the fort, and this was done in a spirit of derision. The schooner Vancouver—the first ship of that name—(150 tons burthen), built on the coast, was wrecked five years after, and became a total loss.

In the same year as the wreck of the *William and Ann*, it Was strongly impressed upon the traders that a sawmill should be erected to supply the material for building new vessels. Chief Factor McLoughlin determined to push this on. He chose as a site a point on the Willamette River, a tributary of the Columbia from the south, where Oregon city now stands. He began a farm in connection with the mill, and in a year or two undertook the construction of the mill race by blasting in the rock, and erected cottages for his men and new settlers. The Indians, displeased with the signs of permanent residence, burnt McLoughlin's huts. It is said it was this enterprise that turned the Hudson's Bay Company Committee in London against the veteran trader. Years afterwards, Edward Ellice, the fur-trade magnate residing in England, said, "Dr. McLoughlin was rather an amphibious and independent personage. He was a very able man, and, I believe, a very good man; but he had a fancy that he would like to have interests in both countries, both in United States and in English territory . . . While he remained with the Hudson's Bay Company he was an excellent servant."

Among the traders far up in the interior, in command of Fort Kamloops, which was at the junction of the North and South Thompson, was a Scotchman named Samuel Black. There came as a visitor to his fort a man of science and a countryman of his own. This man was David Douglas. He was an enthusiast in the search for plants and birds. He was indefatigable as a naturalist, did much service to the botany of

Western America, and has his name preserved in the characteristic tree of the Pacific slope—the Douglas Fir. Douglas, on visiting Black, was very firm in the expression of his opinions against the Company, saying, "The Hudson's Bay Company is simply a mercenary corporation; there is not an officer in it with a soul above a beaver's skin." Black's Caledonian blood was roused, for he was a leading spirit among the traders, having on the union of the Companies been presented with a ring with the inscription on it, "To the most worthy of the worthy Nor'-Westers." He challenged the botanist to a duel. The scientist deferred the meeting till the morning, but early next day Black tapped at the parchment window of the room where Douglas was sleeping, crying, "Mister Douglas, are ye ready?" Douglas disregarded the invitation. David Douglas some time after visited Hawaii, where, in examining the snares for catching wild cattle, he fell into the pit, and was trampled to death by a wild bullock.

The death of Samuel Black was tragic. In 1841, Tran-quille, a chief of the Shushwaps, who dwelt near Kamloops, died. The friends of the chief blamed the magic or "evil medicine" of the white man for his death. A nephew of Tranquille waited his opportunity and shot Chief Trader Black. The Hudson's Bay Company was aroused to most vigorous action. A writer says: "The murderer escaped. The news spread rapidly to the neighbouring posts. The natives were scarcely less disturbed than the white men. The act was abhorred, even by the friends and relatives of Tranquille. Anderson was at Nisqually at the time. Old John Tod came over from Fort Alexandria, McLean from Fort Colville, and McKinley and Ermatinger from Fort Okanagan. From Fort Vancouver McLoughlin sent men. . . . Cameron was to assist Tod in taking charge of Kamloops. All traffic was stopped.

"Tod informed the assembled Shushwaps that the murderer must be delivered up. The address of Nicola, chief of the Okanagans, gives a fine example of Indian eloquence. He said: 'The winter is cold. On all the hills around the deer are plenty; and yet I hear your children crying for food. Why is this? You ask for powder and ball, they refuse you with a scowl. Why do the white men let your children starve? Look there! Beneath yon mound of earth lies him who was your friend, your father. The powder and ball he gave you that you might get food for your famishing wives and children, you turned against him. Great heavens! And are the Shushwaps such cowards, dastardly to shoot their benefactor in the back while his face was turned? Yes, alas, you have killed your father! A mountain has fallen! The earth is shaken! The sun is darkened! My heart is sad. I cannot look at myself in the glass. I cannot look at you, my neighbours and friends. He is dead, and we poor Indians shall never see his like again. He was just and generous. His heart was larger than yonder mountain, and clearer than the waters of the lake. Warriors do not weep, but sore is my breast, and our wives shall wail for him. Wherefore did you kill him? But you did not. You loved him. And now you must not rest until you have brought to justice his murderer.'

"The old man was so rigid in expression that his whole frame and features seemed turned to stone.

"Archibald McKinley said, 'Never shall I forget it; it the grandest speech I ever heard.'

"The murderer was soon secured and placed in irons, but in crossing a river he succeeded in upsetting the boat in the sight of Nicola and his assembled Indians. The murderer floated down the stream, but died, his death song hushed by the crack of rifles from the shore."

Thus by courage and prudence, alas! not without the sacrifice of valuable lives, was the power of the Hudson's Bay Company and the prestige of Great Britain established on the Pacific Coast.

CHAPTER XL.

FROM OREGON TO VANCOUVER ISLAND

Fort Vancouver on American soil—Chief Factor Douglas chooses a new site—Young McLoughlin killed—Liquor selling prohibited—Dealing with the Songhies—A Jesuit father—Fort Victoria—Finlayson's skill—Chinook jargon—The brothers Ermatinger—A fur-trading Junius—"Fifty-four, forty, or fight"—Oregon Treaty— Hudson's Bay Company indemnified—The waggon road—A colony established— First governor—Gold fever—British Columbia—Fort Simpson—Hudson's Bay Company in the interior—The forts—A group of worthies—Service to Britain—The coast become Canadian.

THE Columbia River grew to be a source of wealth to the Hudson's Bay Company. Its farming facilities were great, and its products afforded a large store for supplying the Russian settlements of Alaska. But as on the Rod River, so here the influx of agricultural settlers sounded a note of warning to the fur trader that his day was soon to pass away. With the purpose of securing the northern trade, Fort Langley had been built on the Fraser River. The arrival of Sir George Simpson on the coast on his journey round the world was the occasion of the Company taking a most important stop in order to hold the trade of Alaska.

In the year following Sir George's visit, Chief Factor Douglas crossed Puget Sound and examined the southern extremity of Vancouver Island as to its suitability for the erection of a new fort to take the place in due time of Fort Vancouver. Douglas found an excellent site, close beside the splendid harbour of Esquimalt, and reported to the assembled council of chief factors and traders at Fort Vancouver that the advantages afforded by the site, especially that of its contiguity to the sea, would place the new fort, for all their purposes, in a much better position than Fort Vancouver. The enterprise was accordingly determined on for the next season.

A tragic incident took place at this time on the Pacific Coast, which tended to make the policy of expansion adopted appear to be a wise and reasonable one. This was the violent death of a young trader, the son of Chief Trader McLoughlin, at Fort Taku on the coast of Alaska, in the territory leased from the Russians by the Hudson's Bay Company. The murder was the result of a drunken dispute among the Indians, in which, accidentally, young McLoughlin had been shot.

Sir George Simpson had just returned to the fort from his visit to the Sandwich Islands, and was startled at seeing the Russian and British ships, with flags at half-mast, on account of the young trader's death. The Indians, on the arrival of the Governor, expressed the greatest penitence, but the stern Lycurgus could not be appeased, and this calamity, along with one of a similar kind, which had shortly before occurred on the Stikine River, led Sir George Simpson and the Russian Governor Etholin to come to an agreement to discontinue at once the sale of spirituous liquor in trading with the Indians. The Indians for a time resorted to every device, such as withholding their furs unless liquor was given them, but the traders were unyielding, and the trade on the coast became safer and more profitable on account of the disuse of strong drink.

The decision to build a new fort having been reached in the next spring, the moving spirit of the trade on the coast, James Douglas, with fifteen men, fully supplied with food and necessary implements, crossed in the *Beaver* from Nisqually, like another Eneas leaving his untenable city behind to build a new Troy elsewhere. On the next day, March 13th, the vessel came to anchor opposite the new site.

A graphic writer has given us the description of the beautiful spot: "The view landwards was enchanting. Before them lay a vast body of land, upon which no white man then stood. Not a human habitation was in sight; not a beast, scarcely a bird. Even the gentle murmur of the voiceless wood was drowned by the gentle beating of the surf upon the shore. There was something specially charming, bewitching in the place. Though wholly natural it did not seem so. It was not at all like pure art, but it was as though nature and art had combined to map out and make one of the most pleasing prospects in the world."

The visitor looking at the City of Victoria in British Columbia to-day will say that the description is in no way overdrawn. Not only is the site one of the most charming on the earth, but as the spectator turns about he is entranced with the view on the mainland, of Mount Olympia, so named by that doughty captain, John Meares, more than fifty years before the founding of this fort.

The place had been already chosen for a village and fortification by the resident tribe, the Songhies, and went by the Indian name of Camosun. The Indian village was a mile-distant from the entrance to the harbour. When the *Beaver* came to anchor, a gun was fired, which caused a commotion among the natives, who were afraid to draw near the intruding vessel. Next morning, however, the sea was alive with canoes of the Songhies.

The trader immediately landed, chose the site for his post, and found at a short distance tall and straight cedar-trees, which afforded material for the stockades of the fort. Douglas explained to the Indians the purpose of his coming, and held up to them bright visions of the beautiful things he would bring them to exchange for their furs. He also employed the Indians in obtaining for him the cedar posts needed for his palisades.

The trader showed his usual tact in employing a most potent means of gaining an influence over the savages by bringing the Jesuit Father Balduc, who had been upon the island before and was known to the natives. Gathering the three tribes of the south of the island, the Songhies, Clallams, and Cowichins, into a great rustic chapel which had been prepared, Father Balduc hold an impressive religious service, and shortly after visited a settlement of the Skagits, a thousand strong, and there too, in a building erected for public worship, performed the important religious rites of his Church before the wondering savages.

It was the intention of the Hudson's Bay Company to make the new fort at Camosun, which they first called Fort Albert, and afterwards Fort Victoria—the name now borne by the city, the chief trading depot on the coast.

As soon as the buildings were well under way, Chief Factor Douglas sailed northward along the coast to re-arrange the trade. Fort Simpson, which was on the mainland, some fifteen degrees north of the new fort and situated between the Portland Canal and the mouth of the Skeena River, was to be retained as necessary for the Alaska trade, but the promising officer, Roderick Finlayson, a young Scotchman, who had shown his skill and honesty in the northern post, was removed from it and given an important place in the new establishment. Living a useful and blameless life, he was allowed to see the new fort become before his death a considerable city. Charles Ross, the master of Fort McLoughlin, being senior to Finlayson, was for the time being placed in charge of the new venture. The three minor forts, Taku, Stikine, and McLoughlin, were now closed, and the policy of consolidation led to Fort Victoria at once rising into importance.

On the return of the chief factor from his northern expedition, with all the employés and stores from the deserted posts, the work at Fort Victoria went on apace. The energetic master had now at his disposal fifty good men, and while some were engaged at the buildings—either storehouses or dwellings—others built the defences. Two bastions of solid block work were erected, thirty feet high, and these were connected by palisades or stockades of posts twenty feet high, driven into the earth side by side. The natives encamped alongside the new work, looked on with interest, but as they had not their wives and children with them, the traders viewed them with suspicion. On account of the watchfulness of the builders, the Indians, beyond a few acts of petty theft, did not interfere with the newcomers in their enterprise.

Three months saw the main features of the fort completed. On entering the western gate of the fort, to the right was to be seen a cottage-shaped building, the post office, then the smithy; further along the walls were the large storehouse, carpenter's shop, men's dormitory, and the boarding-house for the raw recruits. Along the east wall wore the chapel, chaplain's house, then the officers' dining-room, and cook-house attached. Along the north wall was a double row of storehouses for furs and goods, and behind them the gunpowder magazine. In the north-west corner was the cottage residence of the chief factor and his family.

The defences of the fort were important, consisting of two bastions on the western angles, and these contained six or eight nine-pounders. The south tower was the real fort from which salutes were fired; the north tower was a prison; and near the western or front gate stood the belfry erection and on its top the flag-staff. Such was the first Fort St. Albert or Victoria.

Victoria rapidly grew into notice, and in due time Roderick Finlayson, the man of adaptation and force, on the death of his superior officer, became chief factor in charge. The writer met the aged fur trader years after he had retired from active service, and spent with him some hours of cheerful discourse. Large and commanding in form, Finlayson had the marks of governing ability about him. He lacked the adroitness of McLoughlin, the instability of Tod, and the genius of Douglas, but he was a typical Scotchman, steady, patient, and trustworthy. Like an old patriarch, he spent his last days in Victoria, keeping a large extent of vacant city property in a common. Urged again and again to sell it when it had become valuable, the sturdy pioneer replied that he "needed it to pasture his 'coo.' "

One of the things most striking in all the early traders was their ability to master language. Many of the officers of the Company were able to speak four languages. On the Pacific Coast, on account of the many Indian tongues differing much from each other, there grew up a language of commerce, known as the Chinook jargon. It was a most remarkable phenomenon; it is still largely in use. The tribe most familiar to the traders at the beginning of the century was the Chinooks. English-speaking, French, and United States traders met with them, and along with them the Kanakas, or Sandwich Island workmen, with many bands of coast Indians.

A trade has developed upon the Pacific Coast, the Chin jargon has grown, and now numbers some five hundred words. Of these, nearly half were Chinook in origin, a number were from other Indian languages, almost a hundred were French, and less than seventy English, while several were doubtful. The then leading elements among the traders were known in the jargon as respectively, Pasai-ooks, French, a corruption of Francais; King Chautchman (King George man), English; and Boston, American. The following will show the origin and meaning of a few words, showing changes made in consonants which the Indians cannot pronounce.

Frenc	Jargon.	Meaning.
Le mouton.	Lemoots.	Sheep.
Chapeau.	Seahpo.	Hat.
Sauvage.	Siwash.	Indian.

English.	Jargon.	Meaning.
Fire.	Piah.	Fire or cook.
Coffee.	Kaupy.	Coffee.
Handkerchief.	Hat'atshum.	Handkerchief.

Chinook.	Jargon.	Meaning.
Tkalaitanam.	Kali-tan.	Arrow.
Thliakso.	Yokso.	Hair.
	Klootchman.	Woman.

Songs, hymns, sermons, and translations of portions of the Bible are made in the jargon, and used by missionaries and teachers. Several dictionaries of the dialect have been published.

Among the out-standing men who were contemporaries upon the Pacific Coast of Finlayson were the two brothers Ermatinger. Already it has been stated that they were nephews of the famous old trader of Sault Ste. Marie. Their father had preferred England to Canada, and had gone thither. His two sons, Edward and Francis, were, as early as 1818, apprenticed by their father to the Hudson's Bay Company and sent on the Company's ship to Rupert's Land, by way of York Factory.

Edward, whose autobiographical sketch, hitherto unpublished, lies before us, tells us that he spent ten years in the fur trade, being engaged at York Factory, Oxford House, Red River, and on the Columbia River. Desirous of returning to the service after he had gone back to Canada, he had received an appointment to Rupert's Land again from Governor Simpson. This was cancelled by the Governor on account of a grievous quarrel with old Charles, the young trader's uncle, on a sea voyage with the Governor to Britain. For many years, however, Edward Ermatinger lived at St. Thomas, Ontario, where his son, the respected Judge Ermatinger, still resides. The old gentleman became a great authority on Hudson's Bay affairs, and received many letters from the traders, especially, it would seem, from those who had grievances against the Company or against its strong-willed Governor.

Francis Ermatinger, the other brother, spent between thirty and forty years in the Far West, especially on the Pacific Coast. An unpublished journal of Francis Ermatinger lies before us. It is a clear and vivid account of an expedition to revenge the death of a trader, Alexander Mackenzie, and four men who had been basely murdered (1828) by the tribe of Clallam Indians. The party, under Chief Factor Alexander McLeod, attacked one band of Indians and severely punished them; then from the ship *Cadboro* on the coast, a bombardment of the Indian village took place, in which many of the tribe of the murderers were killed, but whether the criminals suffered was never known.

That Francis Ermatinger was one of the most hardy, determined, and capable of the traders is shown by a remarkable journey made by him, under orders from Sir George Simpson on his famous journey round the world. Ermatinger had left Fort Vancouver in charge of a party of trappers to visit the interior of California. Sir George, having heard of him in the upper waters of one of the rivers of the coast, ordered him to meet him at Monterey. This Ermatinger undertook to do, and after a terrific journey, crossing snowy chains of mountains, fierce torrents in a country full of pitfalls, reached the imperious Governor. Ermatinger had assumed the disguise of a Spanish caballero, and was recognized by his superior officer with some difficulty. Ermatinger wrote numerous letters to his brothers in Canada, which contained details of the hard but exciting life he was leading.

Most unique and peculiar of all the traders on the Pacific Coast was John Tod, who first appeared as a trader in the Selkirk settlement and wrote a number of the Hargrave letters. In 1823 he was sent by Governor Simpson, it is said, to New Caledonia as to the penal settlement of the fur traders, but the young Scotchman cheerfully accepted his appointment. He became the most noted letter-writer of the Pacific Coast, indeed he might be called the prince of controversialists among the traders. There lies before the writer a bundle of long letters written over a number of years by Tod to Edward Ermatinger. Tod, probably for the sake of argument, advocated loose views as to the validity of the Scriptures, disbelief of many of the cardinal Christian doctrines, and in general claimed the greatest latitude of belief. It is very interesting to see how the solemn-minded and orthodox Ermatinger strives to load him into the true way. Tod certainly had little effect upon his faithful correspondent, and shows the greatest regard for his admonitions.

The time of Sir George Simpson's visit to the coast on his journey round the world was one of much agitation as to the boundary line between the British and United States possessions on the Pacific Coast. By the treaty of 1825 Russia and Britain had come to an agreement that the Russian strip along the coast should reach southward only to 54 deg. 40′ N. lat. The United States mentioned its claim to the coast as far north as the Russian boundary. However preposterous it may seem, yet it was maintained by the advocates of the Munroe doctrine that Great Britain had no share of the coast at all. The urgency of the American claim became so great that the popular mind seemed disposed to favour contesting this claim with arms. Thus originated the famous saying, "Fifty-four, forty, or fight." The Hudson's Bay Company was closely associated with the dispute, the more that Fort Vancouver on the Columbia River might be south of the boundary line, though their action of building Fort Victoria was shown to be a wise and timely step. At length in 1846 the treaty between Great Britain and the United States was made and the boundary line established. The Oregon Treaty, known in some quarters as the Ashburton Treaty, provided that the 49th parallel of latitude should on the mainland be the boundary, thus handing over Fort Vancouver, Walla Walla, Colville, Nisqually, and Okanagan to the United States, and taking them from their rightful owners, the Hudson's Bay Company. Article two of the great treaty, however, stated that the Company should enjoy free navigation of the Columbia River, while the third article provided that the possessory rights of the Hudson's Bay Company and all other British subjects on the south side of the boundary line should be respected.

The decision in regard to the boundary led to changes in the Hudson's Bay Company establishments. Dr. McLoughlin, having lost the confidence of the Company, threw in his lot with his United States homo, and retired in the year of the treaty to Oregon City, where he died a few years after. His name is remembered as that of an impulsive, good-hearted, somewhat rash, but always well-meaning man.

Though Fort Victoria became the depot for the coast of the trade of the Company, Fort Vancouver, with a reduced staff, was maintained for a number of years by the Company. While under charge of Chief Trader Wark, a part of the fields belonging to the Company at Fort Vancouver were in a most highhanded manner seized by the United States for military purposes. The senior officer, Mr. Grahame, on his return from an absence, protested against the invasion. In June, 1860, however, the Hudson's Bay Company withdrew from the Columbia. The great herd of wild cattle which had grown up on the Columbia were disposed of by the Company to a merchant of Oregon. The Company thus retired to the British side of the boundary line during the three years closing with 1860.

Steps were taken by the Hudson's Bay Company to obtain compensation from the United States authorities. A long and wearisome investigation took place; witnesses were called and great diversity of opinion prevailed as to the value of the interest of the Company in its forts. The Hudson's Bay Company claimed indemnity amounting to the sum of 2,000,000 dols. Witnesses for the United States gave one-tenth of that amount as a fair value. Compensation of a moderate kind was at length made to the Company by the United States.

On its withdrawal from Oregon the Hudson's Bay Company decided on opening up communication with the interior of the mainland up the Fraser River. This was a task of no small magnitude, on account of the rugged and forbidding banks of this great river. A. Caulfield Anderson, an officer who had been in the Company's service for some fourteen years before the date of the Oregon Treaty and was in charge of a post on the Fraser River, was given the duty of finding the road to the interior. He was successful in tracing a road from Fort Langley to Kamloops. The Indians offered opposition to Anderson, but he succeeded in spite of all hindrances, and though other routes were sought for and suggested, yet Anderson's road by way of the present town of Hope and Lake Nicola to Kamloops afterwards became one great waggon road to the interior. No sooner had the boundary line been fixed than agitation arose to prepare the territory north of the line for a possible influx of agriculturists or miners and also to maintain the coast true to British connection. The Hudson's Bay Company applied to the British Government for a grant of Vancouver Island, which they held under a lease good for twelve years more. Mr. Gladstone opposed the application, but considering it the best thing to be done in the circumstances, the Government made the grant (1847) to the Company under certain conditions. The Company agreed to colonize the island, to sell the lands at moderate rates to settlers, and to apply nine-tenths of the receipts toward public improvements. The Company entered heartily into the project, issued a prospectus for settlers, and hoped in five years to have a considerable colony established on the Island.

Steps were taken by the British Government to organize the new colony. The head of the Government applied to the Governor of the Company to name a Governor. Chief Factor Douglas was suggested, but probably thinking an independent man would be more suitable, the Government gave the appointment to a man of respectability, Richard Blanshard, in the end of 1849.

The new Governor arrived, but no preparations had been made for his reception. No salary was provided for his maintenance, and the attitude of the Hudson's Bay Company officially at Fort Victoria was decidedly lacking in heartiness. Governor Blanshard's position was nothing more than an empty show. He issued orders and proclamations which were disregarded. He visited Fort Rupert, which had been founded by the Company on the north-east angle of the island, and there held an investigation of a murder of three sailors by the Newitty Indians. Governor Blanshard spent much of his time writing pessimistic reports of the country to Britain, and after a residence of a year and a half returned to England, thoroughly soured on account of his treatment by the officers of the Company.

The colonization of Vancouver Island proved very slow. A company of miners for Nanaimo, and another of farmers for Sooke, near Victoria, came, but during Governor Blanshard's rule only one *bonâ-fide* sale of land was made, and five years after the cession to the Company there were less than five hundred colonists. Chief Factor Douglas succeeded to the governorship and threw his accustomed energy into his administration. The cry of monopoly, ever a popular one, was raised, and inasmuch as the colony was not increasing sufficiently to satisfy the Imperial Government, the great Committee of the House of Commons of 1857 was appointed to examine the whole relation of the Company to Rupert's Land and the Indian territories. The result of the inquiry was that it was decided to relieve the Hudson's Bay Company of the charge of Vancouver Island at the time of expiry of their lease. The Hudson's Bay Company thus withdrew on the Pacific Coast to the position of a private trading company, though Sir James Douglas, who was knighted in 1863, continued Governor of the Crown Colony of Vancouver Island, with the added responsibility of the territory on the mainland.

At this juncture the gold discovery in the mainland called much attention to the country. Thousands of miners rushed at once to the British possessions on the Pacific Coast. Fort Victoria, from being a lonely traders' post, grew as if by magic into a city. Thousands of miners betook themselves to the Fraser River, and sought the inland gold-fields. All this compelled a more complete organization than the mere oversight of the mainland by Governor Douglas in his capacity as head of the fur trade. Accordingly the British Government determined to relieve the Hudson's Bay Company of responsibility for the mainland, which they hold under a licence soon to expire, and to erect Now Caledonia and the Indian territories of the coast into a separate Crown Colony under the name of British Columbia. In Lord Lytton's dispatches to Governor Douglas, to whom the governorship of both of the colonies of Vancouver Island and British Columbia was offered, the condition is plainly stated that he would be required to sever his connection with the Hudson's Bay Company and the Puget Sound Agricultural Company, and to be independent of all local interests. Here we leave Sir James Douglas immersed in his public duties of governing the two colonies, which in time became one province under the name of British Columbia, thus giving up the guidance of the fur-trading stations for whose up-building he had striven for fifty years.

The posts of the Hudson's Bay Company on the Pacific Coast in 1857 were:—

Vancouver Island—

    Fort Victoria.

    Fort Rupert.

    Nanaimo.

Fraser River—

    Fort Langley.

Thompson River—

North-West Coast—

    Fort Simpson.

New Caledonia—

    Stuart Lake.

    McLeod Lake.

    Fraser Lake.

    Alexandria.

Kamloops.

Fort Hope.

Fort George.

Babines.

Connolly Lake.

CHAPTER XLI.

WHEREVER British influence has gone throughout the world the Christian faith of the British people has followed. It is true, for one hundred and fifty years the ships to Hudson Bay crossed regularly to the forts on the Bay, and beyond certain suggestions as to service to the employés, no recognition of religion took place on Hudson Bay, and no Christian clergyman or missionary visitor found his way thither. The Company was primarily a trading company, its forts were far apart, and there were few men at any one point.

The first heralds of the Cross, indeed, to reach Rupert's Land were the French priests who accompanied Verandrye, though they seem to have made no settlements in the territory. It is said that after the conquest of Canada, when the French traders had withdrawn from the North-West, except a few traditions in one of the tribes, no trace of Christianity was left behind.

The first clergyman to arrive in Rupert's Land was in connection with Lord Selkirk's colony in 1811. A party of Lord Selkirk's first colonists having come from Sligo, the founder sent one Father Bourke to accompany the party to Red River. The wintering at York Factory seems to have developed some unsatisfactory traits in the spiritual adviser, and he did not proceed further than the shore of the Bay, but returned to his native land.

The necessity of providing certain spiritual oversight for his Scottish colonists occupied Lord Selkirk's mind. In 1815 James Sutherland, an elder authorized by the Church of Scotland to baptize and marry, arrived with one of the bands of colonists at Red River. The first point in the agreement between Lord Selkirk and his colonists was "to have the services of a minister of their own church." This was Lord Selkirk's wish, and Mr. Sutherland was sent as locum tenens. For three years this devout man performed the duties of his sacred office, until in the conflict between the rival Companies he was forcibly taken away to Canada by the North-West Company.

Lord Selkirk entered into correspondence with the Roman Catholic authorities in Lower Canada as to their appointing priests to take charge of the French and De Meurons of his colony. We have already seen in the sketch of John McLeod that two French priests, Joseph Norbert Provencher and Severe Dumoulin, proceeded to the North-West and took up a position on the east side of Red River nearly opposite the site of the demolished Fort Gibraltar. On account of the preponderance of the German-speaking De Meurons, the settlement was called St. Boniface, after the German patron saint. Though these pioneer priests endured hardships and poverty, they energetically undertook their work, and maintained a school in which, shortly after, we are told, there were scholars in the "Humanities."

With great zeal the Roman Catholic Church has carried its missions to the Indians, even to distant Athabasca and Mackenzie River. In 1822 the Priest Provencher was made a bishop under the title of Bishop of Juliopolis (in partibus infidelium). His jurisdiction included Rupert's Land and the North-West or Indian territories. Besides the work among the Indians, the Bishop organized the French settlements along the Red and Assiniboine Rivers into parishes. In addition to St. Boniface, some of these were St. Norbert, St. François Xavier, St. Charles, St. Vital, and the like, until, at the close of the Hudson's Bay Company's rule in 1869, there were nine French parishes.

The Indian missions have been largely carried on by a Society of the Roman Catholic Church known as the Oblate Fathers. A sisterhood of the Grey Nuns have also taken a strong hold of the North-West.

In the year 1844 a young French priest named Alexandre Antonin Taché came to the North-West and led the way in carrying the faith among the Indians of the Mackenzie River. A most interesting work of Father Taché, called "Vingt Années de Missions," gives the life and trials of this devoted missionary. In a few years the young priest was appointed coadjutor of Bishop Provencher, and on the death of that prelate in 1853, young Monseigneur Taché succeeded to the see under the name of the Bishop of St. Boniface. Bishop Taché became a notable man of the Red River settlement. He was a man of much breadth of view, kindliness of manner, and of great religious zeal. As an educational and public man, he wielded, during the whole time of the Hudson's Bay Company's later régime, a potent influence. A year or two after the elevation of Bishop Taché to the vacant place of Bishop Provencher, Bishop Grandin was appointed a bishop of the interior and took up his abode at Ile à la Crosse. The Roman Catholic Church has done much in bringing many wild tribes under the civilizing influence of Christianity.

Though Lord Selkirk was compelled to betake himself to France in 1820 in search of health, he did not forget his promise to his Scottish colonists on Red River. He entrusted the task of procuring a clergyman for them to Mr. John Pritchard, who, we have seen, had entered the service of his Lordship. Pritchard, acting under the direction of the committee of the Hudson's Bay Company, seems to have taken a course that Lord Selkirk would hardly have approved. To some extent disregarding the promise made to the Scottish settlers, either the agent or the committee applied to the Church Missionary Society to appoint a chaplain for the Hudson's Bay Company at Red River.

The choice made was a most judicious one, being that of Rev. John West, who wrote a very readable book on his experiences, in which the condition of the settlement, along with an account of his missionary labours, are described. A little volume, written by Miss Tucker, under the name of "The Rainbow of the North," also gives an interesting account of the founding of the Protestant faith in the settlement.

Mr. West arrived in Red River settlement in October, 1820, and at once began his labours by holding services in Fort Garry. For a time he was fully occupied in marrying many who had formerly lived as man and wife, though already married after the Indian fashion, and in baptizing the children. He at once opened a school. Mr. West made an exploratory journey five or six hundred miles westward, visiting Indian tribes. In 1823 he erected the first Protestant place of worship on the Red River, and in the same year was joined by Rev. David Jones, who was left in charge when Mr. West returned to England.

Two years afterwards Rev. William Cochrane and his wife arrived at Red River. Mr. Cochrane, afterward Archdeacon Cochrane, was a man of striking personality, and to him has been given the credit of laying the foundation of the Church of England in the Red River settlement. The Indians to the north of the settlement on Red River were visited and yielded readily to the solicitations of the missionaries. Early among these self-denying Indian missionaries was the Rev. A., afterwards Archdeacon, Cowley. Churches were erected in the parishes that were set apart in the same way as the French parishes; St. John's, St. Paul's, St. Andrew's, St. Clement's, St. James, Headingly, and the like, to the number of ten, were each provided with church and school.

Rev. Mr. Jones did not neglect the educational interests of his wide charge. Having become convinced of the necessity of establishing a boarding-school to meet the wants of the scattered families of Rupert's Land, Mr. Jones brought out Mr. John McCallum, a student of King's College, Aberdeen, who had found his way to London. Coming to Red River in 1833, McCallum began the school which has since become St. John's College. At first this school was under the Church Missionary Society, but a decade after its founding it was conducted by McCallum himself, with an allowance from the Company.

In 1844 an episcopal visit was made to Red River by the first Protestant Bishop who could reach the remote spot. This was Dr. Mountain, Bishop of Montreal. He published a small work giving an account of his visit. Many confirmations took place by the Bishop, and Mr. Cowley was made a priest. John McCallum had taken such a hold upon the Selkirk settlers that it was deemed advisable to ordain him, and for several years he carried on the school along with the incumbency of the parish church. McCallum only lived for five years after the Bishop's visit.

In 1838 James Leith, a wealthy chief factor of the Hudson's Bay Company, bequeathed in his will twelve thousand pounds to be expended for the benefit of the Indian missions in Rupert's Land. Leith's family bitterly opposed this disposition of their patrimony, but the Master of the Rolls, hearing that the Hudson's Bay Company was willing to add three hundred pounds annually to the interest accruing from the Leith bequest, gave the decision against them, and thus secured an income to the see of seven hundred pounds a year. In 1849 the diocese of Rupert's Land was established by the Crown, and Rev. David Anderson, of Oxford University, was consecrated first Bishop of Rupert's Land. In the autumn of the same year Bishop Anderson arrived at Red River, by way of York Factory, and his first public duty was to conduct the funeral of the lamented John McCallum. After an incumbency of fifteen years Bishop Anderson returned to England and resigned the bishopric.

In 1865 Dr. Robert Machray arrived at Red River, having been consecrated Bishop by the Archbishop of Canterbury. Under Bishop Anderson the college successfully begun by McCallum languished, for the Bishop seemed more intent on mission work than education. In the year after his arrival, Bishop Machray revived the institution under the name of St. John's College. It was of much service to the colony.

By the time of the passing away of the power of the Hudson's Bay Company, four years after the arrival of Bishop Machray, substantial stone churches and school-houses had been erected in almost all of the parishes mentioned as organized by the Church of England. To the Church of England belonged nearly all the English-speaking half-breed population of the colony, as well as a large number of the Hudson's Bay Company officers.

Bishop Machray's diocese covered a vast area. From Hudson Bay to the Rocky Mountains was under his jurisdiction. Much work was done amongst the Indian tribes. At Moose Factory on the Bay, another devoted labourer was working diligently. It is true the missions were widely scattered, but of the twenty-four clergymen belonging to the diocese of Rupert's Land, fifteen were among the Indians at the time of the cessation of the Hudson's Bay Company's rule. The remainder were in the parishes of Red River such as St. John's, St. Andrew's, St. Paul's, Headingly, Poplar Point, and Portage la Prairie.

The assistance rendered not only by the Church Missionary Society, but also by the Society for the Propagation of the Gospel in Foreign Parts, the Colonial and Continental Church Society, and the Society for the Promotion of Christian Knowledge, was very great, and future generations will be indebted to the benevolence and liberality of the English people in sending spiritual assistance to Rupert's Land.

A perusal of the work, "Red River Settlement," by Alexander Ross, shows that a long and somewhat disappointing struggle was maintained by the Selkirk settlers to obtain the fulfilment of Lord Selkirk's promise to send them a minister of their own faith. Scottish governors came and departed, but no Scottish minister came. Sir George Simpson arrived on his yearly visits at Fort Garry, and was often interviewed by the settlers of Kildonan, but the Governor, though pleasant and plausible enough, was impenetrable as the sphinx. Petitions were sent to the Hudson's Bay Company and to the Scottish General Assembly, but they seldom reached their destination and effected nothing.

The people conformed to the service of the Church of England in the vicinity of their parish. They were treated by the Episcopal clergy with much consideration. Their own psalter was used in their worship, the service was made as simple as they could well desire, but the people, with Highland tenacity, held to their own tenets for forty years, and maintained among themselves regular cottage meetings for prayer and praise.

At length the question arose as to the possession of the church property and the right of burial in St. John's burial-ground. The Scottish settlers maintained their right to the church and churchyard. A very acrimonious discussion arose. In the end the matter was referred to Mr. Eden Colville, a Company director, who was in the settlement on business. Mr. Colville informed the writer that he claimed the credit of settling the dispute. Another site on the river bank two or three miles to the north of St. John's, called La Grenouillère, or Frog Plain, consisting of several hundred acres, was handed over to the Scottish settlers for church, manse, and glebe. This was in 1851, and though the Kildonan people were still given the right to bury their dead in St. John's, in the future their chief interest centred in the new plot.

The presence in Red River of Mr. Ballenden, a countryman of the Kildonan people, as Hudson's Bay Company Governor of Fort Garry, led to an application being made to their friends in Scotland to send them a minister. Indeed, the call had been made again and again for a generation. This request was transmitted to Canada to Dr. Robert Burns, a man of warm missionary zeal and great wisdom. Sir George Simpson had been communicated with, and deemed it wise to reverse his former policy of inaction and promised certain aid and countenance, should a Presbyterian minister be found to care for the parish of Kildonan.

Dr. Burns had among his acquaintances a recent graduate of Knox College, Toronto, named John Black. Him the zealous doctor urged, if not commanded, to go to Red River. This trust was accepted, and after a tedious and uncertain journey Rev. John Black arrived at Red River, September, 1851. The Kildonan people immediately rallied around their new clergyman, who, though not able to speak Gaelic as they desired, yet became an idol to his people. In 1853 a church was erected, with the aid of a small grant from the Hudson's Bay Company, and the foundations of Presbyterianism were laid.

In 1865 Rev. James Nisbet, who had come a few years before to assist Mr. Black, organized a mission to the Cree Indians, and named his mission church on the banks of the Saskatchewan, Prince Albert. Growing by slow degrees, the Presbyterian interest increased and was represented at the end of the Hudson's Bay Company's rule by four or five clergymen. Schools as maintained by voluntary contributions were erected in the Presbyterian parishes of Kildonan and Little Britain.

Manitoba College was planned and arranged for in the closing year of the Hudson's Bay Company's regime.

The Methodists, with the fervour and missionary zeal which has always characterized them, determined to aid in evangelizing the Indians of Rupert's Land. It was the English Methodists who first showed a desire in this direction. They agreed to send the Indians a clergyman suited for the work, if the Canadian Methodist Church would send a few labourers trained in Indian work in Canada.

James Evans, an Englishman who had been long in Canada, and had laboured for years among the Indians of Upper Canada, consented to go to Rupert's Land and take the superintendence of the others sent out. Leaving Montreal with the three English missionaries and two educated young Ojibe-ways, Peter Jacobs and Henry B. Steinhauser, the party went by canoes up the lakes and then along the old fur traders' route, and arrived at Norway House, at the foot of Lake Winnipeg, in 1840. Evans made Norway House his head-quarters, George Barnley went to Moose Factory, William Mason to Rainy Lake and River Winnipeg, and Robert T. Rundle to Edmonton.

The missions to the Hudson Bay and Rainy Lake were soon given up, but Rossville and Oxford House, on Lake Winnipeg, and several points near Edmonton, are the evidence to-day of the faithful self-denying work done by these early Methodist pioneers. Having no whites in the country, the operations of the Methodist Church in Rupert's Land were, up to the time of the Hudson's Bay Company's transfer, confined to the Indians of Rupert's Land.

Mr. Evans, the superintendent of these missions, became very celebrated by the invention of a syllabic system of writing introduced among the Crees. The plan is simple, and an intelligent Indian who has never seen the system can in a short time learn to read and write the syllabic. The syllabic has spread widely over Rupert's Land, and the different Churches use, especially among the Crees, this ingenious invention in printing the Bible and service books. When Lord Dufferin, a number of years ago, visited the North-West as Governor-General of Canada, on hearing of Evans' invention he remarked, "The nation has given many a man a title and a pension and a resting-place in Westminster Abbey who never did half so much for his fellow-creatures."

Some claim has been made for Mason as being the inventor of this character, but there seems to be no ground for the claim.

John Ryerson, a Canadian Methodist divine, in 1854 visited Rupert's Land from Canada, and after seeing the missions on Lake Winnipeg, went from York Factory to England. The taking over of the mission by the Canadian Methodist Church resulted from this visit.

These are the main movements of a religious kind that took place within the borders of Rupert's Land and the territories east of the Rocky Mountains up to the end of the Hudson's Bay Company's regime. A great service was rendered to the whites and Indians alike, to the Hudson's Bay Company, to the Kildonan settlers, and all the native people by the patient work of the four churches named. The best feeling, and in many cases active co-operation, were given by these churches to each other. The work done by these churches laid the foundation for the general morality and advanced social life which prevailed in Red River and in the regions beyond.

On the Pacific slope the Hudson's Bay Company took an immediate control of the religious and educational instruction of the people, upon the organization of Vancouver Island as a colony (1849). The Rev.

Robert Staines was sent as chaplain and teacher to Fort Victoria, and was given a salary and an allowance for carrying on a boarding-school in which he was assisted by his wife. Mr. Staines did not agree with the Company, wont to Britain as a delegate from the dissatisfied employés, but died of injuries received on his homeward voyage.

Mr. Staines' successor was the Rev. Edward Cridge. The new chaplain was well provided for by the Company, being secured a parsonage and glebe of one hundred acres, and three hundred pounds a year, one hundred pounds annually being as chaplain of the Company. Mr. Cridge became a prominent clergyman of the colony, but in later years left his mother Church to become bishop of the Reformed Episcopal Church. In 1859 Bishop Hills was made first bishop of the united colonies of Vancouver Island and British Columbia. Twenty years afterward the diocese was divided into (1) Vancouver Island and the islands, as *Diocese of Columbia*, (2) the southern mainland as *Diocese of New Westminster*, and (3) the northern mainland as *Diocese of New Caledonia*. The Church of England in British Columbia has enjoyed large gifts from the Baroness Burdett-Coutts.

One of the most remarkable missions of modern times is that of Metlakahtla, begun under the auspices of the Church of England by William Duncan. The village he founded became an example of civilization among the Indians, as well as a handmaid to the Christian work done. Unfortunately, the model Indian village has been largely broken up by a misunderstanding between Mr. Duncan and his bishop.

The first missionary of note of the Roman Catholic Church on the coast was Father Demers, who became Bishop of Vancouver Island and New Caledonia. The Oblate Fathers were early on the ground in British Columbia, the first of the Order having baptized upwards of three thousand men, women, and children of Indian tribes, the Songhies, Saanechs, and Cowichins, near Victoria. Many churches, schools, and hospitals have been founded by the energetic and self-denying Roman Catholics who have made British Columbia their home. Bishop Seghers succeeded the venerable Bishop Demers in his diocese.

Ten years after the formation of Vancouver Island as a Crown colony, Revs. Dr. Evans, L. Robson, and two other ministers undertook work for the Methodist Church on the coast. Good foundations were laid by the clergymen named, and still better by Rev. Thomas Crosby, who joined them after a few years' service, and entered heartily into efforts to evangelize the Indians. He had great success among the Flathead Indians.

In 1861 the first Presbyterian minister arrived—Rev. John Hall, from Ireland, and he undertook work in Victoria. In the year following, Rev. Robert Jamieson came from Canada as a representative of the Canadian Presbyterian Church and settled at New Westminster. Churches were soon built in Victoria, Nanaimo, and New Westminster, that now contain strong and vigorous congregations.

All of the churches were under deep obligations to the Hudson's Bay Company for protection, assistance, and sympathy in their undertakings on the coast. The inrush of gold seekers threw a great responsibility upon all the churches, and it was well that the Company, merely for motives of self-interest, should regard the influence of the missionaries among the fierce tribes of the mountains, of both island and mainland, as of the greatest importance. The record of self-denying missionaries of the churches has justified all the patronage and favour rendered them by the Hudson's Bay Company.

CHAPTER XLII.

THE HUDSON'S BAY COMPANY AND THE INDIANS

The Company's Indian policy—Character of officers—A race of hunters—Plan of advances—Charges against the Company—Liquor restriction—Capital punishment—Starving Indians—Diseased and helpless—Education and religion—The age of missions—Sturdy Saulteaux—The Muskegons—Wood Crees—Wandering Plain Crees—The Chipewyans—Wild Assiniboines—Blackfeet Indians—Polyglot coast tribes—Eskimos—No Indian war—No police—Pliable and docile—Success of the Company.

FROM time to time the opponents of the Company have sought to find grounds for the overthrow of the licence to trade granted by the Government of Britain over the Indian territories. One of the most frequent lines of attack was in regard to the treatment of the Indians by the fur traders. It may be readily conceded that the ideal of the Company's officials was in many cases not the highest. The aim of Governor Simpson in his long reign of forty years was that of a keen trader. A politic man, the leader of the traders when in Montreal conformed to the sentiment of the city, abroad in the wilds he did very little to encourage his subordinates to cultivate higher aims among the natives. Often the missionary was found raising questions very disturbing to the monopoly, and this brought the Company officers into a hostile attitude to him. Undoubtedly in some cases the missionaries were officious and unfair in their criticisms.

But, on the other hand, the men and officers of the Company were generally moral. Men of education and reading the officers usually were, and their sentiment was likely to be in the right direction. The spirit of the monopoly—the golden character of silence, and the need of being secretive and uncommunicative—was instilled into every clerk, trapper, and trader.

But the tradition of the Company was to keep the Indian a hunter. There was no effort to encourage the native to agriculture or to any industry. To make a good collector of fur was the chief aim. For this the Indian required no education, for this the wandering habit needed to be cultivated rather than discouraged, and for this it was well to have the home ties as brittle as possible. Hence the tent and teepee were favoured for the Indian hunter more than the log cottage or village house.

It was one of the most common charges against the Company that in order to keep the Indian in subjection advances were made on the catch of furs of the coming season, in order that, being in debt, he might be less independent. The experience of the writer in Red River settlement in former days leads him to doubt this, and certainly the fur traders deny the allegation. The improvident or half-breed Indian went to the Company's store to obtain all that he could. The traders at the forts had difficulty in checking the extravagance of their wards. Frequently the storekeeper refused to make advances lest he should fail in recovering the value of the articles advanced. Fitzgerald, a writer who took part in the agitation of 1849, makes the assertion in the most flippant manner that to keep the Indians in debt was the invariable policy of the Company. No evidence is cited to support this statement, and it would seem to be very hard to prove.

The same writer undertakes, along the line of destructive criticism, to show that the Hudson's Bay Company does not deserve the credit given it of discouraging the traffic in strong drink, and asserts that "a beaver skin was never lost to the Company for want of a pint of rum." This is a very grave charge, and in the opinion of the writer cannot be substantiated. The Bishop of Montreal, R. M. Ballantyne, and the agents of the missionary societies are said either to have little experience or to be unwilling to tell on this subject what they knew. This critic then quotes various statements of writers, extending back in some cases thirty or forty years, to show that spirituous liquors were sold by the Company. It is undoubted that at times in the history of the fur trade, especially at the beginning of the century, when the three Companies were engaged in a most exacting competition, as we have fully shown, in several cases much damage was done. On the Pacific Coast, too, eight or ten years before this critic wrote, there was, as we have seen, excess. At other times, also, at points in the wide field of operations, over half a continent, intoxicating liquor was plentiful and very injurious, but no feeling was stronger in a Hudson's Bay Company trader's mind than that he was in a country without police, without military, without laws, and that his own and his people's lives were in danger should drunkenness prevail. Self-preservation inclined every trader to prevent the use of spirits among the Indians. The writer is of opinion that while there may have been many violations of sobriety, yet the record of the Hudson's Bay Company has been on the whole creditable in this matter.

The charges of executing capital punishment and of neglecting the Indians in years of starvation may be taken together. The criticism of the people of Red River was that the Company was weak in the execution of the penalties of the law. They complained that the Company was uncertain of its powers and that the hand of justice was chained. The marvel to an unprejudiced observer is that the Company succeeded in ruling so vast a territory with so few reprisals or executions. In the matter of assisting the Indians in years of scarcity, it was the interest of the fur company to save the lives of its trappers and workers. But those unacquainted with the vast wastes of Rupert's Land and the Far North little know the difficulties of at times obtaining food. The readers of Milton and Cheadle's graphic story or our account of Robert Campbell's adventures on the Stikine, know the hardships and the near approach to starvation of these travellers. Dr. Cheadle, on a visit to Winnipeg a few years ago, said to the writer that on his first visit the greatest difficulty his party had was to secure supplies. There are years in which game and fish are so scarce that in remote northern districts death is inevitable for many. The conditions make it impossible for the Company to save the lives of the natives. Relief for the diseased and aged is at times hard to obtain. Small-pox and other epidemics have the most deadly effect upon the semi-civilized people of the far-off hunter's territory.

The charge made up to 1849 that the Hudson's Bay Company had done little for the education and religious training of the Indians was probably true enough. Outside of Red River and British Columbia they did not sufficiently realize their responsibility as a company. Since that time, with the approval and co-operation in many ways of the Company, the various missionary societies have grappled with the problem. The Indians about Hudson Bay, on Lake Winnipeg, in the Mackenzie River, throughout British Columbia, and on the great prairies of Assiniboia, are to-day largely Christianized and receiving education.

The Saulteaux, or Indians who formerly lived at Sault Ste. Marie, but wandered west along the shore of Lake Superior and even up to Lake Winnipeg, are a branch of the Algonquin Ojibeways. Hardy and persevering, most conservative in preserving old customs, hard to influence by religious ideas, they have been pensioners of the Hudson's Bay Company, but their country is very barren, and they have advanced but little.

Very interesting, among their relations of Algonquin origin, are the Muskegons, or Swampy Crees, who have long occupied the region around Hudson Bay and have extended inland to Lake Winnipeg. Docile and peaceful, they have been largely influenced by Christianity. Under missionary and Company guidance they have gathered around the posts, and find a living on the game of the country and in trapping the wild animals.

Related to the Muskegons are the Wood Crees, who live along the rivers and on the belts of wood which skirt lakes and hills. They cling to the birch-bark wigwam, use the bark canoe, and are nomadic in habit. They may be called the gipsies of the West, and being in scattered families have boon little reached by better influences.

Another branch of the Algonquin stock is the Plain Crees. These Indians are a most adventurous and energetic people. Leaving behind their canoes and Huskie dogs, they obtained horses and cayuses and hied them over the prairies. Birch-bark being unobtainable, they made their tents, better fitted for protecting them from the searching winds of the prairies and the cold of winter, from tanned skins of the buffalo and moose-deer. For seven hundred miles from the mouth of the Saskatchewan they extend to the foot hills of the Rocky Mountains. Meeting in their great camps, seemingly untameable as a race of plain hunters, they were, up to the time of the transfer to Canada, almost untouched by missionary influence, but in the last thirty years they have been placed on reserves by the Canadian Government and are in almost all cases yielding to Christianizing agencies.

North of the country of the Crees live tribes with very wide connections. They call themselves "Tinné" or "People," but to others they are known as Chipewyans, or Athabascans. They seem to be less copper-coloured than the other Indians, and are docile in disposition. This nation stretches from Fort Churchill, on Hudson Bay, along the English River, up to Lake Athabasca, along the Peace River into the very heart of the Rocky Mountains, and even beyond to the coast. They have proved teachable and yield to ameliorating influences.

Probably the oldest and best known name of the interior of Rupert's Land, the name after which Lord Selkirk called his Colony of Assiniboia, is that belonging to the Wild Assiniboines or Stony River Sioux. The river at the mouth of which stands the city of Winnipeg was their northern boundary, and they extended southward toward the great Indian confederacy of the Sioux natives or Dakotas, of which indeed they were at one time a branch. Tall, handsome, with firmly formed faces, agile and revengeful, they are an intelligent and capable race. These Indians, known familiarly as the "Stonies," have greatly diminished in numbers since the time of Alexander Henry, jun., who describes them fully. In later years they have been cut down with pulmonary and other diseases, and are to-day but the fragment of a great tribe. They have long been friendly with the Plain Crees, but are not very open to Christianity, though there are one or two small communities which are exceptions in this respect.

Very little under Hudson's Bay Company control were the Blackfoot nation, along the foot hills of the Rocky Mountains, ear the national boundary. Ethnically they are related to the Crees, but they have always been difficult to approach. Living in large camps during Hudson's Bay Company days, they spent a wild, happy, comfortable life among the herds of wandering buffalo of their district. Since the beginning of the Canadian régime they have become more susceptible to civilizing agencies, and live in great reserves in the south-west of their old hunting grounds.

A perfect chaos of races meets us among the Indians of British Columbia and Alaska, and their language is polyglot. Seemingly the result of innumerable immigrations from Malayan and Mongolian sources in Asia, they have come at different times. One of the best known tribes of the coast is the Haidas, numbering some six thousand souls. The Nutka Indians occupy Vancouver Island, and have many tribal divisions. To the Selish or Flatheads belong many of the tribes of the Lower Fraser River, while the Shushwaps hold the country on the Columbia and Okanagan Rivers. Mention has been made already of the small but influential tribe of Chinooks near the mouth of the Columbia River.

While differing in many ways from each other, the Indians of the Pacific Coast have always been turbulent and excitable. From first to last more murders and riots have taken place among them than throughout all the vast territory held by the Hudson's Bay Company east of the Rocky Mountains. While missionary zeal has accomplished much among the Western Coast Indians, yet the "bad Indian" element has been a recognized and appreciable quantity among them so far as the Company is concerned.

Last among the natives who have been under Hudson's Bay Company influence are the Eskimos or Innuits of the Far North. They are found on the Labrador Coast, on Coppermine River, on the shore of the Arctic Sea, and on the Alaskan peninsula. Dressed in sealskin clothing and dwelling in huts of snow, hastening from place to place in their sledges drawn by wolf-like dogs called "Eskies" or "Huskies," these people have found themselves comparatively independent of Hudson's

Bay Company assistance. Living largely on the products of the sea, they have shown great ingenuity in manufacturing articles and implements for themselves. The usual experience of the Company from Ungava, through the Mackenzie River posts, and the trading houses in Alaska has been that they were starved out and were compelled to give up their trading houses among them. Little has been done, unless in the Yukon country, to evangelize the Eskimos.

The marvel to the historian, as he surveys the two centuries and a quarter of the history of the Hudson's Bay Company, is their successful management of the Indian tribes. There has never been an Indian war in Rupert's Land or the Indian territories—nothing beyond a temporary *émeute* or incidental outbreak. Thousands of miles from the nearest British garrison or soldier, trade has been carried on in scores and scores of forts and factories with perfect confidence. The Indians have always respected the "Kingchauch man." He was to them the representative of superior ability and financial strength, but more than this, he was the embodiment of civilization and of fair and just dealing. High prices may have been imposed on the Indians, but the Company's expenses were enormous. There are points among the most remote trading posts from which the returns in money were not possible in less than nine years from the time the goods left the Fenchurch Street or Lime Street warehouses. With all his keen bargaining and his so-called exacting motto, "Pro pelle cutem," the trader was looked upon by the Indians as a benefactor, bringing into his barren, remote, inhospitable home the commodities to supply his wants and make his life happier. While the Indians came to recognize this in their docile and pliable acceptance of the trader's decisions, the trader also became fond of the Red man, and many an old fur trader freely declares his affection for his Indian ward, so faithful to his promise, unswerving in his attachment, and celebrated for never forgetting a kindness shown him.

The success of the Company was largely due to honourable, capable, and patient officers, clerks, and employés, who with tact and justice managed their Indian dependents, many of whom rejoiced in the title of "A Hudson's Bay Company Indian."

CHAPTER XLIII.

UNREST IN RUPERT'S LAND (1844-1869).

Discontent on Red River—Queries to the Governor—A courageous Recorder—Free trade in furs held illegal—Imprisonment—New land deed—Enormous freights—Petty revenge—Turbulent pensioners—Heart-burnings—Heroic Isbister—Half-breed memorial—Mr. Beaver's letter—Hudson's Bay Company notified—Lord Elgin's reply—Voluminous correspondence—Company's full answer—Colonel Crofton's statement—Major Caldwell, a partisan—French petition—Nearly a thousand signatures—Love, a factor—The elder Riel—A court scene—Violence—"Vive la liberté"—The Recorder checked—A new judge—Unruly Corbett—The prison broken—Another rescue—A valiant doctor—A Red River Nestor.

THE fuller organization of Assiniboia, after its purchase by the Hudson's Bay Company from the heirs of the Earl of Selkirk, encouraged the authorities at Red River to assert the rights which the Company had always claimed—viz. the monopoly of the fur trade in Rupert's Land and the imposition of heavy freights on imports and exports by way of Hudson Bay. The privilege of exporting tallow, the product of the buffalo, had been accorded on reasonable terms to a prominent resident of the Red River, named James Sinclair. The first venture, a small one, succeeded; but a second larger consignment was refused by the Company, and, after lying nearly two years at York Factory, the cargo was sold to the Company.

Twenty loading half-breeds then petitioned the Company to be allowed to export their tallow and to be given a reasonable freight charge. No answer was returned to this letter. The half-breeds were thus rising in intelligence and means; being frequently employed as middlemen in trafficking in furs, they learned something of the trade and traffic. The half-breed settlers of the Red River settlement have always claimed special privileges in Rupert's Land as being descended from the aboriginal owners. It was under such circumstances that Governor Christie, following, it is supposed, legal direction, in 1844 issued two proclamations, the first, requiring that each settler, before the Company would carry any goods for him, should be required to declare that he had not been engaged in the fur trade; the second, that the writer of every letter write his name on the outside of it, in order that, should he be suspected of dealing in furs, it might be opened and examined.

This was a direct issue, and they determined to bring the matter to a crisis. Twenty leading natives (half-breeds of Red River settlement), among them a number well known, such as James Sinclair, John Dease, John Vincent, William Bird, and Peter Garrioch, in 1845 approached Alexander Christie, Governor of the settlement, requesting answers to fourteen queries. These questions required satisfaction as to whether half-breeds could hunt, buy, sell, or traffic in furs, and also what were the restrictions in this matter upon Europeans, &c. A pacific and soothing reply was made by Governor Christie, but the Company soon began to take steps to repress the free trade in furs, and the Council of Rupert's Land passed certain regulations, among others one placing a duty of twenty per cent. upon imports, but exempting from their tax settlers who were free of the charge of trading in furs. This was a vexatious regulation and roused great opposition.

All these devices had a legal smack about them, and were no doubt the suggestions of Judge Thom, the Recorder of Red River, a remarkable man, who, six years before this time, had come from Montreal to put legal matters in order in the Red River settlement. The Recorder entered *con amore* into the matter, and advised the assertion of claims that had fallen into disuse for many years among the different classes of residents in the settlement. The redoubtable Judge, who, it will be remembered, was said to have been at the elbow of Sir George Simpson in writing his "Journey Round the World," now evolved another tyrannical expedient.

A new land deed was devised, and whosoever wished to hold land in the settlement was compelled to sign it. This indenture provided that if the land-holder should invade any privileges of the Company and fail to contribute to the maintenance of clergy and schools, or omit to do his work upon the public roads, or carry on trade in skins, furs, peltry, or dressed leather, such offender should forfeit his lands.

This was certainly un-British and severe, and we may look upon it as the plan of the Judge, who failed to understand the spirit of his age, and would have readily fallen in with a system of feudal tenure. The writer in after years met this judge, then very old, in London, and found him a kindly man, though with Scottish determination, willing to follow out his opinions logically, however rash or out of place such a course might be. If the Hudson's Bay Company found itself in a sea of trouble, and hostile to public sentiment in the settlement, it had to blame its own creation, the valorous Recorder of Rod River.

The imposition of enormous freights, adopted at this time for carrying goods by way of York Factory to England, in order to check trade, was a part of the same policy of "Thorough" recommended by this legal adviser. Sinclair, already mentioned, became the "Village Hampden" in this crisis. Taking an active part in his opposition to this policy of restriction, he found that he was to be punished, by the "Company's Ship" from England to York Factory refusing to carry for him any freight. It was partly the Oregon question and partly the unsettled state of public opinion in Red River that led to a British regiment being for a time stationed at the Red River settlement. On the removal of these troops the pensioners, a turbulent band of old discharged soldiers, came from Britain and were settled upon the Assiniboine, above Fort Garry. A writer who knew them well ventures to suggest that they were of the same troublesome disposition as the former De Meurons of Lord Selkirk. Coming ostensibly to introduce peace they brought a sword. Sooner or later the discontent and irritation produced by Judge Thorn's inspiration was sure to reach its culmination, and this it did in the Sayer affair afterwards described.

The cause of the complaints from the Rod River settlement found a willing and powerful advocate in Mr. Alexander K. Isbister, a young London barrister, and afterwards a prominent educationalist. He was a native of Rupert's Land, and had a dash of Indian blood in his veins, and so took up the brief for his compatriots in a formidable series of documents. Mr. Isbister's advocacy gave standing and weight to the contention of the Red River half-breeds, and a brave and heroic fight was made, even though the point of view was at times quite unjust to the Company.

In 1847, Isbister, with five other half-breeds of Red River, forwarded, to the Secretary of State for the Colonies, a long and able memorial, setting forth the grievances of the petitioners. The document sets forth in short that the Company had "amassed a princely revenue" at the expense of the natives, allowed their wards to pass their lives in the darkest heathenism, broke their pledges to exclude strong drink from the Indian trade, were careless of the growing evil of want and suffering in the territory, paid little for the furs, and persecuted the natives by checking them in their barter of furs, and followed a short-sighted and pernicious policy.

This was assuredly a serious list of charges. Earl Grey in due time called on Isbister and his friends for a more specific statement of the grievances, and wrote to the Governor of Assiniboia, to the London Governor of the Hudson's Bay Company, and to the Governor-General of Canada, Lord Elgin, asking their attention to the allegations of the petition.

Some two months after Lord Grey's letter was received, the Hudson's Bay Company Governor, Sir J. H. Pelly, submitted a long and minute answer to the various charges of the petitioners. As is usually the case, both parties had some advantages. As to the enormous profits, the Company were able to show that they had unfortunately not been able to make "more than the ordinary rate of mercantile profit." They replied as to the religious interests of the natives, that their sole objects, as stated in the Charter, were trade and the discovery of a North-West Passage, but that they had helped at a considerable annual expense the Church Missionary Society, Wesleyan Missionary Society, and a Roman Catholic Missionary Society. The Company gives a most indignant denial to the charge that they had resumed the trade in spirituous liquors with the Indians, though admitting in the neighbourhood of Red River the use of small quantities of strong drink in meeting the American traders.

This answer did not, however, quiet the storm. Isbister returned to the attack, giving the evidence of Mr. Alexander Simpson, a trader on the Pacific Coast, and the extensive and strong letter of the Rev. Herbert Beaver, the former chaplain of the Hudson's Bay Company at Fort Vancouver. Isbister also raised the question of the validity of the Company's Charter. The Company again replied, and so the battle raged, reply and rejoinder, quotations and evidence *ad libitum*. Isbister may not have proved his case, but his championship won the approbation of many independent observers.

Lord Elgin, the efficient and popular Governor-General of Canada, gave such reply as he was able. He states that the distance of Red River was so great and the intercourse so little, that taking into account the peculiar jurisdiction of the Company, he found it difficult to obtain the information sought. As to the complaints about the religious neglect of the Indians, Lord Elgin states that disappointments in this matter occur in other quarters as well as in the Hudson's Bay Company territories, but declares that the result of his inquiries in the matter "is highly favourable to the Company, and that it has left in his mind the impression that the authority which they exercise over the vast and inhospitable region subject to their jurisdiction is on the whole very advantageous to the Indians."

Lord Elgin states that he is much indebted for his information to Colonel Crofton, the commander of the 6th Royal Regiment, which we have seen was stationed for a time at Red River. Colonel Crofton afterwards gave to the Colonial Secretary what one would say was rather an unjudicial reply. He said, "I unhesitatingly assert that the government of the Hudson's Bay Company is mild and protective, and admirably adapted, in my opinion, for the state of society existing in Rupert's Land, where Indians, half-breeds, or Europeans are happily governed, and live protected by laws which I know were mercifully and impartially administered by Mr. Thorn, the Recorder, and by the magistrates of the land." In regard to this opinion, while no doubt an honest expression of views, it is plain that Colonel Crofton did not understand the aspiration for self-government which prevails in Western communities. The reply of the Governor of Assiniboia, Major Caldwell, was likewise favourable to the Company. Alexander Ross, in his "Red River Settlement," criticizes the method taken by Major Caldwell to obtain information. According to Ross, the Governor sent around queries to a few select individuals, accepting no one "below what the Major considered a gentleman." This, the critic says, was the action of a man" who had never studied the art of governing a people." Ross, who did not admire the Company greatly, however, sums up the whole matter by saying, "The allegations of harsh conduct or maladministration preferred against the Hudson's Bay Company by Mr. Isbister and his party were in general totally unfounded and disproved," and therefore neither Major Caldwell's inquiries nor the inspiration of his genius were required.

Notwithstanding Major Caldwell's optimism and Lord Elgin's favourable reply, there was really a serious condition of affairs in Red River settlement. Along with the petition of Isbister and his five English half-breed compatriots, there was one far more formidable from the French half-breeds, who to the number of nine hundred and seventy-seven subscribed their names. Presented to Her Majesty the Queen, in most excellent terms, in the French language, their petition sought, decrying the monopoly as severe:—

1. That as good subjects they might be governed by the principles of the British Constitution;

2. That as British subjects they demanded their right to enjoy the liberty of commerce;

3. They requested the sale of lands to strangers, and that a portion of the proceeds should be applied to improve the means of transport.

French and English half-breeds were now united in a common purpose. A strange story is related as to the way in which the English-speaking half-breeds came to throw in their lot with their French fellow-countrymen. A Company officer had left his two daughters at Fort Garry to be educated. One of them was the object of the affection of a young Scotch half-breed, and at the same time of a young Highlander. The young lady is said to have preferred the Metis, but the stern parent favoured the Highlander, The Scotchman, fortified by the father's approval, proceeded to upbraid the Metis for his temerity in aspiring to the hand of one so high in society as the lady. As love ruined Troy, so it is said this affair joined French and English half-breeds in a union to defeat the Company.

The agitation went on, as Isbister and his friends corresponded with the people of Red River and succeeded so well in gaining the ear of the British Government. Among the French people one of the fiercest and most noisy leaders was Louis Riel, the revolutionary "miller of the Seine." This man, the father of the rebel chief of later years, was a French half-breed. A tribune of the people, he had a strong ascendency over the ignorant half-breeds. He was ready for any emergency.

It is often the case that some trifling incident serves to bring on a serious crisis in affairs. A French settler, named Guillaume Sayer, half-breed son of an old bourgeois in the North-West Company, had bought a quantity of goods, intending to go on a trading expedition to Lake Manitoba. The Company proceeded to arrest him, and, after a stiff resistance, he was overcome by force and imprisoned at Fort Garry.

As the day of trial drew near the excitement grew intense. Governor Caldwell was a well-known martinet; the Recorder was regarded as the originator of the policy of restriction. He was, moreover, believed to be a Francophobe, having written a famous series of newspaper communications in Montreal, known as the "Antigallic Letters." The day of trial had been fixed for Ascension Day, May 17th, and this was taken as a religious affront by the French. The Court was to meet in the morning.

On the day of the trial hundreds of French Metis, armed, came from all the settlements to St. Boniface Church, and, leaving their guns at the church door, entered for service. At the close they gathered together, and were addressed in a fiery oration by Riel. A French Canadian admirer, writing of the matter, says, "Louis Riel obtained a veritable triumph on that occasion, and long and loud the hurrahs were repeated by the echoes of the Red River."

Crossing by way of Point Douglas, the Metis surrounded the unguarded Court House at Fort Garry. The governor, judge, and magistrate arrived, and took their seats at eleven o'clock. A curious scene now ensued: the magistrates protested against the violence; Riel in loud tones declared that they would give the tribunal one hour, and that if justice were not done them, they would do it themselves. An altercation then took place between Judge Thorn and Riel, and with his loud declaration, "Et je déclare que de ce moment Sayer est libre——" drowned by the shouts of the Metis, the trial was over. Sayer and his fellow-prisoners betook themselves to freedom, while the departing Metis cried out, "Le commerce est libre! le commerce est libre! Vive la liberté!" This crisis was a serious one. Judge Thorn, so instructed by Governor Simpson, never acted as Recorder again. The five years' struggle was over.

The movement for liberty continued to stimulate the people. Five years afterward the plan of the agitators was to obtain the intervention of Canada. Accordingly a petition, signed by Roderick Kennedy and five hundred and seventy-four others, was presented to the Legislative Assembly of Canada. The grievances of the people of Red River were recited. It was stated that application had been made to the Imperial Parliament without result, and this through "the chicanery of the Company and its false representations." In 1857 the Toronto Board of Trade petitioned the Canadian Assembly to open the Hudson's Bay Company territories to trade. Restlessness and uncertainty largely prevailed in Red River, though there were many of the colonists who paid little attention to what they considered the infatuated conduct of the agitators.

No truer test of the success of government can be found than the respect and obedience shown by the people for the law. Red River settlement, judged by this standard, had a woful record at this time. After the unfortunate Sayer affair, Recorder Thorn was superseded, and for a time (1855 to 1858) Judge Johnson, of Montreal, came to Fort Garry to administer justice and to act as Governor.

Judge Black, a capable trader who had received a legal training, was appointed to the office of Recorder, but soon found a case that tried his judicial ability and skill. A clergyman named Corbett, who had been bitterly hostile to the Company, testified to certain extreme statements against the Company in the great investigation of 1857. He then returned to his parish of Headingly in the settlement- A criminal charge was brought against him, for which he was found guilty in the courts and sentenced to six months' imprisonment. The opponents of the Company, seemingly without ground, but none the less fiercely, declared that the trial was a persecution by the Company and that Corbett was innocent. Strong in this belief, the mob surrounded the prison at Fort Garry, overawed the old French jailor, and, rescuing Corbett, took him home to his parish.

Among those who had been prominent in the rescue was James Stewart, long afterward a druggist and meteorological observer in Winnipeg. Stewart and some of his companions were arrested for jail-breaking and cast into prison. Some forty or fifty friends of Stewart threatened violence should he be kept a prisoner. The Governor, bishop, and three magistrates met to overawe the insurgents, but the determined rescuers tore up the pickets enclosing the prison yard, broke open the jail, and made the prisoner a free man.

Such insubordination and tumult marked the decline of the Company's power as a governing body. This lawlessness was no doubt stimulated by the establishment of a newspaper in 1859—*The Nor'-Wester*—which from the first was hostile to the Company. The system of government by the Council of Assiniboia had always been a vulnerable point in the management by the Company, and the newspaper constantly fanned the spirit of discontent. In the year 1868, when the Hudson. Bay Company regime was approaching its end, another violent and disturbing affair took place. This was the arrest of Dr. Schultz, a Canadian leader of great bodily strength and determination, who had thrown in his lot with the Red River people. As a result of a business dispute, Schultz was proceeded against in the Court, and an order issued for seizure of his goods. On his resisting the sheriff in the execution of his duty, he was, after a severe struggle, overpowered, taken captive, and confined in Fort Garry jail.

On the following day the wife of Dr. Schultz and some fifteen men forcibly entered the prison, overpowered the guards, and, breaking open his cell, rescued the redoubtable doctor. Hargrave says, "This done, the party adjourned along with him to his house, where report says, 'They made a night of it.'"

These events represented the decadence of the Company's rule; they indicated the rise of new forces that were to compel a change; and however harmful to those immediately involved they declared unmistakably that the old order changeth, giving place to new.

Typical of his times, there sat through the court scenes of these troublous days the old "clerk of court and council," William Robert Smith. With long grey beard he held his post, and was the genius of the place. He was the Nestor of Red River. A Bluecoat boy from London, he had come from school far back in 1813, to enter on the fur trade in Rupert's Land. At Oxford House, Ile à la Crosse, Little Slave Lake, and Norway House, he served eleven faithful years as a clerk, when he retired and became a settler of Red River. He was the first to settle near Lower Fort Garry, and named the spot "Little Britain," from one of his old London localities. Farming, teaching, catechizing for the church, acting precentor, a local encyclopaedia, and collector of Customs, he passed his versatile life, till, the year before the Sayer *émeute*, he became Clerk of Court, which place, with slight interruption, he held for twenty years. How remarkable to think of the man of all work, the Company's factotum, reaching in his experience from the beginning to well-nigh the ending of the Selkirk settlement! One who knew him says, "From his long residence in the settlement he has seen governors, Judges, bishops, and clergymen, not to mention such birds of passage as the Company's local officers, who come and go, himself remaining to record their doings to their successors."

CHAPTER XLIV.

CANADA COVETS THE HUDSON'S BAY TERRITORY

Renewal of licence—Labouchere's letter—Canada claims to Pacific Ocean—
Commissioner Chief-Justice Draper—Rests on Quebec Act, 1774—Quebec overlaps
Indian territories—Company loses Vancouver Island—Cauchon's memorandum—
Committee of 1857—Company on trial—A brilliant committee—Four hundred folios
of evidence—To transfer Red River and Saskatchewan—Death of Sir George—
Governor Dallas—A cunning scheme—Secret negotiations—The Watkin Company
floated—Angry winterers—Dallas's soothing circular—The old order still—Ermatin-
ger's letters—McDougall's resolutions—Cartier and McDougall as delegates—
Company accepts the terms.

As is well known to those who have followed the history of the Hudson's
Bay Company, while the possession of Rupert's Land was secured by
charter, the territory outside Rupert's Land was secured to the
Company by licence. This licence ended every twenty-one years. The
licence in force at the time of the troubles which have been described
was to terminate in 1859. Accordingly, three or four years before this
date, as their Athabasca, New Caledonia, and British Columbia
possessions had become of great value to them, the Company with due
foresight approached the British Government with a request for the
renewal of their tenure. Men of understanding on both sides of the
Atlantic saw the possible danger of a refusal to their request, on
account of the popular ferment which had taken place both in Red River
and British Columbia. Others thought the time had come for ending the
power of the Company.

Sir Henry Labouchero, Secretary of State for the Colonies, entered
into correspondence with Sir Edmund Head, Governor-General of
Canada, on the subject. Anxious about the state of things in every part
of the Empire as the Colonial Office always is, the turbulence and
defiance of law in Red River settlement called for special attention.
Accordingly the Governor-General was informed that it was the
intention of the Home Government to have, not only the question of the
licence discussed, but also the "general position and prospects" of the

Company considered, by a Committee of the House of Commons. The Canadian Government was therefore cordially invited to have its views, as well as those of the Canadian community, represented before the Committee.

This invitation was the thing for which Canada had been waiting. A despatch was sent by the Canadian Government, in less than seven weeks from the time when the invitation left Downing Street, accepting the proposal of the Mother Country. The Canadian Ministry was pleased that British-American affairs were receiving such prominent notice in England. It suggested the importance of determining the limits of Canada on the side towards Rupert's Land, and went on to state that the general opinion strongly held in the New World was "that the western boundary of Canada extends to the Pacific Ocean." Reference is made to the danger of complications arising with the United States, and the statement advanced that the "question of the jurisdiction and title claimed by the Hudson's Bay Company is to Canada of paramount importance."

In 1857 Chief Justice Draper crossed to Great Britain as Canadian representative, with a very wide commission to advance Canadian interests. He was called before the Committee appointed by the House of Commons, and answered nearly two hundred questions relating to Canada and to the Hudson's Bay Company interests in Rupert's Land and beyond. The capable and active-minded Chief Justice kept before the Committee these points:—

(1) What he conceived to be the true western boundary of Canada, and in so doing gave his opinion, based on the Quebec Act of 1774, that Canada should be allowed to extend to the Rocky Mountains and should have the privilege of exploring and building roads in that region.

(2) The earnest desire of the Canadian people that Rupert's Land and the Indian territories should be maintained as British territory.

(3) That Canada should be allowed to extend her settlements into these territories.

Chief Justice Draper argued his case with great clearness and cogency, and made an excellent impression upon the Committee.

The matter of the Company's hold on Vancouver Island seems to have been settled without any great difficulty. Mr. Richard Blanshard, the former Governor, who received so cool a reception in Vancouver Island, gave a plain and unvarnished tale. The Company had evidently made up its mind to surrender all its claims to Vancouver Island. And the island, as we have seen, became independent.

Canada entered with great spirit into the case presented before the Committee. The question of the licence was quite overshadowed by the wider discussion covering the validity of the Hudson's Bay Company charter, the original boundary line of the province of Canada, and the manner in which the Company had carried out its responsibilities. An industrious minister of the Canadian Government, Hon. Joseph Cauchon, with true Gallic fire and a French Canadian spirit, prepared a memorandum of a most elaborate kind on the Hudson's Bay Company's claim and status. In this, Mr. Cauchon goes back to the earliest times, shows the limits of occupation by the French explorers, follows down the line of connection established by the North-West traders, deals with the troubles of Lord Selkirk, and concludes that the Red River and the Saskatchewan are not within the limits of the Company's charter. This vigorous writer then deals with the Treaty of Paris, the Quebec Act, and the discoveries of Canadian subjects as giving Canada a jurisdiction even to the Rocky Mountains.

As might have been expected, the Committee of 1857 became a famous one. The whole economy of the Company was discussed. The ground gone over by Isbister and others during the preceding decade supplied the members with material, and the proceedings of the Committee became notable for their interest. The Committee held eighteen meetings, examined twenty-nine witnesses, and thoroughly sifted the evidence.

The *personnel* of the Committee was brilliant. The Secretary of State was Chairman. Mr. Roebuck and Mr. Gladstone represented the inquiring and aggressive element. Lord Stanley and Lord John Russell added their experience, Edward Ellice—"the Old Bear"—watched the case for the Company, and Mr. Lowe and Sir John Pakington took a lively interest in the proceedings and often interposed. Altogether the Committee was constituted for active service, and every nook and cranny of Rupert's Land and the adjoining territories was thoroughly investigated.

Among the witnesses was the distinguished Governor Simpson. He was at his best. Mr. Roebuck and he had many a skirmish, and although Sir George was often driven into a corner, yet with surprising agility he recovered himself. Old explorers such as John Ross, Dr. Rae, Col. Lefroy, Sir John Richardson, Col. Crofton, Bishop Anderson, Col. Caldwell, and Dr. King, gave information as to having visited Rupert's Land at different periods. Their evidence was fair, with, as could be expected in most cases, a "good word" for the Company. Rev. Mr. Corbett gave testimony against the Company, Governor Blanshard in the same strain, A. K. Isbister, considerably moderated in his opposition, gave evidence as a native who had travelled in the country, while John McLoughlin, a rash and heady agitator, told of the excitement in Red River settlement. Edward Ellice became a witness as well as a member of the Committee, and with adroitness covered the retreat of any of his witnesses when necessity arose.

From time to time, from February to the end of July, the Committee met, and gathered a vast amount of evidence, making four hundred pages of printed matter. It is a thesaurus of Hudson's Bay Company material. It revealed not only the localities of this unknown land to England and the world, but made everyone familiar with the secret methods, devices, and working of the fur trade over a space of well-nigh half a continent. The Committee decided to recommend to Parliament that it is "important to meet the just and reasonable wishes of Canada to assume such territory as may be useful for settlement; that the districts of the Red River and the Saskatchewan seem the most available; and that for the order and good government of the country," arrangements should be made for their cession to Canada. It was also agreed that those regions where settlement is impossible be left to the exclusive control of the Hudson's Bay Company for the fur trade. The Committee not only recommended that Vancouver Island should be made independent, but that the territory of the mainland in British Columbia should be united with it.

Four years after the sitting of this Committee, which gave such anxiety to the Hudson's Bay Company, Sir George Simpson, after a very short illness, passed away, having served as Governor for forty years. In an earlier chapter his place and influence have been estimated and his merits and defects shown.

Sir George, in his high office as Governor of Rupert's Land, was succeeded by A. J. Dallas, a Scottish merchant, who had been in business in China, had retired, and afterwards acted as Chief Factor of the Hudson's Bay Company at Fort Victoria, in Vancouver Island, and had then married the daughter of Governor James Douglas. Dallas had shown great nerve and judgment in British Columbia, in a serious brush with the United States authorities in 1859. Three years after this event he was called to succeed the great Governor of Rupert's Land. On his appointment to this high position, he took up his residence at Fort Garry, and had, in conjunction with the local Governor, William McTavish, to face the rising tide of dissatisfaction which showed itself in the Corbett and Stewart rescues. Writers of the period state that Dallas lacked the dignity and tact of old Sir George. In his letters, however, Governor Dallas shows that he thoroughly appreciated the serious state of matters. He says: "I have had great difficulty in persuading the magistrates to continue to act. Mr. William McTavish, Governor of Assiniboia, has resigned his post." Governor Dallas says he "finds himself with all the responsibility and semblance of authority over a vast territory, but unsupported, if not ignored, by the Crown." He states that people do not object to the *personnel* of the Hudson's Bay Company government, but to the "system of government." He fears the formation of a provisional government, and a movement for annexation to the United States, which had been threatened. He is of opinion that the "territorial right should revert to the Crown." These are strong, honest words for an official of the Company whose rule had prevailed for some two centuries.

And now Governor Dallas appears co-operating in an ingenious and adroit financial scheme with Mr. E. W. Watkin, a member of the British House of Commons, by which the Hudson's Bay Company property changed hands. Edward Watkin was a financial agent, who had much to do with the Grand Trunk Railway of Canada, and had an intimate knowledge of Canadian affairs. He had succeeded in interesting the Colonial Secretary of State, the Duke of Newcastle, in a railway, road, and telegraphic scheme for connecting the British possessions in North America.

Difficulties having arisen in inducing staid old Governor Berens, the London head of the Company, to accept modern ideas, a plan was broached of buying out the whole Hudson's Bay Company possessions and rights. Difficulty after difficulty was met and surmounted, and though many a time the scheme seemed hopeless, yet in the end it succeeded, though not without much friction and heart-burning. Watkin describes graphically the first interview between throe members of the Hudson's Bay Company, Berens, Eden Colville, and Lyall, of the first part, and Glynn, Newmarch, himself, and three other capitalists of the second part. The meeting took place in the Hudson's Bay Company House, Fenchurch Street, February 1st, 1862. "The room was the 'Court' room, dark and dirty, faded green cloth, old chairs almost black, and a fine picture of Prince Rupert. Governor Berens, an old man and obstinate, was somewhat insulting in his manner. We took it patiently." It was a day of fate for the old Company.

Many interviews afterwards took place between Watkin and the accountant and solicitors of the Company. The Company would hear of no dealings, except on the basis of a cash payment. The men of capital accordingly succeeded in interesting the "International Financial

Association," a new corporation looking for some great scheme to lay before the public.

At length the whole shares, property, and rights of the Hudson's Bay Company were taken over, the final arrange-ments being made by Mr. Richard Potter on June 1st, 1863. Thus the Company begun in so small a way by Prince Rupert and his associates nearly two centuries before, sold out, and the purchase money of one and a half millions of pounds was paid over the counter to the old Company by the new Association.

A new company was now to be organized whose stock would be open for purchase, and the International Association would, on such organization being formed, hand over the Company's assets to the new stockholders. In a short time the Company was reconstituted, Sir Edmund Head being the new Governor, with, as prominent members of the Board of Directors, Richard Potter, Eden Colville, E. B. Watkin, and an American fur trader of experience, Sir Curtis Lampson.

Secretly as the negotiations for the formation of a new company had been conducted, the news of the affair reached Canada and Rupert's Land, and led to anxious inquiries being made and to a memorial from the Company's officers being presented to the Board of Directors asking for information. So thoroughly secret had the interviews between the London parties been carried on that the officials of the London office know nothing of them, and stated in their reply to the memorialists that the rumours were incorrect. In July, when the transfer had been consummated and the news of it appeared in the public press, it created surprise and indignation among the chief factors and chief traders, who, under the deed poll or Company arrangement which had been adopted in 1821, though somewhat modified thirteen years later, had been regarded as having certain partnership rights in the Company.

Mr. Edward Watkin informs us, in his interesting "Reminiscences," that he had intended that the "wintering partners," as the officers in Rupert's Land were called, should have been individually communicated with, but that on account of his hasty departure to Canada the matter had been overlooked. It certainly was irritating to the officers of the fur trade to learn for the first time from the public press of an arrangement being perfected involving their whole private Watkin expresses his great apprehension lest the news in a distorted form should reach the distant regions of the fur country, where the Company had one hundred and forty-four posts, covering the continent from Labrador to Sitka, Vancouver Island and San Francisco. He feared also that there would be a new company formed to occupy the ground with the old.

On reaching Canada, Mr. Watkin was agreeably surprised at the arrival of Governor Dallas from Red River in Montreal. After consultation it was decided on that the Governor should send a conciliatory circular to the commissioned officers of the Company, explaining the objects of the new Company, and stating that all the interests of the wintering partners would be conserved. It is evident that the attitude of the officers had alarmed even such stout-hearted men as Watkin and Dallas. There lies before the writer also a personal letter, dated London, July 23rd, 1863, signed by Edmund Head, Governor, to a chief trader of the Company, stating that it was the intention of the Committee "to carry on the fur trade as it has been hitherto carried on, under the provisions of the deed poll." None of the collateral objects of the Company "should interfere with the fur trade." He begs the officers to "have with him free and unreserved communication through the usual channel." Evidently the echo of the angry voices in Athabasca had been heard in London.

The old deed poll, which they had intended to suspend, as shown by Watkin, was thus preserved. This document secured them as follows: According to both deed polls of 1821 and 1834, forty per cent. of the net profits of the trade, divided into eighty-five shares of equal amount, were distributed annually among the wintering partners of the Company. A chief trader received an eighty-fifth share of the profits, and a chief factor two eighty-fifth shares. Both had certain rights after retiring.

The proposed abolition of these terms of the deed poll and the substitution therefor of certain salaries with the avowed purpose of reducing the expenses, of course meant loss to every wintering partner. The interests thus involved justified the most strenuous opposition on the part of the partners, and, unless the proposal were modified, would almost certainly have led to a disruption of the Company.

In harmony with Governor Head's circular letter no action in the direction contemplated was taken until 1871, when, on the receipt of the three hundred thousand pounds voted by Canada to the Company, the sum of one hundred and seven thousand and fifty-five pounds was applied to buying out the vested rights of the wintering partners, and the agitation was quieted.

The effect of the arrangement made for the payment of officers of the Company since 1871, as compared with their previous remuneration, has been a subject of discussion.

There lies before the writer an elaborate calculation by an old Hudson's Bay Company officer to the effect that under the old deed poll a chief factor would receive two eighty-fifth shares, his total average being seven hundred and twenty pounds per annum; and under the new (taking the average of twenty-five years) two and one half-hundredths shares, amounting to five hundred and thirty-two pounds annually, or a loss nearly of one hundred and eighty-eight pounds; similarly that a chief trader would receive three hundred and nineteen pounds, as against three hundred and sixty formerly, or a loss per annum of forty-one pounds.

Besides this, the number of higher commissioned officers was reduced when the old deed poll was cancelled, so that the stockholders received the advantage from there being fewer officials, also the chances of promotion to higher offices were diminished.

During the progress of these internal dissensions of the Hudson's Bay Company public opinion had been gradually maturing in Canada in favour of acquiring at least a portion of Rupert's Land. At the time of the Special Committee of 1857, it will be remembered the Hind-

Gladman expedition had gone to spy out the land. A company, called the North-West Transportation Company, was about the same time organized in Toronto to carry goods and open communication from Fort William by way of the old fur traders' route to Fort Garry.

The merits and demerits of the north-western prairies were discussed in the public press of Canada. Edward Ermatinger, whose name has been already mentioned, was a steady supporter of the claim of the Hudson's Bay Company in a series of well-written letters in the *Hamilton Spectator*, a journal of Upper Canada. Taking the usual line of argument followed by the Company, he showed the small value of the country, its inhospitable climate, its inaccessibility, and magnified the legal claim of the Hudson's Bay Company against the Canadian contention. It is amusing to read in after years, when his opinion of Sir George Simpson was changed, his declaration of regret at having been led to so strenuously present his views in the Spectator.

Ten years had passed after the setting of the great Committee of 1857, and nothing practical as to the transfer of the country to Canada had been accomplished. The confederation movement had now widened the horizon of Canadian public men. In the very year of the confederation of the Canadian provinces (1867), Hon. William McDougall, who had been a persistent advocate of the Canadian claim to the North-West, moved in the Dominion Parliament a series of resolutions, which were carried. These resolutions showed the advantage, both to Canada and the Empire, of the Dominion being extended to the Pacific Ocean; that settlement, commerce, and development of the resources of the country are dependent on a stable Government being established; that the welfare of the Red River settlers would be enhanced by this means; that provision was contained in the British North-American Act for the admission of Rupert's Land and the North-West territory to the Dominion; that this wide country should be united to Canada; that in case of union the legal rights of any corporation, as the Hudson's Bay Company, association, or individual should be respected; that this should be settled judicially or by agreement; that the Indian title should be legally extinguished; and that an address be made to Her Majesty to this effect. The resolutions were carried by a large majority of the House. This was a bold and well-conceived step, and the era of discussion and hesitancy seemed to have passed away in favour of a policy of action.

The Hudson's Bay Company, however, insisted on an understanding being come to as to terms before giving consent to the proposed action, and a despatch to the Dominion Government from Her Majesty's Government called attention to this fact. As soon as convenient, a delegation, consisting of Hon, George E. Cartier and Hon. William McDougall, proceeded to England to negotiate with the Company as to terms. The path of the delegates on reaching England proved a thorny one. The attitude of the Imperial Government was plainly in favour of recognizing some legal value in the chartered rights of the Company, a thing denied by some, specially Mr. McDougall. No progress was being made. At this juncture D'Israeli's Government was defeated, and a delay resulted in waiting for a new Government. Earl Granville was the new Secretary of State for the Colonies. While negotiations were going on, the Hudson's Bay Company sent in to the Secretary of State a rather hot complaint that Canadian surveyors and road builders had entered upon their territory to the west of the Lake of the Woods. This was quite true, but the action had been taken by the Canadian Government under the impression that all parties would willingly agree to it. Not being at this juncture able to settle anything, the commissioners returned to Canada.

The Imperial Government was, however, in earnest in the matter, and pressed the Hudson's Bay Company to consent to reasonable terms, the more that the government by the Company in Red River was not satisfactory—an indisputable fact. At length the Company felt bound to accept the proposed terms. The main provisions of bargain were that the Company should surrender all rights in Rupert's Land; that Canada pay the Company the sum of three hundred thousand pounds; that the Company be allowed certain blocks of land around their posts; that they be given one-twentieth of the arable land of the country; and that the Company should be allowed every privilege in carrying on trade as a regular trading company. Thus was the concession of generous Charles the Second surrendered after two centuries of honourable occupation.

CHAPTER XLV.

Transfer Act passed—A moribund government—The Canadian surveying party—Causes of the rebellion—Turbulent Metis—American interference—Disloyal ecclesiastics—Governor McDougall—Riel and his rebel band—A blameworthy Governor—The "blawsted fence"—Seizure of Fort Garry—Kiel's ambitions—Loyal rising—Three wise men from the East—*The New Nation*—A winter meeting—Bill of Rights—Canadian shot—The Wolseley expedition—Three renegades slink away—The end of Company rule—The new Province of Manitoba.

THE old Company had agreed to the bargain, and the Imperial Act was passed authorizing the transfer of the vast territory east of the Rocky Mountains to Canada. Canada, with the strengthening national spirit rising from the young confederation, with pleasure saw the Dominion Government place in the estimates the three hundred thousand pounds for the payment of the Hudson's Bay Company, and an Act was passed by the Dominion Parliament providing for a government of the northwest territories, which would secure the administration of justice, and the peace, order, and good government of Her Majesty's subjects and others. It was enacted, however, that all laws of the territory at the time of the passing of the Act should remain in force until amended or repealed, and all officers except the chief to continue in office until others were appointed.

And now began the most miserable and disreputable exhibition of decrepitude, imbecility, jesuitry, foreign interference, blundering, and rash patriotism ever witnessed in the fur traders' country. This was known as the Red River rebellion. The writer arrived in Fort Garry the year following this wretched affair, made the acquaintance of many of the actors in the rebellion, and heard their stories. The real, deep significance of this rebellion has never been fully made known. Whether the writer will succeed in telling the whole tale remains to be seen.

The Hudson's Bay Company officials at Red River were still the government. This fact must be distinctly borne in mind. It has been stated, however, that this government had become hopelessly weak and inefficient. Governor Dallas, in the words quoted, admitted this and lamented over it. Were there any doubt in regard to this statement, it was shown by the utter defiance of the law in the breaking of jail in the three cases of Corbett, Stewart, and Dr. Schultz. No government could retain respect when the solemn behests of its courts were laughed at and despised. This is the real reason lying at the root of the apathy of the English-speaking people of the Red River in dealing with the rebellion. They were not cowards; they sprang from ancestors who had fought Britain's battles; they were intelligent and moral; they loved their homes and were prepared to defend them; but they had no guarantee of leadership; they had no assurance that their efforts would be given even the colour of legality; the broken-down jail outside Fort Garry, its uprooted stockades and helpless old jailor, were the symbol of governmental decrepitude and were the sport of any determined law-breaker.

It has been the habit of their opponents to refer to the annoyance of the Hudson's Bay Company Committee in London with Canada for in 1869 sending surveyors to examine the country before the transfer was made. Reference has also been made to the dissatisfaction of the local officers at the action taken by the Company in dealing with the deed poll in 1863; some have said that the Hudson's Bay Company officials at Fort Garry did not admire the Canadian leaders as they saw them; and others have maintained that these officers cared nothing for the country, provided they received large enough dividends as wintering partners.

Now, there may be something in these contentions, but they do not touch the core of the matter. The Hudson's Bay Company, both in London and Fort Garry, wore thoroughly loyal to British institutions; the officers were educated, responsible, and high-minded men; they had acted up to their light in a thoroughly honourable manner, and no mere prejudice, or fancied grievance, or personal dislike would have made them untrue to their trusts. But the government had become decrepit; vacillation and uncertainty characterized every act; had the people been behind them, had they not felt that the people distrusted them, they would have taken action, as it was their duty to do.

The chronic condition of helplessness and governmental decay was emphasized and increased by a sad circumstance. Governor William McTavish, an honourable and well-meaning man, was sick. In the midst of the troubles of 1863 he would willingly have resigned, as Governor Dallas assures us; now he was physically incapable of the energy and decision requisite under the circumstances. Moreover, as we shall see, there was a most insidious and dangerous influence dogging his every step. His subordinates would not act without him, he could not act without them, and thus an absolute deadlock . ensued. Moreover, the Council of Assiniboia, an appointed body, had felt itself for years out of touch with the sentiment of the colony, and its efforts at legislation resulted in no improvement of the condition of things. Woe to a country ruled by an oligarchy, however well-meaning or reputable such a body may be!

Turn now from this picture of pitiful weakness to the unaccountable and culpable blundering of the Canadian Government. Cartier and McDougall found out in England that sending in a party of surveyors before the country was transferred was offensive to the Hudson's Bay Company. More offensive still was the method of conducting the expedition. It was a mark of sublime stupidity to profess, as the Canadian Government did, to look upon the money spent on this survey as a benevolent device for relieving the people suffering from the grasshopper visitation. The genius who originated the plan of combining charity with gain should have been canonized. Moreover, the plan of contractor Snow of paying poor wages, delaying payment, and giving harsh treatment to such a people as the half-breeds are known to be was most ill advised. The evidently selfish and grasping spirit shown in this expedition sent to survey and build the Dawson Road, yet turning aside to claim unoccupied lands, to sow the seeds of doubt and suspicion in the minds of a people hitherto secluded from the world, was most unpatriotic and dangerous. It cannot be denied, in addition, that while many of the small band of Canadians were reputable and hard-working men, the course of a few prominent leaders, who had made an illegitimate use of the Nor'-Wester newspaper, had tended to keep the community in a state of alienation and turmoil.

What, then, were the conditions? A helpless, moribund government, without decision, without actual authority on the one hand, and on the other an irritating, selfish, and aggressive expedition, taking possession of the land before it was transferred to Canada, and assuming the air of conquerors.

Look now at the combustible elements awaiting this combination. The French half-breeds, descendants of the turbulent Bois Brûlés of Lord Selkirk's times; the old men, companions of Sayer and the elder Riel, who defied the authority of the court, and left it shouting, "Vive la liberté!" now irritated by the Dawson Road being built in the way just described; the road running through the seigniory given by Lord Selkirk to the Roman Catholic bishop, the road in rear of their largest settlements, and passing through another French settlement at Pointe des Chenes! Further, the lands adjacent to these settlements, and naturally connected with them, being seized by the intruders! Furthermore, the natives, antagonized by the action of certain Canadians who had for years maintained the country in a state of turmoil! Were there not all the elements of an explosion of a serious and dangerous kind?

Two other most important forces in this complicated state of things cannot be left out. The first of these is a matter which requires careful statement, but yet it is a most potential factor in the rebellion. This is the attitude of certain persons in the United States. For twenty years and more the trade of the Red River settlement had been largely carried on by way of St. Paul, in the State of Minnestota. The Hudson Bay route and York boat brigade were unable to compote with the facilities offered by the approach of the railway to the Mississippi River. Accordingly long lines of Red River carts took loads of furs to St. Paul and brought back freight for the Company. The Red River trade was a recognized source of profit in St. Paul. Familiarity in trade led to an interest on the part of the Americans in the public affairs of Red River. Hot-headed and sordid people in Red River settlement had actually spoken of the settlement being connected with the United States.

Now that irritation was manifested at Red River, steps were taken by private parties from the United States to fan the flame. At Pembina, on the border between Rupert's Land and the United States, lived a nest of desperadoes willing to take any steps to accomplish their purposes. They had access to all the mails which came from England to Canada marked "Viâ Pembina." Pembina was an outpost refuge for lawbreakers and outcasts from the United States. Its people used all their power to disturb the peace of Red River settlement. In addition, a considerable number of Americans had come to the little village of Winnipeg, now being begun near the walls of Fort Garry. These men held their private meetings, all looking to the creation of trouble and the provocation of feeling that might lead to change of allegiance. Furthermore, the writer is able to state, on the information of a man high in the service of Canada, and a man not unknown in Manitoba, that there was a large sum of money, of which an amount was named as high as one million dollars, which was available in St. Paul for the purpose of securing a hold by the Americans on the fertile plains of Rupert's Land.

Here, then, was an agency of most dangerous proportions, an element in the village of Winnipeg able to control the election of the first delegate to the convention, a desperate body of men on the border, who with Machiavelian persistence fanned the flame of discontent, and a reserve of power in St. Paul ready to take advantage of any emergency.

A still more insidious and threatening influence was at work. Here again the writer is aware of the gravity of the statement he is making, but he has evidence of the clearest kind for his position. A dangerous religious element in the country—ecclesiastics from old France—who had no love for Britain, no love for Canada, no love for any country, no love for society, no love for peace! These plotters were in close association with the half-breeds, dictated their policy, and freely mingled with the rebels- One of them was an intimate friend of the loader of the rebellion, consulted with him in his plans, and exercised a marked influence on his movements. This same foreign priest, with Jesuitical cunning, gave close attendance on the sick Governor, and through his family exercised a constant and detrimental power upon the only source of authority then in the land. Furthermore, an Irish student and teacher, with a Fenian hatred of all things British, was a "familiar" of the leader of the rebellion, and with true Milesian zeal advanced the cause of the revolt.

Can a more terrible combination be imagined than this? A decrepit government with the executive officer sick; a rebellious and chronically dissatisfied Metis element; a government at Ottawa far removed by distance, committing with unvarying regularity blunder after blunder; a greedy and foreign cabal planning to seize the country, and a secret Jesuitical plot to keep the Governor from action and to incite the fiery Metis to revolt!

The drama opens with the appointment, in September, 1869, by the Dominion Government, of the Hon. William McDougall as Lieutenant-Governor of the north-west territories, his departure from Toronto, and his arrival at Pembina, in the Dakota territory, in the end of October. He was accompanied by his family, a small staff, and three hundred stand of arms with ammunition. He had been preceded by the Hon. Joseph Howe, of the Dominion Government, who visited the Red River settlement ostensibly to feel the pulse of public opinion, but as Commissioner gaining little information. Mr. McDougall's commission as Governor was to take effect after the formal transfer of the territory. He reached Pembina, where he was served with a notice not to enter the territory, yet he crossed the boundary line at Pembina, and took possession of the Hudson's Bay Fort of West Lynn, two miles north of the boundary.

Meanwhile a storm was brewing along Red River. A young French half-breed, Louis Riel, son of the excitable miller of the Seine of whom mention was made—a young man, educated by the Roman Catholic Bishop Taché, of St. Boniface, for a time, and afterwards in Montreal, was regarded as the hope of the Metis. He was a young man of fair ability, but proud, vain, and assertive, and had the ambition to be a Caesar or Napoleon. He with his followers had stopped the surveyors in their work, and threatened to throw off the approaching tyranny. Professing to be loyal to Britain but hostile to Canada, he succeeded, in October, in getting a small body of French half-breeds to seize the main highway at St. Norbert, some nine miles south of Fort Garry.

The message to Mr. McDougall not to enter the territory was forwarded by this body, that already considered itself the *de facto* government. A Canadian settler at once swore an affidavit before the officer in charge of Fort Garry that an armed party of French half-breeds had assembled to oppose the entrance of the Governor.

Here, then, was the hour of destiny. An outbreak had taken place, it was illegal to oppose any man entering the country, not to say a Governor, the fact of revolt was immediately brought to Fort Garry, and no amount of casuistry or apology can ever justify Governor McTavish, sick though he was, from immediately not taking action, and compelling his council to take action by summoning the law-abiding people to surround him and repress the revolt. But the government that would allow the defiance of the law by permitting men to live at liberty who had broken jail could not be expected to take action. To have done so would have been to work a miracle.

The rebellion went on apace; two of the so-called Governor's staff pushed on to the barricade erected at St. Norbert. Captain Cameron, one of them, with eyeglass in poise, and with affected authority, gave command, "Remove that blawsted fence," but the half-breeds were unyielding. The two messengers returned to Pembina, where they found Mr. McDougall likewise driven back and across the boundary. Did ever British prestige suffer a more humiliating blow?

The act of rebellion, usually dangerous, proved in this case a trivial one, and Kiel's little band of forty or fifty badly-armed Metis began to grow. The mails were seized, freight coming into the country became booty, and the experiment of a rising was successful. In the meantime the authorities of Fort Garry were inactive. The rumour came that Riel thought of seizing the fort. An affidavit of the chief of police under the Government shows that he urged the master of Fort Garry to meet the danger, and asked authority to call upon a portion of the special police force sworn in, shortly before, to preserve the peace. No Governor spoke; no one even closed the fort as a precaution; its gates stood wide open to friend or foe.

This exhibition of helplessness encouraged the conspirators, and Riel and one hundred of his followers (November 2nd) unopposed took possession of the fort and quartered themselves upon the Company. In the front part of the fort lived the Governor; he was now flanked by a bodyguard of rebels; the master of the fort, a burly son of Britain, though very gruff and out of sorts, could do nothing, and the young Napoleon of the Metis fattened on the best of the land.

Riel now issued a proclamation, calling on the English-speaking parishes of the settlement to elect twelve representatives to meet the President and representatives of the French-speaking population, appointing a meeting for twelve days afterwards.

Mr. McDougall, on hearing of the seizure of the fort, wrote to Governor McTavish stating that as the Hudson Bay Company was still the government, action should be taken to disperse the rebels. A number of loyal inhabitants also petitioned Governor McTavish to issue his proclamation calling on the rebels to disperse. The sick and helpless Governor, fourteen days after the seizure of the fort and twenty-three days after the affidavit of the rising, issued a tardy proclamation condemning the rebels and calling upon them to disperse. The Convention met November 16th, the English parishes having been cajoled into electing delegates, thinking thus to soothe the troubled land. After meeting and discussing in hot and useless words the state of affairs, the Convention adjourned till December 1st, it being evident, however, that Riel desired to form a provisional government of which he should be the joy and pride.

The day for the reassembling of the Convention arrived. Riel and his party insisted on ruling the meeting, and passed a "Bill of Rights" consisting of fifteen provisions. The English people refused to accept these propositions, and, after vainly endeavouring to take steps to meet Mr. McDougall, withdrew to their homes, ashamed and confounded.

Meanwhile Mr. McDougall was chafing at the strange and humiliating situation in which he found himself. With his family and staff poorly housed at Pembina and the severe winter coming on, he could scarcely be blamed for irritation and discontent. December 1st was the day on which he expected his commission as Governor to come into effect, and wonder of wonders, he, a lawyer, a privy councillor, and an experienced statesman, went so far on this mere supposition as to issue a proclamation announcing his appointment as Governor. As a matter of fact, far away from communication with Ottawa, he was mistaken as to the transfer. On account of the rise of the rebellion this had not been made, and Mr. McDougall, in issuing a spurious proclamation, became a thing of contempt to the insurgents, an object of pity to the loyalists, and the laughing-stock of the whole world. His proclamation at the same time authorizing Colonel Dennis, the Canadian surveyor in Red River settlement, to raise a force to put down the rebellion, was simply a *brutum fulmen*, and was the cause to innocent, well-meaning men of trouble and loss. Colonel Dennis succeeded in raising a force of some four hundred men, and would not probably have failed had it not transpired that the two proclamations were illegal and that the levies were consequently unauthorized. Such a thing to be carried out by William McDougall and Colonel Dennis, men of experience and ability! Surely there could be no greater fiasco!

The Canadian people were now in a state of the greatest excitement, and the Canadian Government, aware of its blundering and stupidity, hastened to rectify its mistakes. Commissioners were sent to negotiate with the various parties in Red River settlement. These were Vicar-General Thibault, who had spent long years in the Roman Catholic Missions of the North-West, Colonel de Salaberry, a French Canadian, and Mr. Donald A. Smith, the chief officer of the Hudson's Bay Company, then at Montreal. On the last of these Commissioners, who had been clothed with very wide powers, lay the chief responsibility, as will be readily seen.

A number of Canadians—nearly fifty—had been assembled in the store of Dr. Schultz, at the village of Winnipeg, and, on the failure of Mr. McDougall's proclamation, were left in a very awkward condition. With arms in their hands, they were looked upon by Riel as dangerous, and with promises of freedom and of the intention of Riel to meet McDougall and settle the whole matter, they (December 7th) surrendered. Safely in the fort and in the prison outside the wall, the prisoners were kept by the truce-breaker, and the Metis contingent celebrated the victory by numerous potations of rum taken from the Hudson's Bay Company stores.

Riel now took a step forward in issuing a proclamation, which has generally been attributed to the crippled postmaster at Pembina, one of the dangerous foreign clique longing to seize the settlement. He also hoisted a new flag, with the fleur-de-lis worked upon it, thus giving evidence of his disloyalty and impudence. Other acts of injustice, such as seizing Company funds and interfering with personal liberty, were committed by him.

On December 27th—a memorable day—Mr. Donald A. Smith arrived. His commission and papers were left at Pembina, and he went directly to Fort Garry, where Riel received him. The interview, given in Mr. Smith's own words, was a remarkable one. Riel vainly sought to induce the Commissioner to recognize his government, and yet was afraid to show disrespect to so high and honoured an officer. For about two months Commissioner Smith lived at Fort Garry, in a part of the same building as Governor McTavish.

Mr. Smith says of this period, "The state of matters at this time was most unsatisfactory and truly humiliating. Upwards of fifty British subjects were held in close confinement as political prisoners; security for persons or property there was none. . . . The leaders of the French half-breeds had declared their determination to use every effort for the purpose of annexing the territory to the United States."

Mr. Smith acted with great wisdom and decision. His plan evidently was to have no formal breach with Riel but gradually to undermine him, and secure a combination by which he could be overthrown. Many of the influential men of the settlement called upon Mr, Smith, and the affairs of the country were discussed. Riel was restless and at times impertinent, but the Commissioner exercised his Scottish caution, and bided his time.

At this time a newspaper, called The New Nation, appeared as the organ of the provisional government. This paper openly advocated annexation to the United States, thus show the really dangerous nature of the movement embodied in the rebellion.

During all these months of the rebellion, Bishop Taché, the influential head of the Roman Catholic Church, had been absent in Rome at the great Council of that year. One of his most active priests left behind was Father Lestanc, the prince of plotters, who has generally been credited with belonging to the Jesuit Order. Lestanc had sedulously haunted the presence of the Governor; he was a daring and extreme man, and to him and his fellow-Frenchman, the cure of St. Norbert, much of Kiel's obstinacy has been attributed. Commissioner Smith now used his opportunity to weaken Riel. He offered to send for his commission to Pembina, if he were allowed to meet the people. Riel consented to this. The commission was sent for, and Riel tried to intercept the messenger, but failed to do so. The meeting took place on January 19th. It was a date of note for Red River settlement. One thousand people assembled, and as there was no building capable of holding the people, the meeting took place in the open air, the temperature being twenty below zero.

The outcome of this meeting was the election and subsequent assembling of forty representatives—one half French, the other half English—to consider the matter of Commissioner Smith's message. Six days after the open-air meeting the Convention met. A second "Bill of Rights" was adopted, and it was agreed to send delegates to Ottawa to meet the Dominion Government. A provisional government was formed, at the request, it is said, of Governor McTavish, and Riel gained the height of his ambition in being made President, while the fledgling Fenian priest, O'Donoghue, became "Secretary of the Treasury."

The retention of the prisoners in captivity aroused a deep feeling in the country, and a movement originated in Portage La Prairie to rescue the unfortunates. This force was joined by recruits at Kildonan, making up six hundred in all. Awed by this gathering, Riel released the prisoners, though he was guilty of an act of deepest treachery in arresting nearly fifty of the Assiniboine levy as they were returning to their homes. Among them was Major Boulton, who afterwards narrowly escaped execution, and who has written an interesting account of the rebellion.

The failure of the two parties of loyalists, and their easy capture by Riel, raises the question of the wisdom of these efforts. No doubt the inspiring motive of these levies was in many cases true patriotism, and it reflects credit on them as men of British blood and British pluck, but the management of both was so unfortunate and so lacking in skill, that one is disposed, though lamenting their failures, to put these expeditions down as dictated by the greatest rashness.

The elevation of Riel served to awaken high ambitions. The late Archbishop Taché, in a later rebellion, characterized Riel as a remarkable example of inflated ambition, and called his state of mind that of "megalomania." Riel now became more irritable and domineering. He seemed also bitter against the English for the signs of insubordination appearing in all the parishes. The influence of the violent and dastardly Lestanc was strong upon him. The anxious President now determined to awe the English, and condemned for execution a young Irish Canadian prisoner named Thomas Scott. Commissioner Smith and a number of influential inhabitants did everything possible to dissuade Riel, but he persisted, and Scott was publicly executed near Fort Garry on March 4th, 1870.

"Whom the gods destroy, they first make mod." The execution of Scott was the death-knell of Riel's hopes. Canada was roused to its centre. Determined to have no further communication with Riel, Commissioner Smith as soon as possible left Fort Garry and returned to Canada.

The arrival of Bishop Taché, who had returned at the request of the Canadian Government, took place in due time. Probably the real attitude of Bishop Taché will never be known, though, his strong French Canadian associations and love of British connection make it seem hardly possible that he could have been implicated in the rebellion. Bishop Tache endeavoured to overcome the terrible mistake of Riel. Commissioners were despatched to Ottawa, the most important of them Father Ritchot, of St. Norbert, whose hand had been in the plot from the beginning. Carrying down a "Bill of Rights" from the provisional government, which, however, there is clear evidence Ritchot and others took the liberty of altering, they were instrumental in having a bill passed through the Dominion Parliament, establishing Manitoba as a province.

For the establishment of peace, an expedition was organized by Canada, consisting of British regulars and Canadian volunteers, under Colonel Wolseley. Coming from Canada up the fur-traders' route, through Lake of the Woods, down Winnipeg River, across Lake Winnipeg, and up the Red River, the expedition arrived, to the great joy of the suffering people of the settlement, on August 24th, 1870. After eleven months of the most torturing anxiety had been endured, the sight of the rescuing soldiery sent the blood pulsing again through their veins. As the troops approached Fort Garry, three slinking figures were seen to leave the fort and escape across the Assiniboine. These were the "President Riel," "Adjutant-General" Lepine, and the scoundrel

O'Donoghue. "They folded their tents like the Arabs, and as silently stole away." Colonel Wolseley says, "The troops then formed line outside the fort, the Union Jack was hoisted, a royal salute fired, and three cheers were given for the Queen, which were caught up and heartily re-echoed by many of the civilians and settlers who had followed the troops from the village."

The transfer of Rupert's Land had been completed, and the governing power of the famous old Company was a thing of the past.

CHAPTER XLVI.

PRESENT STATUS OF THE COMPANY

A great land Company—Fort Garry dismantled—The new buildings—New v. Old—
New life in the Company—Palmy days are recalled—Governors of ability—The
present distinguished Governor—Vaster operations—Its eye not dimmed.

RELIEVED of the burden of government, the Hudson's Bay Company threw itself heartily into the work of developing its resources. Mr. Donald A. Smith, who had done so much to undermine the power of Riel, returned to Manitoba as Chief Commissioner of the Company, and proceeded to manage its affairs in the altered conditions of the country. Representing enormous interests in the North-West, Mr. Smith entered the first local legislature at Winnipeg, and soon after became for a time a member of the Canadian House of Commons. One of the most important matters needing attention was the land interests of the Company. The Company claimed five hundred acres around Fort Garry. This great tract of land, covering now one of the most important parts of the City of Winnipeg, was used as a camping-ground, where the traders from the far west posts, even as far as Edmonton, made their "corrals" and camped during their stay at the capital. Some opposition was developed to this claim, but the block of land was at length handed over to the Company, fifty acres being reserved for public purposes.

The allotment of wild land to the Company of one-twentieth went on in each township as it was surveyed, and though all this land is taxable, yet it has become a great source of revenue to the Company. Important sites and parcels of land all over the country have helped to swell its resources.

The great matter of adapting its agencies to meet the changed conditions of trade was a difficult thing. The methods of two centuries could not be changed in a day. The greatest difficulty lay in the officers and men remote from the important centres. It was reported that in many of the posts no thorough method of book-keeping prevailed. The dissatisfaction arising from the sale made by the Company in 1863, and the uncertainty as to the deed poll, no doubt introduced an element of fault-finding and discontent into the Company's business. Some of the most trusted officers retired from the service. The resources of the Company were, however, enormous, its credit being practically unlimited, and this gave it a great advantage in competing with the Canadian merchants coming to the country, the majority of whom had little capital. Ten years after the transfer Fort Garry was sold, and though it came back on the hands of the Company, yet *miserabile dictu* the fort had been dismantled, thrown down, and even the stone removed, with the exception of the front gate, which still remains. This gate, with a portion of ground about it, has been given by the Hudson's Bay Company to the City of Winnipeg as a small historic park. Since the time of sale, large warehouses have been erected, not filled, as were the old shops, with bright coloured cloths, moccasins, and beads, fitted for the Indian and native trade, but aiming at full departments after the model of Maple and Shoolbred, of the mother city of London. These shops are represented in the plate accompanying this description.

The trade thus modified has been under the direction of men of ability, who succeeded Mr. Donald A. Smith, such as Messrs. Wrigley, Brydges, and a number of able subordinates. The extension of trade has gone on in many of the rising towns of the Canadian West, where the Hudson's Bay Company was not before represented, such as Portage La Prairie, Calgary, Lethbridge, Prince Albert, Vancouver, &c. In all these points the Company's influence has been a very real and important one.

The methods of trade, now employed, require a skill and knowledge never needed in the old fur-trading days. The present successful Commissioner, C. C. Chipman, Esq., resident in Winnipeg, controls and directs interests far greater than Sir George Simpson was called upon to deal with. Present and Past presents a contrast between ceaseless competition and a sleepy monopoly.

The portions of the country not reached, or likely to be reached by settlement, have remained in possession of the Hudson's Bay Company almost solely. The Canadian Government has negotiated treaties with the Indians as far north as Lake Athabasca, leaving many of the Chipewyans and Eskimos still to the entire management of the Company.

The impression among the officers of the Company is that under the deed poll of 1871 they are not so well remunerated as under the former regime. It is difficult to estimate the exact relation of the present to the past, inasmuch as the opening up of the country, the improvement of transportation facilities, and the cheapening of all agricultural supplies has changed the relative value of money in the country. Under this arrangement, which has been in force for twenty-four years, the profits of the wintering partners are divided on the basis of one-hundredth of a share. Of this an inspecting chief factor receives three shares; a chief factor two and a half; a factor two; and a chief trader one and a half shares. The average for the twenty-five years of the one-hundredth share has been 213*l*. 12*s*. 2½*d*. Since 1890 a more liberal provision has been made for officers retiring, and since that time an officer on withdrawing in good standing receives two years' full pay and six years' half pay. Later years have seen a further increase.

A visit to the Hudson's Bay House on the corner of Leaden-hall and Lime Streets, London, still gives one a sense of the presence of the old Company. While in the New World great changes have taken place, and the visitor is struck with the complete departure from the low-ceiling store, with goods in disorder and confusion, with Metis smoking "kinni-kinnik" till the atmosphere is opaque—all this to the palatial buildings with the most perfect arrangements and greatest taste; yet in London "the old order changeth" but slowly. It is true the old building on Fenchurch Street, London, where "the old Lady" was said by the Nor'-Westers to sit, was sold in 1859, and the proceeds divided among the shareholders and officers for four years thereafter. But the portraits of Prince Rupert, Sir George Simpson, and the copy of the Company Charter were transferred bodily to the directors' room in the building on Lime Street. The strong room contains the same rows of minutes, the same dusty piles of documents, and the journals of bygone years, but the business of a vast region is still managed there, and the old gentlemen who control the Hudson's Bay Company affairs pass their dividends as comfortably as in years gone by, with, in an occasional year, some restless spirit stirring up the echoes, to be promptly repressed and the current of events to go on as before.

Since 1871, however, it is easy to see that men of greater financial ability have been at the head of the councils of the Hudson's Bay Company, recalling the palmy days of the first operations of the Company. After five years' service, Sir Edmund Head, the first Governor under the new deed poll, gave way, to be followed for a year by the distinguished politician and statesman, the Earl of Kimberley. For five years thereafter, Sir Stafford Northcote, who held high Government office in the service of the Empire, occupied this position. He was followed for six years by one who has since gained a very high reputation for financial ability, the Rt. Hon. G. J. Goschen. Eden Colville, who seems to carry us back to the former generation—a man of brisk and alert mind, and singularly free from the prejudices and immobility of Governor Berens, the last of the barons of the old regime—held office for three years after Mr. Goschen.

For the last ten years the veteran of kindly manner, warm heart, and genial disposition, Lord Strathcona and Mount Royal, has occupied this high place. The clerk, junior officer, and chief factor of thirty hard years on the inhospitable shores of Hudson Bay and Labrador, the Commissioner who, as Donald A. Smith, soothed the Riel rebellion, and for years directed the reorganization of the Company's affairs at Fort Garry and the whole North-West, the daring speculator who took hold, with his friends, of the Minnesota and Manitoba Railway, and with Midas touch turned the enterprise to gold, a projector and a builder of the Canadian Pacific Railway, the patron of art and education, has worthily filled the office of Governor of the Hudson's Bay Company, and with much success reorganized its administration and directed its affairs.

The Company's operations are vaster than ever before. The greatest mercantile enterprise of the Greater Canada west of Lake Superior; a strong land Company, still keeping up its traditions and conducting a large trade in furs; owning vessels and transportation facilities; able to take large contracts; exercising a fatherly care over the Indian tribes; the helper and assistant of the vast missionary organizations scattered over Northern Canada, the Company since the transfer of Rupert's Land to Canada has taken a new lease of life; its eye is not dim, nor its natural force abated.

CHAPTER XLVII.

IN 1871, soon after Rupert's Land and the Indian territories were transferred to Canada, it was the fortune of the writer to take up his abode in Winnipeg, as the village in the neighbourhood of Fort Garry was already called. The railway was in that year still four hundred miles from Winnipeg. From the terminus in Minnesota the stage coach drawn by four horses, with relays every twenty miles, sped rapidly over prairies smooth as a lawn to the site of the future City of the Plains.

The fort was in its glory. Its stone walls, round bastions, threatening pieces of artillery and rows of portholes, spoke of a place of some strength, though even then a portion of stone wall had been taken down to give easier access to the "Hudson's Bay Store." It was still the seat of government, for the Canadian Governor lived within its walls, as the last Company Governor, McTavish, had done. It was still the scene of gaiety, as the better class of the old settlers united with the leaders of the new Canadian society in social joys, under the hospitable roof of Governor Archibald.

Since that time forty years have well-nigh passed. The stage coach, the Red River cart, and the shagganappe pony are things of the past, and great railways with richly furnished trains connect St. Paul and Minnesota with the City of Winnipeg. More important still, the skill of the engineer has blasted a way through the Archaean rocks to Fort William, Lake Superior, more direct than the old fur-traders' route; the tremendous cliffs of the north shore of Lake Superior have been levelled and the chasm bridged. To the west the prairies have been gridironed with numerous lines of railway, the enormous ascents of the four Rocky Mountain ranges rising a mile above the sea level have been crossed, and the giddy heights of the Fraser River canon traversed. The iron band of the Canadian Pacific Railway, one of whose chief promoters was Lord Strathcona and Mount Royal, the present Governor of the Company, has joined ocean to ocean. The Canadian Northern Railway runs its line from Lake Superior through Winnipeg and Edmonton to British Columbia. It has in prospect a transcontinental Railway from the Atlantic to the Pacific Ocean. The Grand Trunk Pacific Railway has in operation a perfectly built line from Lake Superior through Winnipeg and Edmonton to the Rocky Mountains, and with the backing of the Canadian Government guarantees a most complete connection between the eastern and western shores of the continent.

A wonderful transformation has taken place in the land since the days of Sir George Simpson and his band of active chief factors and traders. It is true, portions of the wide territory reaching from Labrador to the Pacific Ocean will always be the domain of the fur-trader. The Labrador, Ungava, and Arctic shores of Canada will always remain inhospitable, but the Archaean region on the south and west of Hudson Bay undoubtedly contains great mineral treasures. The Canadian Government pledges itself to a completed railway from the prairie wheat fields to York Factory on Hudson Bay. This will bring the seaport on Hudson Bay as near Britain as is New York, and will make an enormous saving in transportation to Western Canada. What a mighty change from the day when the pessimistic French King spoke of all Canada, as "only a few orpents of snow." Mackenzie River district is still the famous scene of the fur trade, and may long continue so, though there is always the possibility of any portion of the vast waste of the Far North developing, as the Yukon territory has done, mineral wealth rivalling the famous sands of Pactolus or the riches of King Solomon's mines.

Under Canadian sway, law and order are preserved throughout this wide domain, although the Hudson's Bay Company officers still administer law and in many cases are magistrates or officers for the Government, receiving their commissions from Ottawa. Peace and order prevail; the arm of the law has been felt in Keewatin, the Mackenzie River, and distant Yukon.

But it is to the fertile prairies of the West and valleys and slopes of the Pacific Coast we look for the extension of the Greater Canada. While the Hon. William McDougall was arguing the value of the prairie land of the West, his Canadian and other opponents maintained "that in the North-West the soil never thawed out in summer, and that the potato or cabbage would not mature." With this opinion many of the Hudson's Bay Company officers agreed, though it is puzzling to the resident of the prairie to-day to see how such honourable and observing men could have made such statements. The fertile plains have been divided into four sections, the Province of Manitoba and the three wide territories of Assiniboia, Alberta, and Saskatchewan, these being known as the North-West Territories. Manitoba, which at the time of the closing of the Hudson's Bay Company régime, numbered its twenty-five thousand people, more than one half Indians and the remainder whites and half-breeds, has multiplied ten times up to its present population, estimated at a quarter of a million. The North-West Territories are said to have ninety-five thousand inhabitants, and British Columbia, including Indians, upwards of one hundred thousand; making in all west of Lake Superior well nigh one half of a million of people dwelling in the old of the fur-traders.

The City of Winnipeg, which, when the writer first saw the hamlet bearing that name, had less than three hundred souls, is estimated now at the end of the century to have a population of from forty-five to fifty thousand. The Hudson's Bay Company store was a low building, a wooden erection made of lumber sawn by whip-saw or by some rude contrivance, having what was known in the old Red River days as a "pavilion roof." Its highly-coloured fabrics suited to the trade of the country did not relieve its dingy interior. To-day the great departmental stores and offices, built of dark red St. Louis brick, speak of the enormous progress made in the development of the country. Every town upon the prairies bears testimony, by its towering elevators, to the overflowing abundance of what the old fur-traders contended could not be produced, viz. agricultural products of every kind characteristic of the north temperate zone. The returns made by the Government show that Manitoba, with a population not exceeding a quarter of a million, and of these not more than twenty-five thousand being farmers, produced in the last year of record sixty millions of bushels of cereals, valued at, say, twenty-five millions of dollars. Not less remarkable is the development of the North-West territories. Assiniboia shows a remarkable production of grains, and the Far West abounds in great herds of cattle, exceeding in its ranching capabilities even many parts of Manitoba.

British Columbia, including the New Caledonia, Kootenay Country, and Vancouver Island of the fur-traders, is a land of great resources. Its population has increased many times over. Its great salmon fisheries, trade in timber, coal mines, agricultural productiveness, and genial climate have long made it a favourite dwelling-place for English-speaking colonists.

In late years much prominence has been given to this province by the discovery of its mineral products. Gold, silver, and lead mines in the Kootenay region, which was discovered by old David Thompson, and in the Cariboo district, have lately attracted many immigrants to British Columbia; the adjoining territory of the Yukon, brought to the knowledge of the world by Chief Factor Robert Campbell, has surpassed all other parts of the fur-traders' land in rich productiveness, although the region lying between the Lake of the Woods and Lake Superior, along the very route of the fur-traders, is becoming famous by its production of gold, silver, and other valuable metals.

Throughout the wide West great deposits of coal and iron are found, the basis of future manufactures, and in many districts great forests to supply to the world material for increasing development.

What, then, is to be the future of this Canadian West? The possibilities are illimitable. The Anglo-Saxon race, with its energy and pluck, has laid hold of the land so long shut in by the wall built round it by the fur-traders. This race, with its dominating forcefulness, will absorb and harmonize elements coming from all parts of the world to enjoy the fertile fields and mineral treasures of a land whose laws are just, whose educational policy is thorough and progressive, whose moral and religious aspirations are high and noble, and which gives a hearty welcome to the industrious and deserving from all lands.

Winnipeg, it is said, now ranks third in its commercial standing, as represented by banking statistics, among the cities of Canada, and will be one of her three great cities. Those who are hopeful of its future, and who forecast its position as the financial, commercial, educational, and religious centre of the great prairie land, speak of it as the Chicago of Western Canada.

On the shores of Burrard Inlet on the Pacific Ocean another place of great importance is rising—Vancouver City, the terminus of the Canadian Pacific Railway. Victoria, begun, as we have seen, by Chief Factor Douglas as the chief fort along the Pacific Coast, long held its own as the commercial as well as the political capital of British Columbia, but in the meantime Vancouver has surpassed it in population, if not in influence.

All goes to show that the Hudson's Bay Company was preserving for the generations to come a most valuable heritage. The leaders of opinion in Canada have frequently, within the last five years of the century, expressed their opinion that the second generation of the twentieth century may see a larger Canadian population to the West of Lake Superior than will be found in the provinces of the East. William Cullen Bryant's lines, spoken of other prairies, will surely come true of the wide Canadian plains:—

> "I listen long
> . . . . and think I hear
> The sound of that advancing multitude
> Which soon shall fill these deserts. From the ground
> Comes up the laugh of children, the soft voice
> Of maidens, and the sweet and solemn hymn
> Of Sabbath worshippers. The low of herds

> Blends with the rustling of the heavy grain
> Over the dark brown furrows."

The French explorers are a reminiscence of a century and a half ago; the lords of the lakes and forests, with all their wild energy, are gone for ever; the Astorians are no more; no longer do the French Canadian voyageurs make the rivers vocal with their chansons; the pomp and circumstance of the emperor of the fur-traders has been resolved into the ordinary forms of commercial life; and the rude barter of the early trader has passed into the fulfilment of the poet's dream, of the "argosies of magic sails," and the "costly bales" of an increasing commerce. The Hudson's Bay Company still lives and takes its new place as one of the potent forces of the Canadian West.

Printed in Great Britain
by Amazon

22809932R00278